THE LAW OF DAMAGES IN INTERNATIONAL SALES

The second edition of this internationally acclaimed book explores damages for breach of an international sales contract, one of the most important and frequently invoked remedies. The focus is on the international contract law instruments such as the Convention on Contracts for the International Sale of Goods (CISG), the UNIDROIT Principles of International Commercial Contracts and the Principles of European Contract Law. The book draws on the experience of some major legal systems and engages with legal scholarship on the international instruments and on contract damages, providing the most comprehensive, in-depth and thorough examination of damages under the instruments to date. The second edition is updated, reflecting the latest developments in legal thinking on contract damages. It incorporates about 60 new cases and now covers more than 370 cases decided by courts and arbitration tribunals from around the world. The new edition is substantially revised, covering new topics such as damages for a documentary breach. Truly international in spirit, this book is analytically rigorous and practically oriented, offering distinctive analyses of and solutions to some of the most challenging problems surrounding contract damages. This book will be of interest to practitioners involved in international commercial transactions, scholars and students worldwide interested in international commercial and comparative contract law.

The Law of Damages in International Sales

The CISG and Other International Instruments

Second Edition

Djakhongir Saidov

•HART•

OXFORD • LONDON • NEW YORK • NEW DELHI • SYDNEY

HART PUBLISHING

Bloomsbury Publishing Plc

Kemp House, Chawley Park, Cumnor Hill, Oxford, OX2 9PH, UK

1385 Broadway, New York, NY 10018, USA

29 Earlsfort Terrace, Dublin 2, Ireland

HART PUBLISHING, the Hart/Stag logo, BLOOMSBURY and the Diana logo are trademarks of Bloomsbury Publishing Plc

First published in Great Britain 2021

A catalogue record for this book is available from the British Library.

Library of Congress Cataloging-in-Publication data

Names: Saidov, Djakhongir, author.

Title: The law of damages in international sales : the CISG and other international instruments / Djakhongir Saidov.

Description: Second edition. | Oxford, UK ; New York, NY : Hart Publishing, an imprint of Bloomsbury Publishing, 2021. | Includes bibliographical references and index.

Identifiers: LCCN 2020056160 (print) | LCCN 2020056161 (ebook) | ISBN 9781509922741 (hardback) | ISBN 9781509947133 (paperback) | ISBN 9781509922734 (pdf) | ISBN 9781509922758 (Epub)

Subjects: LCSH: Export sales contracts. | Damages.

Classification: LCC K1030 .S247 2021 (print) | LCC K1030 (ebook) | DDC 343.08/7—dc23

LC record available at https://lccn.loc.gov/2020056160

LC ebook record available at https://lccn.loc.gov/2020056161

ISBN: HB: 978-1-50992-274-1
ePDF: 978-1-50992-273-4
ePub: 978-1-50992-275-8

Typeset by Compuscript Ltd, Shannon

To find out more about our authors and books visit www.hartpublishing.co.uk. Here you will find extracts, author information, details of forthcoming events and the option to sign up for our newsletters.

To my parents and the memory of Oijon

Preface to the Second Edition

There have been many developments in the law of contract damages since the publication of the first edition of this book more than a decade ago. The legal scene surrounding the international instruments, that are the subject of this book, has also advanced. A substantial number of cases on damages for breach of contract has been decided under the UN Convention on Contracts for the International Sale of Goods 1980 (CISG) since the first edition was published. Approximately 60 additional cases (decided mainly under the CISG) are included in this edition. The CISG Advisory Council has adopted its second Opinion on damages (CISG-AC Opinion No 8) which is now taken into account. At the time of the initial publication of this book, the UNIDROIT Principles of International Commercial Contracts (UPICC) were in their (second) 2004 edition, whereas now they are in their (fourth) 2016 edition. Although the subsequent two revisions of the UPICC have not affected the remedy of damages for breach of contract, this book draws on the latest version of the UPICC and, of course, on any new cases on damages decided under the UPICC.

The book in this second edition is substantially revised and updated. There is a new section on damages for a documentary breach. Some notable revisions include those dealing with: the 'performance interest' and gain-based damages; some categories of loss, such as 'fixed' and 'variable' costs and lost profits; the 'commodities trading' context; the impact of trade terms on the assessment of damages (with Incoterms 2020 taken into account); aspects of causation and mitigation; the assessment of the buyer's damages for non-conforming goods. The comparative angle is strengthened further as some of the latest cases in English sales and contract law are drawn on, providing further insights (additional to those flowing from the experience of the international instruments) into the complexities that surround contract damages and international sales. Turning specifically to the CISG, this new edition reveals, even more strongly and fully than the first, how detailed and well-developed the CISG regime on damages has become. This point becomes evident if the Convention's provisions, cases decided under it and legal scholarship that incorporates the most advanced legal thinking on contract damages are viewed in an integrated way. From this perspective, the Convention's regime on damages has proven to be robust and viable, making the CISG a highly competitive and effective international sales law. Because the CISG is regularly applied in numerous fora worldwide, it is tested in a wider range of and more diverse commercial and legal contexts than those in which national sales laws are applied. This means that all legal systems will find something valuable to learn from the Convention's rich experience on damages.

This book is based on the materials that were available to me as at 31 August 2020.

Djakhongir Saidov
London, 5 September 2020

Preface to the First Edition

RECENT DECADES HAVE witnessed an increasing scholarly interest in the law of contract damages in the context of various legal systems. This book seeks to contribute to the existing body of scholarship on this subject by exploring the remedy of damages under the UN Convention on Contracts for the International Sale of Goods (CISG) and, to a somewhat lesser extent, under the UNIDROIT Principles of International Commercial Contracts (UPICC) and the Principles of European Contract Law (PECL). In writing it, I aimed to provide a comprehensive treatment of these instruments' provisions on damages for breach of contract taking into account cases that have thus far been decided under the instruments in various domestic jurisdictions and arbitration tribunals. Having been written against the background of the experience of some major legal systems, the book engages with the issues and problems raised in domestic systems to the extent relevant to the international instruments' remedy of damages. I hope that the book will be of use not only to scholars, practitioners and students interested in the law of the international instruments but also to those interested in contract damages.

This book is a product of several years of research. During that period, I have benefited greatly from the help, comments and criticism of many people. I would like to thank Alastair Mullis, Michael Bridge, Ralph Cunnington, Albert Kritzer, Nelson Enonchong, Sarah Green, TT Arvind, Kyriaki Noussia, and Frank Meisel – all of whom, at various points in time, have kindly read earlier chapters of this book. I am very grateful to Tanya Corrigan for her immense help in preparing the book for publication. I also wish to thank the Birmingham Law School, University of Birmingham, for generously granting me the study leave which enabled me to complete this project. I owe much to Richard Hart for his encouragement, support and patience. Above all, I would like to thank my parents and parents-in-law, my wife, Sanam, daughter, Malika, and sister, Anora, without whom none of this would have been possible.

The book is based on the materials that were available to me up to 31 January 2008.

Djakhongir Saidov
Birmingham, 31 January 2008

Contents

PART II
METHODS OF LIMITING DAMAGES

PART III
PROOF OF LOSS AND CALCULATION OF DAMAGES

About the Author

Djakhongir Saidov is Professor of Commercial Law at The Dickson Poon School of Law, King's College London, UK, a Consultant to Helmsman LLC, Advocates & Solicitors, Singapore, and an Academic Fellow at the Centre for Maritime Law at the National University of Singapore.

Table of Cases

Court of Arbitration of the International Chamber of Commerce

Australia

Austria

Belgium

Brazil

Canada

China

England & Wales

Estonia

Finland

France

Germany

Iran-United States Claims Tribunal

Italy

Korea

Lithuania

Mexico

Netherlands

Panama

Poland

Russia

Spain

Serbia

Sweden

Switzerland

Ukraine

United States of America

1

Introduction

1. GENERAL

RECENT DECADES HAVE seen a steady growth in international trade and, with it, increasing efforts to harmonise and unify commercial law. The harmonisation and unification of commercial law are often seen as desirable and even necessary in the conditions of the globalisation of commerce and markets because they are thought to: facilitate commerce and trade by lifting legal barriers and reducing transaction costs; produce legal regimes which are neutral and specifically tailored to the needs of international commerce; dispense with a need to resort to conflict of laws rules and reduce forum shopping; fill a legal vacuum by creating legal regimes in a field not covered or not well regulated by domestic legal systems; increase legal certainty, security and predictability in international transactions; trigger law reforms in domestic legal systems;[1] and contribute to world peace and security by encouraging the settlement of disputes by amicable and peaceful means.[2] Although this perspective on the harmonisation and unification of law[3] is not shared by all,[4] the process of 'transnationalisation' of commercial law[5] has advanced considerably. That said, international commercial law remains fragmented[6] and in contrast

[1] See, eg, L Mistelis, 'Is Harmonisation a Necessary Evil? The Future of Harmonisation and New Sources of International Trade Law' in I Fletcher, L Mistelis and M Cremona (eds), *Foundations and Perspectives of International Trade Law* (London, Sweet & Maxwell, 2001) 3, 20–1.

[2] See R Goode, H Kronke and E McKendrick, *Transnational Commercial Law: Text, Cases, and Materials*, 2nd edn (Oxford, OUP, 2015) 164 ('it was thought that armed conflicts could be best avoided if there was trust and understanding among nations; that such trust and understanding were effectively fostered by more trade; and, that more trade and, consequently, economic opportunities, for all would be facilitated by a framework of harmonized and, therefore, reliable rules of commercial law'). See also ch 2.

[3] For a recent examination of the phenomenon of unification of sales law, see L Spagnolo, 'Unification, Disintegration or Optimization: Purposes of Modern Sales Law' in D Saidov (ed), *Research Handbook on International and Comparative Law Sale of Goods Law* (Cheltenham, Edward Elgar, 2019).

[4] For a well-known example, see JS Hobhouse, 'International Conventions and Commercial Law: The Pursuit of Uniformity' (1990) 106 *LQR* 530; and for a helpful summary of arguments, see Mistelis (n 1) 22.

[5] See, eg, KP Berger, 'Transnational Commercial Law in the Age of Globalization', available at w3.uniroma1.it/idc/centro/publications/42berger.pdf.

[6] MJ Bonell, *An International Restatement of Contract Law: The UNIDROIT Principles of International Commercial Contracts*, 3rd edn (Ardsley, NY, Transnational Publishers Inc, 2005) 16.

with domestic legal systems, international instruments do not yet exist within a 'common legal environment'.[7]

In the area of contract law this problem has been considerably alleviated by three instruments: the UN Convention on Contracts for the International Sale of Goods (CISG) and the UNIDROIT Principles of International Commercial Contracts (UPICC) at the international level and the Principles of European Contract Law (PECL) at a regional level.[8] Some commentators regard these instruments with great enthusiasm by treating them as 'an emerging jus commune, the gospels for the future world law of contract'.[9] Whatever the true characterisation of the instruments, each of them has marked an important step in the development of commercial and contract law at the international and regional levels. They are now firmly entrenched in the world of commercial and contract law by: being regularly applied by judges and arbitrators; being used as models for legal reform in many countries; being used in the drafting of international contracts;[10] and influencing legal thinking across the world. There is an immense body of literature exploring these instruments[11] and only a brief overview of their historical background, nature, aims and structure will be presented in this book.

2. THE CISG

The CISG[12] is a product of lengthy attempts to unify the law of international sales. Its general aims are set out in the Preamble, which provides that in the adoption of the Convention the following considerations were taken into account:

> the broad objectives in the resolutions adopted by the sixth special session of the General Assembly of the United Nations on the establishment of a New International

[7] O Lando, 'European Contract Law' (1983) 31 *AJCL* 654.

[8] See also the (European) Draft Common Frame of Reference (DCFR) and other regional harmonisation initiatives such as: Principles of Asian Contract Law (PACL) (on which see, eg, S Han, 'Principles of Asian Contract Law: An Endeavor of Regional Harmonization of Contract Law in East Asia' (2013) 58 *Villanova L Rev* 589); the Principles of Latin American Contract Law (PLACL) (on which see, eg, R Momberg and S Vogenauer (eds), *The Principles of Latin American Contract Law* (Oxford, Hart, 2017)).

[9] O Lando, 'Comparative Law and Lawmaking' (2000–2001) 75 *Tulane L Rev* 1015, 1016.

[10] See, eg, MJ Bonell, 'UNIDROIT Principles 2004 – The New Edition of the Principles of International Commercial Contracts Adopted by the International Institute for the Unification of Private Law' (2004) 45 *Uniform L Rev* 5, 6–17.

[11] For an extensive list of sources, see, eg, www.cisg.law.pace.edu/cisg/biblio/full-biblio.html.

[12] The Convention on Contracts for the International Sale of Goods was signed in Vienna on 11 April 1980. It entered into force on 1 January 1988. The Convention consists of 101 Articles and is organised into four parts: Part I outlines the Convention's sphere of application and its general provisions; Part II deals with formation of the sales contract; Part III provides for the substantive rules of the sales contract itself; Part IV contains the Final Provisions on the Obligations of the Contracting States.

> Economic Order, ... the development of international trade on the basis of equality and mutual benefit is an important element in promoting friendly relations among States, ... that the adoption of uniform rules which govern contracts for the international sale of goods and take into account the different social, economic and legal systems would contribute to the removal of legal barriers in international trade and promote the development of international trade.

The CISG is not the first international instrument purporting to govern international sales. In 1964, two instruments – a Uniform Law on the International Sale of Goods (ULIS) and a Uniform Law on the Formation of Contracts for the International Sale of Goods (ULFS) – were adopted. These instruments failed to achieve a worldwide unification and were ratified only by a small number of states.[13] In this respect, the CISG is far more successful having been ratified, as at the time of writing, by 94 states.[14] The CISG is routinely applied by courts and arbitration tribunals as the source of law for international sales contracts.[15] The CISG is a piece of 'international legislation', being an 'international treaty' within the meaning of art 2 of the Vienna Convention on the Law of Treaties 1969.[16] If the conditions for its applicability are met[17] and the parties have not excluded it in their contract,[18] the CISG will be the governing sales law regime.

It is often pointed out that the Convention is fraught with many compromises that had to be made to enable the representatives of various political, legal, economic and social systems to agree on a unified sales law. This has affected the CISG in at least two ways. First, a number of its provisions are based on general standards and rules, such as reasonableness or a fundamental breach.[19] Second, the CISG is what may be called a 'skeleton' or 'minimalist' instrument,[20] lacking in detailed regulation. A key feature of many international private law conventions is the requirement that their international character be

[13] Belgium, Federal Republic of Germany, Italy, Luxembourg, Netherlands, San Marino, UK, Gambia, and Israel.

[14] See uncitral.un.org/en/texts/salegoods/conventions/sale_of_goods/cisg/status.

[15] For the databases containing the CISG cases see, eg: www. cisg.law.pace.edu; www.uncitral.org; www.unilex.info; www.cisg-online.ch. See also *UNCITRAL Digest of Case Law on the United Nations Convention on Contracts for the International Sale of Goods*, 2016 edn, available at www.uncitral.org/pdf/english/clout/CISG_Digest_2016.pdf.

[16] '"[T]reaty" means an international agreement concluded between States in written form and governed by international law, whether embodied in a single instrument or in two or more related instruments and whatever its particular designation' (art 2(1)(a) of the Vienna Convention on the Law of Treaties 1969).

[17] Article 1(1) CISG provides that the 'Convention applies to contracts of sale of goods between parties whose places of business are in different States: (a) when the States are Contracting States; or (b) when the rules of private international law lead to the application of the law of a Contracting State'.

[18] See art 6 CISG.

[19] See, eg, CP Gillette and RE Scott, 'The Political Economy of International Sales Law' (2005) 25 *Int'l Rev L Economics* 446, 473–5.

[20] See, eg, AH Kritzer, 'Observations on the Use of the Principles of European Contract Law as an Aid to CISG Research', available at cisgw3.law.pace.edu/cisg/text/peclcomp.html.

respected and that uniformity in their application be promoted.[21] This means that like other Conventions, the CISG must be interpreted 'autonomously', that is, within its own legal and conceptual framework. Domestic legal systems must have no role to play in the interpretation and application of the Convention in respect of matters governed by it.[22] This requirement is expressed in art 7(1) CISG:

> In the interpretation of this Convention, regard is to be had to its international character and to the need to promote uniformity in its application and the observance of good faith in international trade.

The following paragraph of the same article is no less important as it provides guidance on what needs to be done if a matter is not expressly addressed by the Convention:

> Questions concerning matters governed by this Convention which are not expressly settled in it are to be settled in conformity with the general principles on which it is based or, in the absence of such principles, in conformity with the law applicable by virtue of the rules of private international law.[23]

Thus, if a particular matter is not expressly dealt with by the CISG, the first step is to determine whether the matter is *governed* by the Convention (ie, if it falls within the Convention's scope). The Convention's guidance is that it 'governs only the formation of the contract of sale and the rights and obligations of the seller and the buyer arising from such a contract'.[24] Considering the multiplicity of issues that may potentially arise, it is not of much use to attempt to discuss in the abstract what issues do or do not fall within the Convention's scope. Several such issues will arise in the course of this book and each of them will be addressed in the relevant chapters. If the matter is governed by the CISG, the next step is to identify a relevant general principle and some uncertainty still exists as to what are the general principles underlying the Convention. It is probably safe to say that party autonomy, equality of the contracting parties, reasonableness and full compensation for the loss suffered are some of the Convention's general principles.[25] Much controversy has surrounded the question whether 'good faith', specified in art 7(1) as a method of interpreting the CISG, can be regarded as a general principle. There are strong objections to treating good faith as a general principle. One is that doing so contravenes the compromise made by the Convention's drafters, whereby good faith was intended to be nothing more than a method of interpreting the Convention. Another is that, owing to the difficulty

[21] See, eg, art 6 of the Convention on International Financial Leasing (1988); art 4 of the Convention on International Factoring (1988); art 5 of the Convention on International Interests in Mobile Equipment (2001).

[22] See, eg, M Gebauer, 'Uniform Law, General Principles and Autonomous Interpretation' (2000) 5 *Uniform L Rev* 683, 686–7.

[23] Article 7(2) CISG.

[24] Article 4 CISG.

[25] The main text mentions only those principles that are relevant to this book.

of articulating coherent and specific content from the good faith concept, recognising it as a general principle would undermine the Convention's objective of promoting certainty and predictability in international trade. Despite these objections, this book adopts the view that good faith *is* a general principle of the CISG because, despite the drafters' compromise to the contrary, it is difficult to deny that the idea of good faith emanates from numerous provisions of the CISG.[26] Finally, if there is no relevant general principle to govern the matter or if the matter is outside the Convention's scope, it is to be resolved based on the law applicable by virtue of private international law.[27]

3. THE UPICC

In contrast with the CISG, the UPICC[28] are an instrument of a different nature, representing a 'totally new product of international trade law'.[29] The Principles are neither a state-made piece of 'international legislation' nor a model law which becomes effective by being implemented into national legislation. The UPICC were intended to become a non-binding instrument, a source of 'soft law'[30] of international commercial contracts.[31] They are a kind of restatement of world contract law,[32] playing a role on the international arena similar to that

[26] See arts 16(2)(b), 21(2), 29(2), 37, 40, 44, 46, 64(2), 77, 82, 85–88 CISG. See also O Lando, 'CISG and Its Followers: A Proposal to Adopt Some International Principles of Contract Law' (2005) 53 *AJCL* 379, 391 ('[I]t is not possible in practice to distinguish a problem of interpretation from one of supplementation. It is not reasonable that a question of interpretation of a rule in the Convention is, and the interpretation of a term in the sales contract is not to be governed by the principle of good faith').

[27] Art 7(2) CISG.

[28] The first edition of the UPICC was adopted in 1994 by the International Institute for the Unification of Private Law (UNIDROIT). The second edition was adopted in 2004, the third in 2010 and the current fourth edition in 2016. The fourth edition consists of the Preamble and 211 Articles, divided into the following chapters: ch 1 – 'General Provisions'; ch 2 – 'Formation' (Section 1) and 'Authority of Agents' (Section 2); ch 3 – 'Validity'; ch 4 – 'Interpretation'; ch 5 – 'Content' (Section 1), 'Third Party Rights' (Section 2) and 'Conditions' (Section 3); ch 6 – 'Performance in General' (Section 1) and 'Hardship' (Section 2); ch 7 – 'Non-performance in General' (Section 1), 'Right to Performance' (Section 2), 'Termination' (Section 3) and 'Damages (Section 4); ch 8 – 'Set-Off'; ch 9 – 'Assignment of Rights' (Section 1), 'Transfer of Obligations' (Section 2) and 'Assignment of Contracts' (Section 3); ch 10 – 'Limitation Periods'; ch 11 – 'Plurality of Obligors and of Obligees'.

[29] KP Berger, 'The Lex Mercatoria Doctrine and the UNIDROIT Principles of International Commercial Contracts' (1997) 28 *L Policy Int'l Business* 943, 945 (with further reference).

[30] R Goode, 'International Restatements of Contract and English Contract Law' in EZ Lomnicka and CGJ Morse (eds), *Contemporary Issues in Commercial Law – Essays in Honour of Professor AG Guest* (London, Sweet & Maxwell, 1997) 65.

[31] For the history of preparation of the UPICC, see Bonell (n 6) 9–56.

[32] 'However, to the extent that [the UPICC] do not follow the common-core but the best-solution approach the even more felicitous characterisation is pre-statement: the drafters take on the role of an enlightened legislature to enact the most functional, modern and internationally acceptable rule' (H Kronke, 'The UN Sales Convention, The UNIDROIT Contract Principles and the Way Beyond' (2005–2006) 25 *J L Commerce* 451, 457–8).

of the Restatement of Contracts in the United States.[33] It has been suggested that this non-binding nature of the UPICC is a better way to achieve harmonisation of international commercial and contract law than doing so by means of international 'legislative' instruments.[34] The scope of the UPICC is much broader than that of the CISG because they are not confined to any particular commercial contract. The objectives of the UPICC are set out in their Preamble:

— [The] Principles set forth general rules for international commercial contracts.
— They shall be applied when the parties have agreed that their contract be governed by them.
— They may be applied when the parties have agreed that their contract be governed by general principles of law, the *lex mercatoria* or the like.
— They may be applied when the parties have not chosen any law to govern their contract.
— They may be used to interpret or supplement international uniform law instruments.
— They may be used to interpret or supplement domestic law.
— They may serve as a model for national and international legislators.

By assigning these functions to the UPICC[35] the drafters intended the UPICC to help remedy the fragmentary nature and scope of international conventions[36] by creating an 'international legal environment'. They are based not only on the principles and rules found in most legal systems but also on solutions perceived as most suitable to the needs of international commerce. The UPICC can also help bring some clarity and conceptual order to the vague concept of *lex mercatoria*, although there is no agreement as to the interrelationship between the

[33] See EA Farnsworth, 'An International Restatement: the UNIDROIT Principles of International Commercial Contracts' (1996–1997) 26 *U Baltimore L Rev* 1, 2–3; JM Perillo, 'UNIDROIT Principles of International Commercial Contracts: The Black Letter Text and a Review' (1994) 63 *Fordham L Rev* 281, 283; A Rosett, 'The UNIDROIT Principles of International Commercial Contracts: A New Approach to International Commercial Contracts, Part I' (1998) 46 *AJCL* 348. For a different view, see R Hyland, 'On Setting Forth the Law of Contract: A Foreword' (1992) 40 *AJCL* 541, 542 ('[The UPICC] are … not a restatement – either of the oft-mentioned common core of existing legal systems or of the lex mercatoria. Certain of the rules formulated in the Principles doubtlessly reflect ideas that are generally accepted in modern systems of contract law. Other rules reflect the standard practice in international trade. Yet neither the common core – if in fact one exists – nor the lex mercatoria has been sufficiently elaborated to provide a basis either for restatement or for codification').

[34] See Rosett (n 33) 349; Goode (n 30) 65–6.

[35] For some other cases where the UPICC can perhaps be used see, eg, AM Garro, 'The Contribution of the UNIDROIT Principles to the Advancement of International Commercial Arbitration' (1994) 3 *Tulane J Int'l Comparative L* 93, 114–25; H van Houtte, 'The UNIDROIT Principles of International Commercial Contracts' (1995) 11 *Arbitration Int'l* 373, 380–1.

[36] Bonell (n 6) 16.

UPICC and *lex mercatoria*.[37] Similar to the CISG, the UPICC provide that in their interpretation 'regard is to be had to their international character and to their purposes including the need to promote uniformity in their application'.[38] If a matter is not expressly settled in the UPICC but is nevertheless within their scope, it is 'as far as possible to be settled in accordance with their underlying general principles'.[39] In contrast with the CISG, the UPICC expressly impose a duty to act 'in accordance with good faith and fair dealing in international trade'.[40]

4. THE PECL

The PECL[41] have much in common with the UPICC. Like the UPICC, the PECL are non-binding instrument[42] and the two instruments largely cover the same issues.[43] There are also similarities in the style and presentation because the two groups of drafters have influenced each other's work.[44] However, there are some differences between the two sets of Principles. The essential difference is that while the UPICC are intended to be applied worldwide, the PECL only target the countries of the European Community. In accordance with art 1:101, the PECL are to be applied as general rules of contract law in the Communities.[45] The purpose behind the adoption of the PECL was to launch the process of harmonisation of the law of contract within the European Communities. This aspiration was based on the idea that a variety of laws stands in the way of

[37] See, eg, Berger (n 29) 952; G Baron, 'Do the UNIDROIT Principles of International Commercial Contracts form a New Lex Mercatoria?', available at www.cisg.law.pace.edu/cisg/biblio/baron.html; H Veytia, 'The Requirement of Justice and Equity in Contracts' (1994–1995) 69 *Tulane L Rev* 1191; MPP Viscasillas, 'UNIDROIT Principles of International Commercial Contracts: Sphere of Application and General Provisions' (1996) 13 *Arizona J Int'l and Comparative L* 381; O Lando, 'Assessing the Role of the UNIDROIT Principles in the Harmonization of Arbitration Law' (1994) 3 *Tulane J Int'l Comparative L* 129.

[38] Article 1.6(1) UPICC.

[39] Article 1.6(2) UPICC.

[40] Article 1.7(1) UPICC. The parties cannot limit or exclude this duty (art 1.7(2)).

[41] The Principles of European Contract Law (PECL) were prepared by the self-appointed Commission on European Contract Law (CECL), also referred to as the 'Lando Commission' in honour of its founder and chairman Professor Ole Lando. The Commission, which, in essence, represented a body of scholars, was set up and started its work in 1982. At present, the PECL consists of the following chapters: ch 1 – 'General Provisions'; ch 2 – 'Formation'; ch 3 – 'Authority of Agents'; ch 4 – 'Validity'; ch 5 – 'Interpretation'; ch 6 – 'Contents and Effects'; ch 7 – 'Performance'; ch 8 – 'Non-Performance and Remedies in General'; ch 9 – 'Particular Remedies for Non-Performance'; ch 10 – 'Plurality of Parties'; ch 11 – 'Assignment of Claims'; ch 12 – 'Substitution of New Debtor: Transfer of Contract'; ch 13 – 'Set-Off'; ch 14 – 'Prescription'; ch 15 – 'Illegality'; ch 16 – 'Conditions'; ch 17 – 'Capitalisation of Interest'.

[42] See Lando (n 7) 656.

[43] See Lando (n 9) 1019.

[44] See Bonell (n 6) 338.

[45] See art 1:101 PECL.

European Economic Integration.[46] Quite naturally, the PECL are designed as 'European law' because 'European communities [had] to be offered principles of contract law which [met] their requirements and those of the communities, and which [did] not have to pay heed to the traditions and views of nations with a political social and economic background widely different from that of the EEC countries'.[47] The purposes of the PECL are formulated thus:

— to facilitate cross-border transactions with Europe;
— to strengthen the Single European Market;
— to create an infrastructure for Community laws governing contracts;
— to provide guidelines for national courts and legislatures and fill gaps in national laws;
— to construct a linkage between the Civil and the Common law;
— to provide a modern formulation of 'general principles of law' or *lex mercatoria* relating to contracts.[48]

There are a number of other differences between the PECL and the UPICC. Although the PECL are narrower in geographical scope, they are wider in some other respects. In contrast with the UPICC, which are concerned with 'international commercial contracts', the PECL apply to contracts in general, whether domestic or international, commercial or non-commercial.[49] There are also some differences in the way the rules of the applicability are formulated.[50] Article 1:101 PECL provides that:

> (2) These Principles will apply when the parties have agreed to incorporate them into their contract or that their contract is to be governed by them.
> (3) These Principles may be applied when the parties:
>
> (a) have agreed that their contract is to be governed by 'general principles of law', the 'lex mercatoria' or the like; or
> (b) have not chosen any system or rules of law to govern their contract.
>
> (4) These Principles may provide a solution to the issue raised where the system or rules of law applicable do not do so.

The rules of interpretation and gap filling do not differ greatly from those in the UPICC. Article 1:106 PECL provides:

> (1) These Principles should be interpreted and developed in accordance with their purposes. In particular, regard should be had to the need to promote good faith and fair dealing, certainty in contractual relationships and uniformity of application.

[46] See Lando (n 7) 658.
[47] Ibid, 656.
[48] Goode (n 30) 67.
[49] See Bonell (n 6) 348–9; Goode (n 30) 67.
[50] For a detailed comparison of the UPICC with the PECL, see Bonell (n 6) 339–52.

(2) Issues within the scope of these Principles but not expressly settled by them are so far as possible to be settled in accordance with the ideas underlying the Principles. Failing this, the legal system applicable by virtue of the rules of private international law is to be applied.

Finally, like the UPICC, the PECL impose duties of good faith and fair dealing on the parties.[51]

5. SCOPE AND STRUCTURE OF THE BOOK

The focus of this book is on the remedy of damages for breach of contract under the CISG and, to a somewhat lesser extent, under the UPICC and PECL (hereafter referred to as the 'international instruments' or the 'instruments'). This focus also explains why the scope of the book is confined to international sales contracts. This book provides a comprehensive and detailed examination of the remedy of damages based on the instruments' nature, purposes, underlying values and policies, principles and rules. At the same time, the book is as much about damages as it is about the life of the instruments. The analysis of the specific remedy of damages sheds light on whether the instruments have been successful in achieving their underlying purposes.[52]

Damages are one of the most important remedies for breach of contract, as demonstrated by a continuous interest in damages of the legal community throughout the world.[53] Much of the interest stems from the reciprocal relationship between the law of damages and the wider policies and purposes pursued by the law. The examination of the law of damages helps identify the law's underlying purposes and values. As one commentator notes, '[n]o aspect of a system of contract law is more revealing of its underlying assumptions than is the law that prescribes the relief available for breach'.[54] At the same time, our understanding of values and policies of the law often influences our judgements about how a particular problem on damages should be resolved. A lawyer's fascination with contract damages also emanates from the realisation of the important practical role that damages play. Remedies, and damages in particular, are vital for the effective operation of contract law. Without them the law of contract would lose much of its force and value[55] and the market economy and trade, which contract

[51] Article 1:201 PECL.

[52] For a recent discussion of this question in the CISG context, see UG Schroeter, 'Has the UN Sales Convention Achieved its Key Purpose(s)?' in Saidov (n 3).

[53] See D Saidov and R Cunnington, 'Current Themes in the Law of Contract Damages: Introductory Remarks' in D Saidov and R Cunnington (eds), *Contract Damages: Domestic and International Perspectives* (Oxford, Hart Publishing, 2008) 1.

[54] EA Farnsworth, 'Damages and Specific Relief' (1979) 27 *AJCL* 247.

[55] See, eg, AL Corbin, *Corbin on Contracts: A Comprehensive Treatise on the Working Rules of Contract Law*, vol 5 (St Paul, Minn, West Publishing Co, 2002) 2.

law supports and facilitates,[56] would be substantially undermined.[57] Damages are also the most frequently invoked remedy for the simple reason that business persons are predominantly concerned with pecuniary matters and aim to achieve the end results in monetary terms.[58]

This book takes both a practical and an analytical perspective. Driven by a sense of commercial realism, it tests and analyses the instruments in various factual and commercial settings. The book develops the rationale of the instruments' provisions on damages and demonstrates the relevance of the rationale of a particular rule to resolving specific and often technical questions on damages. While the problems arising under the instruments are often similar to those addressed by domestic legal systems, international sales transactions raise a number of legal issues that are specific to the cross-border nature of such transactions. For example, losses arising as a result of changes in the values of currencies are likely to arise much more frequently in international than in domestic transactions. Some types of loss, such as the seller's payment of a penalty to state authorities for its non-return (or untimely return) of foreign currency due to the buyer's failure to pay, are altogether unlikely to arise from domestic sales contracts. Where damages are awarded to an injured party in a domestic transaction, the question of the currency of damages is unlikely to be relevant, whereas it often arises in international transactions.

A greater diversity of markets or trade sectors on the international arena is another consideration that can be relevant to calculating damages (eg, in terms of what constitutes a 'market', whether there is a relevant 'market' or 'current' price).[59] Some legal systems, such as English law, have an immensely rich experience of governing international sales and in recent years there has been much discussion about whether the CISG is as well suited to governing the so-called 'trade in commodities' as English law. It has been argued that while the CISG may be better suited to trade sectors involving goods bought for commercial consumption, English law is a better law for commodity sales involving highly volatile markets where traders often enter into contracts for the purpose of speculation.[60] This debate covers all aspects of sales law and engaging with it

[56] H Collins, *The Law of Contract*, 4th edn (London, Butterworths, 2003) 9; J Jackson, 'Global Economics and International Economic Law' (1998) 1 *JIEL* 1, 5; A Rosett, 'Unification, Harmonization, Restatement, Codification, and Reform in International Commercial Law' (1992) 40 *AJCL* 683.

[57] See ch 2 for further discussion of these ideas.

[58] See Saidov and Cunnington (n 53) 2.

[59] See ch 8.

[60] See, eg, MG Bridge, 'A Law for International Sales' (2007) 37 *Hong Kong L J* 17; MG Bridge, 'Uniformity and Diversity in the Law of International Sale' (2003) 15 *Pace Int'l L Rev* 55; A Mullis, 'Avoidance for Breach under the Vienna Convention; A Critical Analysis of Some of the Early Cases' in M Andenas and N Jareborg (eds), *Anglo-Swedish Studies in Law* (Uppsala, Iustus Förlag, 1999) 326; *cf* P Schlechtriem, 'Interpretation, Gap-Filling and Further Development of the UN Sales Convention', available at cisgw3.law.pace.edu/cisg/biblio/schlechtriem6.html; I Schwenzer, 'Avoidance of the Contract in Case of Non-Conforming Goods (Article 49(1)(a) CISG)' (2005–2006) 25 *J L Commerce* 437.

fully would lie outside the book's scope. Nevertheless, the debate was taken into account in the course of writing this book and some chapters[61] explore how the CISG should be applied in the commodities trade context.

The Convention's journey to uniformity has not been smooth, for which there are several inter-related reasons. One is that its provisions lack detail and the interpretation of these general provisions by numerous fora worldwide has generated many inconsistent and conflicting decisions. Another reason relates to the quality and style of many of the reported decisions. In the absence of the centralised institution responsible for giving authoritative interpretations and given the diversity of judicial styles and legal cultures,[62] it is sometimes difficult to understand the rationale underlying a particular decision under the CISG,[63] not to mention those decisions that do not even explain the facts with sufficient clarity and detail. This, coupled with the question of what value should be accorded to prior decisions, has naturally hampered the development of a coherent and well-reasoned body of cases on damages that would send a clear signal to the international commercial and legal community as to what they can expect if they claim damages under the CISG. Despite these difficulties, this book's message is that of optimism and recognition of the Convention's success as a major *truly international* commercial law instrument,[64] but much work needs to be continued to be done by the international legal community to alleviate these difficulties. For its part, by revealing the instruments' experience in respect of damages, distilling and analysing cases decided under the CISG and other instruments and engaging with the rich discourse on damages under the instruments and beyond, this book shows that the instruments have generated a well-developed, highly detailed and robust legal regime on damages for breach of contract.

Continuing with the theme of the Convention's uniform application, it has been correctly noted that the CISG does not mandate an 'absolutist approach to uniformity' but rather 'a process and a mind set' – 'regard' to 'the need to

[61] See chs 3, 8 and 9.

[62] See, eg, MG Bridge, 'Issues Arising under Articles 64, 72 and 73 of the United Nations Convention on Contracts for the International Sale of Goods' (2005–2006) 25 *J L Commerce* 405, 406.

[63] 'How can I write intelligently about case law from different national legal traditions when so many of those cases give sparse reasons for their decisions and often assert propositions in a conclusive, rather than a reasoned, way? … The fate of … laconic case law is to be banished from the main text of commentaries and consigned to an obscure place in the footnotes. If a more discursive style of judgment were to emerge, the case law would be enriched and the weight of the legal culture surrounding the Convention increased. It would no longer be possible, if it ever was, to classify cases as right or wrong. A more nuanced, relative reading would be required' (ibid, 406).

[64] See, eg, Goode, Kronke and McKendrick (n 2) 309 ('The CISG must be considered to be a considerable success. It has been ratified by most of the major trading nations of the world; it has been tested in thousands of cases and arbitral hearings in many of the world's jurisdictions and it has been the subject of exhaustive academic commentary … In general it can be said that the CISG has proved to be a workable instrument in practice which produces sensible results in the vast majority of cases'); R Goode, *Commercial Law in the Next Millennium* (London, Sweet & Maxwell, 1998) 95.

promote uniformity'.[65] The former approach would 'undermine the flexibility required to allow the CISG to deal with the vast diversity of trading conditions around the world ... and ... sacrifice the sometimes slow development of well-conceived and just principles to the false god of absolute uniformity'.[66] A true achievement of the CISG is its spreading of what has been called 'an international law methodology', that is:

> a methodology that, by mandating knowledge of and respect for (but not necessarily submission to) the perspectives of legal systems beyond one's national boundaries, clears the way for more ambitious ventures in international law. As Professor Honnold has written, 'international acceptance of the same rules gives us a common medium for communication – a *lingua franca* – for the international exchange of experience and ideas. It is not too much to expect that this dialogue will contribute to a more cosmopolitan and enlightened approach to law'.[67]

The skeleton structure of the Convention's provisions makes it necessary that the discourse on damages concentrates not on what is a superficial exercise of examining what the Convention provides for – for it is impossible to find 'the law on damages in the text of statutory rules'[68] – but on exploring how the CISG would and should apply to various factual settings.[69] To do so, this book relies not only on cases decided under the international instruments but also on the 'rich storehouse of experience'[70] of major domestic legal systems. This comparative method is very useful, if not essential, for several reasons. First, the experience of domestic legal systems helps identify practical and conceptual problems that may need to be resolved. Second, it provides a range of possible solutions that can be used to resolve these problems. Third, the cases decided in domestic legal systems are in a sense a 'window', additional to that provided by cases decided under the international instruments, into commercial reality. Used this way, the experience of domestic systems can advance our understanding of how certain trade or commercial sectors operate (as is the case, for example, with English sales law that reveals so extensively the specific features of the commodities trade) and how best to interpret and apply the instruments in those commercial contexts. Finally, this comparative exercise is also of value to those interested in domestic legal systems because a comprehensive analysis of

[65] HM Flechtner, 'The Several Texts of the CISG in a Decentralized System: Observations on Translations, Reservations and Other Challenges to the Uniformity Principle in Article 7(1)' (1998) 17 *J L Commerce* 187, 217, also at www.cisg.law.pace.edu/cisg/biblio/flecht1.html.

[66] Ibid. See also S Eiselen, 'Adopting the Vienna Sales Convention: Reflections Eight Years down the Line' (2007) 19 *SA Mercantile L J* 14–17.

[67] Ibid.

[68] MG Bridge, 'The Market Rule of Damages Assessment' in Saidov and Cunnington (n 53) 435.

[69] 'true knowledge of this area of law can only derive from a clear understanding of the complexity and variety of problems surrounding modern commercial transactions' (Saidov and Cunnington (n 53) 4).

[70] See JS Ziegel, 'The Remedial Provisions in the Vienna Sales Convention: Some Common Law Perspectives' in Galston and Smit (eds), *International Sales: The United Nations Convention on Contracts for the International Sale of Goods* (NY, Matthew Bender, 1984) 9-1, 9-2.

the instruments' experience equally reveals problems, questions and solutions earlier unknown to or insufficiently addressed by a domestic system.[71]

The focus on three international instruments naturally involves the comparison between them. In relation to the CISG and UPICC this exercise goes beyond mere comparison. As noted, the preamble to the UPICC provides that the Principles can be used to supplement uniform law instruments like the CISG and the question arises as to the extent to which it is permissible to do so. The provisions of the UPICC on damages are more detailed than those of the CISG. Allowing them to supplement the CISG would mean that the provisions which the Convention itself does not contain would, in effect, be read into it. This approach has rightly been questioned:

> The UNIDROIT Principles were, after all, drawn up subsequent to the coming into effect of the CISG and it is not altogether easy to see the basis on which it can be said that the interpretation of one Convention can be influenced by a document drawn up at a later point in time which does not itself have the force of law.[72]

Simply because the UPICC provide that they can supplement uniform law instruments is not a sufficient basis for doing so, although this function of the UPICC cannot be ruled out altogether. It is submitted that in addressing the relationship between the two instruments, the first step is to consider whether the CISG is capable of resolving the issue *within its own framework*. Where so, there is no need to supplement the CISG with the UPICC.

It is only where no such possibility exists that the question of supplementation is relevant. At this point, may be helpful to distinguish between the case where the instruments' provisions contain the same concepts but where the provisions of the UPICC are more detailed by setting out additional criteria and clarifying the meaning of a particular concept,[73] *and* the case where the issue is a 'gap' under the CISG but which is addressed in the UPICC. Although in the former case supplementing the CISG with the UPICC may be justifiable, the issue in both cases must ultimately be resolved on a case-by-case basis. The critical question is whether the provisions of the UPICC reflect or are based on the same general principles, ideas, legal structures, values and policies as those underlying the CISG.[74] If so, supplementing the CISG with the UPICC is

[71] See Saidov and Cunnington (n 53) 6.

[72] See Goode, Kronke and McKendrick (n 2) 243 (but see also ibid., 477 and 479); see also JY Gotanda, 'Using the UNIDROIT Principles to Fill Gaps in the CISG' in Saidov and Cunnington (n 53) 166 ('it goes too far to apply the UNIDROIT Principles as the primary source of authority for filling a gap in the CISG').

[73] One example relates to the instruments' provisions on fundamental breach (see arts 25 CISG, 7.3.1 UPICC). See further MJ Bonell, 'The UNIDROIT Principles of International Commercial Contracts and CISG – Alternatives or Complementary Instruments?', available at www.cisg.law.pace.edu/cisg/biblio/ulr96.html; *cf* R Koch, 'Commentary on Whether the UNIDROIT Principles of International Commercial Contracts May Be Used to Interpret or Supplement Article 25 CISG', available at www.cisg.law.pace.edu/cisg/biblio/koch1.html#rki.

[74] For an example of where this is arguably not the case, see 7.4.3(3) UPICC which, as this book will argue, reflects a different policy choice to that of the CISG (see ch 7).

arguably justifiable. Contrary to the view that both instruments are based on the same ideas because the UPICC are 'a component part of the "general principles" underlying the Convention',[75] it cannot be assumed that the UPICC as a whole reflect the Convention's general principles.[76]

When it comes to damages for breach of contract, the UPICC potentially provide a lot of opportunities for supplementing the CISG. However, the analysis in this book demonstrates that most unresolved problems on damages under the CISG (which are 'gaps' under the Convention but which are addressed by the UPICC) are capable of being resolved by the Convention itself. This relates to such issues as the problems of the recoverability of loss of a chance, future losses, damage to reputation and goodwill, standard of proof and the currency of damages. Therefore, in this context there is not much room for supplementing the CISG with the UPICC. The UPICC can still be useful to the CISG by informing the meaning of and adding precision to the formulation of the newly developed principles and rules under the CISG.[77]

The instruments' provisions on damages offer, by and large, only general guidance on how the remedy of damages operates. It has been argued that such general rules may no longer be adequate in the light of modern commercial practices, sophisticated transactions and the 'complex mathematical formulae used by economists in providing their calculation of damages'.[78] With this consideration in mind, this book places special emphasis on the calculation of damages.[79] So far as its structure is concerned, the book begins by examining the general aspects of the law of damages, which includes the definition and purposes of damages, the basis for the right to claim damages, basic principles underlying the award of damages and the idea of limiting damages.[80] The chapter on categories of loss[81] analyses the problem of the recoverability of different heads of loss and explores various losses that can arise in international sales contracts. The following chapters examine the methods of limiting damages, such as causation,[82] foreseeability[83] and mitigation.[84] The book concludes by examining the problems of proving losses[85] and calculating damages.[86]

[75] AM Garro, 'The Gap-Filling Role of the UNIDROIT Principles in International Sales Law: Some Comments on the Interplay between the Principles and the CISG' (1994–1995) 69 *Tulane L Rev* 1156.

[76] See Gotanda (n 72); see also F Ferrari, 'General Principles and International Uniform Commercial Law Conventions: A Study of the 1980 Vienna Sales Convention and the 1988 UNIDROIT Conventions on International Factoring and Leasing' (1997) 2 *in* 451, 459–60.

[77] For a similar view, see Gotanda (n 72).

[78] See A Komarov, 'The Limitation of Contract Damages in Domestic Legal Systems and International Instruments' in Saidov and Cunnington (n 53) 246.

[79] See, in particular, chs 8 and 9.

[80] See ch 2.

[81] See ch 3.

[82] See ch 4.

[83] See ch 5.

[84] See ch 6.

[85] See ch 7.

[86] See chs 8 and 9.

Part I

General Part

2

General Part of the Law of Damages

1. DEFINITION AND PURPOSE OF DAMAGES

DAMAGES FOR BREACH of contract under the international instruments can be defined as a *monetary compensation for the loss suffered* by the injured party.[1] While it is easy to formulate the compensatory purpose of damages, it is much more difficult to implement it. The difficulty stems from the problem of defining a loss, and this problem must be addressed at different levels.[2] One level is that of different heads of loss and the question is whether a particular type of loss is sufficiently real and important to qualify for legal protection. Another level is that of the dilemma, faced by every legal system, between the so-called 'concrete' and 'abstract' approaches to calculating damages. This dilemma also poses, in an acute form, questions about the role to be played by some methods of limiting damages, such as mitigation or causation. The next level, interlinked with the previous two, relates to the nature and role of the 'performance interest'. Yet another level, again linked with some of those already mentioned, centres on the extent to which the law should take into account any gains made by the breaching party as a result of the breach in calculating the injured party's loss. Each of the levels is explored in various parts of this book.

While compensation is undoubtedly the central purpose of damages under the instruments, from a policy perspective damages can also be said to pursue a number of other purposes. First, remedies in general, and damages in particular, have been said to serve the goal of keeping peace through the prevention of private wars. It has been suggested that if there were no remedies, the injured parties could 'seek justice' by starting private wars against the breaching parties.[3] While preventing private wars may not be a primary concern in

[1] See arts 74 CISG, 7.4.2 UPICC and 9:502 PECL. The definition of contract damages has been undergoing considerable evolution in some legal systems, see, eg, J Edelman, S Colton and J Varuhas (eds), *McGregor on Damages*, 20th edn (London, Sweet & Maxwell, 2019) [1-001]; also D Saidov and R Cunnington, 'Current Themes in the Law of Contract Damages: Introductory Remarks' in D Saidov and R Cunnington (eds), *Contract Damages: Domestic and International Perspectives* (Oxford, Hart Publishing, 2008) 9–12.

[2] See Saidov and Cunnington (n 1) 17.

[3] See AL Corbin, *Corbin on Contracts: A Comprehensive Treatise on the Working Rules of Contract Law*, vol 5 (St Paul, Minn, West Publishing Co, 2002) 29; AI Ogus, *The Law of Damages* (London, Butterworths, 1973) 5.

the context of international commercial transactions, this goal should not be dismissed altogether considering that commercial law plays an important role in facilitating and supporting international trade which, in turn, is still regarded as an important means of maintaining world peace and friendly relations amongst countries.[4] By requiring '[i]nternational collaboration in the cause of uniformity', the international instruments can also be said to 'assist ... mutual understanding and encourage ... neighbourliness'.[5] Second, the remedies, and in particular damages, are vital for the effective operation of contract law.[6] If no remedies were available, the market economy and international trade which contract law supports[7] would be substantially undermined. Third, in the light of a general need for security in commercial transactions and the instruments' values of *pacta sunt servanda* (contract must be performed)[8] and *favour contractus* (keeping the contract in existence as long as possible)[9] the goal of deterring parties from breaching their contracts is undoubtedly valuable. Although the extent to which damages deter parties from breaching the contract is disputed,[10]

[4] See ch 1.

[5] MG Bridge, 'Uniformity and Diversity in the Law of International Sale' (2003) 15 *Pace Int'l L Rev* 55, 56.

[6] '[W]here no remedy is provided, there is neither right nor duty ... [The recognition of rights and duties] is made effective by providing and enforcing a remedy for breach. Until this has been done, there is no sufficient reason for saying that rights and duties exist as a part of any legal system' (Corbin (n 3) 2); B Coote, 'Contractual Damages, *Ruxley*, and the Performance Interest' (1997) 56 *Cambridge LJ* 537, 541.

[7] H Collins, *The Law of Contract*, 4th edn (London, Butterworths, 2003) 9; J Jackson, 'Global Economics and International Economic Law' (1998) 1 *JIEL* 1, 5; A Rosett, 'Unification, Harmonization, Restatement, Codification, and Reform in International Commercial Law' (1992) 40 *AJCL* 683.

[8] See art 1.3 UPICC and Comment thereon; although the rule is not expressly mentioned in the CISG and PECL, there is little doubt that it is implicit in them (see, eg, arts 30, 53, 79 CISG and 6:111 PECL; see also U Magnus, 'General Principles of UN-Sales Law', available at www.cisg.law.pace.edu/cisg/text/magnus.html; P Huber, 'CISG – The Structure of Remedies' (2007) 71 *Rabels Zeitschrift für ausländisches und internationales Privatrecht* 13, 17–20; O Lando, 'Salient Features of the Principles of European Contract Law: A Comparison with the UCC' (2001) 13 *Pace Int'l L Rev* 339, 343–4, 360–1).

[9] MJ Bonell, 'Art. 7 CISG' in CM Bianca and MJ Bonell, *Commentary on the International Sales Law: The 1980 Vienna Sales Convention* (Milan, Giuffrè, 1987) 80; MJ Bonell, *An International Restatement of Contract Law: The UNIDROIT Principles of International Commercial Contracts*, 3rd edn (Ardsley, NY, Transnational Publishers Inc, 2005) 102–26, JM Perillo, 'UNIDROIT Principles of International Commercial Contracts: The Black Letter Text and a Review' (1994) 63 *Fordham L Rev* 281, 303; Lando (n 8) 360–1.

[10] The ability of damages to deter a breach and induce performance has been doubted. One argument is that it is not a formal legal sanction that deters a breach but various non-legal sanctions (eg, reputational loss) that have a true deterrent effect (see H Collins, *Regulating Contracts* (Oxford, OUP, 1999) 97–126; CP Gillette, 'Reputation and Intermediaries in Electronic Commerce' (2001–2002) 62 *La L Rev* 1165; L Bernstein, 'Opting out of the Legal System: Extralegal Contractual Relations in the Diamond Industry' (1992) 21 *JLS* 115; L Bernstein, 'Private Commercial Law in the Cotton Industry: Creating Cooperation through Rules, Norms, and Institutions' (2000–2001) 99 *Mich L Rev* 1724). Another is that the need to establish the preconditions for an award of damages and uncertainties involved in proving losses may in fact create incentives to break a contract (see D Harris, 'Incentives to Perform, or Break Contracts' (1992) 45 *Current Legal Problems* 29). From the law and economics perspective, it has been argued that the 'expectation' measure often encourages a party to breach the contract where, by doing so, it will be able to fully compensate the other

damages, being in a sense a legal sanction for breach, may nevertheless have a deterrent effect.[11]

Fourth, it is submitted that economic considerations of wealth maximisation and economic efficiency are not irrelevant to the international instruments and arguably constitute an important part of values that the instruments promote.[12] The value of free trade, which the international instruments facilitate, is often justified on the basis of efficient allocation of resources.[13] In addition, the goals of uniformity and harmonisation pursued by the instruments are believed to encourage trade by means of reducing transaction costs.[14] Specific principles and rules underlying the law of damages such as the protection of the expectation/performance interest, foreseeability and mitigation are also in line with the goal of efficient allocation of resources.[15] Therefore, at least to some extent the remedy of damages can be justified from the law and economics perspective. But not all components of the traditional law and economics analysis are acceptable to the ethos of the international instruments. This relates to the doctrine of 'efficient breach', which refers to a situation where it is *efficient* for a party to breach its contract because by doing so it will be able to fully compensate the injured party for the loss suffered and be left with a benefit greater than that which it would have received had it performed the contract.[16] This doctrine, it is suggested, does not sit easily with the already-mentioned values, underlying the instruments, of *pacta sunt servanda* and *favour contractus*. Finally, sales contracts are not only concerned with the passing of property in the goods but also perform an important function of allocating market risks[17] and the remedy

party for the loss suffered *and* be left with a greater gain than that it would have received had it performed the contract ('efficient breach') (see, eg, AI Ogus, 'The Economic Basis of Damages for Breach of Contract: Inducement and Expectation' in Saidov and Cunnington (n 1) 126–9; D Harris, D Campbell and R Halson, *Remedies in Contract and Tort*, 2nd edn (Cambridge, CUP, 2002) 77).

[11] See R Demogue, 'Validity of the Theory of Compensatory Damages' (1917–1918) 27 *Yale L J* 591; for a similar view, see Corbin (n 3) 29.

[12] 'Ultimately, it is economics that drives the demand for international trade, and international trade that drives the demand for transnational contract law. International legal institutions should accordingly attend to the economic underpinnings of the transactions they govern, in order to facilitate their underlying purposes' (AW Katz, 'Remedies for Breach of Contract under the CISG' (2006) 25 *Int'l Rev L Economics* 378, 394).

[13] See, eg, JH Jackson, WJ Davey and AO Sykes, Jr, *Legal Problems of International Economic Relations: Cases, Materials and International Regulation of Transnational Economic Relations*, 3rd edn (St Paul, Minn, West Publishing Co, 1995) 7–14.

[14] For a critical analysis, see G Cuniberti, 'Is the CISG Benefiting Anybody?' (2006) 39 *Vanderbilt J Transnational L* 1511.

[15] See the respective parts of the book where each of these rules is examined.

[16] For an overview, see Ogus (n 10).

[17] 'The function of contract has shifted: instead of simply being the method of transferring title to specific property, a contract promising future delivery became a means of ensuring an expected future market return. Executory contracts became important as instruments for futures agreements, designed to transfer risk from those wishing to insure against market fluctuations in supply and price to those wishing to speculate' (D Simon and GA Novack, 'Limiting the Buyer's Market Damages to Lost Profits: Challenge to the Enforceability of Market Contracts' (1978–1979) 92 *Harvard L Rev* 1395, 1399). See also MR Cohen, 'The Basis of Contract' (1932–1933) 46 *Harvard L Rev* 584–5.

of damages plays an important role in ensuring that such risks are allocated in accordance with the instruments' policies and values.

2. BASIS FOR THE RIGHT TO CLAIM DAMAGES

2.1. General

A claim for damages can arise in several types of case which include situations involving a breach of contract, problems of validity of the contract,[18] and pre-contractual relationships.[19] This book is only concerned with claims arising from a breach of contract. To succeed in its claim for damages for breach of contract, the injured party must prove that: the other party has committed a *breach* of contract; it has suffered *loss*, recognised by the instruments as recoverable; and the loss has occurred *as a consequence of the breach*. The loss will be recovered only to the extent to which it was foreseeable by the breaching party at the time of the conclusion of the contract and the burden of proving foreseeability lies with the injured party.[20] The injured party is also required to take all reasonable steps to mitigate its loss and this requirement is a further limitation on damages. In contrast with the foreseeability requirement, it is the breaching party who bears the initial burden of proving the injured party's failure to mitigate.[21] The issues of recoverable heads of loss, causation, foreseeability, mitigation and proof are considered in later chapters. This section only makes some remarks in relation to the breach of contract as the basis for the right to claim damages.

In contrast with some civil law systems,[22] the international instruments rely upon a comprehensive and uniform concept of breach (or non-performance) of

[18] The issues of validity are outside the scope of the CISG (see art 4); see ch 3 UPICC (on the measure of damages, see art 3.2.16); see ch 4 PECL (on the measure of damages see art 4:117).

[19] See arts 2.1.15, 2.1.16 UPICC and 2:301, 2:302 PECL. For the discussion of legal issues which may arise in the course of pre-contractual dealings, see J Dietrich, 'Classifying Precontractual Liability: A Comparative Analysis' (2001) 21 *LS* 156; EA Farnsworth, 'Precontractual Liability and Preliminary Agreements: Fair Dealing and Failed Negotiations' (1987) 87 *Columbia L Rev* 217; F Kessler and E Fine, 'Culpa in Contrahendo, Bargaining in Good Faith, and Freedom of Contract: A Comparative Study' (1963–1964) 77 *Harvard L Rev* 401; NE Nedzel, 'A Comparative Study of Good Faith, Fair Dealing, and Precontractual Liability' (1997) 12 *Tulane European Civil L Forum* 97. On pre-contractual liability and the CISG (see, eg, I Schwenzer and P Hachem, 'Arts 1–6 CISG' in I Schwenzer (ed), *Schlechtriem and Schwenzer Commentary on the UN Convention on the International Sale of Goods (CISG)*, 4th edn (Oxford, OUP, 2016) 80–81; DM Goderre, 'International Negotiations Gone Sour: Precontractual Liability under the United Nations Sales Convention' (1997) 66 *U Cincinnati L Rev* 257, 274–80; J Klein and C Bachechi, 'Precontractual Liability and the Duty of Good Faith Negotiation in International Transactions' (1994–1995) 17 *Houston J Int'l L* 1, 19–26).

[20] See ch 5.

[21] See ch 6.

[22] See GH Treitel, *Remedies for Breach of Contract: A Comparative Account* (Oxford, Clarendon Press, 1988) 129; J Basedow, 'Towards a Universal Doctrine of Breach of Contract: The Impact of the CISG' (2005) 25 *Int'l Rev L Economics* 487, 489–91.

contract: *any* breach or non-performance[23] gives an aggrieved party the right to claim damages. According to the CISG, '[i]f the seller fails to perform any of his obligations under the contract or this Convention, the buyer may … claim damages as provided for in articles 74 to 77'.[24] Similarly, '[i]f the buyer fails to perform any of his obligations under the contract or this Convention, the seller may … claim damages as provided in articles 74 to 77'.[25] The UPICC provide that '[a]ny non-performance gives the aggrieved party a right to damages either exclusively or in conjunction with any other remedies'.[26] Likewise, the PECL provide that '[t]he aggrieved party is entitled to damages for loss caused by the other party's non-performance'.[27] The character and gravity of the breach or its consequences are irrelevant to the right to claim damages.

2.2. The Role of Fault

In contrast with some civil law systems,[28] the party's right to damages under the instruments does not depend on the breaching party's fault.[29] Nevertheless, some elements, of which the notion of fault can consist, may play a role in determining whether a breach of contract has occurred. In those legal systems which utilise the concept of fault, two forms of fault are identified: actual fault and negligence.[30] The former is fault in the subjective sense because it refers to the

[23] The CISG uses the terms 'breach' or 'failure to perform' and the UPICC and the PECL use the term 'non-performance'.

[24] Article 45(1)(b) CISG; see also Case No 10 Ob 518/95 Supreme Court (Austria) 6 February 1996 (Propane), available at cisgw3.law.pace.edu/cases/960206a3.html; Case No 8 U 46/97 Appellate Court Zweibrücken (Germany) 31 March 1998 (Vine wax), available at cisgw3.law.pace.edu/cases/980331g1.html; Case No 4 O 113/90 District Court Baden-Baden (Germany) 14 August 1991 (Wall tiles), available at cisgw3.law.pace.edu/cases/910814g1.html.

[25] Article 61(1)(b) CISG; see also Case No 2 U 27/99 Appellate Court Braunschweig (Germany) 28 October 1999 (Frozen meat), available at cisgw3.law.pace.edu/cases/991028g1.html; Case No 43 O 136/92 District Court Aachen (Germany) 14 May 1993 (Electronic hearing aid), available at cisgw3.law.pace.edu/cases/930514g1.html.

[26] Article 7.4.1 UPICC.

[27] Article 9:501 PECL; see also art 8:101(1) providing that '[w]henever a party does not perform an obligation under the contract and the non-performance is not excused under Art 8.108, the aggrieved party may resort to any of the remedies.'

[28] '[T]he contract in the civil law world primarily is a mutual promise of a certain behaviour whereas the common law would consider the contract rather as a guarantee made by each party of the result achieved by the performance of its undertaking. What the party owes under common law is a certain state of affairs, while the obligation is directed towards a certain behaviour in civil law jurisdictions. Consequently, the breach of contract under common law consists in the divergence between the result promised under the contract and the real state of affairs, it is a matter of objective assessment. In itself, this divergence is not sufficient to qualify as a breach in the perspective of civil law jurisdictions; since the obligation is focused on the debtor's behaviour a breach can only be assessed if the debtor could reasonably have been expected to behave in a different way. Therefore, the fault principle is often considered to be an indispensable part of the law of obligations in civil law countries' (Basedow (n 22) 495 with further reference).

[29] See, eg, I Schwenzer, 'Arts 74–77' in Schwenzer (n 19) 1058.

[30] Treitel (n 22) 8, 11–13; MI Braginskiy and VV Vitryanskiy, *Contract Law: General Provisions (Dogovornoye pravo: Obshiye polozheniya)* (Moscow, Statut, 1998) 595–97, 613.

breaching party acting intentionally or deliberately.[31] The latter, which in different systems can have different degrees,[32] is fault in the objective sense: it denotes a failure to exercise the required degree of care or skill.[33] Actual fault (in the subjective sense) looks at the actual intent of the party while negligence (fault in the objective sense) requires compliance with a certain standard of conduct and this means that 'a defendant may … be liable even though he was not guilty of any actual (or subjective) fault'.[34] With regard to the question whether a breach, to constitute the basis for the right to claim damages, must be accompanied by fault, it is the notion of fault in the objective sense that may be relevant. Take the UPICC that distinguish between a duty 'to achieve a specific result' and a duty 'to exert best efforts': 'To the extent that an obligation of a party involves a duty to achieve a specific result, that party is bound to achieve that result'[35] and '[t]o the extent that an obligation of a party involves a duty of best efforts in the performance of an activity, that party is bound to make such efforts as would be made by a reasonable person of the same kind in the same circumstances'.[36] This distinction has its roots in French law,[37] where a failure to comply with the duty of best efforts (*obligation de moyen*) – that is, to show 'the degree of care to be expected of a reasonable person'[38] – is regarded as fault in the objective sense.[39] The same line of reasoning is applicable to the UPICC: to prove a breach of duty of 'best efforts' it must be demonstrated that the other party's conduct was not in compliance with the standard fixed in the UPICC, namely, 'such efforts as would be made by a reasonable person of the same kind in the

[31] Treitel (n 22) 12; Braginskiy and Vitryanskiy (n 30) 595, 613. For example, in the Russian doctrine of civil law 'wilful fault' is defined as 'intentional acts or failure to act with a view not to perform an obligation or not to perform an obligation properly' (ibid, 613) (translation of the author).

[32] 'Civil law systems … distinguish between ordinary (or 'slight') and gross negligence' (Treitel (n 22) 11); also Braginskiy and Vitryanskiy (n 30) 595, 613.

[33] Treitel (n 22) 11–12; Braginskiy and Vitryanskiy (n 30) 595, 613.

[34] Treitel (n 22) 12.

[35] Article 5.1.4(1) UPICC.

[36] Article 5.1.4(2) UPICC.

[37] See M Fontaine, 'Content and Performance' (1992) 40 *AJCL* 648. For the discussion of the classification in French law, see B Nicholas, *The French Law of Contract*, 2nd edn (Oxford, Clarendon Press, 1992) 50–56; B Nicholas, 'Rules and Terms – Civil and Common Law' (1973–1974) 48 *Tulane L R* 946, 952–5; Treitel (n 22) 9–10. This distinction is also used in other legal systems (see note 2 in Comment on art 8:101 in O Lando and H Beale (eds), *Principles of European Contract Law: Parts I and II* (prepared by the Commission on European Contract Law (The Hague, Kluwer Law International, 2000) 361).

[38] Treitel (n 22) 11.

[39] See Treitel (n 22) 9 ('A party claiming damages for breach of [*obligation de moyens*] must prove that the other party was guilty of fault'); Nicholas (n 37) 52; ICC No 7006, 1992 (decided on the basis of French law) (in *Collection of ICC Arbitral Awards: 1991–1995: Recueil des Sentences Arbitrales de la CCI 1991–1995*, compiled by JJ Arnaldez Y Derains and D Hascher (The Hague, Kluwer Academic Law Publishers, 1997) 203); F Werro and EM Belser, 'Switzerland' in MJ Bonell (eds), *A New Approach to International Commercial Contracts: The UNIDROIT Principles of International Commercial Contract* (The Netherlands, Kluwer Law International, 1999) 368 ('When … the obligor merely owes her best efforts, proof of nonperformance overlaps with the proof of the obligor's fault').

same circumstances'.[40] Therefore, proving a breach of duty of 'best efforts' under the UPICC is similar to what French law would regard as proving the other party's *fault* in the objective sense. Contracts governed by the CISG[41] and PECL[42] may also provide for obligations of 'best efforts' and, where so, establishing a breach of such an obligation will also involve demonstrating what some legal systems would treat as objective fault.

There may also be cases, governed by the instruments, where fault becomes relevant by virtue of the parties' agreement. Because parties are free to derogate from the instruments' provisions,[43] they can contractually incorporate additional preconditions for the right to claim damages, such as fault. In one CISG case,[44] the seller's warranty terms, which were a part of the contract, provided that the buyer could not have the right to claim damages for non-conformity in the goods, unless 'the damage resulted from or ... the defect resulted from *wilful or harshly negligent* action on [the seller]'s side'. Notwithstanding the Convention's principle of strict liability, the court had to treat fault as a necessary precondition for the right to damages: 'the parties are free to agree on the content of the warranty and its effect on the liability for non-conformity'.[45]

2.3. Anticipatory Breach

The instruments recognise not only the breach which has *actually* occurred but also an 'anticipatory breach'[46] or 'anticipatory non-performance'.[47] This refers to a situation where *before* the due date for performance the innocent party has grounds to expect that the other party's performance *at* the due date will not be forthcoming. The recognition of an 'anticipatory breach' makes it possible for a party to be liable even before the due date for the performance of its obligation.[48] The anticipatory breach concept forms the basis of several

[40] Article 5.1.4(2) UPICC.

[41] See also B Nicholas, 'Fault and Breach of Contract' in J Beatson and D Friedmann (eds), *Good Faith and Fault in Contract Law* (Oxford, Clarendon Press, 1995) 352 (interpreting art 60 CISG as containing an obligation of best efforts).

[42] See Comment on Article 5:101 PECL in Lando and Beale (n 37) 286.

[43] See art 6 CISG, art 1.1 UPICC and art 1:102 PECL.

[44] Turku Court of Appeal (Finland) 12 April 2002 (Forestry equipment), available at cisgw3.law.pace.edu/cases/020412f5.html.

[45] See also Arbitration No 48, 2005 (Ukraine), available at cisgw3.law.pace.edu/cases/050000u5.html.

[46] The term used in the CISG.

[47] The term used in the UPICC and in the PECL.

[48] For the discussion of the concept of anticipatory breach, see JC Gulotta, Jr, 'Anticipatory Breach – A Comparative Analysis' (1976) 50 *Tulane L Rev* 927; MG Strub, 'The Convention on the International Sale of Goods: Anticipatory Repudiation Provisions and Developing Countries' (1989) 38 *ICLQ* 475; D Saidov, 'Anticipatory Non-Performance and Underlying Values of the UNIDROIT Principles' (2006) 11 *Uniform L Rev* 795; D Saidov, 'Arts 71–73' in S Kröll, L Mistelis and P Viscasillas (eds), *The United Nations Convention on Contracts for the International Sale of Goods*, 2nd edn (München, C.H. Beck and Oxford, Hart 2018).

provisions in the CISG. First, according to art 71, 'if after the conclusion of the contract, it becomes apparent that the other party will not perform a substantial part of his obligations',[49] the innocent party is entitled to suspend its obligations.[50] Article 71(2) also provides for a remedy, specifically designed for the seller, of preventing the handing over of the goods to the buyer if the seller had dispatched the goods before it knew of the grounds indicating danger of a future 'substantial nonperformance'. The party suspending performance also has an obligation to 'immediately give notice of the suspension to the other party and [to] continue with performance if the other party provides adequate assurance of his performance'.[51] Second, according to art 72(1), '[i]f prior to the date for performance of the contract it is clear that one of the parties will commit a fundamental breach of contract, the other party may declare the contract avoided'.[52] The article further provides that '[i]f time allows, the party intending to declare the contract avoided must give reasonable notice to the other party in order to permit him to provide adequate assurance of his performance'.[53] This requirement does not apply 'if the other party has declared that he will not perform his obligations'.[54]

It is submitted that an anticipatory breach can constitute a basis for claiming damages where the innocent party *avoids* the contract under art 72(1).[55] Where the contract is not or cannot be avoided under art 72(1), no right to claim damages should be available. First, it is only the avoidance of the contract that crystallises the parties' legal positions in that neither party can change its mind: if the contract remains in existence, there is still a possibility that the party under suspicion will be able to perform. Allowing a claim for damages *only* where the contract is avoided helps achieve finality and certainty in resolving disputes. Second, the innocent party cannot be allowed to claim damages for loss of a bargain while maintaining that the other party must still perform the contract. It is also worth reiterating that while the innocent party has the right to suspend its performance of the contract (where it is apparent that the other party will not perform a substantial part of its obligations), it must immediately give notice of suspension to enable the other party to provide adequate assurance of performance. A failure to do so is a sufficient basis for that other party

[49] The criteria for determining whether there is a danger of a future 'substantial nonperformance' are 'a serious deficiency in [the other party's] ability to perform or [this party's] creditworthiness; [the other party's] conduct in preparing to perform or performing the contract' (art 71(1)(a) and (b)).

[50] See art 71(1); suspension must be understood as meaning not only actual performance, but also preparation to perform (see P Schlechtriem, *Uniform Sales Law: The UN-Convention on Contracts for the International Sale of Goods* (Vienna, Manz Verlag, 1986) 93).

[51] Article 71(3).

[52] Article 72(1).

[53] Article 72(2) CISG.

[54] Article 72(3) CISG.

[55] See also art 73 CISG. The arguments are based on those developed in the context of the common law in Q Liu, 'Claiming Damages upon an Anticipatory Breach: Why Should an Acceptance Be Necessary?' (2005) 25 *LS* 559, 566.

to claim damages.[56] The same can be said about the notification requirement in art 72(2) CISG.[57] The UPICC and PECL also enable an innocent party to suspend performance[58] or terminate the contract[59] in cases of anticipatory non-performance. For the reasons just given, it is similarly submitted that damages should only be available under these instruments where the contract has been terminated.

3. BASIC MEASURE OF DAMAGES

3.1. General

The basic measure of damages establishes the principle(s) based on which the amount of compensation must be determined. The measure expressly provided for by the instruments is that the injured party is entitled to damages for the loss suffered, including loss of profit (or gains prevented).[60] The PECL also provide that '[t]he general measure of damages is such sum as will put the aggrieved party as nearly as possible into the position in which it would have been if the contract had been duly performed'.[61] The former principle, known as the principle of 'full compensation',[62] has its roots in Roman law where recoverable damages were classified as both *damnum emergens* (actual loss) and *lucrum cessans* (lost profit),[63] and is widely used by many civil law systems.[64] The principle is relatively simple – an injured party is entitled to claim *full* compensation for the losses it has suffered and gains of which it was deprived as a result of the breach.[65]

[56] See Netherlands Arbitration Institute No 2319, 15 October 2002 (Condensate crude oil mix), available at cisgw3.law.pace.edu/cases/021015n1.html.

[57] See Strub (n 48) 498.

[58] Article 7.3.4 UPICC (first sentence): 'A party who reasonably believes that there will be a fundamental non-performance by the other party may demand adequate assurance of due performance and may meanwhile withhold its own performance'; art 9:201(2) PECL: 'A party may similarly withhold performance for as long as it is clear that there will be a non-performance by the other party when the other party's performance becomes due.'

[59] Article 7.3.3 UPICC: 'Where prior to the date for performance by one of the parties it is clear that there will be a fundamental non-performance by that party, the other party may terminate the contract' (see also art 7.3.4 UPICC second sentence); art 9:304: 'Where prior to the time for performance by a party it is clear that there will be a fundamental non-performance by it the other party may terminate the contract.'

[60] See arts 74 CISG, 7.4.2 UPICC, 9:502 PECL.

[61] Article 9:502 PECL.

[62] See, eg, arts 14 of the Civil Code of Uzbekistan and 15 of the Civil Code of the Russian Federation; see also Braginskiy and Vitryanskiy (n 30) 516; AP Sergeyev and YK Tolstoy, *Civil Law* (*Grazhdanskoye pravo*) Part 1 (Moscow, Prospect Publishing House, 1998) 554.

[63] See IS Peretyorskiy and IB Novitskiy, *Roman Private Law* (*Rimskoye Chastnoye Pravo*) (Moscow, Yurist, 1999).

[64] See Lando and Beale (n 37) 439.

[65] This simplicity probably explains why relatively little attention has been paid to the discussion of this principle in civil law. See, eg, Nicholas (n 37) 226 (stating that French writers make nothing of the distinction between *damnum emergens* and *lucrum cessans*).

The latter principle, known as the protection of the 'expectation',[66] 'performance',[67] or 'positive'[68] interest, derives from those legal systems (mainly those of the common law)[69] which view 'the remedies for breach of contract through the "interests" that the remedies serve to protect'.[70] The protection of the expectation/performance interest compensates the injured party for loss of the bargain.[71]

Suppose that A contracts with B to manufacture and sell a piece of machinery for £100,000. The cost of manufacture is £80,000. Before A incurs any costs B refuses to perform. The 'net' profit that A expected to gain from the contract was £20,000 and the protection of the expectation/performance interest would lead to the award of £20,000 because this is the amount with which A would have been left had B performed the contract. Despite different formulations of the basic measure of damages, there is no doubt that both the principle of full compensation and the protection of the expectation/performance interest are based on the very same idea:[72] it is only by being *fully* compensated for its loss (including loss of profit) that the party is placed in the position in which it would have been had the contract been performed.[73] This explains why art 74 CISG, for example, is interpreted as based on both the principle of full compensation[74]

[66] See LL Fuller and WR Perdue, Jr, 'The Reliance Interest in Contract Damages' (1936) 46 *Yale L J* 53. The term 'expectation interest' has been heavily criticised: 'The expectation interest is simply an inappropriate term describing the performance interest … If we understand 'interest' to reflect the purpose or the reason for entering the contract, then performance is the only genuine contractual interest.' 'Expectancy' is often used to describe a prospect or a probability of receiving a benefit in the future, *when this possibility is not supported by a legal right*' (D Friedmann, 'The Performance Interest in Contract Damages' (1995) 111 *LQR* 628, 632, 634).

[67] See Friedmann (n 66).

[68] See Lando and Beale (n 37) 439.

[69] See *Robinson v Harman* (1848) 1 Exch 850; § 344(a) Restatement (Second) of Contracts (1981).

[70] A Burrows, 'Contract, Tort and Restitution – A Satisfactory Division or Not?' (1983) 99 *LQR* 218. In English law, the principle of putting the injured party in the position in which it would have been had the contract been properly performed had existed before it was labelled as the protection of the 'expectation' or 'performance' interest (see *Robinson v Harman* (n 69)).

[71] See Treitel (n 22) 82.

[72] '[Art 9:502] combines the widely accepted "expectation interest" basis of damages and the traditional rule of "*damnum emergens*" and "*lucrum cessans*" of Roman law' (Lando and Beale (n 37) 437).

[73] This statement finds support in Roman law where the formula, based on the distinction between *damnum emergens* and *lucrum cessans* ('interesse') meant the 'difference' between the position of the creditor in which it would have been had the obligation been performed and the actual position in which it found itself as a result of the breach (see Peretyorskiy and Novitskiy (n 63)). The basic measure under the CISG is sometimes interpreted in the same way (see Schwenzer (n 29) 1059, with further references and criticism of such an approach).

[74] See, eg, V Knapp, 'Arts. 74–77 CISG' in CM Bianca and MJ Bonell (eds), *Commentary on the International Sales Law: The 1980 Vienna Sales Convention* (Giuffrè, Milan 1987) 543; M Djordjević, 'Arts 74–77' in S Kröll, L Mistelis and P Viscasillas (eds), *The United Nations Convention on Contracts for the International Sale of Goods*, 2nd edn (München, C.H. Beck and Oxford, Hart, 2018) 958; E Visser, 'Gaps in the CISG: In General and with Specific Emphasis on the Interpretation of the Remedial Provisions of the Convention in the Light of the General Principles of the CISG', available at www.cisg.law.pace.edu/cisg/biblio/visser.html; Vienna Arbitration SCH–4318,

and the protection of the expectation/performance interest.[75] A convenient way of conceptualising the relationship between the two principles is to view the protection of the expectation/performance interests as the *goal* that damages seek to achieve, whilst treating the principle of full compensation as the *means* of achieving that goal.[76]

The aim of protecting the expectation/performance interest has been justified in various ways. First, the binding nature of the contract suggests that the party has a *legal right* to the other party's performance of an obligation. If the obligation is not performed, it arguably flows from the innocent party's legal right to performance that damages must be measured with reference to the value of that obligation.[77] There is little doubt that 'the very recognition of a legal right entails some consequences regarding the remedy, one of which relates to the initial point of inquiry. This initial point relates to the value of legal right.'[78] It is suggested that this reason in itself is sufficiently strong to justify the goal of protecting the expectation/performance interest.[79] Second, this goal has been justified from the perspective of the morality of promise keeping. It is said that 'promises are sacred *per se*, that there is something inherently despicable about not keeping a promise, and a properly organized society should not tolerate this … [C]ommon sense does generally find something revolting about the breaking of a promise, and this, if a fact, must be taken into account by the law.'[80] It follows from this view that because a promise and the innocent party's expectations are important, the law should provide the party with the value of the broken promise.

15 June 1994 (Rolled metal sheets), available at cisgw3.law.pace.edu/cases/940615a4.html; Vienna Arbitration SCH–4366, 15 June 1994 (Rolled metal sheets) cisgw3.law.pace.edu/cases/940615a3.html; ICC No 7585, 1992 (Foamed board machinery), available at cisgw3.law.pace.edu/cases/927585i1.html.

[75] Commentary to art 70 of the 1978 Draft, para 3; Knapp (n 74) 543; JS Sutton, 'Measuring Damages under the United Nations Convention on the International Sale of Goods' (1989) 50 *Ohio State L J* 737, also at: www.cisg.law.pace.edu/cisg/biblio/sutton.html; EC Schneider, 'Measuring Damages under the CISG', available at www.cisg.law.pace.edu/cisg/text/cross/cross-74.html.

[76] For further discussion of the relationship between the two principles, see Nicholas (n 37) 226 and D Tallon, 'French Report' in D Harris and D Tallon (eds), *Contract Law Today: Anglo-French Comparisons* (Oxford, Clarendon Press, 1991) 274.

[77] The most obvious example is that of damages for the buyer's non-payment of the price to the seller who has performed its contractual obligations. These damages (awarded in *Norfolk Railway v Power Source Supply, Inc*, 2008 WL 2884102) become very similar to the seller's exercise of its right to specific performance (see, eg, art 62 CISG). Similarly, it may be that despite best efforts the innocent seller is unable to resell the goods, not accepted and paid for by the buyer, which results in the deterioration of the goods. In this case, again, the contract price (subject to any saved costs) represents the value of the seller's contractual right to the buyer's performance (see ICAC No 37/2006, 11 October 2006 in PD Savkin (ed), *Praktika MKAS pri TPP RF: 2004–2016 – K 85-letiyu MKAS* (Nauka Prava – Elektronnaya biblioteka, Moskva, 2017) 391).

[78] See Friedmann (n 66) 637.

[79] For a similar position, see A Von Mehren, 'General View of Contract' in *International Encyclopedia of Comparative Law* (vol VII, 1981) 92.

[80] Cohen (n 17) 571–2. See also C Fried, *Contract as a Promise: A Theory of Contractual Obligation* (Cambridge, Mass, Harvard University Press, 1981).

The third justification emphasises not the morality of a promise, but the psychological expectation of the innocent party, which is described thus: 'The breach of a promise arouses in the promise a sense of injury … [T]he promise has formed an attitude of expectancy such that a breach of the promise causes him to feel that he has been "deprived" of something which was "his".'[81] However, this argument cannot fully justify the protection of the expectation/performance interest because no legal system protects every kind of promise and every kind of expectation.[82] Another justification is that since 'expectation damages' provide the injured party with the benefit of the bargain, the remedy of damages based on the protection of the expectation/performance interest increases security in commercial transactions by reducing the risks associated with the breach of contract and encourages contracting and exchange.[83] This, in turn, provides the necessary support for the market economy by making it possible for goods and services to end up where they are valued most.[84] In a similar vein, it can be argued that the protection of the expectation/performance interest is essential for maintaining the system of credit, an important part of the economic system in the modern world:

> The essence of a credit economy lies in the fact that it tends to eliminate the distinction between present and future (promised) goods. Expectations of future values become, for purposes of trade, present values. In a society in which credit has become a significant and pervasive institution, it is inevitable that the expectancy created by an enforceable promise should be regarded as a kind of property, and breach of the promise as an injury to that property. In such a society the breach of a promise works an 'actual' diminution of the promisee's assets – 'actual' in the sense that it would be so appraised according to modes of thought which enter into the very fiber of our economic system.[85]

Protecting the party's expectation/performance interest has also been encouraged from the law and economics perspective. One reason is that the economic goal of wealth maximisation requires that resources be put to their most valuable use and, as noted, the 'expectation' damages aim to do just that. In other words, because a voluntary exchange is usually thought to lead to an efficient allocation of resources, 'expectation damages' play an important role in achieving such an allocation by providing incentives for parties to enter into transactions.[86]

[81] Fuller and Perdue (n 66) 57.

[82] See ibid, 57–8.

[83] See, eg, DW Barnes, 'The Net Expectation Interest in Contractual Damages (1999) 48 *Emory L J* 1159–60.

[84] See Fuller and Perdue (n 66) 60–62; A Burrows, *Remedies for Torts, Breach of Contract and Equitable Wrongs*, 4th edn (Oxford, OUP, 2019) 40.

[85] Fuller and Perdue (n 66) 59.

[86] 'Say, for example, A contracts to sell to B for £100,000 a machine that is worth £110,000 to B (ie that would yield him a profit of £10,000). Before delivery C comes to A and offers him £109,000 for that machine. A would be encouraged to breach the contract with B were he not liable to pay B £10,000 expectation damages. Given that damages do protect the expectation rather than the

A further reason relates to the 'efficient breach' doctrine, a significant part of the economic analysis of contract law. For a breach to be efficient, not only must the breaching party be made better off but also no one must be made worse off (Pareto efficiency) and the 'expectation damages' generally meet these criteria. In the efficient breach situation, the injured party by being awarded a full value of the promised performance is not, as a rule, worse off as a result of the breach while the breaching party is better off.[87] While, as explained, the 'efficient breach' doctrine does not sit easily with the instruments' values of *pacta sunt servanda* and *favour contractus*, the perspective that focuses on the incentives for parties to enter into a voluntary exchange is in line with the instruments' policy of promoting international commerce and trade.[88]

3.2. 'Gains Made' and 'Costs Saved' as a Result of the Breach

By providing the basic measure of compensation, the principles of full compensation and the protection of the party's expectation/performance interest also set a limit on how much the injured party can recover. In other words, these principles dictate that the party cannot be awarded damages which exceed the amount of its loss and be put in a better position than the one in which it would have been had the contract been performed. This means that to prevent over-compensation, all gains made and costs saved as a consequence of the breach must be taken into account when calculating damages.[89] Suppose that after the buyer's failure to pay £2,000 for the manufacture of jewellery the manufacturer uses the resources, initially allocated to performing the contract with the buyer, to fulfil another order which would not have been accepted had the buyer performed the contract. If the seller expected to receive a 'net' profit margin of £500 (£1,500 being the cost of manufacture) from its contract with the buyer and if the seller's 'net' profit from a substitute order was £300, the seller would be entitled to an award of £200 because £300 would represent gains made as a result of the breach.

'Costs saved' as a result of the breach are relevant where it is 'gross' profit, as opposed to 'net' profit, that is the starting point for calculating damages.[90]

reliance interest, C will not be able to induce a breach of A's contract with B unless he offers A more than £110,000 thereby indicating that the machine really is worth more to him than to B. The expectation rule thus ensures that the machine ends up where it is most valuable' (Burrows (n 84) 40).

[87] For an overview, see Ogus (n 10).

[88] See the discussion above.

[89] See, eg, art 7.4.2(1) UPICC and Comment 3 thereon; CISG Advisory Council (CISG–AC) Opinion No 6, 'Calculation of Damages under CISG Article 74', available at www.cisg.law.pace.edu/cisg/CISG-AC-op6.html; Comment C on Article 9:502 PECL (see Lando and Beale (n 37) 438–9).

[90] See CISG–AC (n 89); Comment C on art 9:502 PECL (see Lando and Beale (n 37) 438–9). See also Case No 11 O 4261/94 District Court Kassel (Germany) 21 September 1995 (Wooden poles), available at cisgw3.law.pace.edu/cases/950921g1.html ('[the Buyer's inability to perform its sub-sale contract] caused in the first place a loss of revenue of US $608,879.77 which however must not be

To return to the previous example, suppose that all that is known at the start of the calculation process is the seller's contract price of £2,000 (gross profit). In this case, all the costs the seller would have incurred to deliver the jewellery must be identified. Suppose the seller has actually spent £800 on procuring precious stones and that, had the buyer performed, it would have also spent £500 to employ a specialist and £200 to pay for other necessary materials. The seller's profit from the contract with the buyer cannot just be the difference between the contract price and the cost actually incurred (£1,200 (2,000 – 800)) because had the buyer performed, the seller would have also spent another £700 (500 + 200) to earn the contract price. Although £700 has not been actually incurred, it is a 'cost saved' by the breach, which must be deducted from the amount of gross profit to determine the 'net' profit the seller would have made but for the breach, that is, £500 (2,000 – 800 – 700).[91]

Similarly, take an example involving an injured buyer who had contracted to resell the goods that the seller failed to deliver. In one CISG case,[92] the court determined that had the seller performed the contract and the buyer resold the goods to its sub-buyer, the buyer would have earned $6,806,000 by means of its gross profit. However, since the buyer had not paid the seller the full contract price ($5,166,000) for the goods (saved cost), the buyer's 'net profit' margin under its sub-sale was determined by subtracting the contract price from the intended gross profit: $6,806,000 – $5,166,000 = $1,640,000. Finally, the court rightly added the partial down payment ($787,500) that the buyer had already made, resulting in the damages of $2,427,500 ($1,640,000 + $787,500).[93]

considered as the profit subject to compensation. Experience [shows] that the execution of a transaction of the [same] kind as the present [transaction] causes additional expenses which lead to a lower profit and which have been saved in the case at hand. For example, it is undisputed that [the Buyer] was to bear the costs of the owed examination of poles by inspectors of company E, which would have cost it US $1,000 in each case. Furthermore, [the Buyer] had to have a number of letters of credit opened which in turn generally leads to considerable bank fees that have now been saved as well. Finally, [the Buyer] itself at least temporarily had to pre-fund the amounts due to payment, which generally causes expenses. If these savings are taken into account … it appears justifiable to award [the Buyer] damages in the amount of US$580,000.').

[91] For further discussion, see ch 3. See also Case No 6 U 53/07 Appellate Court Brandenburg (Germany) 18 November 2008, available at cisgw3.law.pace.edu/cases/081118g1.html, where the buyer failed to order the contractually specified minimum quantities of beer and the seller, a brewery, was awarded damages for its loss of profit, which rightly took account of costs saved by the seller ('The quantity shortage of 91,022 hectoliters of canned beer … constitutes damages of EUR 330,668.90. This is equivalent to the sum which [the Seller] has suffered as a loss of profit. Spared own costs have already been deducted.').

[92] See *Al Hewar Environmental & Public Health Establishment v Southeast Ranch, LLC and Joel Gutierre* (S.D. Fla. 2011).

[93] See ibid, [18]–[19]. The buyer was also awarded damages for the loss of the guarantee (performance bond) that the buyer was contractually required to provide to its sub-buyer (Ibid, [20]–[21]; see further ch 3).

3.3. The Role of the 'Reliance Interest'

Besides protecting the expectation/performance interest, some legal systems also protect the so-called 'reliance'[94] or 'negative' interest by placing the innocent party in the position in which it would have been had there been no contract.[95] This is done by compensating the party for expenses incurred in reliance on the contract. These expenses primarily include those which are necessary for preparing to perform or performing the contract. Simply put, these costs, known as 'essential reliance',[96] are the 'price' the injured party pays to obtain the other party's performance and benefits flowing from it. 'Essential reliance' is contrasted with 'incidental reliance', which does not, strictly speaking, involve costs necessary for the performance of the contract[97] but which nevertheless aims to advance benefits expected to flow from using the subject-matter of the contract.[98] For example, incidental reliance includes costs the buyer incurs to make some modifications to the goods or to advertise them to increase either the goods' ability to generate profits or the buyer's ability to sell them.[99] Another type of loss, a part of the reliance interest, is the loss the injured party suffers by foregoing other opportunities. When the injured party is placed in the position in which it would have been had there been no contract, it can be argued that at that point in time it had an *opportunity* to enter into other similar transactions. Because the breach deprives the injured party of that opportunity, the protection of the reliance interest would require the injured party to be compensated for the lost opportunity.[100]

There is certainly a degree of overlap between the expectation/performance interest, on the one hand, and the reliance interest, on the other. For the former interest to be protected, the party needs to be compensated for 'net' loss of profit *and* for losses incurred in relying on the contract. Suppose that A contracts with B to manufacture and sell a piece of machinery for £100,000 with the expectation that it will incur £80,000 in costs in performing the contract. If A had incurred, say, £50,000 in costs towards performing the contract (and assuming that the result of this expenditure is worthless), A would have to be awarded £70,000 to be placed in the position in which it would have been had B performed the contract (£20,000 ('net' lost profit) + £50,000 (essential reliance loss actually incurred)). It has also been said that the two interests approach one another at the point where the loss of foregone opportunities is awarded as part of the

[94] See Fuller and Perdue (n 66) 54.
[95] See ibid; Treitel (n 22) 83; § 344 Restatement (Second) of Contracts.
[96] Fuller and Perdue (n 66) 78.
[97] Ibid.
[98] See RE Hudec, 'Restating the "Reliance Interest"' (1982) 67 *Cornell L Rev* 724.
[99] For a more detailed discussion, see ch 3.
[100] Fuller and Perdue (n 66) 74.

reliance interest.[101] It has been suggested that if in a competitive market the injured party had entered into alternative contracts with third parties, it would have made the same profit as that which it expected to gain from the contract with the breaching party.[102] Two points need to be made. First, this assertion equates loss of foregone opportunities with 'loss of profit' and this does not seem to be entirely accurate because 'loss of foregone opportunities' is probably best described as loss of a 'chance' to profit on another transaction. The difference is that damages for the latter are likely to be lower than damages for lost profit, since compensation is awarded for a *chance* to profit and not for the profit itself. Second, even if loss of foregone opportunities does mean loss of profit, rarely will alternative lost profits be the same as profits lost under the contract with the breaching party: 'unless there is a perfect market, one cannot say that by entering into the contract with the defendant, the plaintiff has foregone the opportunity to make exactly the same gain in a contract with somebody else'.[103]

Despite these points of overlap and similarity, the expectation/performance interest and reliance interest are distinct, taking different perspectives on the measure of damages: the former is a forward-looking measure while the latter is backward-looking. The question arises, then, whether the expectation/performance and the reliance measures constitute alternative bases for the recovery of damages under the instruments.[104] The instruments' measure of damages for breach of contract is that of protecting the party's expectation/performance interest. However, as is well known, this does not prevent the reliance interest from constituting a separate basis for recovery where the injured party cannot prove its loss of profit and does not have any choice but to claim its reliance losses.[105] In this case, an award of reliance damages is not in conflict with the protection of the expectation/performance. The conflict will arise, however, if damages are awarded for 'foregone opportunities' because this award will require making an assumption that the *contract had not come into existence.* Take a CISG case,[106] where the buyer claimed damages for *loss of profit*, arguing that it could have deposited the money used to open the letter of credit under the contract with the bank under the deposit rate. The tribunal allowed the claim because the buyer had proven the calculation of that alleged profit. It seems,

[101] Ibid.

[102] SA Smith, *Contract Theory* (Oxford, OUP, 2004) 415 ('For example, in reliance on a supplier's promise to provide a purchaser with widgets, the purchaser will not attempt to obtain widgets from other suppliers. Assuming the market for widgets is reasonably competitive, the economic value of the buyer's lost opportunity is equivalent to the economic value of the original contract').

[103] Burrows (n 70) 223.

[104] See JS Ziegel, 'The Remedial Provisions in the Vienna Sales Convention: Some Common Law Perspectives' in NM Galston and H Smit (eds), *International Sales: The United Nations Convention on Contracts for the International Sale of Goods* (NY, Matthew Bender, 1984) 9-38 note 104 (raising this question in the context of the CISG). There is no uniformity amongst legal systems in this respect (see Treitel (n 22) 89–98). English law generally gives the injured party a choice between the two measures (see *CCC Films (London) Ltd v Impact Quadrant Films Ltd* [1985] QB 16).

[105] For a well-known example in English law, see *Anglia Television v Reed* [1972] 1 QB 60.

[106] ICAC No 238/1998, 7 June 1999, available at cisgw3.law.pace.edu/cases/990607r1.html.

however, that although the claim was formulated in terms of *loss of profit*, it was in essence a claim for 'foregone opportunities'. The buyer could have earned profit from the money it had spent on performing the contract *only* if it had not entered into the contract with the seller. Similarly, in another CISG case,[107] the buyer argued that had it not entered into the contract with the seller, it would have entered into contracts with other parties and claimed damages for the loss of that foregone opportunity. Treating this claim as part of the 'reliance loss' claim, the court would have allowed this claim had it not been for the buyer's failure to prove that loss.[108] It is submitted that the approach taken in these cases is inconsistent with the measure provided for in art 74 CISG. Both decisions contravene the assumption, which must be drawn under the damages provisions of the CISG, that the *contract had been performed*.[109]

Finally, where reliance losses are claimed and where the claim is consistent with the instruments' 'expectation/performance interest' measure, reliance damages cannot be awarded if it is evident that had the contract been performed, the innocent party would have made a loss.[110] To return to an earlier example, suppose that although A planned to make a £20,000 profit by manufacturing and selling machinery to B for £100,000, A realised, after the contract had been made, that it would have to spend £110,000 (and not £80,000 as it had originally planned) to perform the contract. If by the time of B's breach A has incurred £50,000 in costs, A should not be allowed to claim £50,000 since such an award would put A in a better position than the one in which it would have been had B performed the contract.

3.4. The Role of Gain-Based Damages

Because the purpose of the instruments' remedy of damages for breach of contract is to compensate the injured party for the loss, benefits received or gains made by the breaching party as a result of the breach are generally irrelevant for measuring damages. Therefore, the so-called 'restitution interest',[111] which focuses not on the injured party's loss but on the breaching party's gain to prevent that party from being unjustly enriched,[112] is not protected by

[107] *Castel Electronics Pty Ltd v Toshiba Singapore Pte Ltd* [2011] FCAFC 55.

[108] Ibid, [16]: 'It was incumbent on Castel to establish on the balance of probabilities that it had lost a valuable opportunity. If Castel satisfied the burden of proof it bore on this issue, the Court could proceed to value that opportunity in accordance with the degree of likelihood that the opportunity would have ensued to Castel's pecuniary gain'.

[109] *Cf* P Koneru, 'The International Interpretation of the UN Convention on Contracts for the International Sale of Goods: An Approach Based on General Principles' (1997) 6 *Minnesota J Global Trade* 105.

[110] See Fuller and Perdue (n 66) 76.

[111] See ibid, 53.

[112] Gains can be of two kinds: the value of what has been received under the contract (goods or purchase price) and the value derived from putting the subject-matter of the performance to a profitable use. The instruments contain provisions relating to the return of what has been received under

the instruments.[113] Nevertheless, it is submitted that the benefits received by the breaching party as a result of its breach cannot always be dismissed as irrelevant for calculating *compensatory* damages because, in some cases, damages reflecting the breaching party's gains may be an appropriate way of implementing the compensatory purpose of damages.[114] It is also arguable that the instruments cannot ignore the issue of gain-based damages because otherwise courts may apply concurrent domestic remedies to those cases with which the instruments were designed to deal.[115] If this happens, not only will the instruments be 'undermined in one of [their] core areas'[116] but also the goal of uniformity will be impaired.

Cases where it may be appropriate to rely on the breaching party's gains to implement the compensatory purpose of damages are those where: the innocent party's contractual right to the performance of an obligation that was breached is damaged (damage to the 'performance interest');[117] and conventional ways of calculating damages are incapable of compensating the innocent party or the latter is not in the position to prove its loss.[118] As argued in the next chapter, to determine whether the innocent party has truly suffered damage to its 'performance interest' (including where it should be compensated with reference to the breaching party's gains), it is useful to ask whether this party has a legitimate interest in the breaching party's performance and preventing the breaching party from benefiting from its breach.[119] In ascertaining whether the party has such a legitimate interest, it may also be relevant whether the breach

the contract where the contract has been avoided (see arts 81, 82 CISG; arts 7.3.6 and 7.3.7 UPICC; and arts 9:307, 9:308 PECL).

[113] For a recent overview of the developments in the common law in respect of gain-based damages for breach of contract, see K Barnett, 'Gain-Based Damages' in R Halson and D Campbell (eds), *Research Handbook on Remedies in Private Law* (Cheltenham UK – Northampton, MA, USA, Edward Elgar, 2019); for a critical analysis, see R Cunnington, 'The Measure and Availability of Gain-Based Damages for Breach of Contract' in Saidov and Cunnington (n 1).

[114] A similar point is made in I Schwenzer and P Hachem, 'The Scope of the CISG Provisions on Damages' in Saidov and Cunnington (n 1) 100–102. For the view and arguments to the contrary, see Djordjević (n 74) 978–80.

[115] Ibid.

[116] Ibid.

[117] For a detailed discussion, see chs 3 and 8.

[118] For other views in favour of some scope for cases where compensatory damages under the CISG can be assessed with reference to the breaching party's gains, see, eg, Schwenzer (n 29) 1075–76; E Muñoz and DO Ament-Guemez, 'Calculation of Damages on the Basis of the Breaching Party's Profits under The CISG' (2017) 8 *George Mason J Int'l Commercial L* 201 (rationalising this position with reference to good faith: 'In circumstances where there is no way of calculating exactly how much the buyer would have made with the goods he did not receive, the principle of good faith, which means reasonable standards of fair dealing and a common ethical sense, offers the justification for applying a more easily identified baseline to calculate such profits, i.e., the breaching party's profits' (ibid, 209)).

[119] This guideline has been put forward in English law to help identify cases where 'gain-based' damages are available as an independent measure (and alternative to the expectation damages) for breach of contract (see *Attorney-General v Blake* [2001] AC 268, 285). But see now *Court Morris-Garner v One Step (Support) Ltd* [2018] UKSC 20.

was cynical, opportunistic or committed in bad faith.[120] While these guiding criteria are admittedly vague, there are examples where they were at play and where an award based on the breaching party's gains was justifiable.

In one CISG case,[121] the seller agreed to supply pressure sensors to the buyer and to license the use and integration of these pressure sensors with the buyer's other products. Since the performance of the contract involved the buyer's exposure to significant amounts of the seller's confidential and proprietary information, the contract contained a confidentiality clause whereby the parties agreed that neither party would obtain rights to the confidential and proprietary information of the other party and undertook not to disclose such information to third parties. The seller argued that the buyer committed a breach of both those obligations and 'never had the genuine intention to perform its obligations [and] entered into the Agreement as a tactical step to obtain access [to the Seller]'s confidential and proprietary technology in order to develop, manufacture and sell the pressure sensors which will directly compete with those manufactured and sold by [the Seller]'.[122] The arbitrator found that the buyer had indeed copied the seller's information and awarded damages based on the profits the buyer earned by using the seller's technology.

In another CISG case,[123] the seller agreed to sell jeans to a US buyer on the condition that they would not be resold on the European market and it was agreed that the goods would only be resold in South America and Africa. During the pre-contractual negotiations and after the conclusion of the contract, the seller repeatedly demanded that the buyer provide proof of the destination of the goods. The buyer breached the contract by selling the goods in Spain. The rationale for the seller's interest in the destination of the goods was described thus:

> [The seller] is bound by contracts with many foreign distributors and, more specifically in the case of Spain where the brand name 'Jeans Bonaventure' is sought after, it has an interest in not allowing a parallel network of sale [parallel imports]. [The seller] adds that it has received numerous complaints by its Spanish distributors who complain that Bonaventure Jeans have flooded the market and that it has encountered counterfeiting problems. It adds that, with respect to the USA, it is not the owner of the trade mark 'Bonaventure' and that it risks having its products seized.[124]

[120] It is suggested that a relevant policy should not be to penalise the breaching party (as that would be contrary to the compensatory purpose of damages) but to deter such cynical or bad faith breaches. Some commentators also appear to take a similar position, expressly or implicitly, when, for instance, they give an example of a seller who intentionally sells the same goods twice to different buyers (Schwenzer (n 29) 1076; Muñoz and Ament-Guemez (n 118) 205 (but also taking this position explicitly based on the good faith rationale).

[121] Stockholm Chamber of Commerce 5 April 2007 (Pressure sensors), available at cisgw3.law.pace.edu/cases/070405s5.html.

[122] Ibid.

[123] See *SARL BRI Production 'Bonaventure' v Société Pan African Export* Appellate Court Grenoble (France) 22 February 1995, available at cisgw3.law.pace.edu/cases/950222f1.html. For a similar discussion of this case, see Schwenzer and Hachem (n 114).

[124] Ibid.

Although damages were awarded on an unclear ground of 'abuse of process', the court held that the buyer did not act in good faith. It can be argued that profits made by the buyer by reselling the goods in Spain would constitute an appropriate measure of compensatory damages particularly because they would most likely reflect the profits the seller lost as a result of the breach.[125]

Another example is where the buyer, conscious of human rights, agrees to buy goods from a seller on the condition that no child labour would be used in the production of the goods and pays a price higher than the current price for these goods to ensure compliance with this condition.[126] It has been correctly argued that, given the difficulty of placing a value on the buyer's interest in performance, the savings made by the seller as a result of its breach can help measure the buyer's loss.[127] In short, it is submitted that in all these types of case, damages based on the breaching party's gains are justifiable as long as the loss could not be quantified by conventional methods of calculating damages or the innocent party was not in the position to prove its loss. In all three cases, the injured party arguably had a legitimate interest in the performance. By being well aware of the importance the innocent party placed on the performance and yet breaching the contract solely to make a gain, the other party's breach can be described as 'cynical' and, possibly, as having been committed in 'bad faith'.[128]

4. THE IDEA OF LIMITING DAMAGES

Like most legal systems,[129] the instruments are not relentless in pursuing the goals of full compensation and the protection of the injured party's expectation/performance interest. The party's claim is subject to several other requirements that have the effect of limiting damages. These requirements, often referred to as the 'methods of limiting damages', include causation, foreseeability, mitigation and, to some extent, the standard of proof. The literature on the law of damages may create an impression that all these methods derive from one single idea of the necessity of limiting damages. But this is only true to some extent and, to explain why, it is necessary to explore the reasons advanced to explain why damages need to be limited.

First, it has been argued that it is necessary to limit damages because losses can be unexpectedly high and it is not fair to the breaching party to be held liable for such losses. The argument runs as follows. Relentless adherence to full

[125] See Schwenzer and Hachem (n 114).

[126] The example is given in ibid.; see also Schwenzer (n 29) 1075–76. The example is also discussed in chs 3 and 9.

[127] See Schwenzer and Hachem (n 114).

[128] For another example in the context of sale of goods, see the English case *Esso Petroleum Co Ltd v Niad Ltd* [2001] All ER 324.

[129] For a comparative overview, see A Komarov, 'The Limitation of Contract Damages in Domestic Legal Systems and International Instruments' in Saidov and Cunnington (n 1).

compensation may result in a breaching party's liability for all losses resulting from the breach, 'however improbable, however unpredictable'.[130] The risk of 'unusual' and 'unpredictable' liability is all the more real in commercial transactions where 'the provision of opportunities for gain may have a snowball effect: opportunities breed further opportunities'.[131] Saddling the breaching party with such losses would be unjust.[132] This argument is particularly relevant where the party has not assumed the risk of such losses under the contract. Second, the idea of limiting damages has been put forward in the context of losses which are disproportionate to the amount of the benefit received by the breaching party under the contract.[133] In this case, the necessity of limiting damages can be explained by 'an impulse to preserve some proportion between the liability imposed on the defendant and the compensation which was paid him under the contract'.[134] Finally, it has been argued that unqualified adherence to full compensation would 'operate as too strong a disincentive to the assumption of contractual obligations, or to an undue raising of charges to cover such unlimited liability'.[135] It is evident that the justification of the idea of limiting damages has not been uniform. Even if it is accepted that all these reasons are an integral part of a single idea of limiting damages, they are insufficient to justify *all* methods of limiting damages. Each method is based, to a significant extent, on the considerations and policies that are specific to it. That said, it is true that, broadly speaking, the notions of fairness[136] and reasonableness[137] inevitably permeate both the justification and application of each method.

[130] *Victoria Laundry (Windsor) Ltd v Newman Industries Ltd Coulson and Co Ltd (Third Parties)* [1949] 2 KB 528, 539.

[131] HLA Hart and T Honore, *Causation in the Law*, 2nd edn (Oxford, Clarendon Press, 1985) 312.

[132] CT McCormick, *Handbook on the Law of Damages* (St Paul, Minn, West Publishing Co, 1935) 565.

[133] Fuller and Perdue (n 66) 87; A Von Mehren and JR Gordley, *The Civil Law System: An Introduction to the Comparative Study of Law*, 2nd edn (Boston, Little, Brown & Co, 1977) 1114.

[134] Fuller and Perdue (n 66) 88.

[135] Treitel (n 22) 143; Comment, 'Lost Profits as Contract Damages: Problems of Proof and Limitations on Recovery' (1955–1956) 65 *Yale L J* 992, 995–6.

[136] For a somewhat similar view, see Corbin (n 3) 16 (seemingly explaining the necessity of limiting damages by the idea of 'justice').

[137] See Ogus (n 3) 290 (justifying the methods of limiting damages from the perspective of justice and reasonableness).

3

Categories of Loss

1. GENERAL

THE PROBLEM OF meaning and definition of loss lies at the heart of the law of damages and this chapter explores only *one* set of issues relating to how the notion of 'loss' should be interpreted under the international instruments – that is, what losses are, as a matter of law, recoverable? In other words, what types of loss are considered sufficiently 'real' and serious to qualify for legal protection? These questions are important because by considering them we inevitably enter the debate about the values and policies underlying the instruments. To answer these questions, losses are considered, for the sake of convenience, under several broad headings and no classification of losses found in legal literature is relied upon.[1] The only classification worth recognising is that adopted by the instruments themselves: that is the distinction, dating back to Roman law and widely used by many civil law systems,[2] between 'loss suffered' and 'gains prevented (loss of profit)'[3] (or, to use a well-known Latin terminology, *damnum emergens* and *lucrum cessans*).

'Loss suffered' is the reduction in the innocent party's existing assets, property, or financial situation.[4] 'Loss of profit', in contrast, refers to what the party has never had but would have had if the contract had been performed.[5]

[1] See I Schwenzer, 'Arts 74–77 CISG' in I Schwenzer (ed), *Schlechtriem and Schwenzer Commentary on the UN Convention on the International Sale of Goods (CISG)*, 4th edn (Oxford, OUP, 2016) 1064, stating that '[r]ecoverable types of loss include non-performance loss, incidental loss, and consequential loss resulting from breach of contract'. It is doubtful whether such classifications are helpful. Concepts such as 'incidental' and 'consequential' damages are widely used in some legal systems (see, eg, §§ 2-710 and 2-715 UCC). The term 'consequential damages' is used in a number of different senses (see, eg, GH Treitel, *Remedies for Breach of Contract: A Comparative Account* (Oxford, Clarendon Press, 1988) 87; see, eg, RR Anderson, 'Incidental and Consequential Damages' (1987) 7 *J L Commerce* 330; U Draetta, 'The Notion of Consequential Damages in the International Trade Practice: A Merger of Common Law and Civil Law Concepts' (1991) 4 *Int'l Business L J* 491). Relying on such concepts in the CISG context advances neither the Convention's international character nor the promotion of uniformity in its application.

[2] See, eg, Treitel (n 1) 84; B Nicholas, *The French Law of Contract*, 2nd edn (Oxford, Clarendon Press, 1992) 226–7.

[3] See art 74 CISG, art 7.4.2 UPICC and art 9:502 PECL.

[4] See, eg, Comment 2 on art 7.4.2 UPICC; OS Ioffe, *Otvetstvennost' po Sovetskomu Grazhdanskomu Pravu* (Leningrad, LGU, 1955) 205–6.

[5] In ICAC No 174/2003, 12 November 2004 (reported in Russian in PD Savkin (ed), *Praktika MKAS pri TPP RF: 2004–2016 – K 85-letiyu MKAS* (Nauka Prava – Elektronnaya biblioteka,

What is the purpose of this distinction? One answer is that, in the case of the CISG at least, there are instances where loss of profit cannot be claimed and they concern the provision in art 44 which allows disregarding the provisions in arts 39[6] and 43[7] if the buyer has a reasonable excuse for the failure to give the required notice. Where so, and the buyer claims damages, loss of profit cannot be claimed.[8] Another answer, applicable to all international instruments, is that because not all legal systems allow damages for loss of profit (gains prevented),[9] this type of loss is specifically mentioned to indicate its recoverability.[10]

2. EXPENDITURE WASTED AS A RESULT OF THE BREACH

A party often incurs expenses which constitute part of its performance of (or preparation to perform) the contract in the expectation that they will be recouped from the value received from the other party's performance. If that other party fails to do so, these expenses may, wholly or in part, turn out to be wasted, causing loss. What items can be regarded as 'as expenses wasted as a result of the breach' depends on the nature of the injured party's performance. The seller may incur costs relating to the manufacture, such as the costs of labour and materials, or packaging[11] of the goods which it intended to deliver

Moskva 2017) 260–81), where the tribunal defined 'loss of profit' with reference to the applicable domestic law (the Russian Civil Code) because of the absence of the definition in the CISG (ibid, 278). Doing so was clearly incorrect given that the recoverability of loss of profit is a matter governed by the CISG and its precise definition ought to be developed within the CISG (see arts 4 and 7 CISG).

[6] Article 39(1) CISG: 'The buyer loses the right to rely on a lack of conformity of the goods if he does not give notice to the seller specifying the nature of the lack of conformity within a reasonable time after he has discovered it or ought to have discovered it.'

[7] Article 43(1) CISG: 'The buyer loses the right to rely on the provisions of article 41 or article 42 if he does not give notice to the seller specifying the nature of the right or claim of the third party within a reasonable time after he has become aware or ought to have become aware of the right or claim.'

[8] Article 44 CISG: 'Notwithstanding the provisions of paragraph (1) of article 39 and paragraph (1) of article 43, the buyer may reduce the price in accordance with article 50 or claim damages, except for loss of profit, if he has a reasonable excuse for his failure to give the required notice.'

[9] It has been reported that such legal systems include, eg, those of Jordan and United Arab Emirates (see JY Gotanda, 'Damages in Lieu of Performance because of Breach of Contract' (Villanova University School of Law Working Paper Series, 2006, Paper 53), available at law.bepress.com/cgi/viewcontent.cgi?article=1053&context=villanovalwps).

[10] See para 3 on art 70 of the Secretariat Commentary of the 1978 Draft of the Convention; V Knapp, 'Arts. 74–77 CISG' in CM Bianca and MJ Bonell (eds), *Commentary on the International Sales Law: The 1980 Vienna Sales Convention* (Milan, Giuffrè, 1987) 543; Comment 2 on art 7.4.2 UPICC. But see JY Gotanda, 'Recovering Lost Profits in International Disputes' (2004) 36 *Georgetown J Int'l L* 61, 86 ('[the] principle of recovery [of lost profit] is so well settled that it can be said it has become a general rule of private international law').

[11] See Case No T-6/08 Foreign Trade Court, the Serbian Chamber of Commerce (Serbia) 19 October 2009, available at cisgw3.law.pace.edu/cases/091019sb.html, where the contract of sale of mineral water required the buyer to provide replacement packaging (bottles, crates and pallets). The buyer failed to do so and the seller was awarded damages for the value of such replacement packaging.

to the buyer.[12] The injured buyer may also incur a variety of costs in performing the contract, including the fees for the opening of a letter of credit[13] or the costs arising from importing the goods[14] (such as paying import duties, clearing customs or transporting the goods)[15] or paying insurance fees.[16] The question whether a particular cost is an essential part of performing the contract ('essential reliance') is important for calculating damages because, if it is, it must be taken into account. Crucially, double compensation must be avoided at this point: if the cost has *actually* been incurred it can only be compensated together with the amount of '*net profit*', as opposed to 'gross profit', for the latter already comprises the entire cost of the performance. By the same token, if a claim is based on 'gross profit' where a particular cost of 'essential reliance' has *not* been incurred, that cost (being, this time, a 'cost saved' as a result of the breach) must be deducted from the amount of 'gross profit'. For example, where as a result of the buyer's failure to accept the goods the seller resells the goods and thereby avoids paying a commission to a broker which it would have paid had the buyer accepted the goods, the amount of the commission, being a 'saved cost', must be deducted from the difference between the contract price and the resale price.[17]

Where the seller fails to deliver the goods and the buyer is awarded damages under the instruments' 'concrete' or 'abstract' formulae,[18] the costs of 'essential reliance' should not be recoverable because the buyer either has the goods on hand[19] or has the monetary value enabling it to purchase substitute goods.[20] In both cases the buyer is put in the position that enables it to carry on with its plans (resale or manufacture). The same should be the case where the buyer who resells non-conforming goods at a reduced price is awarded the loss in its profit

[12] See Case No 2 U 30/77 Appellate Court Hamm (Germany) 23 March 1978 (Brass poles), available at cisgw3.law.pace.edu/cases/780323g1.html.

[13] See, eg, CIETAC 14 March 1996 (Dried sweet potatoes), available at cisgw3.law.pace.edu/cases/960314c1.html.

[14] See *China Xhanghai Dongda Import & Export Corp v Germany Laubholz-Meyer Corp* Shanghai Yangpu District People's Court 2002 (China), available at cisgw3.law.pace.edu/cases/ 020000c1.html; Case No A21-2330/2018 Arbitration Court Kaliningrad Region (Russia) 7 February 2019, available at ras.arbitr.ru (in Russian).

[15] See CIETAC 26 October 1996 (Cotton bath towel), available at cisgw3. law.pace.edu/cases/961026c1.html; Arbitration Court Kaliningrad Region 7 February 2019 (n 14).

[16] CIETAC 30 October 1991 (Roll aluminium and aluminium parts), available at www.cisg.law.pace.edu/cisg/wais/db/cases2/911030c1.html.

[17] See *Downs Investments Pty Ltd v Perwaja Steel SDN BHD* [2000] QSC 421.

[18] See arts 75 and 76 CISG; arts 7.4.5 and 7.4.6 UPICC; and arts 9:506 and 9:507 PECL. See further ch 8.

[19] For cases where the buyer procured substitute goods and where the fees it had paid to open (and/or modify) a letter of credit were denied, see CIETAC 14 March 1996 (n 13); CIETAC 7 May 1997 (Horsebean), available at cisgw3.law.pace. edu/cases/970507c1.html. However, if as a result of the breach, the buyer had to pay that fee twice, then it should be recoverable (see CIETAC 4 September 1996 (Natural rubber), available at cisgw3.law.pace.edu/cases/960904c1.html ('[The] Buyer signed Contract … to purchase substitute goods and paid a security deposit and issuing fee for the L/C [and this] caused the L/Cs to be issued twice for buying the goods … The expense of the first L/C is additional expense to buy the goods …')).

[20] CIETAC 25 December 1998 (Basic pig iron), available at cisgw3.law. pace.edu/cases/981225c2.html.

margin (that is, the difference between the reduced price at the actual resale and the price at which it would have sold the goods had they been conforming).[21] It is clear that in such cases, the costs of 'essential reliance' are not wasted. The same applies to cases where the seller delays the delivery of the goods and the buyer is awarded the cost of hiring an immediate replacement for the period of delay. In this case, even if the buyer has incurred certain costs of 'essential reliance', such costs are not 'wasted' because the buyer is able to execute its plans. It is where it is not possible for the buyer to procure a replacement (such as where no market exists, where goods are unique, or where the buyer suffers loss of volume) that 'essential reliance' costs can be recoverable. Even then, however, it must be proven that had the seller performed the contract the buyer would have been able to put the goods to profitable use, thereby recouping such costs.[22]

To be relevant to the calculation of damages, a cost needs to be 'essential' to the performance of the contract, that is, a cost without which performance would not be possible. There are expenses which do not constitute an essential part of the performance, but which are nevertheless incurred in the expectation that they will bring benefit relating to the subject-matter of the contract. For example, it may be that before the goods were found to be defective, the buyer had spent money on advertising the goods,[23] preparing to take part in an exhibition,[24] or making certain modifications to the goods (such as painting a machine).[25] It is suggested that, subject to two requirements, such costs are, in principle, recoverable. First, they must be shown to be reasonably connected with a further use of the subject-matter of the contract. If, for instance, it is found that an advertisement or an exhibition had little to do with the contract goods and were aimed at promoting some other product(s), it is appropriate to deny compensation for these costs.[26] Second, such costs must be reasonable or expedient in the circumstances. If a car dealer repainted a car, which turned out to be defective, and where there were no reasonable grounds to expect that re-painting would increase the chances of selling the car or selling it at a higher price, the cost of doing so should not be recoverable.[27] It goes without saying

[21] CIETAC 11 April 1997 (Silicon metal), available at cisgw3.law.pace.edu/cases/970411c1.html ('The first SGS inspection cost, the cost of establishing the L/C and the cost of packing the goods are normal costs in international trade; since the profit losses and damages suffered by [the] Buyer are confirmed and to be compensated, the requests for the above costs claimed by [the] Buyer cannot be granted').

[22] For similar views in the context of the common law, on avoiding double compensation in cases involving 'essential reliance' costs, see S Waddams, *The Law of Damages*, 4th edn (Toronto, Canada Law Book Inc, 2004) 103–4.

[23] See Case No 10 O 72/00 District Court Darmstadt (Germany) 9 May 2000 (Video recorders), available at cisgw3.law.pace.edu/cases/000509g1.html.

[24] See CIETAC 21 May 1999 (Excavator), available at cisgw3.law. pace.edu/cases/990521c1.html.

[25] See the English case *Cullinane v British 'Rema' Manufacturing Co Ltd* [1954] 1 QB 292.

[26] '[The] Buyer's claim for the exhibition expenses, RMB 18,000 is not related to this case and cannot be upheld' (CIETAC 21 May 1999 (n 24)).

[27] See AS Komarov, *Otvetstvennost' v kommercheskom oborote* (Moscow, Juridical Literature, 1991) 202 (discussing the case, decided by the USSR Foreign Trading Commission, where the costs

that if the injured party has received benefits as a result of incurring such costs, these benefits must be taken into account in calculating damages. In one CISG case[28] where the seller failed to deliver a pipe extrusion production line, the buyer claimed compensation for numerous items of accessory equipment bought to enhance the use of the production line. The tribunal awarded damages for such costs only in part on the ground that those items of accessory equipment did not wholly 'lose their use value'.

Another question relates to the so-called 'overhead' or 'fixed' costs, as opposed to 'variable' costs. While the latter are 'costs which may be identified as belonging to a specific contract or product of sale',[29] the former are costs which do not directly relate to any particular contract and are necessary to maintaining the business as a whole – they can include, for example, insurance protection, power, lighting, rental payments and work time of employees.[30] The question is whether such 'fixed' costs are sufficiently connected with the breached contract so as to be taken into account in calculating damages. If so, this can have the following consequences. Because fixed costs are, as a rule, incurred *regardless of* the breach, they can rarely become a 'saved cost' which would reduce the amount of lost profits. It seems that it is only in rare cases where a breach of contract prevents the very possibility of incurring certain fixed costs (eg, where a breach causes the destruction of the factory or the suspension of the production, making it unnecessary for the party to incur utility costs) that the amount of lost profits would need to be reduced by the amount of fixed costs thus 'saved'.[31]

Another consequence is that recognising a part of the overall fixed costs as having a sufficient connection with a particular contract leads to the possibility

incurred by the injured party were denied on the ground that, when incurring them, the party was not confident that benefits would result from such an investment; the tribunal held that the party had acted at its own risk).

[28] CIETAC 6 November 2002 (Pipe extrusion), available at cisgw3.law. pace.edu/cases/021106c1.html.

[29] R Childress and R Burgess, 'Seller's Remedies: The Primacy of UCC 2-708(2)' (1973) 48 *New York University L Rev* 833, 840.

[30] See *Hewlett-Packard France v Matrox Graphics Inc*, 2020 QCCS 78, [192]–[227] (various examples of employee and related costs); *Castel Electronics Pty Ltd v Toshiba Singapore Pte Ltd* [2011] FCAFC 55, [99], [226]–[251] (distinguishing between the cost of permanent employees, not held recoverable, and the cost of additional employees employed to deal with the consequences of a breach).

[31] For this reason, it is difficult to understand the view (see Secretariat Commentary on article 70 of the 1978 Draft, Example 70A; *Delchi Carrier SpA v Rotorex Corp* 71 F.3d 1024-1031) that if fixed costs *are not* recoverable, they must *not* reduce the amount of lost profits. It is submitted that the same result would be reached even if fixed costs *are* recognised as recoverable because they are, almost by definition, *incurred* and not 'saved' and should not therefore reduce lost profits (see Case No 1 U 31/99 Appellate Court Hamburg 26 November 1999 (Germany) (Jeans), available at cisgw3.law.pace.edu/cases/991126g1.html). In other words, once a particular cost is recognised as relevant to calculating damages, it will only be taken to reduce damages where it is a 'saved' cost because once it has been incurred, it would require that damages be awarded for it. Because fixed costs are usually incurred, that part of lost profits which bears a pro rata relation to the overall fixed costs needs to be compensated.

of claiming compensation for such costs[32] as 'reliance damages'. This would clearly not be possible if fixed costs were treated as irrelevant for calculating damages. There is no agreement on whether fixed (overhead) costs need to be taken into account under the international instruments.[33] Whilst it can be argued that these costs should not be recoverable because they would be incurred even if there were no breach of contract,[34] it is suggested that they should be regarded as costs sufficiently related to a particular contract since by enabling a business to run, they enable each contract to be performed. In principle, therefore, fixed costs need to be allocated to a particular contract 'in the same proportion which the contract price bears to the total revenues'.[35] In practical terms, it is not easy to implement this principle as 'the calculation of overheads is not an exact science'[36] and, consequently, there is no agreement amongst accountants as to what constitutes overhead costs.[37] More so, what is an overhead to one manufacturer may be a variable cost to another and it may be the case that the same cost may be both a variable and a fixed cost to the same manufacturer depending on its volume of manufacture and sales.[38] For these reasons, the amount of overheads attributable to a particular contract may depend 'on more or less arbitrary management accounting decisions'.[39]

A breach may result in an increase in fixed costs, in which case the margin of increase may be recoverable.[40] It may also be the case that an apparent fixed cost reflects a foregone opportunity cost. If so, it is arguably correct that this cost should be recoverable to the extent of its being a foregone opportunity cost. In a case,[41] involving the delivery of defective computer graphics cards, the court

[32] More precisely, a part of the overall fixed costs to which profits under a particular contract would have contributed on a pro rata basis.

[33] For a CISG case seemingly in favour of this position, see, eg, Appellate Court Hamburg (Germany) 26 November 1999 (n 28). For the contrary position, see Federal Appellate Court (2nd Circuit) 6 December 1995 (n 28); *TeeVee Tunes Inc et al v Gerhard Schubert GmbH* not reported in F.Supp.2d 2006, WL 2463537 (SDNY) (No. 00 Civ 5189 (RCC)).

[34] *Castel Electronics Pty Ltd v Toshiba Singapore Pte Ltd* (n 30) [234] ('There is no doubt that if these costs would have been incurred in any event then the costs cannot found a claim for damages.'); Case No 6 U 53/07 Appellate Court Brandenburg (Germany) 18 November 2008, available at cisgw3.law.pace.edu/cases/081118g1.html ('According to the jurisprudence of the German Federal Supreme Court, fixed costs can generally not be included in the calculation of damages'; if the reference is made to non-CISG jurisprudence of the German Supreme Court, then relying on it to interpret the CISG contravenes art 7 CISG).

[35] Childress and Burgess (n 30) 843.

[36] E McKendrick, *Goode on Commercial Law*, 5th edn (London, Penguin, 2016) [15.50]. See also *Borealis AB v Geogas Trading SA* [2010] EWHC 2789 (Comm) [149].

[37] JJ White and RS Summers, *Uniform Commercial Code*, 5th edn (St Paul, Minn, West Publishing Co, 2000) 289.

[38] Childress and Burgess (n 29) 841.

[39] McKendrick (n 36); similarly, R Speidel and K Clay, 'Seller's Recovery of Overhead Under UCC Section 2-708 (2): Economic Cost Theory and Contract Remedial Policy' (1972) 57 *Cornell L Rev* 689.

[40] Appellate Court Brandenburg (n 34) ('An exception to this principle [of non-recoverability of fixed costs] may apply only where the individual purchases by the buyer have required additional investments by the seller, thus leading to an increase in fixed costs.').

[41] *Hewlett-Packard France v Matrox Graphics Inc* (n 30).

was prepared to award as damages a 'limited portion' of certain management and employee costs, claimed by the buyer. The decision is mainly based on the opportunity cost reasoning:

> It is not unusual to include a certain amount in damages to reflect the time that a company's management and employees must dedicate to a crisis resulting from a third party's product or conduct. Clearly the graphic card epidemic imposed such a time burden on HPF management and employees ... One must acknowledge that 'but for' the defective graphic cards, HPF's management would have been focusing on its regular business functions and on seeking ways to improve the business.[42]

In addition, the court took the view that it would be 'inappropriate' and 'gratuitous' for the seller 'to assert that no damage is suffered because there is no "but for" increase in management and employees time involvement and that the salary has not been shown to change or overtime to have been paid'.[43] This part of the reasoning may seem questionable as it is driven more by a moral stance against the breaching seller than by the causal reasoning. However, as the next chapter shows,[44] the question of causation can sometimes be difficult to disentangle from moral considerations, such as justice and fairness. Finally, both parts of this reasoning demonstrate that courts and tribunals inevitably have some discretion in deciding on the extent to which a fixed cost is recoverable in a given case, as the court in this case expressly acknowledged:

> The Court has a certain discretion in awarding damages, and that is certainly no less true in relation to the full compensation principle envisaged by Article 74 CISG ... [M]athematical precision is certainly not required under the CISG. Considering the actual amounts claimed, the proof and the analysis ... as regards employees, engineer ... and division management, the Court considers that a global award of US$75,000 would be justified in this regard and in keeping with the proof and the principles expressed in [CISG].[45]

3. ADDITIONAL EXPENDITURE INCURRED AS A RESULT OF THE BREACH

Losses under this heading include expenses which are not part of the performance of the contract but are *additional* losses incurred by the injured party as a consequence of the breach. Numerous examples can be given. It is often the case that the injured party incurs costs in attempting to mitigate its losses.[46] For instance, where the buyer rejects the goods, the seller may have to incur additional storage and/or maintenance charges and costs of modifying the goods

[42] Ibid, [244]–[245].
[43] Ibid, [245].
[44] See ch 4.
[45] *Hewlett-Packard France v Matrox Graphics Inc* (n 30) [248]–[249].
[46] For a detailed discussion, see ch 6.

for the needs of a new buyer[47] or, where there is no need to do so, it may have to incur additional transportation, broker's and sales promotion fees.[48] Where the seller fails to deliver, the injured buyer may similarly incur costs in attempting to find and conclude a replacement transaction.[49] If the buyer receives non-conforming goods which it does not reject, it may be reasonable for the buyer to attempt to cure the non-conformity[50] and/or deal with complaints from its customers, to whom the contract goods or the goods, incorporating the contract goods, were sold.[51] All these costs, subject to being reasonable, have been held recoverable.[52] If there is a delay in delivery, it may be reasonable for the buyer to hire a replacement for the period of delay[53] and the cost of doing so should also be recoverable.

It is clear that expenses arising from attempts to mitigate losses are recoverable as long as they are reasonable and it is certainly true that the same requirement applies to expenses other than those arising from mitigation.[54] However, in addition to the requirement of reasonableness, a new criterion has emerged in the CISG cases, according to which costs incurred after the breach must be *necessary* or *unavoidable* to be recoverable.[55] It is suggested that this criterion can be considered a part of the broader reasonableness requirement for if the cost is truly necessary or unavoidable, it is certainly reasonable and therefore recoverable.[56] Both the considerations of reasonableness and necessity have

[47] See ICC No 7585, 1992 (Foamed board machinery), available at cisgw3.law. pace.edu/cases/927585i1.html; ICAC No 142/94, 25 September 1995, available at cisgw3.law.pace.edu/cases/950425r2.html; Vienna Arbitration SCH-4366, 15 June 1994 (Rolled metal sheets), available at cisgw3.law.pace.edu/cases/940615a3.html; *Vital Berry Marketing NV v Dira-Frost NV* District Court Hasselt (Belgium) 2 May 1995, available at cisgw3.law.pace.edu/cases/950502b1.html.

[48] See *China Yituo Group Company v Germany Gerhard Freyso Ltd GmbH and Co* Second Intermediate People's Court (District Court) of Shanghai (China) 22 June 1998, available at cisgw3.law.pace.edu/cases/980622c1.html; see also Case No OR.96.0-0013 Commercial Court Aargau (Switzerland) 26 September 1997 (transportation costs apparently incurred after and as a result of the breach) (Cutlery), available at cisgw3.law.pace.edu/cases/970926s1.html.

[49] See, eg, Case No 27 U 58/96 Appellate Court Köln (Germany) 8 January 1997 (Tannery machines), available at cisgw3.law.pace.edu/cases/970108g1.html.

[50] For an example of various attempts to cure by the buyer who received defective computer cards, installed in computers supplied by the buyer worldwide, see *Hewlett-Packard France v Matrox Graphics Inc* (n 30) (the measures included the repair and replacement of graphic cards in cards that have failed as well as 'preventative repairs' of cards that have not yet failed (see further n 57)).

[51] See *Castel Electronics Pty Ltd v Toshiba Singapore Pte Ltd* (n 30) [233]–[251] (the cost of hiring 'additional' staff to deal with issues arising from defects in the goods were recoverable; see further nn 30 and 34 and the main text accompanying them).

[52] See ICC No 8740, October 1996 (Russian coal), available at cisgw3.law. pace.edu/cases/968740i1.html. For a more extensive discussion, see ch 8.

[53] See Case No 7 Ob 301/01t Supreme Court (Austria) 14 January 2002 (Cooling system), available at cisgw3.law.pace.edu/cases/020114a3.html.

[54] See Case No 295401/HA ZA 07-2802 District Court Rotterdam (Netherlands) 15 October 2008, available at cisgw3.law.pace.edu/cases/081015n2.html.

[55] For references and further discussion, see ch 4.

[56] See Case No 6 O 171/08 District Court Potsdam (Germany) 7 April 2009, available at cisgw3.law.pace.edu/cases/090407g1.html, where the cost of employing an attorney before the trial was deemed 'necessary' and recoverable under art 74 CISG; Case No 759/2008 Appellate Court Madrid

been relied upon to deal with the question whether the amount of the injured party's liability to third parties should be recoverable as damages.[57] For example, as a result of the seller's non-delivery the buyer may have to reach a settlement with its sub-buyer and, in one CISG case,[58] the amount of such a settlement was held recoverable as it was 'reasonable and legally binding'. In another case of non-delivery,[59] the buyer was awarded damages for its liability to its sub-buyer on the ground that paying damages to the sub-buyer was 'inevitable'.[60] Paying damages to a sub-buyer is certainly 'inevitable' or 'unavoidable' where the buyer is required to do so by a legally binding settlement or a court or arbitration decision.[61] It goes without saying that the settlement itself must be reasonable or, where a claim is brought against the buyer, the buyer needs to take reasonable steps to defend it. This flows from the mitigation rule or, more broadly, from the instruments' general principle of reasonableness. It is noteworthy that, in one case,[62] reasonableness is taken as far as to deny the recovery of the injured buyer's costs incurred prior to the litigation with its sub-buyer because the buyer had failed to engage the breaching seller in the pre-litigation process which, in the court's opinion, could have helped the buyer deal with the sub-buyer's claim.

It is not always the case that a mere fact of reaching a reasonable settlement with a sub-buyer will make the seller liable for the full amount of the settlement as it may have been the parties' intention to share liability for this loss. In one CISG case,[63] the seller had stated, after the conclusion of the contract, that it would be willing to bear a part of the buyer's responsibility to its customer subject to certain conditions and although no definite agreement at that point had been reached, the tribunal inferred from such a statement that it was the

(Spain) 10 March 2009, available at cisgw3.law.pace.edu/cases/090310s4.html, where shipping non-conforming wine back to the seller was deemed a measure taken at the buyer's sole discretion and the necessity of having had to incur that cost was not established.

57 The question has arisen in other situations too. In *Hewlett-Packard France v Matrox Graphics Inc* (n 30), as a result of the defects in computer graphics installed in computers supplied worldwide, the buyer, amongst other measures, carried out 'preventative' repairs of the graphic cards. The costs of such preventative repairs were held recoverable, having been implicitly treated as reasonable and, quite possibly, necessary (ibid, [154]–[155]).

58 See CIETAC 17 October 1996 (Tinplate), available at cisgw3.law.pace. edu/cases/961017c1.htm.

59 CIETAC 14 March 1996 (n 13).

60 See also *Al Hewar Environmental & Public Health Establishment v Southeast Ranch, LLC and Joel Gutierre* (S.D. Fla. 2011), [20]–[21], where damages for the 'loss of the performance bond' that the buyer was contractually required to provide to its sub-buyer were awarded as a result of the seller's failure to deliver the goods, which the buyer contracted to sell and deliver to its sub-buyer. Although the court did not analyse this cost from the perspective of whether it was inevitable, that must have been the position of the court that focused on the foreseeability test and held that the seller ought to have foreseen this loss as a possible consequence of its breach. For the link between foreseeability and causation, see ch 5.

61 See CIETAC 25 October 1994 (High tensile steel bar), available at cisgw3.law.pace.edu/cases/941025c1.html (where the buyer's liability to its sub-buyer was based on both the court decision and the settlement with the sub-buyer).

62 See Case No P 1997/482 Civil Court Basel (Switzerland) 1 March 2002 (Soyprotein products), available at cisgw3.law.pace.edu/cases/020301s1.html. This case is also discussed in ch 4.

63 CIETAC 29 March 1999 (Flanges), available at cisgw3.law.pace. edu/cases/990329c1.html.

parties' intention to bear joint responsibility for settlements the buyer would reach with its sub-buyers. A difficult situation may arise where there is a chain of buyers following the buyer's sub-sale and where, as a result of the seller's breach, each buyer claims damages against its preceding buyer. The question is whether the first buyer can claim damages against the seller for the entire amount of these accumulated items of liability. It is submitted that although in principle the seller can be held liable for such damages, methods of limiting damages, such as causation, foreseeability and mitigation have a special role to play in such circumstances: the chain of liability may be broken by unreasonable actions of one of the buyers in the chain;[64] the seller may not have been in the position to foresee either the chain itself or its extent;[65] or the buyer may have been able to prevent such a snowball accumulation of liability.[66]

A breach of contract may lead not only to the injured party's liability to its customers but also to liability, that may arise from the applicable law, vis-a-vis state authorities. The unpaid seller may have to pay a penalty to state authorities for its failure to sell foreign currency on time[67] or to ensure the receipt of payment in foreign currency in the seller's account in the specified bank within the time limits specified by the applicable law,[68] or the buyer may have to pay a penalty to customs authorities if the seller fails to deliver the goods.[69] There have been suggestions that in the former type of case, damages for the seller's liability to state authorities are not recoverable because the seller had incurred liability not as a subject of private contractual relations but as a taxpayer, ie as a subject of administrative public relations.[70] It is argued, however, that there is no reason

[64] ibid. For general considerations in such cases, see ch 4.

[65] See the argument made by the breaching seller in CIETAC 5 August 1997 (Cold-rolled coils), available at cisgw3.law.pace.edu/cases/970805c1.html.

[66] This was the basis for the tribunal's curious division of responsibility in ibid ('The Tribunal … notes [that] as the market price then was in downward trend, and the [Buyer's] principal … had already sold the goods to downstream customers, [the Buyer] should have taken steps for substitute goods within a reasonable time, in order to avoid further damages. Although [the Buyer] claims that the contract goods of cold-rolled steel of 0.5 mm x 1250 mm x COIL are a special product, the Tribunal has determined that this [was] not the case. Therefore, [the Buyer] should bear some responsibility for the losses because it did not take reasonable measures to find substitute goods. Therefore … [the Seller] should be responsible for 70% … of the sum [the Buyer] has paid to its downstream customer as liquidated damages and relevant legal fees; the rest, or the 30%, … should be borne by [Buyer] itself.').

[67] See, eg, Arbitration 9 July 1999 (Ukraine) (Metal production goods), available at cisgw3.law.pace.edu/cases/990709u5.html; Arbitration 27 October 2004 (Ukraine) (Lavatory paper), available at cisgw3.law.pace.edu/cases/041027u5.html; Arbitration 10 May 1999 (Ukraine) (Sunflower seeds meal), available at cisgw3.law.pace.edu/cases/ 990510u5.html.

[68] Case No A53-11062/16 Arbitration Court Rostov Region (Russia) 7 July 2016, available at ras.arbitr.ru (in Russian), where damages for this loss were denied on the basis that it was unforeseeable under art 74 CISG to the breaching buyer and that the latter failed to mitigate this loss (see, similarly, Case No A53-11062/2016 Arbitration Court North Caucasus Region (Russia) 1 December 2016, available at ras.arbitr.ru (in Russian)).

[69] ICAC No 85/2002, 26 June 2003, available at cisgw3.law.pace.edu/cases/ 030626r1.html.

[70] *Gildia Ltd v Gaiski GOK* Federal Arbitration Court for the Moscow Circuit (Resolution of the cassation instance on whether the decisions of arbitration courts are legal and substantiated), No KG-A40/5498-00 (Russia) 6 December 2000, available at cisgw3.law.pace.edu/cases/001206r1.html.

in principle why such damages cannot be recoverable so long as the requirements of limiting damages are met and this position is rightly taken in the majority of CISG cases.[71] These losses are specific to international sales transactions and some other examples of losses which are unlikely to occur in domestic sales can be given.

For instance, because of the seller's delay, the buyer may have to pay a higher import tariff than the one it would have paid had there been a timely delivery and damages for the difference between the two rates have been awarded in a CISG case.[72] In a similar vein, where the seller fails to deliver the goods of the contractually specified origin, causing the buyer to pay a higher import duty, the amount of such a duty can be recovered as damages.[73] One CISG case[74] involved the sale of agricultural tools which were, according the applicable regulations in the United States, treated as 'dumped products'. To avoid the imposition of an import anti-dumping duty by the US authorities, the so-called 'reconsideration application' ought to have been filed with the authorities. The tribunal held that it was an obligation of the Chinese seller to file such an application and because its failure to do so had caused the US buyer to pay an import anti-dumping duty, the buyer was awarded damages for the amount of that duty. In another CISG case, the US buyer had breached the contract by not providing the Russian seller, within the fixed time limit, with documents which would have enabled the seller to claim exemption from the payment of value added tax (VAT) and the tribunal granted damages for the amount of the VAT.[75] In yet another CISG case,[76] the buyer's non-payment resulted in the Chinese seller losing the 'duty drawback', which seemed to refer to a refund of an import duty where the goods initially imported into China (or finished products manufactured from them) were to be subsequently exported from China. The seller was awarded damages for this loss.

Some other costs incurred as a result of the breach that (subject to the criterion of reasonableness) may be recoverable as damages include the seller's cost of taking out a loan (in cases of: the buyer's non-payment or late payment;[77]

[71] See cases referred to in D Saidov, 'Cases on the Sales Convention and the UNIDROIT Principles Decided in the Russian Federation: An Update' (2005) 9 *Vindobona J Int'l Commercial L Arbitration* 1, note 30.

[72] See ICAC No 437/1992, 6 May 1994 (see MG Rozenberg, *Kontrakt mezhdunarodnoy kupli-prodazhi* (Moscow 1998) 53).

[73] See Case No 8 O 118/02 District Court Saarbrücken (Germany) 1 June 2004 (Pallets), available at cisgw3.law.pace.edu/cases/040601g1.html.

[74] See CIETAC 10 December 2003 (Agricultural tools), available at cisgw3.law.pace.edu/cases/031210c1.html.

[75] See ICAC No 91/1997, 29 May 1998 in MG Rozenberg, *Arbitrazhnaya praktika mezhdunarodnogo kommercheskogo arbitrazhnogo suda pri TPP RF za 1998 g* (Moscow, Statut, 1999).

[76] CIETAC 18 April 2003 (Desulfurization reagent), available at cisgw3.law.pace.edu/cases/030418c1.html.

[77] CIETAC Arbitration 21 July 1997 (Yam-dyed fabric), available at cisgw3.law.pace.edu/cases/970721c1.html; CIETAC 7 November 1996 (Stone products), available at cisgw3.law.pace.edu/cases/961107c1.html.

or the buyer's non-performance of its contractual obligation to replace the packaging of the goods delivered by the seller, resulting in the seller having to take out a loan to purchase replacement packaging[78]) or the seller's loss of use of money.[79] A controversial question is whether the seller's cost of employing a debt collection agency is recoverable. It is suggested that the criteria of reasonableness and expediency point in the direction of these costs not being generally recoverable under the instruments. Because debt collection agencies do not have any special powers of enforcing the seller's claim to the price[80] and the legal means available to such agencies are not generally superior to those available to the seller,[81] it cannot be assumed that employing such services is a normal (and certainly not necessary or unavoidable, to use a guideline discussed earlier) way of enforcing the seller's rights.[82] However, given that some courts have been prepared to recognise the recoverability of such costs,[83] the way forward may be to establish a rebuttable presumption that such costs are unreasonable, unnecessary and, for that reason, non-recoverable and it should then be up to the injured party to prove otherwise.

The buyer's use of non-conforming goods delivered by the seller may cause damage to the buyer's property and although the CISG expressly excludes liability for death and personal injury,[84] there is little doubt that damage to the buyer's property is recoverable under the Convention.[85] Because there is nothing in the

[78] Foreign Trade Court, the Serbian Chamber of Commerce (Serbia) 19 October 2009 (n 11), where the seller was awarded interest as damages ('in international trade the [Seller] is entitled to the interest rate equal to the average interest rate that applies to short-term loans for the currency in which the payment would be made, in the country where the [Seller] has its seat. This solution is inspired by the similar solutions in international trade, contained, for example, in the UNIDROIT Principles of International Commercial Contracts from 2004 (Article 7.4.9) and the Principles of European Contract Law from 2009 (Article 9.508).').

[79] Although claiming interest for the sum in arrears (art 78 CISG) may be a more appropriate and convenient way of compensating for this loss, there are CISG cases where the seller specifically claimed damages for this loss and where the arbitrators recognised it as recoverable (see ICAC No 107/2002, 16 February 2004, available at cisgw3.law.pace. edu/cases/040216r1.html). There is also no reason why damages under art 74 cannot be calculated on the basis of an interest rate (see Case No 3 KfH O 97/89 District Court Stuttgart (Germany) 31 August 1989, available at cisgw3.law.pace.edu/cases/890831g1.html). Even if the seller is awarded interest either under art 78 CISG or as damages under art 74, the seller's loss suffered as a result of non-payment or delay in payment may still exceed the amount, arrived at by applying the applicable interest rate. In such a case, the remainder of the seller's loss, not covered by interest, should still be recoverable as damages under art 74 (Case No 5 C 73/89 Lower Court Oldenburg in Holstein (Germany) 24 April 1990, available at cisgw3.law.pace.edu/cases/890831g1.html ('the seller may claim excess interest by way of damages, the interest damage arising from the seller's not being able to profitably invest the purchase price, or from his needing to take up a loan as a consequence of the failed payment')).

[80] See, somewhat similarly, Schwenzer (n 1) 1070.

[81] See Case No 3/11 O 3/91 District Court Frankfurt (Germany) 16 September 1991 (Shoes), available at cisgw3.law.pace.edu/cases/910916g1.html.

[82] For an extensive list of references to relevant cases, see, eg, Schwenzer (n 1) 1070.

[83] For an example, see *Gaba BV v Direct NV* District Court Hasselt (Belgium) 12 January 2005, available at cisgw3.law.pace.edu/cases/050112b1.html.

[84] See art 5 CISG.

[85] See, eg, CISG Advisory Council Opinion (CISG-AC) No 12, 'Liability of the Seller for Damages Arising out of Personal Injuries And Property Damage Caused by Goods and Services under the CISG',

UPICC and PECL to exclude this loss, it seems safe to assume that it is also recoverable under the two sets of Principles.[86] Another issue that has arisen under the CISG concerns the relationship between agreed damages clauses (liquidated damages/penalty clauses)[87] and the right to claim damages under the instruments. The difficulty arises where the injured party claims that the amount of liquidated damages is lower than its actual loss and the question is whether the injured party is entitled to damages under the CISG in the amount not covered by liquidated damages. The first question is whether the relationship between liquidated damages and the Convention's remedy of damages is a matter governed by the CISG. It is suggested that, contrary to some CISG cases,[88] this matter falls within the Convention's scope. If this proposed position is taken, a conflict may be inevitable between the Convention's right to damages and the policy of some legal systems of not allowing ordinary compensatory damages *in addition* to the amount flowing from an agreed damages clause where the latter does not fully compensate the party for its actual loss.[89] This conflict can be avoided,[90] if it can be inferred from the contract[91] that the issue of compensation was intended to be governed solely by the agreed damages clause.[92] It is only where no intention can be derived that the conflict between the Convention's right to damages and the applicable domestic law may arise. The former should prevail over the latter because the applicable domestic law should not be allowed to prevail over a right provided for by an international treaty, particularly if the country in question has ratified the Convention.[93] Furthermore, this should be so because

available at www.cisgac.com/cisgac-opinion-no12, Rule 3.1 (see further Rule 3.2: 'If the damage is caused to the goods themselves, the liability of the seller is governed by the CISG to the exclusion of any claims based on domestic law, whether contractual or not. The same applies if the damage is caused to property which is attached to the goods, or with which the goods are combined or commingled, or which are processed by the goods, in the normal course of business or in the course of normal use.'; and Rule 3.3: 'However, if the damage is caused to other property of the buyer, any liability under the applicable domestic law is not excluded by the CISG.'); Case No HG 920670 Commercial Court Zürich (Switzerland) 26 April 1995 (Saltwater isolation tank), available at cisgw3.law.pace.edu/cases/950426s1.html; W Khoo, 'Arts. 2–5 CISG' in Bianca and Bonell (n 10) 49.

[86] See O Lando and H Beale (eds), *Principles of European Contract Law: Parts I and II* prepared by the Commission on European Contract Law (The Hague, Kluwer Law International, 2000) 439.

[87] For an overview on this subject, see, eg, A Komarov, 'The Limitation of Contract Damages in Domestic Legal Systems and International Instruments' in D Saidov and R Cunnington (eds), *Contract Damages: Domestic and International Perspectives* (Oxford, Hart Publishing, 2008) 257–9, 262–4; see also Treitel (n 1) 208–44; P Benjamin, 'Penalties, Liquidated Damages and Penal Clauses in Commercial Contract: A Comparative Study of English and Continental Law' (1960) 9 *ICLQ* 600.

[88] See ICAC No 95/2004 27 May 2005, available at cisgw3.law.pace.edu/cases/ 050527r1.html.

[89] See *Dunlop Pneumatic Tyre Co Ltd v New Garage and Motor Co Ltd* [1915] AC 79.

[90] See CIETAC 1 April 1993 (Steel products), available at cisgw3.law.pace.edu/cases/930401c1.html.

[91] See art 6 CISG.

[92] Presumably, the reverse is also true – that is, that the parties are allowed to specify their intention to allow the injured party to claim damages under the CISG where agreed damages do not fully compensate the party for the loss.

[93] See arts 26, 27 of the Vienna Convention on the Law of Treaties.

of the need to respect the Convention's requirement[94] that regard be had to its international character and the need to promote uniformity in its application.[95]

Much controversy has surrounded the question whether the costs of legal proceedings and attorney's fees incurred as a result of the breach are recoverable as damages under the CISG. There is no uniformity, either amongst legal systems or in international commercial arbitration, regarding the treatment of such costs[96] and the Convention itself is silent on the matter. Against this background, it is not surprising that opinions are divided. On the one hand, it has been argued that costs of litigation (arbitration) and the resulting attorney's fees constitute a 'loss' under art 74 CISG because such an interpretation follows from a plain reading of this article: because such costs are incurred as 'a consequence of the breach', the principles of full compensation and the protection of the party's expectation/performance interest dictate that these costs be recoverable.[97] This argument has been further supported on the grounds of policy by suggesting that such an interpretation is dictated by the need for uniformity in the Convention's application.[98] On the other hand, it has been suggested that the recoverability of such costs is outside the Convention's scope and should be left to the applicable law.[99] Various reasons are put forward to

[94] See art 7(1) CISG.

[95] See also CIETAC 13 June 1989 (Sesame/urea), available at cisgw3.law. pace.edu/cases/890613c1. html (the decision is somewhat unfortunate because in awarding damages in addition to the amount fixed by the agreed damages clause the tribunal relied not only on the CISG but also on the applicable domestic statute).

[96] See, eg, JY Gotanda, 'Awarding Costs and Attorney's Fees in International Commercial Arbitrations' (1999) 21 *Mich J Int'l L* 1.

[97] J Felemegas, 'The award of counsel's fees under Article 74 CISG, in *Zapata Hermanos Sucesores v Hearthside Baking Co* (2001)' (2002) 6 *Vindobona J Int'l Commercial L Arbitration* 30, 32, 37–8. For cases where legal fees were held to be recoverable under art 74 CISG, see, eg, Case No 1 C 419/01 Lower Court Viechtach (Germany) 11 April 2002 (Pallets), available at cisgw3.law. pace.edu/cases/020411g1. html; Case No 99 O 123/92 District Court Berlin (Germany) 30 September 1992 (Shoes), available at cisgw3.law.pace.edu/cases/920930g1.html; Appellate Court Düsseldorf (Germany) 14 January 1994 (Shoes), available at cisgw3.law.pace.edu/cases/ 940114g1.html.

[98] See B Zeller, 'Interpretation of Article 74 – *Zapata Hermanos Sucesores v Hearthside Baking* – Where Next?' (2004) 1 *Nordic J Commercial L*, available at www.njcl.fi/1_2004/commentary1.pdf.

[99] This position is taken in numerous cases. See, eg, *Zapata Hermanos Sucesores v Hearthside Baking Co* 13 F.3d 385; *Norfolk Railway v Power Source Supply, Inc*, 2008 WL 2884102 (following *Zapata Hermanos Sucesores v Hearthside Baking Co* (n 104)); *San Lucio S.r.l. v. Import & Storage Services LLC* (D.N.J. Apr. 15, 2009) (articulating also the policy underlying the approach of the US law: 'The U.S. legal system deliberately requires parties to pay their own legal fees in almost all situations, so as not to discourage parties from litigation and to remove barriers to entry into the judicial system.'); Case No C1 04 162 Appellate Court Valais/Wallis (Switzerland) 21 February 2005 (CNC machine), available at cisgw3.law.pace.edu/cases/050221s1.html; ICAC No 97/2004, 23 December 2004, available at cisgw3.law.pace.edu/cases/041223r1. html; Case No 12 HKO 4174/99 District Court München (Germany) 6 April 2000 (Furniture), available at cisgw3.law.pace.edu/ cases/000406g1.html; see also *Zodiac Seats US LLC v Synergy Aerospace Corp* (E.D. Tex. Apr. 23, 2019), where the parties claimed the recovery of attorney's fees on the basis of a specific domestic statute, rather than the CISG, and where *Zapata Hermanos Sucesores v Hearthside Baking Co* (n 99) was discussed. For further references to cases both in favour and against the recoverability of legal fees, see, eg, *UNCITRAL Digest of Case Law on the United Nations Convention on Contracts for the International Sale of Goods*, 2016 edn, available at www.uncitral.org/pdf/english/clout/ CISG_Digest_2016.pdf.

support this suggestion. One reason is that the matter is a procedural issue and should be outside the CISG because the Convention is only concerned with the matters of substantive law.[100] The view is expressed in a much-discussed CISG case:

> The Convention is about contracts, not about procedure. The principles for determining when a losing party must reimburse the winner for the latter's expense of litigation are usually not a part of a substantive body of law, such as contract law, but a part of procedural law.[101]

Another reason is that treating such costs and fees as damages under the CISG will give rise to an anomaly where damages will be awarded to the *winning claimant* but not to the *prevailing respondent party* who successfully defends a breach of contract claim because damages are only awarded for breach of contract. This result undermines the equality of the parties[102] and it is this argument that best explains why the recoverability of costs of legal proceedings and attorney's fees should lie outside the Convention's scope. It has been suggested that the anomaly can be resolved by awarding damages to the prevailing respondent party on the basis that the claimant breached its 'duty of loyalty to the contract' by 'filing a suit for a breach of contract where a court later holds that party's suit to be lacking a proper foundation'.[103] This suggestion, however, lacks support in the CISG[104] and is far too stretched to constitute a solid basis for awarding of damages to the prevailing respondent.[105] To return briefly to the first reason, it is now increasingly recognised that resolving issues under the CISG merely with reference to the distinction between procedural and substantive law is unhelpful: whether a particular matter is classified as a substantive or procedural issue varies from one legal system to another.[106] Consequently, this distinction is not an appropriate framework for dealing with the issue of legal costs and fees. Thus, whether costs of legal proceedings and attorney's fees are

[100] See H Flechtner and J Lookofsky, 'Viva Zapata! American Procedure and CISG Substance in a US Circuit Court of Appeal' (2003) 7 *Vindobona J Int'l Commercial L Arbitration* 93, 94.

[101] *Zapata Hermanos Sucesores v Hearthside Baking Co* (n 99) 388.

[102] The principle of equality can be derived from the Convention's preamble and from its generally symmetrical structure in relation to the rights, obligations, and remedies of the seller and the buyer.

[103] J Felemegas, 'An Interpretation of Article 74 CISG by the US Circuit Court of Appeals' (2003) 15 *Pace Int'l L Rev* 91, available at www.cisg.law.pace.edu/cisg/biblio/felemegas4.html.

[104] See A Mullis, 'Twenty-Five Years On – The United Kingdom, Damages and the Vienna Sales Convention' (2007) 71 *Rabels Zeitschrift für ausländisches und internationales Privatrecht* 35, 44.

[105] 'An approach that requires such a result-oriented jurisprudential stretch … in order to avoid egregious partiality … does not recommend itself' (HM Flechtner, 'Recovering Attorneys' Fees as Damages under the UN Sales Convention: A Case Study on the New International Commercial Practice and the Role of Case Law in CISG Jurisprudence, with Comments on *Zapata Hermanos Sucesores SA v Hearthside Baking Co*' (2002) 22 *Northwestern J Int'l L Business* 121, 151).

[106] See generally, CG Orlandi, 'Procedural Law Issues and Law Conventions' (2000) 5 *Uniform L Rev* 23, available at www.cisg.law.pace.edu/cisg/biblio/orlandi.html. See also ch 7.

recoverable lies outside the CISG because it undermines the equality between the parties and should be resolved based on the applicable law.[107]

The same does not necessarily apply to legal costs incurred *prior* to litigation (arbitration). Some such legal costs, such as those incurred in mitigating losses, are recoverable under the CISG.[108] There may, however, be certain pre-litigation costs which cannot be neatly separated from costs of litigation such as 'the legal costs for the provisional assessment of the legal situation, of the possible outcome of any litigation and settlement negotiations'.[109] It has been correctly suggested that such costs can be very similar to costs arising from litigation and, where so, the consideration of equality of the parties again seems to require that they should not be recoverable.[110] Put differently, the pre-litigation costs incurred in order to prepare for litigation (or reach a settlement)[111] will, if recoverable under the CISG, be recovered as damages by the winning claimant but will not be recovered as damages by the respondent who successfully defended the claim.[112]

4. DAMAGE TO THE 'PERFORMANCE INTEREST'

It can be argued that where one party does not perform its contractual obligation, the other party's interest in the performance of that obligation

[107] See also T Kelly, 'How Does the Cookie Crumble? Legal Costs under a Uniform Interpretation of the United Nations Convention on Contracts for the International Sale of Goods' (2003) 1 *Nordic J Commercial L*, available at www.njcl.fi/1_2003/commentary2.pdf; J Vanto, 'Attorney's Fees as Damages in International Commercial Litigation' (2003) 15 *Pace Int'l L Rev* 203, available at www.cisg.law.pace.edu/cisg/biblio/vanto1.html; M Djordjević, 'Arts 74–77' in S Kröll, L Mistelis and P Viscasillas (eds), *The United Nations Convention on Contracts for the International Sale of Goods*, 2nd edn (München, CH Beck and Oxford, Hart 2018) 988 (against the recoverability of this loss for a different reason: 'the issue is excluded from the CISG ambit since it does not constitute a loss suffered by the aggrieved party 'as a consequence of the breach' but rather as a consequence of litigation (arbitration).')

[108] *Zapata Hermanos Sucesores v Hearthside Baking Co* (n 99); District Court Potsdam (n 56) ('Due to Art. 74 CISG, [the Seller] is … entitled to reimbursement of its attorneys' fees that were incurred before the trial.'); Case No A3 2004 112 District Court Zug (Switzerland) 27 November 2008, available at cisgw3.law.pace.edu/cases/081127s1.html ('Doctrine and jurisprudence generally argue that reimbursement for such pre-trial enforcement costs is subject to the CISG because such costs are hard to separate from claims regarding damages and in domestic law they are often not separated. However, such costs may be reimbursed only if they are business-related expenses in a legal sense, incurred as a result of the debtor's conduct violating the contract and which the debtor could foresee as a reasonable reaction to its conduct'); Case No A56-23325/2015 Arbitration Court St Petersburg and Leningrad Region (Russia) 27 March 2019, available at ras.artbitr.ru (in Russian), where the buyer recovered, amongst others, the cost of employing a law firm in the seller's country (Korea) to resolve a difference with the seller (regarding the parties' contractual performance), who for a certain time was not providing the buyer with the required documents that would enable the goods to be exported from Korea.

[109] I Schwenzer and P Hachem, 'The Scope of the CISG Provisions on Damages' in Saidov and Cunnington (n 87) 105.

[110] Ibid.

[111] Ibid.

[112] See, similarly, Schwenzer (n 1) 1070.

('performance interest') is damaged because the party does not get what it is entitled to receive under the contract.[113] It follows from this argument that every breach can be said to damage the innocent party's interest in and right to performance, and a striking consequence of such a description of the party's loss is that whenever there is a breach there is necessarily a loss.[114] Adopting such a position in full would arguably run counter to the traditional understanding of the law of damages (including that in the context of international instruments)[115] that rests on the fundamental premise that an innocent party must identify and prove its loss and therefore does not presume that every breach necessarily results in a loss.[116] The full-scale recognition of this position can also encourage innocent parties to inflate their claims by valuing damage to their 'contractual right' or 'performance interest' higher than the amount of damages based on other heads of loss.[117] Not only would the possible proliferation of such claims shift the focus away from losses that are in truth more 'real', making the law of damages more 'artificial', but would also create the risk of over-compensating these parties and contravening the compensatory purpose of damages.

At the same time, it is submitted that the concept of the performance interest cannot be abandoned altogether because there are cases where it is necessary to so conceptualise or characterise an innocent party's loss. Because legal thinking and the experience of the international instruments (and of some legal systems) concerning this concept are still in the state of flux,[118] it is not easy to

[113] An obvious example is where the buyer fails to pay the contract price and damages are awarded for the full amount of the contract price. Such damages were awarded in: *Norfolk Railway v Power Source Supply, Inc* (n 994)), where the seller performed its part of the contract; and in ICAC No 37/2006, 11 October 2006 in PD Savkin (ed), *Praktika MKAS pri TPP RF: 2004–2016 – K 85-letiyu MKAS* (Nauka Prava – Elektronnaya biblioteka, Moskva, 2017) 391, where, despite best efforts, the seller was unable to resell the goods which resulted in their deterioration and loss of all commercial value. These damages should be subject to any costs saved by the seller.

[114] See A Burrows, 'Are 'Damages on the *Wrotham Park* Basis Compensatory, Restitutionary, or Neither?' in Saidov and Cunnington (n 87) 173.

[115] See ibid (stating, in the context of the common law, that if this approach is logically followed through 'one would end up with the infringement of every type of right leading to substantial compensation for the value of the "lost right". That is not our present law and acceptance of it would shatter our conventional approach to damages'.).

[116] English law, for example, distinguishes between nominal and substantial damages. See, eg, H Beale (ed), *Chitty on Contracts*, 33rd edn, vol 1 (London, Sweet & Maxwell, 2019) [26-010] ('A regular use of nominal damages … is to establish the infringement of the claimant's legal right, and sometimes the award of nominal damages is a mere peg on which to hang costs.').

[117] In the context of English law, see the UK Supreme Court case *Court Morris-Garner v One Step (Support) Ltd* [2018] UKSC 20, involving the breach of a 'non-compete' clause where the claimant claimed 'negotiating' damages based on the amount that would have been negotiated and paid for the release of the breaching party from its obligations under the non-compete clause. The claimed damages were a higher amount (between £5.6m and £6.3m) than the estimated loss of profit arising from the breach of that clause (between £3.4m and £4.6m).

[118] For an overview of current debates surrounding the protection of the 'performance interest' in the common law, see, eg, D Winterton, 'Two Conceptions of the 'Performance Interest' in Contract Damages' in R Halson and D Campbell (eds), *Research Handbook on Remedies in Private Law* (Cheltenham UK – Northampton, MA, USA, Edward Elgar, 2019).

exhaustively and definitively identify the types of case that ought to be covered by it. It is suggested that the concept of a 'legitimate interest' in the performance of an obligation, which has been breached, can be a useful guide for identifying cases where it is appropriate to recognise that an innocent party has suffered damage to its performance interest. The very notion of a 'legitimate interest' in the performance of an obligation underscores that it is only cases, where the innocent party has attached particular significance to a certain obligation by the breaching party, that deserve protection by means of damages. Admittedly vague and in the abstract lacking in substantive content,[119] the legitimate interest concept is nevertheless sufficiently flexible to strike the right balance between, one the one hand, the need not to undermine the well-entrenched understanding of the law of damages and, on the other, to recognise that the 'performance interest' loss must have a role to play. It is further suggested that whether a party has such a legitimate interest should be interpreted within narrow boundaries to ensure limited scope for the 'performance interest' loss. Specifically, it is preferable to confine the 'performance interest' damages to cases where it is either impossible for the innocent party to establish its loss by relying on another head of loss[120] and/or the usual 'concrete' and 'abstract' approaches to both defining and calculating a loss do not provide an appropriate or relevant analytical framework.[121]

Further limitations are inherent in the limited types of case to which, as this book argues, the recoverability of the 'performance interest' damages should be confined. The first type of case, where a party can have a legitimate interest in the performance, is where the party's contractual right can in itself be seen as a 'valuable asset' or its breach results in the loss of a 'valuable asset'.[122] Examples include cases involving a breach of: a contractual 'confidentiality' clause that requires, for example, parties not to disclose to third parties the information obtained about each other and the technology involved in the course of performing the contract;[123] a similar contractual clause that provides that neither party obtains rights to the confidential and proprietary information of the other party;[124] a contractual obligation that leads to infringement of intellectual property rights;[125] a contractual 'non-competition' clause requiring, for example, the

[119] See, similarly, S Waddams, 'The Modern History of Remedies for Breach of Contract' in Halson and Campbell (n 118) 28.

[120] For the reasons set out in the previous paragraph of the main text. For a similar position in the common law context, see A Burrows, 'Negotiating Damages' in C Mitchell and S Watterson, *The World of Maritime and Commercial Law: Essays in Honour of Francis Rose* (Oxford – New York, Hart, 2020) 306–07.

[121] See the discussion in this section below.

[122] For a similar position in English law, see *Court Morris-Garner v One Step (Support) Ltd* (n 117) [91]–[93], [95].

[123] For a CISG case, see Stockholm Chamber of Commerce Arbitration 5 April 2007 (Pressure sensors), available at cisgw3.law.pace.edu/cases/070405s5.html (discussed in more detail in ch 2).

[124] See ibid.

[125] See, eg, *Court Morris-Garner v One Step (Support) Ltd* (n 117) [95].

buyer to resell the goods only in specified countries or markets and/or in countries and markets other than those in which the seller or the seller's customers operate.[126] Contractual rights based on clauses of this kind protect valuable economic and commercial assets and can potentially meet the proposed 'legitimate interest' guideline.

The second type of case is where the innocent party places a special subjective or non-economic value on the performance.[127] In such cases, the well-known 'concrete' and 'abstract' approaches to calculation provide an inadequate analytical framework.[128] Suppose that:[129] a builder fails to build a swimming pool of the required depth but this has no impact on its market value;[130] the seller supplies a wedding ring of greater market value than that specified in the contract but which comes as a great disappointment to the buyer because of an emotional attachment to a cheaper ring; a ring cheaper than that contracted for is delivered but the injured party's wife actually prefers the delivered ring to the one provided for by the contract. If an 'abstract' measure is applied to these examples it will produce inconsistent results: the market formula will lead to damages only in the last case for it is only there that there is a difference between the value of subject matter as contracted for and its value as delivered. While the 'concrete' approach (which looks at the party's *actual* circumstances) may lead to the conclusion that the injured party has suffered some kind of loss, this approach *in itself* is unable to explain and rationalise what that loss is. Eventually the question whether the party can be considered to have suffered any loss depends on whether the law is prepared to compensate the party for damage to the 'subjective' value (non-economic interest) it has placed on the performance. Therefore, damage to the performance interest is a separate issue requiring special treatment and should, it is submitted, be viewed as an independent head of loss.

Examples in the commercial context can also be given.[131] While the problems of calculating this loss are addressed in a later chapter,[132] it may be helpful to give a relevant example at this stage. Suppose that a company, conscious of human rights, orders goods under a condition that no child labour will be used in the production of the goods and agrees to pay an additional price to ensure compliance with this condition.[133] Suppose further that child labour was used

[126] *SARL BRI Production 'Bonaventure' v Société Pan African Export* Appellate Court Grenoble (France) 22 February 1995, available at cisgw3.law.pace.edu/cases/070405s5.html (discussed in detail in ch 2).

[127] For a well-known article on this subject, see D Harris, A Ogus, and J Phillips, 'Contract Remedies and the Consumer Surplus' (1979) 95 *LQR* 581.

[128] See D Saidov and R Cunnington, 'Current Themes in the Law of Contract Damages: Introductory Remarks' in Saidov and Cunnington (n 87) 25.

[129] All examples are based on those discussed in ibid.

[130] See *Ruxley Electronics and Construction Ltd v Forsyth* [1996] AC 344 (HL).

[131] See Schwenzer and Hachem (n 109).

[132] See ch 8.

[133] The example is given in Schwenzer and Hachem (n 109).

in manufacturing the goods but this fact does not change the product's tangible properties. A strong case can be made in such circumstances that even if the use of child labour does not affect the market value of the product, the buyer has suffered loss.

A difficult task is identifying those cases where the innocent party has in fact placed a special subjective or non-economic value on the performance. One important factor is whether the party, such as the buyer in our example, has paid an additional price to ensure compliance. There may also be some other clear evidence such as a contractual clause imposing a strict obligation against the use of child labour reinforced by specific and strong statements to this effect during the negotiations between the parties prior or subsequent to the conclusion of the contract, or a relevant trade usage. Another way of both identifying and calculating such losses can be for the court to 'ask itself, hypothetically, if the parties had agreed on a liquidated damages clause, whether ... it would have included compensation for non-pecuniary benefits'.[134] Given the possible difficulties of both identifying cases where a subjective value has been placed on the performance and quantifying damage to that value, the parties are advised to make their intentions clear and, more importantly, to provide their assessment of the value they place on the performance (eg, by including a liquidated damages clause).

5. LOSS CAUSED BY THE CHANGE IN THE VALUE OF CURRENCY

In international transactions, a delay in performance may give rise to losses brought about by a change in the value of the currency(ies). First, there are situations where losses can be caused by a change in the so-called 'internal' or 'real' value of a currency. A change in the internal value of a currency is usually part of inflationary or deflationary processes[135] and represents a change in the domestic purchasing power of a currency.[136] A change in its purchasing power can, in turn, be defined as a change in its value 'against the value of goods and services which can be acquired with it'.[137] Second, losses can also arise from a change in the 'external' or 'international' value of a currency and these terms refer to the value of one currency in relation to the value of another currency.

[134] A Ogus, 'The Economic Basis of Damages for Breach of Contract: Inducement and Expectation' in Saidov and Cunnington (n 87) 135.

[135] 'Inflation and its opposite, deflation, describe changes in a nation's ... currency's domestic purchasing power' (K Rosenn, *Law and Inflation* (University of Pennsylvania Press, Philadelphia 1982) 3). Although there is no universally accepted definition of the term 'inflation', it has been said to refer either to 'a sustained rise in an economy's general level of prices or to a corresponding fall in the domestic purchasing power of an economy's currency' (ibid, 3); also RG Hammond, 'Compensation for the Lost Value of Money: A Canadian Proposal' (1983) 99 *LQR* 71–2 (defining inflation in descriptive and causal senses).

[136] Rosenn (n 135) 3.

[137] A Hudson, 'Money as Property in Financial Transactions' (1999) 14 *J Int'l Banking L* 171.

This relationship influences and is reflected in the 'rate of exchange', ie 'the price of one currency in terms of another'.[138]

The distinction between the two situations is important because a change in one value will not necessarily entail a change in the other value,[139] although in the long term a change in the internal value may well result in a change in the external value.[140] Since, at least in the short term, the two types of value are distinct from one another, a change in those values can give rise to two different types of loss: loss arising from a change in the purchasing power (internal value) of a currency and loss caused by a change in the external value of a currency. The former may occur where, for example, the buyer makes a late payment and the currency has depreciated between the due date and the date of actual payment and, as a result, the seller receives less than what it would have received had the payment been timely. The loss flowing from changes in the external value of currencies may arise in different situations. One example is where the buyer makes a late payment in a currency which the seller intends to exchange for its domestic currency. If the domestic currency has strengthened against the currency of payment or if the latter has devalued against the former between the payment due date and the actual date of payment, the seller receives less than what it would have received had the contract been properly performed.[141]

Should these losses be recoverable under the international instruments? An argument in favour of their recoverability is that they are *real* financial losses and, subject to the requirements of limiting damagess, they should be recoverable. It can also be argued that this result is dictated by the purpose of putting the party in the position in which it would have been had the contract been performed. So far as the case of the 'external' value of currencies is concerned,[142] there

[138] C Proctor, *Mann on the Legal Aspect of Money*, 6th edn (Oxford, OUP, 2005) 74; Rosenn (n 135) 3.

[139] 'It seems that there is no necessary or direct connection between the domestic and the international values of the unit of account; in the late 1970s and the early 1980s, significant rates of inflation eroded the domestic value of the pound, yet its value in terms of the US dollar remained broadly stable' (Proctor (n 138) 75). Therefore, we cannot be as categorical as one court was by stating that 'inflationary value of the money … affects the flexible exchange rates which, as opposed to fixed exchange rates, are determined on the basis of the laws of supply and demand. The flexible exchange rates mirror the respective purchase power of the currency' (Case No O 116/81 District Court Heidelberg (Germany) 27 January 1981, available at cisgw3.law.pace.edu/cases/810127g1.html).

[140] 'In the long run, countries experiencing inflation rates higher than those of customary trading partners, will be forced to devalue; however, in the short run, it is frequently possible for countries to maintain the same exchange rate despite substantial inflation, or to devalue by less than the inflation rate differential' (Rosenn (n 135) 3).

[141] See Case No C1 08 45 Higher Cantonal Court Valais (Switzerland) 28 January 2009, available at cisgw3.law.pace.edu/cases/090128s1.html, where the Swiss buyer paid late in Swiss francs and the German seller exchanged the Swiss francs into Euros, with the resulting amount in Euros having been lower than what it would have been at the payment due date. For other examples and a more extensive discussion, see ch 9.

[142] See also arts 6.1.9(4) UPICC and 7:108(3) PECL (for a specific remedy designed to deal with the problem of exchange rate losses) and the discussion in ch 9.

are no obstacles to this line of argument.[143] The same cannot be said of the 'internal' value of currency where the principal objection to the recoverability of currency depreciation losses is the principle of nominalism.[144] According to this principle, any change in the purchasing power of currency should not be taken into account and it is its face value which should be relied upon.[145] Nominalism is said to be an 'essential part of every stable monetary system'[146] and this idea has already been supported in a case governed by the ULIS, where the court stated the following:

> [The] financial nominalism is derived from considerations of the stability of currency and also the promotion of good faith and legal certainty. If the value of the currency had to be considered in connection with every purchase price debt, this would lead to an accelerated depreciation of the currency and would present the contracting party ... with an incalculable risk ... Recognition of a loss of value of a currency as a compensable loss on grounds of a delayed payment would accelerate the drop of the value of a currency and would intervene in the monetary policies of the Contracting States.[147]

Relying on this principle, the buyer who made a late payment can argue that any decrease in the currency's purchasing power must be ignored because the seller received nominally the same amount as it would have received had the payment been made on time.

It is submitted that despite the principle of nominalism being recognised and entrenched in some legal systems,[148] it should not prevent the currency depreciation loss from being recoverable under the international instruments.[149] This principle is said to be based on the presumed intentions of the parties:[150] by agreeing on a particular currency the parties are presumed to have intended

[143] It has been suggested in one CISG case that '[a] currency devaluation can only be compensated if it leads to damages on the part of the creditor, for instance, if the creditor usually conducts his money transfers in a third currency and therefore always converts other currencies immediately after their receipt. In such a case, the currency devaluation has an unfavorable effect' (Appellate Court Düsseldorf (Germany) 14 January 1994 (n 97). It is argued, however, that this statement cannot be taken as a general position on the recoverability of this loss as its true relevance lies with whether exchange rate losses, when a creditor exchanges the currency of payment into another currency, are foreseeable (for further discussion, see ch 9). For a case where the exchange rate loss was deemed recoverable under the CISG, see Higher Cantonal Court Valais (Switzerland) 28 January 2009 (n 141) ('when the debtor is late and pays in a currency different from the legal currency of the creditor's place of business, it is considered an additional damage due to the fact that the location of the buyer's place of business causes exchange rate loss.').

[144] For reasons why nominalism is not relevant to the exchange rate losses, see RA Brand, 'Exchange Loss Damages and the Uniform-Money Claims Act: The Emperor Hasn't All His Clothes' (1991/1992) 23 *L Policy Int'l Business* 1, 44–5.

[145] See TA Downes, 'Nominalism, Indexation, Excuse and Revalorisation: A Comparative Survey' (1985) 101 *LQR* 98–9.

[146] Waddams (n 22) 383.

[147] Landgericht Heidelberg (n 139).

[148] See Brand (n 144) 43; *Procter & Gamble Co (The) v Svenska Cellulosa Aktiebolaget SCA* [2012] EWCA Civ 1413 [32] (referring to a 'deep-rooted principle of nominalism').

[149] In relation to the exchange rate losses, see also Djordjević (n 107) 982–3.

[150] Proctor (n 138) 242.

their obligations to be discharged on 'a unit for unit basis'.[151] In other words, the presumption is that each unit of performance should correspond to a unit of the currency in question, despite the possibility of the change in this currency's purchasing power. It has also been argued that because the declining value of currency and the contractual devices for protecting against inflation[152] are widely known, it can be presumed that a failure to include such contractual devices should serve as evidence that the creditor has assumed the risk of a decline in the value of money.[153]

In response, it has been correctly argued that while drawing presumptions regarding the parties' intentions may be appropriate in cases involving claims for the payment of the price or similar claims for the payment of a pre-determined sum of money, drawing such presumptions is not relevant where damages are claimed because the 'innocent party had not intended that the contract should be broken'.[154] It is further submitted that a failure to stipulate a device for protecting against inflation may, *in some cases*, be a sufficient reason to presume that the risk of currency depreciation is assumed by the creditor. For instance, if before making the contract the creditor discussed with the other party the risk of inflationary losses, it might be justifiable to conclude that the creditor intended to assume such a risk. However, in international transactions involving business persons of different backgrounds and varying levels of commercial sophistication, a more appropriate and balanced position is to consider each case on its facts with a view to determining whether the parties intended to derogate from the instruments' provisions on damages by allocating the risk of the currency depreciation loss to the creditor.[155] A failure to include an inflation protection device should be no more than a factor in contract interpretation. Thus, the reasons set out in this paragraph together with the need to protect the party's 'expectation/performance' interest and the fact that the currency depreciation loss is a real financial loss dictate that this loss be recoverable under the international instruments.[156]

[151] C Proctor, 'Changes in Monetary Value and the Assessment of Damages' in Saidov and Cunnington (n 87) 464.

[152] These devices include linking payments to an agreed index, escalation clauses and short repayment periods for loans (Waddams (n 22) 384).

[153] Ibid.

[154] Proctor (n 151).

[155] Article 6 CISG, art 1.5 UPICC and art 1:102(2) PECL.

[156] The Comments on the PECL seem to indicate that currency losses are recoverable losses under the PECL: '[T]he aggrieved party's remedy for non-payment or delay in payment is not limited to interest. It extends to additional and other loss recoverable within the limits laid down by the general provisions on damages … This might include, for example, … a fall in the internal value of the money, through inflation, between the due date and the actual date of payment, so far as this fall is not compensated by interest under paragraph (1); and, where the money of payment is not the money of account, loss on exchange' (Comment C to Article 9:508 in Lando and Beale (n 86) 450). For a seemingly different position on this issue, see CISG Advisory Council (CISG-AC) No. 6, 'Calculation of Damages under CISG Article 74', available at www.cisg.law.pace.edu/cisg/CISG-ACop6.html. For cases where currency losses were held recoverable, see ch 9. See also *Gruppo IMARS SpA v Protech Horst* District Court Roermond (Netherlands) 6 May 1993, available at cisgw3.law.pace.

6. DAMAGE TO REPUTATION AND GOODWILL[157]

In contrast with the UPICC and PECL, which expressly recognise the recoverability of non-pecuniary losses,[158] the CISG provides no indication as to the recoverability of such losses. Most such losses are unlikely to be relevant to commercial transactions because those transactions usually give rise to pecuniary or economic considerations and because most commercial players are legal entities, incapable of suffering most types of non-pecuniary loss (such as emotional harm or mental distress).[159] Nevertheless, business reputation and goodwill are those intangible phenomena which may be relevant to commercial transactions and therefore damage to these intangibles cannot be easily dismissed as non-recoverable under the CISG. It has been suggested that only pecuniary losses flowing from damage to intangibles are recoverable,[160] and a similar attitude is expressed in some CISG cases. For example, in one case, the court stated that:

> '[t]he [buyer] cannot claim a loss of turnover, on the one hand – which could be reimbursed in the form of lost profits – and then, on the other hand, try to get additional compensation for a loss in reputation. A damaged reputation is completely insignificant as long as it does not lead to a loss of turnover and consequently lost profits. A businessperson runs his business from a commercial point of view. As long as he has the necessary turnover, he can be completely indifferent towards his image'.[161]

Likewise, another court stated that 'deterioration of commercial image [reputation] is not compensable damages in itself, if it did not entail proved pecuniary damages'.[162] These cases seem to reflect the view that damage to reputation

edu/cases/930506n1.html, where the position of the court was not clear when it stated that 'although under the CISG a devaluation of the currency of the price is in principle at the risk of the seller, in this case, the buyer had to pay damages for devaluation since the seller would not have incurred this loss if the buyer had paid in due time'.

[157] This section is a revised version of D Saidov, 'Damage to Business Reputation and Goodwill under the Vienna Sales Convention' in Saidov and Cunnington (n 87).

[158] Article 7.4.2(2) UPICC and art 9:501(2)(a) PECL. See also The Arbitration Center of Mexico (CAM) Arbitral Award 30 November 2006, available at www.unilex.info, where the UPICC were applicable (the abstract of the decision is available in English). In this case, the tribunal, acknowledging that non-pecuniary losses were recoverable under the UPICC, rejected a distributor's claim for damage to its reputation on the Californian market, allegedly caused by the suppliers failure to supply the goods, because the distributor failed to prove both the existence and amount of such damage.

[159] See National and International Arbitral Tribunal of Milan (Italy) Award No A-1795/51 1 December 1996, available at www.unilex.info/ (where the tribunal, applying the UPICC, excluded compensation for emotional harm and distress because the injured party was a corporate entity).

[160] See CISG-AC (n 156).

[161] Case No 10 O 72/00 District Court Darmstadt (Germany) 9 May 2000 (Video recorders), available at cisgw3.law.pace.edu/cases/000509g1.html.

[162] See *Calzados Magnanni v Shoes General International* Court of Appeal Grenoble (France) 21 October 1999, available at www.cisg.law.pace.edu/cisg/wais/db/cases2/991021f1.html. This decision overruled the decision in the first instance where compensation for loss of reputation had been awarded.

and/or goodwill is not a 'real loss' in itself and that it only becomes such where adverse pecuniary consequences follow.[163]

The question is whether this is a proper approach to take under the CISG. The procedure that the CISG adopts to deal with issues which it does not expressly address is, first, to determine whether the issue is governed by the CISG.[164] If so, the matter needs to be resolved on the basis of the Convention's general principles.[165] To deal with the first part of this procedure, it is submitted that the issue of the recoverability of losses is within the Convention's scope. The Convention expressly deals with the issue of damages and therefore the answer to this question must be found within the Convention itself. Is there a relevant general principle which helps resolve the matter? It is often suggested that the principle of 'full compensation' can be regarded as a general principle[166] and it is sometimes argued that this principle dictates that loss of reputation and goodwill be recoverable.[167] But this is too easy an answer[168] because full compensation would dictate the recovery of damage to intangibles only if such damage is regarded as a (recoverable) 'loss' within the meaning of art 74 in the first place.

The issue then is one of the interpretation of art 74 and the question is whether damage to reputation and goodwill is 'a loss' under the CISG. The answer depends on the Convention's policies which are, in turn, informed by its underlying values.[169] For present purposes, it suffices to state that the CISG aims to support international trade and commerce and provides a balanced set of rules acceptable to international traders. It is often argued that to be able to facilitate commercial development legal rules need to meet the legitimate needs and expectations of commercial people. This line of thinking leads to the question whether business people consider reputation and goodwill as being important to them. Are reputation and goodwill something into which they will invest money, time, and effort? In short, is it reasonable to expect that they would generally

[163] This position is sometimes taken in the context of English law (see N Enonchong, 'Contract Damages for Injury to Reputation' (1996) 59 MLR 592, 597).

[164] The Convention defines its scope in very general terms by referring to the issues of formation and rights and obligations of the parties flowing from the contract (see art 4).

[165] See art 7(2) CISG.

[166] See Comment 3 on Article 70 of the 1978 Draft Convention; see also Vienna Arbitration SCH-4318 15 June 1994 (Rolled metal sheets), available at cisgw3.law.pace.edu/cases/940615a4.html and SCH-4366 15 June 1994 (n 48).

[167] See A Burrows, *Remedies for Torts, Breach of Contract and Equitable Wrongs*, 4th edn (Oxford, OUP, 2019) 271.

[168] The same can be said about the argument that art 7.4.2 UPICC can supplement the CISG in this respect.

[169] The connection between what constitutes loss, on the one hand, and underlying values of a legal system and of society as a whole has been highlighted on a number of occasions (see, eg, E McKendrick and K Worthington, 'Damages for Non-Pecuniary Loss' in N Cohen and E McKendrick (eds), *Comparative Remedies for Breach of Contract* (Oxford, Hart Publishing, 2005) 322; MG Bridge, 'Contractual Damages for Intangible Loss: A Comprehensive Analysis' (1984) 62 *Can Bar Rev* 323, 326–7).

regard reputation and goodwill as important assets? It is the answers to these questions that should be decisive in resolving the question whether damage to reputation and goodwill is recoverable under the CISG.

It is not possible to make generalisations in answering these questions.[170] In some industries or trade sectors reputation or goodwill may be regarded as important assets whereas in others this may not be the case.[171] It may also be that companies with bad reputations are very profitable.[172] Nonetheless, there is a substantial body of evidence, both in law and outside it, which demonstrates that it is *often* the case that reputation and goodwill are viewed by business persons as important commercial assets. Although the reasons are many, they all revolve around the benefits flowing from having a good reputation or goodwill. These benefits include: a company's ability to charge premium prices for their products/services;[173] pay lower prices to its suppliers; incur lower marketing costs; attract top recruits; experience greater loyalty from customers and employees; have more stable profits; face fewer risks in times of crisis; obtain credit more easily; and, generally, have greater freedom in decision making.[174] Because of these potential benefits, good reputation is viewed as a strategic resource enabling a company to have a competitive advantage over its rivals.[175] Legal research[176] also demonstrates that in certain trade sectors, reputation is an important factor in selecting a transactional partner and a non-legal sanction[177] the threat of which may deter a breach or help enforce an arbitral decision. There is little doubt therefore that reputation and goodwill play a significant *multi-functional* role in commercial affairs and it is not surprising that some companies make significant investments in terms of money, time and effort in developing and sustaining their reputations.[178] The importance of reputation

[170] See R Chun, 'Corporate Reputation: Meaning and Measurement' (2005) 7 *Int'l J Management Reviews* 91, 100 ('A good image/reputation is probably better than a bad image, but the results in the literature have in fact been inconsistent').

[171] See NA Gardberg, 'Reputatie, Reputation, Réputation, Reputazione, Ruf: A Cross-Cultural Qualitative Analysis of Construct and Instrument Equivalence' (2006) 9 *Corporate Reputation Rev* 39, 51.

[172] Ibid, 52.

[173] See L Bernstein, 'Private Commercial Law in the Cotton Industry: Creating Cooperation through Rules, Norms, and Institutions' (2000–2001) 99 *Mich L Rev* 1724, 1748–9 nn 104 and 107.

[174] There are numerous sources outlining these benefits (see, eg, C Fombrun, *Reputation: Realizing Value from the Corporate Image* (Boston MA, Harvard Business School Press, 1996) 11, 73, 75).

[175] Ibid, 11 and 28.

[176] See, eg, the following sources with further references: H Collins, *Regulating Contracts* (Oxford, OUP, 1999) 97–126; CP Gillette, 'Reputation and Intermediaries in Electronic Commerce' (2001–2002) 62 *La L Rev* 1165; L Bernstein, 'Opting out of the Legal System: Extralegal Contractual Relations in the Diamond Industry' (1992) 21 *JLS* 115; Bernstein (n 173).

[177] See Case No 32 O 508/04 District Court Bayreuth (Germany) 10 December 2004 (Tiles), available at cisgw3.law.pace.edu/cases/041210g1.html (where the buyer alleged that its customer had warned other customers not to purchase tiles from the buyer).

[178] See EL Black and TA Carnes, 'The Market Valuation of Corporate Reputation' (2000) 3 Corporate Reputation Rev 31; Collins (n 76) 112. Cases provide a number of examples showing that building a solid reputation may require years to develop by expanding business, establishing good relations with other companies (such as, eg, suppliers and retailers), ensuring high quality

and goodwill is further reaffirmed by the fact that companies sometimes prefer paying damages or fines to taking the risk of damaging their reputations.[179] For these reasons, damage to these intangibles can be significant for a company's business standing, even if it does not immediately result in substantial financial losses. This discussion demonstrates that reputation and goodwill can be significant business assets and it is reasonable to assume that business people often treat them as such. It is also reasonable to suggest that if damage to these intangibles is not recoverable, incentives for commercial people to invest in reputation and goodwill will be reduced.[180] All this points in favour of such damage being, in principle, recoverable.

It is important to examine the objections to this position. One is that the recoverability of this type of loss cannot be properly dealt with unless reputation and goodwill are defined precisely.[181] The intangible nature of reputation and goodwill makes it impossible to develop a precise and workable definition of what constitutes damage to these phenomena. This also makes it impossible to identify a specific property to which damage has been done; such damages are too speculative, difficult to prove and not capable of a rational assessment.[182] For these reasons, it can also be argued that making a breaching party pay damages for this loss is simply unfair. According to some courts, this unfair treatment becomes more acute because of the difficulty of setting limits to the recovery of such damages.[183] Another objection is that such losses are never foreseeable as required by art 74 and, for that reason, are not recoverable.[184] Finally, the

of goods/services and proper contractual performance and making much financial investment in hiring new employees, promotion and advertising (see decision by Tampere Court of First Instance (Finland) 17 January 1997 (Canned food), available at cisgw3.law.pace.edu/ cases/970117f5.html (decided under the CISG); *Barrett Co v Panther Rubber Mfg Co* 24 F.2d 329, 331 (C.A.1 1928); *Reo D Stott v Thomas Johnston* (1951) 36 Cal.2d 864, 872–3 (the latter two cases were decided under US law)).

[179] Fombrun (n 174) 84; TW Waelde, 'Contract and Enforceability in International Business: What Works?', available at www.dundee.ac.uk/cepmlp/journal/html/vol5/vol5-8.html.

[180] It can also be argued that the recoverability of damage to reputation may, in some cases, create a disincentive for parties to breach their contracts and this would be in line with the idea of *favor contractus* often said to underlie the CISG (see, eg, U Magnus, 'General Principles of UN-Sales Law', available at www.cisg.law.pace.edu/cisg/biblio/magnus.html).

[181] See D Saidov, 'Damages: The Need for Uniformity' (2005–2006) 25 *J L Commerce* 393, 395. It can also be argued that since the ideal is for the Convention to be applied uniformly around the world, reaching an agreement on a uniform definition is important to achieve a uniform treatment of claims for damage to reputation and goodwill.

[182] See, eg, *Kassab v Central Soya* 246 A.2d 848, 858 (Pa. 1968). Similar points have been made in the context of other disciplines. See SL Wartick, 'Measuring Corporate Reputation: Definition and Data' (2002) 41 *Business & Society* 371, 372 ('[A]ny discussion of measurement must necessarily start with a look at definition. The following thought may be grossly oversimplified, but it seems to me that one cannot talk about measuring something until one knows what that something is').

[183] See *Armstrong Rubber Co Inc v Griffith* 43 F.2d 689, 691 (C.A.2 1930).

[184] For the CISG cases, see CIETAC 26 October 1996 (n 15) (it is not clear, however, whether loss of reputation was simply unforeseeable on the facts or whether the tribunal took the view that this type of loss could never be foreseeable). This argument has also been raised in the context of other legal systems (see Enonchong (n 163) 600; RP Barbarowicz, 'Loss of Goodwill and Business Reputation' (1970–1971) 75 *Dickinson L Rev* 63, 75; RR Anderson, 'Incidental and Consequential Damages' (1987) 7 *J L Commerce* 327, 421).

so-called 'floodgate' argument is often put forward, according to which courts will be swamped with various claims described as loss of reputation/goodwill.[185] Each of these objections is addressed in turn.

The 'definitional' objection requires a closer look at the attempts to define business reputation and goodwill.[186] So far as the former is concerned, no uniform definition exists for the purpose of dealing with claims for damage to reputation either in the Convention or in domestic systems. It seems possible, however, to highlight the essential characteristics of business reputation. First, there is an agreement that *perceptions or impressions* are central to the idea of reputation. Reputation is developed by means of the processing of information about the company's past actions and making judgements about its future prospects by an individual, group or community (whichever is relevant). Therefore, reputation is 'purely perceptual'.[187] The second element relates to relevant observers *making judgements about or assessing* a company's business standing.

Third, who should be regarded as the relevant 'stakeholders' whose perceptions and judgements need to be examined? There are potentially many individuals and groups who might be considered stakeholders and may include customers, other companies whose business activities are connected with the company in question, employees, investors and a broader community. It is probably true that in most cases, it is damage to reputation amongst customers that is alleged. Nevertheless, examples can be found where courts deemed it possible to define concepts not dissimilar to reputation on the basis that customers were not the only stakeholders. In one US case involving a claim for loss of goodwill, the court stated that although goodwill was primarily viewed as 'a function of customer response and ongoing allegiance to a company',[188] the measure of goodwill can also take into consideration 'a firm's relationship with creditors, including relationship with its bank'. The court also alluded to the possibility of taking into account not only the relationship with the company's creditors and banks but also the existence of goodwill in the 'labour market'.[189] This broad approach to defining reputation is also taken in many writings in business and business-related disciplines where reputation is defined as 'a collective representation of a firm's past behaviour and outcomes that depicts the firm's ability to render valued results to multiple stakeholders'.[190] According to a similar definition, business reputation is 'a perceptual representation of a company's

[185] See, eg, Enonchong (n 163) 602 and Barbarowicz (n 184) 68.

[186] Since most players in international trade are companies, the focus is on 'corporate' reputation and goodwill.

[187] Wartick (n 182) 374.

[188] *Toltec Fabrics v August Inc* WL 339280 1, 2 (SDNY 1993).

[189] Ibid, 2.

[190] CJ Fombrun, NA Gardberg and JM Sever, 'The Reputation Quotient[SM]: A multi-Stakeholder Measure of Corporate Reputation' (2000) 7 *J Brand Management* 241, 243. Ibid.

past actions and future prospects that describes the firm's overall appeal to all of its key constituents when compared with other leading rivals'.[191]

There are serious doubts about the workability of such a broad definition and a better approach is to refrain from a comprehensive definition and to admit that *there is no one reputation*. Instead, the relevant questions are: Reputation to whom, for what, and for what purpose?[192] Taking this position would mean that there are many aspects to defining 'reputation'. A claimant may, for example, claim damages only for loss of reputation amongst a very specific group of stakeholders, such as customers or potential investors, and the question 'reputation for what?' would have to be answered with reference to the interest of a particular group. A company's customers presumably focus on the quality of goods and services and other aspects of contractual performance, such as timely delivery. So far as investors are concerned, reputation concerns a company's ability to maintain a financially healthy and stable business. In sum, it is possible to define business reputation in very general terms by referring to its essential characteristics of being based on people's perceptions and judgements. However, it should be left to a claimant to answer the questions 'reputation to whom, for what, and for what purpose?' in the particular context of its case. So far as the definition of goodwill is concerned, research shows that despite a multiplicity of definitions of goodwill,[193] for the purposes of breach of contract claims it should be treated synonymously with business reputation.

The objection that there are serious difficulties of proving and assessing damage to reputation/goodwill is addressed in a later chapter that shows that there *are* reliable means of calculating it.[194] The next argument asserting the difficulty of setting the limits to the recovery is not strong because the Convention contains mechanisms, such as the rules on foreseeability, causation, mitigation[195] and the standard of proof (if it exists under the Convention),[196] which are capable of setting appropriate limits. The argument that such losses are never foreseeable also cannot prevent them from being recoverable. As pointed out on numerous occasions,[197] it is perfectly possible, for example, for a seller to be in

[191] Fombrun (n 174) 72. Although these definitions of reputation are not free from criticism, it appears that they are used more widely than other existing definitions (See, eg, Wartick (n 182) 374–80).

[192] See PG Lewellyn, 'Corporate Reputation: Focusing on Zeitgeist' (2002) 41 *Business & Society* 446, 451.

[193] See, eg, see Djordjević (n 107) 985.

[194] See ch 9.

[195] See *NV Maes Roger v NV Kapa Reynolds* Appellate Court Gent (Belgium) 10 May 2004, available at cisgw3.law.pace.edu/cases/040510b1.html (where the claim for damage to reputation was dismissed on the grounds of causation and mitigation).

[196] See ch 7.

[197] See *EK, L and A v F* Supreme Court (Switzerland) 28 October 1998, available at cisgw3.law.pace. edu/cases/981028s1.html ('it is not possible to establish a general rule which says that certain damages are only foreseeable if they have been expressly dealt with in the contractual negotiations. This is also true for goodwill disadvantages and for damages that are caused because a buyer loses

the position to foresee, at the time when the contract is made, that its delivery of a large quantity of defective goods is likely to damage a buyer's reputation. Like with any other loss, the question whether it was foreseeable must be decided on the facts. Finally, there is also a general agreement that the 'floodgate' argument is not a valid reason to prevent the recoverability of damages to reputation/goodwill. As stated in a well-known English case, 'it will not be right to allow "floodgates" arguments ... to stand in the way of claims which, as a matter of ordinary legal principle, are well founded'.[198] Thus, there is no good reason why damage to reputation/goodwill should not be recoverable[199] and it is submitted that the line of cases recognising this loss as recoverable under the CISG should be followed.[200]

7. LOSS OF PROFIT

7.1. General

Loss of profit, expressly indicated by the instruments as recoverable, can arise in various circumstances. If the seller fails to deliver the goods, the buyer may be prevented from earning a profit by reselling the goods.[201] If the buyer intended to use the goods in manufacture, non-delivery may cause an interruption in the manufacturing process or, in more extreme cases, wholly deprive the buyer of an opportunity of carrying out the manufacturing activity. In both cases, the

a client due to a deficient delivery. Such damages can be foreseeable by the seller if the buyer is obviously an intermediary in a sensitive market and in addition has no possibility to otherwise supply its clients with complying goods within the time limit due to its own precautions'); *Reo D Stott v Thomas Johnston* (n 178) 353; Enonchong (n 163) 75; McKendrick and Worthington (n 169) 315 (in the context of non-pecuniary losses generally).

[198] *Malik v Bank Credit and Commerce International SA* [1998] AC 20, 42.

[199] *Cf* CISG Advisory Council Opinion No. 6, 'Calculation of Damages under CISG Article 74', available at cisgw3.law.pace.edu/cisg/CISG-AC-op6.html. According to Rule 7, '[t]he aggrieved party is entitled to damages for loss of goodwill as a consequence of the breach.' Comment 7.1, however, takes the view that the 'recovery of damages for loss of goodwill is available only if the aggrieved party can establish with reasonable certainty that it suffered a financial loss because of a breach of contract'.

[200] See ICC No 11849, 2003 (Fashion products), available at cisgw3.law.pace. edu/cases/031849i1. html; Case No HG 970238.1 Commercial Court of Zürich (Switzerland) 10 February 1999 (Art books), available at cisgw3.law.pace.edu/cases/990210s1.html; Case No S 00/82 Helsinki Court of Appeals (Finland) 26 October 2000 (Plastic carpets), available at www.cisg.law.pace.edu/cisg/wais/db/cases2/001026f5.html; Appellate Court Gent (n 1953). See also *Hewlett-Packard France v Matrox Graphics Inc* (n 30) [228]–[231] (a claim for damage to reputation was rejected simply on the basis of the buyer's failure to prove this loss).

[201] See *Al Hewar Environmental & Public Health Establishment v Southeast Ranch, LLC and Joel Gutierre* (n 60) [19]; *Macromex Srl v Globex International Inc*, 2008 WL 1752530 (affirmed in 330 F. App'x 241 (2d Cir. 2009)). See also Appellate Court München (Germany) 5 March 2008, available at cisgw3.law.pace.edu/cases/080305g1.html, where the seller sold a stolen car, seized by the police from the buyer and returned to the owner. The buyer, a car dealer, was awarded damages for lost profit it would have made by reselling the car.

buyer may suffer lost profits as a result of its inability to sell the final product during the period of the interruption or to sell anything at all. The buyer may also suffer loss of volume through not being able to supply all the customers whom it would have supplied had there been no breach.[202] Similarly, the seller's delivery of non-conforming goods or late delivery may result in the buyer being prevented from earning the planned profit by reselling the goods because its sub-buyers either reject the goods[203] or buy them at reduced prices.[204] As in the case of non-delivery, the delivery of non-conforming goods (or delay in delivery) may result in the buyer losing profits because due to the non-conformity in the goods the production line of finished goods remains idle[205] or the buyer is unable to produce the goods at all.[206]

If the buyer fails to pay and/or take the goods, the seller can (if the bargain was not a losing one) lose the profit margin it planned to receive by selling the contract goods.[207] As a result of not getting the price on time, the seller may also lose profit by losing an opportunity to invest in a lucrative venture. If the buyer is in breach of its contractual obligation not to resell the contract goods in the country(ies) specified in the contract, the seller, an exclusive supplier of the goods in that (those) country(ies), can suffer the loss of a profit margin because: it is no longer the exclusive supplier; and/or the price for the goods decreases; and/or the seller's buyer(s) in that (those) country(ies) contracted to buy specified quantities of the goods on the basis that the seller was the exclusive supplier and due to the buyer's breach order a lesser quantity from the seller than initially planned.[208] All these types of lost profits are recoverable as damages,

[202] *Delchi Carrier SpA v Rotorex Corp* (n 31) (the case involved the delivery of defective goods but because they were rejected, the case is analogous to a case of non-delivery).

[203] See, eg, Case No VIII ZR 210/78 Supreme Court (Germany) 24 October 1979 (Cheese), available at cisgw3.law.pace.edu/cases/791024g1.html (decided under the ULIS).

[204] ICAC No 054/1999, 24 January 2000, available at cisgw3.law.pace.edu/cases/ 000124r1.html.

[205] ICAC No 310/1996, 26 September 1997 in MG Rozenberg, *Mezhdunarodnaya kuplya-prodazha tovarov: Kommentariy k zakonodatel'stvu i praktike razresheniya sporov* (Moscow, Statut, 2001) 249.

[206] *Topp Paper Company LLC v ETI Converting Equipment*, 2013 WL 12101111 (S.D. Fla. 2013), where due to non-functional machines delivered by the seller the buyer was unable to produce quality labels that the buyer contracted to sell to specific customers.

[207] See Appellate Court Brandenburg (n 35), where the buyer failed to place orders for the minimum specified quantities of beer, as required by the contract with the seller (a brewery), who was awarded damages for the loss of profit it would have made on the sale of those quantities.

[208] This happened in Case No BZ.2007.55 Appellate Court St. Gallen (Switzerland) 13 May 2008, available at cisgw3.law.pace.edu/cases/080513s1.html, where because the buyer had breached its contractual obligation not to resell the contract goods in country Y, the seller's customer (company C) in country Y ordered a lower quantity of the goods than that contracted for due to the resulting price fall, causing the seller to suffer the loss in its expected profit margin ('It is argued that owing to [the Buyer]'s delivery to a competitor in country Y, dumping prices were caused so that company C could only purchase … [965 pairs less than contracted for]). Since company C suffered a violation of its exclusivity rights, [the Seller] could "apparently not bring a claim for the insufficient quantity so purchased" but instead would have to defend itself against claims filed by company C following breach of contract' (ibid)).

subject to the methods of limiting damages (causation,[209] foreseeability[210] and mitigation[211]) and the applicable standards of proof.[212] As later chapters will show, different methods of calculation can be used to quantify lost profits.[213]

Loss of profit often occurs where, as a result of the breach, the injured party loses its customers. A typical case is where the buyer argues[214] that as a result of the delivery of non-conforming goods, its sub-buyers have cancelled the existing orders and/or decided not to do business with the buyer in the future.[215] In such circumstances, damages are sometimes awarded for loss of clientele, orders, or trade.[216] It is submitted that it is misleading to treat loss of custom as a loss in itself. Loss of custom essentially describes a *situation* that has resulted from the breach and that situation, in turn, can give rise to specific losses for which damages may be awarded. Such specific losses are usually lost profits but may also include other types of loss.[217] Clearly, lost profits arising from loss of custom are recoverable (subject to the usual requirements of limiting damages and proof).[218]

7.2. Loss of Volume

An injured party may suffer lost profit as a result of losing 'volume' of sales and there has been some uncertainty regarding whether this type of loss is recoverable. In a 'lost volume'[219] situation, the seller has fewer customers than

[209] See ch 4.
[210] See ch 5.
[211] See ch 6.
[212] See ch 7.
[213] For a detailed discussion, see chs 8 and 9.
[214] For such claims brought under the CISG, see CIETAC 31 January 2000 (Clothes), available at cisgw3.law.pace.edu/cases/000131c1.html (where this loss was held unforeseeable and not sufficiently proven); *Société TCE Diffusion Sarl v Société Elettrotecnica Ricci* Appellate Court Orléans (France) 29 March 2001, available at cisgw3.law.pace. edu/cases/010329f1.html.
[215] See *Castel Electronics Pty Ltd v Toshiba Singapore Pte Ltd* (n 30) [252]–[285], for the buyer's claim for damages for loss of its profit margin resulting from decline in sales of the buyer's computers in which defective computer cards, delivered by the seller, had been installed.
[216] See Swiss Supreme Court (Switzerland) 28 October 1998 (n 197) (the abstract of the case refers to loss of clientele, while the translation of the case refers to loss of profit flowing from loss of clientele). For such damages in English law, see,eg, *Cointat v Myham & Son* [1913] 2 KB 220; *GKN Centrax Gears Ltd v Matbro Ltd* [1976] 2 Lloyds Rep 555).
[217] For instance, in one case, the injured party claimed that 'as a result of losing business relations with one customer he lost a group delivery arrangement which would increase the buyer's future transportation costs' (Supreme Court (Germany) 24 October 1979 (n 203)).
[218] See ibid (where the injured buyer claimed that as a result of the delivery of defective goods, its customers had discontinued business relations with it which had caused lost profits over four years).
[219] The term has been coined by RJ Harris (see RJ Harris 'A General Theory for Measuring Seller's Damages for Total Breach of Contract' (1961–1962) 60 Michigan L Rev 599–605). Loss of volume is recoverable in a number of legal systems: see the English case *Thompson (WL) LD v Robinson (Gunmakers) LD* [1955] Ch 177; EA Farnsworth, *Contracts*, 4th edn (New York, Aspen Publishers, 2004) 773.

it can supply[220] or, in other words, its ability to supply exceeds the demand for its goods. The buyer's refusal to accept and pay for the goods costs the seller 'one sale' or one unit of profit even if it manages to resell the goods. In a true lost volume situation, the seller's resale is not a replacement for the original contract because even if the original contract had been performed, the second buyer would have bought these goods from the seller anyway and the seller loses volume by selling only one item instead of two. Lost volume situations may arise because: the amount the seller is able to supply exceeds the existing demand for the goods; the goods are highly specialised and/or have been manufactured for the needs of a particular buyer;[221] or the goods have to bear the buyer's trademark, logo or signet,[222] eliminating any demand for the seller's goods.

Although it is the seller who is usually prone to experiencing loss of volume, the party who acts as the buyer in the contract with the breaching seller can also find itself in this situation. This can be the case where the buyer, whether a trader or a manufacturer, purchases the goods with a view to either reselling them or using them to manufacture the final product destined for further sale. If the demand for the contract goods exceeds their supply,[223] the buyer may be unable, as a result of the seller's breach, to supply its sub-buyer or manufacture the final product and sell it in the expected volumes. If the buyer makes what may seem to be a cover purchase and resells these goods to its sub-buyer, it can argue that it has lost volume of one sale if it can prove that had the seller performed, it would have bought these goods anyway and resold them to *another* sub-buyer who would also have bought the goods. These situations cannot be lost volume situations involving a buyer *exclusively* because although the injured party acts as the buyer in the first transaction (with the breaching seller), it would not have suffered loss of volume had it not acted as the seller in a subsequent transaction. The reason it loses volume is because of its lack of supply in its capacity as a seller. At the same time, the difference with a lost volume seller, discussed in the previous paragraph, is that in that case the seller's *supply exceeds demand* whereas in the present case loss of volume arises because *demand exceeds supply*. It seems appropriate to refer to the latter situation as involving a lost volume 'buyer-seller'.

The next question is whether loss of volume is recoverable under the instruments. Several objections to its recoverability have been advanced. First, it has been argued that legal recognition of a lost volume seller would not correspond to the realities of commercial life. No seller, the argument runs, can either prove

[220] RR Anderson, 'Damages for Sellers under the Code's Profit Formula' (1986–1987) 40 *Southwestern L J* 1023.

[221] See Case No 1 Ob 292/99v Supreme Court (Austria) 28 April 2000 (Jewellery), available at cisgw3.law.pace.edu/cases/000428a3.html.

[222] See Commercial Court Aargau (Switzerland) 26 September 1997 (n 48) (the situation related only to the sale of knives).

[223] See EA Farnsworth, 'Legal Remedies for Breach of Contract' (1970) 70 *Columbia L Rev* 1196, n 210.

with certainty the specific number of customers it will have in the future or that it has an unlimited capacity to supply because invariably there are periods when the seller is unable to handle new customers and this may be 'due to such things as temporary shortages of goods, limitation on or breakdowns of productive capacity, shortage of warehousing facilities, temporary unavailability of personnel'.[224] The second related objection is based on the economic law of diminishing returns according to which it is inevitable that, as the seller's volume increases, a point will be reached where the marginal cost of producing and selling an additional item will diminish and eventually nullify the seller's return, rendering the production of such an additional item unprofitable.[225] The third argument is that the buyer's breach in fact expands the seller's market because the seller is put in a position to sell the goods to those who otherwise would have been the buyer's customers. Put differently, the buyer's breach removes the threat of the buyer's competition and the volume initially lost as a result of the buyer's breach can be re-captured by selling to the buyer's customers.[226] Finally, because the problem of lost volume is too complex[227] and revolves around economics, it has been argued that judges and arbitrators are not sufficiently equipped to deal with it.[228]

It is suggested that while these arguments refine our understanding of the problem of lost volume, they should not lead to the conclusion that this loss should not be recoverable. The concerns raised by them can and must be addressed at the stage of proving the loss. But once it is shown that the innocent party has found itself in a true lost volume situation, there is no reason why this loss should not be recoverable. After all, what the injured party suffers is a 'loss of profit' and this loss is expressly recognised by the instruments as recoverable. If this loss is not compensated, the injured party will not be placed in the position in which it would have been had the contract been performed.[229] The recoverability of lost profits, arising from loss of volume, is gaining recognition in the CISG cases. In one case, damages for lost profit were awarded to the seller who had agreed to manufacture and sell jewellery to the buyer. The delivery was not made as a result of the buyer's failure to pay and the court stated that the seller's

[224] MG Shanker, 'The Case for a Literal Reading of UCC Section 2-708(2) (One Profit for the Reseller)' (1973) 24 *Case Western Reserve L Rev* 697, 705.

[225] This argument has been made on numerous occasions: see, eg, *RE Davis Chemical Corp v Diasonics, Inc*, 826 F.2d 678 (1987) ('Diasonics I'); Shanker (n 224); White and Summers (n 37) 292.

[226] See RE Scott, 'The Case for Market Damages: Revisiting the Lost Profits Puzzle' (1990) 57 *University Chicago L Rev* 1155, 1165.

[227] 'Do we really want to develop rules of law that require … prescience from our courts? After all, our courts are administered by human beings, not prophets' (Shanker (n 224) 708).

[228] See White and Summers (n 37) 292.

[229] The suggestion that loss of volume is recoverable is widely accepted. See, eg, CISG-AC (n 156); J Ziegel, 'The Remedial Provisions in the Vienna Sales Convention: Some Common Law Perspectives' in NM Galston and H Smit (eds), *International Sales: The United Nations Convention on Contracts for the International Sale of Goods* (NY, Matthew Bender, 1984) 9–41; Djordjević (n 107) 983–4; EA Farnsworth, 'Damages and Specific Relief' (1979) 27 *AJCL* 252.

loss would arise 'regardless of a possible resale of the goods ordered to a subsequent buyer, as the later contract would have been formed independently of the [buyer's] order'.[230] In another case,[231] involving a lost volume 'buyer-seller', as a result of the seller's delivery of defective compressors which the buyer intended to use in its manufacture of air conditioners, the buyer was unable to obtain substitute compressors from other sources thereby producing and selling fewer air conditioners than it would have sold otherwise. The court stated that the CISG permitted the 'recovery of lost profit resulting from a diminished volume of sales'.[232]

What remains to be said relates to the requirements that must be met for a party to be found in a lost volume situation. It is appropriate to begin with a lost volume seller who argues that it would have sold the goods to another buyer(s) even if the first buyer had not breached the contract. To prove this claim, it must be established, first of all, that the seller would have entered into and performed the contract with that other buyer(s)[233] and several factors may need to be taken into account. The fact that the seller has made *special* efforts to carry out the second sale may indicate that, but for the breach, this sale would not have been made. Such special efforts may include advertising the goods or using the services of a broker. If it is established that these efforts are not usually taken by the seller to sell the goods and that the second buyer bought the goods as a result of such special efforts, this may evidence that the seller did not intend to sell the goods to this particular buyer and that this buyer bought the goods only because the first buyer did not perform its contract. The characteristics of the goods and the needs of a particular buyer may also be relevant. Suppose the seller is a car dealer who has many cars to sell. The original buyer ordered one car of a rare colour and the seller made sure that one of its cars was painted as ordered. The original buyer refused to perform the contract and shortly after the second buyer, attracted by the unusual colour of the car, bought it. Although the seller had many cars to sell, it may be that the second buyer bought the car *only* because it saw the unusual colour.[234]

Second, it must be shown that the seller would have had the capacity to perform an additional contract[235] and it may have to be demonstrated that the

[230] Supreme Court (Austria) 28 April 2000 (n 221).

[231] Federal District Court (New York) 9 September 1994 (United States), available at cisgw3.law.pace.edu/cases/940909u1.html (that part of the decision was later upheld by the court of higher instance (see *Delchi Carrier SpA v Rotorex Corp* (n 31)).

[232] See also *Sunrise Foods international Inc v Ryan Hinton Inc*, 2019 WL 3755499 (D Idaho, 2019), where the court would have allowed the seller's claim for damages for loss of profit, arising from the loss of volume of sales, had the seller not failed to prove that it suffered that loss.

[233] See ibid; also RJ Harris, 'A Radical Restatement of the Law of Seller's Damages: Sales Act and Commercial Code Results Compared' (1965–1966) 18 Stanford L Rev 82.

[234] See JB Holisky, 'Finding the "Lost Volume Seller": Two Independent Sales Deserve Two Profits under Illinois Law' (1988) 22 *John Marshall L Rev* 375, 384–5; see also JA Sebert, Jr, 'Remedies under Article Two of the Uniform Commercial Code: An Agenda for Review' (1981–1982) 130 *U Pennsylvania L Rev* 388.

[235] See, similarly, *Sunrise Foods international Inc v Ryan Hinton Inc* (n 232).

seller had, for example, excessive capacity to manufacture the goods or ready access to additional stock.[236] If it cannot do so, it may need to present evidence that it 'would, in fact, have expanded [its] manufacturing operations, or sought and found replacement stock outside [its] regular supply channels'.[237] Third, bearing in mind the objections to the recoverability of lost volume damages, it is submitted that it must also be proven that an additional sale would have been profitable.[238] It seems appropriate to place the initial burden of demonstrating that these requirements are met on the injured party, based on a basic precondition (for the right to claim damages) that the injured party must demonstrate that it has suffered loss. This allocation of the burden of proof is also justifiable because the injured party is in a better position than the breaching party to provide information regarding what *it* would have done had there been no breach.

In a similar vein, the 'buyer-seller' must, first, prove that it would have bought the goods which were sold to the first buyer with a view to selling more of these goods to yet another buyer had there been no breach. Similar to a lost volume seller, it is relevant whether the 'buyer-seller' has made special efforts to find another supplier.[239] If such special efforts were taken, this fact might indicate that had the first supplier not breached the contract, the 'buyer-seller' would *not* have bought the goods from the second supplier and would not have been able to sell more goods to yet another buyer if the first supplier had not breached. Evidence showing that there had already been arrangements between the 'buyer-seller' and the second supplier prior to the breach points in favour of the 'buyer-seller' being in a lost volume situation.[240] If there were no past dealings between the parties, strong evidence may be needed to support the claim that the goods would have been bought from the second supplier regardless of the seller's breach. Conversely, the fact of ongoing business relations between the parties can increase the likelihood that the 'buyer-seller' is in a lost volume situation.

The second question is whether another buyer would have bought the goods had there been no breach and, again, several factors can be relevant. Some earlier arrangements, past dealings or practices between the 'buyer-seller' and that additional buyer may show that the goods would have been sold to the additional buyer. In some cases, the time at which the transaction with the second supplier was made may be important. If another buyer only wanted the goods at the date earlier than the date when the goods were bought from the second supplier, this might indicate that the 'buyer-seller' was not in a lost volume

[236] See Holisky (n 234) 380–1.

[237] Ibid, 381.

[238] For a similar approach in some US cases, see *E Davis Chemical Corp v Diasonics, Inc* (n 225).

[239] Such as hiring a broker or posting an announcement in an attempt to find a supplier.

[240] Such arrangements may include contracts for future delivery and some other evidence confirming the parties' intentions to make such a transaction in future.

situation. It may also be that, even if it is proven that another buyer intended to buy the goods, the type of goods actually bought from the second supplier was not that which that buyer would have purchased. This factor points against the 'buyer-seller' being in a lost volume situation.

8. LOSS OF A CHANCE

Some legal systems allow damages for loss of a chance[241] which compensate the party not for loss of profit but for loss of a chance to profit. The UPICC take a similar approach by providing that '[c]ompensation may be due for the loss of a chance in proportion to the probability of its occurrence'.[242] Although there is no express provision recognising the recoverability of this loss in the CISG or PECL, it is argued that this loss should be recoverable under these instruments. Before this argument is developed, it is necessary to explore the reasons that can justify damages for loss of a chance, bearing in mind that loss of a chance is a curious concept that can be considered from the perspective of both the recoverability of losses and a standard of proving losses. Both perspectives need to be borne in mind when dealing with the question whether loss of a chance should be recoverable.

From the perspective of the recoverability of losses, the crucial question is whether loss of a chance can be regarded as an 'asset' recognised by the instruments. A striking example where this is the case can be found in contract cases where the subject-matter of the contract is *a chance*.[243] But this situation is unlikely to arise in sales transactions where the subject-matter is the sale and delivery of goods. Nevertheless, there can be sales contracts of which a chance is an integral part, such as those involving exhibitions and bidding.[244] For example, the seller's breach may prevent the buyer from taking part in a large-scale exhibition and cause the buyer to lose an opportunity to make lucrative contracts, be ever considered as a potential supplier by important business players[245] or take part in a competition for the best exhibition carrying a substantial

[241] Damages for loss of a chance are allowed in a number of legal systems (see, eg, Komarov (n 27) 202; *Chaplin v Hicks* [1911] 2 KB 786; MA Eisenberg, 'Probability and Chance in Contract Law' (1998) 45 *U California L Rev* 1005, 1049–52; § 346(3) of the Restatement the 2nd of Contracts).

[242] Article 7.4.3(2).

[243] See *Chaplin v Hicks* (n 241).

[244] See MG Bridge, *The Sale of Goods,* 4th edn (Oxford, OUP, 2019) [12.16], arguing that to be recoverable 'lost chance must constitute the subject matter of the transaction or at least an integral part of it'.

[245] See Commercial Court Zürich (Switzerland) 10 February 1999 (n 200), where the buyer argued that owing to the seller's late delivery of art books and catalogues to several presentations, an art exhibition and a press conference, it had never again been considered by sponsors of these events as a potential supplier.

monetary prize.[246] The seller's breach may also cause the buyer to lose an opportunity to make a bid on a large-scale project[247] or to make a supply contract with a construction company which, in turn, intended to bid on a project. In such cases, a chance should arguably be regarded as an 'asset'.[248] First, taking chances is important in business because taking risks and the involvement in speculative ventures are often the primary vehicles of commercial activity. Second, the innocent buyer in our examples, despite the uncertainty of the outcome of taking part either in exhibitions or bidding, may have made substantial investments of time, effort and money in taking a chance and, if so, this demonstrates that business persons regard a chance as an asset on which they place value, despite the assertions that it is 'not something in the real world' or is 'merely a causal likelihood'.[249]

It is also possible to regard loss of a chance as a standard of proving losses. It is often difficult to prove loss of profit with certainty because of the need to enquire into hypothetical future or past events. There may be cases where although lost profit cannot be proven with the required degree of certainty, the court/tribunal is satisfied that some loss has been suffered. The question is whether the injured party should be left with no, rather than some, compensation. It can be argued that while it is unfair to require the breaching party to pay the full amount of the alleged lost profit, it is equally unfair to leave the innocent party with no compensation. Loss of a chance can be a tool that prevents the 'all-or-nothing' result, striking a fair balance between both parties' interests, and deals with uncertainty of losses,[250] being 'a pragmatic response to the uneconomic pursuit of truth in the definition of the plaintiff's true expectation loss'.[251]

Returning to the question whether loss of a chance is recoverable under the CISG and PECL, it is argued that the matter of the recoverability of losses is within the scope of the instruments and must be resolved by interpreting the instruments themselves. One way of doing so is to regard the matter as governed but not expressly addressed by the instruments.[252] The relevant general principle (idea) is full compensation for the loss suffered. But this principle does not explain whether a particular loss should be recoverable. The answer is to be

[246] See an example in S Eiselen 'Unresolved Damages Issues of the CISG: A Comparative Analysis' (2005) 38 *Comparative Int'l L J Southern Africa* 32, 38.

[247] See an example in Schwenzer and Hachem (n 109).

[248] The discussion below is partly based on D Saidov, 'Damages: The Need for Uniformity' (2005–2006) 25 *J L Commerce* 393, 400–02.

[249] See M Hogg, 'Lost Chances in Contract and Delict – Golden Opportunities for Litigation' [1997] *SLT* 71.

[250] S Waddams, 'Damages: Assessment of Uncertainties' (1998) 13 *J Contract Law* 55.

[251] MG Bridge, 'Expectation Damages and Uncertain Future' in J Beatson and D Friedmann (eds), *Good Faith and Fault in Contract Law* (Oxford, OUP, 1995) 438.

[252] See arts 7(2) CISG and 1:106 PECL.

found by interpreting the notion of loss, which ultimately rests on the instruments' underlying policies and values. As explained, there are strong policy reasons in favour of the recoverability of loss of a chance under the CISG[253] and PECL.[254]

The next question is whether loss of *any* chance to profit, no matter how speculative and uncertain, should be recoverable or only a chance that can be considered as 'real' or 'substantial'. The wording of the UPICC does not preclude the former position as it simply refers to valuing a chance with reference to the probability of its occurrence. On this view, even very unlikely events (say, a 2 per cent chance of getting an alleged profit) may provide a basis for damages for loss of chance. It is suggested, however, that this is not the correct approach. Taking it would mean that virtually every breach, unless there was no likelihood whatsoever of earning profit, would result in *some* award of damages. It is also arguable that this approach does not sit well with the rationale of a chance being an 'asset': if a chance of success is not 'real' or 'substantial', it is not reasonable to expect business persons to take risks arising from and make investments in taking such a chance. There are signs that this is how tribunals have interpreted some of the instruments. In one case, where the tribunal referred to the UPICC, it was stated that the claimant had to demonstrate 'a very high probability' of a chance being successful.[255] In a CISG case,[256] the court rejected the buyer's claim for damages for loss of an opportunity to conclude and profit from a supply contract with a construction company which in turn intended to bid on a large-scale construction project by stating that it was 'entirely speculative to conclude that [the buyer] sustained a *substantial* loss with respect to this project'.[257]

How is it to be determined what constitutes a 'real' or 'substantial' chance? It has been argued that such a determination should not be about quantifying probabilities or ascertaining percentages as the latter are only relevant to

[253] Since there is a fine line between loss of a chance and lost profits, the only difference being the degree of uncertainty involved, some commentators argue that the recoverability of loss of a chance is expressly allowed by art 74 CISG, which stresses the recoverability of loss of profit. There is no agreement, in cases or amongst commentators, as to whether loss of a chance is recoverable under the CISG. For those in favour of the recoverability of this loss, see *Mansonville Plastics (BC) Ltd v Kurtz GmbH* 2003 BCSC 1298; Saidov (n 248); Schwenzer and Hachem (n 109). For the view against its recoverability, see Commercial Court Zürich (Switzerland) 10 February 1999 (n 200). For the view that loss of a chance is recoverable only where a chance is a subject-matter of the contract, see CISG-AC (n 156). However, on this view this loss will rarely be recoverable because, as noted, these cases are unlikely to arise in sales transactions.

[254] 'Future loss often takes the form of the loss of a chance' (Comment F on Article 9:501 PECL, see Lando and Beale (n 86) 435).

[255] ICC No 9078, October 2001, available at www.unilex.info. See also ICC No 10346, December 2000, available at www.unilex.info.

[256] *Mansonville Plastics (BC) Ltd v Kurtz GmbH* (n 253) (italics added).

[257] The court further accepted the view expressed in a case decided under Canadian law that the facts precluded 'any real and substantial chance of benefit'. Although the reliance on domestic law with respect to the issue governed by the CISG is incorrect, the decision demonstrates that courts are not prepared to compensate for chances which cannot be viewed as 'real' or 'substantial'.

calculating loss of a chance; the problem of determining whether a chance is 'real' or 'substantial' is only relevant to *establishing liability* in damages.[258] Once a lost chance is found to be 'real' and liability is established, the percentage (of the likelihood of the chance materialising) becomes relevant for the purposes of quantum.[259] In short, the argument is that whether a chance is 'real' is a matter of 'gut instinct', not mathematics.[260] Although this position may well be appropriate in some cases, it is often difficult, if not impossible, to avoid an inquiry into the likelihood (percentage) of the occurrence of a particular event to determine whether a chance of profit was 'real' and 'substantial'.[261] Nevertheless, this does not mean that a particular threshold (eg, 50 per cent chance) should be set to indicate whether a chance is sufficiently 'real' to establish liability in damages.[262] The likelihood of a chance materialising should be a factor, albeit an important one, in deciding whether a chance is 'real' but ultimately it should be left to courts and tribunals to establish liability in the light of the particular circumstances.

Finally, in some legal systems, loss of a chance cannot be claimed where a relevant hypothetical depends on the actions of the innocent party.[263] The distinction between the actions of the innocent party and those of third parties primarily rests on the idea that the innocent party can be expected to produce the best evidence possible of what *its* conduct would have been, whereas the same cannot be said of a third party not least because it may not take part in the proceedings.[264] This consideration seems sufficiently convincing to justify the same approach under the international instruments and cases decided under the instruments appear to have awarded damages for loss of a chance or, at least, acknowledged the recoverability of this loss only where the relevant hypothetical questions depended on the actions of third parties. For instance, in one case,[265] a party breached its obligation to re-transfer to the other party all know-how relating to the equipment and not to manufacture and sell the equipment to third parties.[266] The injured party argued that as a result of the breaching party selling the equipment to third parties, it was deprived of a chance to sell

[258] J Poole, 'Loss of Chance and the Evaluation of Hypotheticals in Contractual Claims' [2007] *LMCLQ* 63, 74–76, 81–82.

[259] Ibid.

[260] Ibid, 74.

[261] See *Mansonville Plastics (BC) Ltd v Kurtz GmbH* (n 253) ('[The buyer] may have lost an opportunity to enter into a supply arrangement with [the construction company] but the opportunity would have led to nothing unless [the latter] was the successful bidder. There is no evidence with which I can properly assess the *possibility or likelihood* of winning the contract'); ICC No 9078, October 2001 (n 255).

[262] In *Mohammed Hanif v Middleweeks (A Firm)* [2000] Lloyd's Rep PN 151, [44], a 20% chance was not regarded as insignificant.

[263] For the position of English law, see, eg, Poole (n 258) 67–69.

[264] Burrows (n 163) 67–68.

[265] ICC No 9078, October 2001 (n 255).

[266] See also *Mansonville Plastics (BC) Ltd v Kurtz GmbH* (n 253); Commercial Court Zürich 10 February 1999 (n 200).

the equipment to third parties. It seems that the tribunal's award of damages for loss of a chance centred on the likelihood of whether *third parties* would have bought the equipment from the injured party.[267]

9. FUTURE LOSSES

It is often the case that the injured party claims damages not only for loss already suffered but also for the loss it will suffer in the future. Future losses are not confined to any one type. For example, the buyer may claim compensation for the liability it will incur to its sub-buyer as a result of the seller's breach or costs of cure it will incur to remedy the non-conformity in the goods. The injured party will also often claim damages for its loss of future profits: the seller's breach of a forward delivery contract soon after its conclusion will often cause the buyer the loss of future profits it intended to receive from the resale or use of the goods. Provided that the requirements of proof and limiting damages are met, future losses are expressly recoverable under the UPICC and PECL.[268]

In contrast, the CISG does not contain a similar provision and, in several cases, it was interpreted as allowing the recovery of only those losses which were *actually* suffered.[269] This interpretation of the CISG seems to be based on two reasons. First, the arbitrators may have been concerned about compensating for uncertain and speculative losses. The second reason seems to relate to the legal background of some of the arbitrators. Two out of the three cases were tried

[267] '[I]n most cases, it would be impossible to prove that the potential customer would have concluded a supply contract with the claiming party, and, further, it would be impossible in most cases to prove at what conditions, respectively prices, such contract might have been concluded. The sole fact that the claiming party has submitted an offer is, by itself, obviously no evidence for the fact that it would have been able to conclude a final contract and no evidence for the conditions at which the contract would have been concluded'. Another case (ICC No 8264, April 1997, available at www.unilex.info; only the abstract was available) may, at first sight, appear to provide evidence to the contrary. In that case, involving the supply of industrial equipment and transfer of know-how, the supplier failed to provide the buyer with the necessary information about the equipment and the buyer claimed that this failure had deprived it of an opportunity to 'develop and adapt its industrial production to the demands of the market'. Although it would seem that the inquiry would have to focus on the buyer's hypothetical actions (ie, whether the buyer would have carried out the alleged development and adaptation), a lost opportunity of the development and adaptation is not in itself the ultimate purpose of the inquiry and it is a lost opportunity of making profits from these works that is relevant to damages for loss of a chance. This ultimate purpose of the inquiry was most likely dependent on the actions of third parties rather than those of the injured party.

[268] Art 7.4.3(1) UPICC and art 9:502(2)(b) PECL.

[269] See ICAC No 131/1996, 14 September 1998 in MG Rozenberg, *Praktika Mezhdunarodnogo Kommercheskogo Arbitrazhnogo Suda: Nauchno-Prakticheskiy Kommentariy* (Moscow, Izd. mezhd. tsentra finansovo-economicheskogo razvitiya, 1997) 165; ICAC No 345/1996, 14 September 1998 (see MP Bardina in MG Rozenberg (eds), *Venskaya Konventsiya OON 1980 g. o dogovorah mezhdunarodnoy kupli-prodazhi tovarov. K 10-letiyu yeyo primeneniya Rossiyei* (Moscow, Statut, 2001) 39; also ICC No 7660, 23 August 1994 (Battery machinery), where damages within the meaning of art 74 were interpreted as covering only those losses which were actually suffered (abstract of the case and editorial remarks by AH Kritzer, available at cisgw3.law.pace.edu/cases/947660i1.html).

by the Russian Federation International Commercial Arbitration Court (ICAC) and the arbitrators appear to have been influenced by both the Russian text of the Convention, which uses past tense for the word 'suffered' ('*ponesyon*'), and the comparison of art 74 CISG with art 15 of the Russian Civil Code, which specifically provides that recoverable losses include those which have been incurred or *will have to be incurred*.[270] The absence of a reference to future losses in art 74 CISG may have led the ICAC arbitrators to conclude that future losses were not recoverable under the Convention. So far as the first reason is concerned, it is argued that although the concern about speculative awards is valid, it should be addressed not by disallowing the recoverability of future losses but by ensuring that the standard of proof is duly applied. The second reason is more difficult. Although the Convention's Russian text uses the past tense for the word 'suffered', excluding future losses is still based, for the reasons set out below, on an unduly restrictive reading of art 74. Interpreting the CISG from the standpoint of the Russian Civil Code also contravenes the Convention's international character and the need to promote uniformity in its application.[271]

It is submitted that future losses must be interpreted as recoverable under the CISG.[272] If the Convention is interpreted otherwise, the injured party will either have to wait until the time when future losses become 'actual' or may be compelled to bring more than one claim for breach of the same contract at different points in time which may not be allowed by the procedural rules of the forum.[273] This result is unfair to an injured party because claiming damages under the CISG is likely to become unduly time-consuming and expensive and may encourage the exclusion of the CISG. These potential consequences are not in line with the Convention's aspiration of becoming a uniform instrument. It can also be argued that because future losses often include lost profit and because art 74 expressly refers to the recoverability of lost profits, this provision can be interpreted as indicating that future losses are recoverable.[274]

10. DAMAGES FOR A DOCUMENTARY BREACH

Documents play an important role in international trade, performing many functions.[275] A transport document, such as a bill of lading: evidences the shipment date, quantity of the goods and aspects of the state and condition in which

[270] According to art 15(2) of the Civil Code of the Russian Federation 'real loss' is defined as 'expenses, which a person whose right has been infringed, has incurred or will have to incur to restore the infringed right, loss or damage to its property'.

[271] See art 7 CISG.

[272] See Mullis (n 104) where the same view is taken.

[273] For example, this is not possible in English law: see *Chitty* (n 116) [26-012].

[274] For a similar view, see Eiselen (n 246) 37.

[275] For a detailed discussion, see ch 8 in D Saidov, *Conformity of Goods and Documents – The Vienna Sales Convention* (Oxford, Hart Publishing 2015).

they were shipped; evidences whether, say, a CIF seller has made a carriage contract on terms that comply with the terms of the contract of sale; may have to comply with certain requirements to transfer the contract of carriage to the buyer;[276] enables the buyer to obtain physical possession of the goods from the carrier; and may have to be issued in a form that enables the buyer to resell the goods. Where the seller is required to procure insurance, an insurance document evidences that the seller has complied with its insurance obligations. In a CIF contract, an insurance document is expected to enable the buyer to bring a claim against the insurer. A commercial invoice – a document which typically sets out the details of the parties, quantity and description of the goods, the price and its structure, the buyer's order or contract number, time and mode of delivery and payment – is invariably required by the sales contract because it is often necessary for the goods to be cleared through customs and identified for the purposes of an import licence or foreign exchange regulations. A commercial invoice is also relied upon to determine whether the goods' description corresponds with that in the letter of credit.[277] A sales contract may also require the seller to supply quality, quantity, weight, health, phytosanitary or other certificates as evidence of the seller's compliance with its obligations as to conformity of the goods. Documents play a particularly prominent role in the so-called 'commodities' trade[278] characterised by: high price fluctuations; high levels of speculative trading in 'strings' or 'chains'; a high degree of standardisation of goods, contracts and documents; the need for speedy decision making and legal certainty that require documents to comply strictly with the documentary requirements. In this trade sector, it is common for traders in chains to buy and sell goods by means of transferring documents[279] that 'symbolise' the goods.

There is thus a close link between the seller's obligations in relation to the goods (physical obligations) and the documents (documentary obligations). Unsurprisingly, the CISG recognises the important and distinct commercial and legal role of documents by making clear that handing over any documents relating to the goods is an obligation of the seller that is separate from its obligation to deliver the goods.[280] There is no doubt therefore that a seller's documentary

[276] See, eg, the UK Carriage of Goods by Sea Act 1992.

[277] See Art 18(c), the Uniform Customs and Practices for Documentary Credits (UCP) 600.

[278] For the introduction to this trade sector, see MG Bridge, *The International Sale of Goods*, 4th edn (Oxford, OUP 2017) ch 1. See also ch 8.

[279] The role of documents in this sector is so prominent that at one point one English court famously pronounced that a CIF sales contract in this context was a 'sale of documents' (*Arnhold Karberg & Co v Blythe, Green, Jourdain & Co* [1915] 2 KB 379, 388; affirmed [1916] 1 KB 495).

[280] See arts 30 ('The seller must deliver the goods, hand over any documents relating to them and transfer the property in the goods, as required by the contract and this Convention') and 34 CISG ('If the seller is bound to hand over documents relating to the goods, he must hand them over at the time and place and in the form required by the contract. If the seller has handed over documents before that time, he may, up to that time, cure any lack of conformity in the documents, if the exercise of this right does not cause the buyer unreasonable inconvenience or unreasonable expense. However, the buyer retains any right to claim damages as provided for in this Convention.').

breach in itself constitutes a basis for the buyer to invoke remedies under the CISG.[281] It is submitted that despite a prominent role of documents in international trade generally and in certain trade sectors in particular, the question whether an innocent buyer is entitled to damages based on a seller's documentary breach should depend on the effect of that breach on the buyer's ability to deal with the *goods*. This should be so because the documents are ultimately a means of selling the goods.[282]

The multiplicity of documents and their functions means that a buyer may suffer a wide range of losses, such as those examined throughout this chapter.[283] For instance, damages have been awarded in the CISG cases for the amount of customs fees and taxes, which the buyer would have been exempt from paying had a contractually required certificate of origin been delivered,[284] or for the demurrage and other costs which the buyer had to incur due to the delay in delivering an export licence.[285] Where a failure to deliver an insurance policy and a quality certificate prevented the buyer from conducting customs clearance and taking over the goods, causing it to breach the currency regulations in its country and pay a fine to state authorities, damages have been awarded for the amount of the fine.[286]

Regardless of whether there is a breach in respect of the goods, a documentary breach in itself may entitle the buyer to refuse to accept the documents[287] and avoid the contract. If the buyer then makes a replacement transaction in a reasonable manner and within a reasonable time, the buyer is entitled to the difference between the contract price and the price in the replacement transaction, together with any further damages, as provided for in the CISG and other international instruments.[288] Similarly, if such a replacement transaction has not been made the buyer is entitled, arguably subject to the mitigation rule,[289] to the difference between the contract price and the current price of the goods, together with any further damages.[290] A lack of conformity in a document,

[281] See further D Saidov, 'Remedies for a Documentary Breach: English Law and the CISG' in K Rowley, L DiMatteo, S Saintier and Q Zhou (eds), Current Issues in Commercial Contracts: Transatlantic Perspectives (New York, CUP, 2013).

[282] See ibid, 462–3.

[283] The precise calculation of damages depends on the specific loss the buyer suffers as a result of a documentary breach. See further chs 8 and 9.

[284] See Case No T-9/07 Foreign Trade Court of Arbitration, Serbian Chamber of Commerce, 23 January 2008, available at cisgw3.law.pace.edu/cases/080123sb.html.

[285] CIETAC 15 December 1998 (Shirt), available at cisgw3.law.pace.edu/cases/981215c1.html. See similarly Arbitration Court St Petersburg and Leningrad Region (Russia) 27 March 2019 (n 108), where due to the seller's non-delivery of the required documents, the buyer was not able to export the goods from Korea which resulted in various losses, such as costs of storage, payment to the shipping agent and employing a legal team in Korea to resolve the matter with the seller.

[286] Arbitration 5 July 2005 (Ukraine) (Medical equipment), available at cisgw3.law.pace.edu/cases/050705u5.html.

[287] For the argument in favour of the existence in the CISG of the buyer's right to reject documents, separate from the right to terminate the contract, see Saidov (n 281) 445–6.

[288] See 75 CISG, 7.4.5 UPICC and 9:506 PECL.

[289] See further ch 8.

[290] See arts 76 CISG, 7.4.6 UPICC and 9:507 PECL.

such as a false statement in a bill of lading about the shipment date of the goods and/or their description,[291] state and condition, the goods may become non-tradeable with the buyer being 'locked in the market'.[292] In this case, the buyer may suffer loss of its profit margin either on a specific sub-sale contract, which the buyer had made or intended to make, or by having lost an opportunity to resell the goods on the market.[293]

As the experience of some legal systems shows,[294] the ability of the buyer to avoid the contract on the basis of a documentary breach can give rise to a claim for damages seeking to compensate the buyer for the loss of its right to avoid the contract, caused by a documentary non-conformity. Suppose that under a CIF contract the goods are shipped outside the contractual shipment period but the bill of lading is falsely dated to show that the goods were shipped within the shipment period. Suppose further that on a falling market the buyer pays against these apparently conforming documents but later, when the right to avoid the contract is no longer available,[295] learns about the true shipment date. The buyer may argue that had the bill of lading been conforming and not concealed the true shipment date, it would have refused to accept the documents, avoided the contract on this basis[296] and re-purchased the goods at a market price lower than the price in the contract with the breaching seller. Having lost the right to avoid the contract, the buyer can claim damages to put itself in the financial position in which it would have been had there been no documentary breach, thereby throwing the risk of the falling market on the seller. Such damages can be based on the difference between the contract price and the price at which the buyer would have been able to purchase the goods on a falling market when the contract would have been avoided following its refusal to accept the documents.[297]

[291] See Saidov (n 275).

[292] In English law, see *Procter & Gamble Philippine Manufacturing Corp v Kurt A Becher GMBH & Co KG* [1988] 2 Lloyd's Rep 21, 32.

[293] If the buyer managed to reasonably resell the goods, say, at a very low price because a documentary non-conformity damaged their tradeability, the price so obtained must be taken into account to reduce the profit margin claimed by the buyer (on the relevance of benefits gained as a result of the breach, see ch 2). If by having lost an opportunity to resell the goods as intended the buyer saved costs, the latter also must be taken into account in assessing damages (on the relevance of costs saved as a result of the breach, see ch 2).

[294] In English law, see *James Finlay & Co, Ltd v NV Kwik Hoo Tong Handel Maatschappij* [1929] 1 KB 400.

[295] The right to avoid under the CISG will be lost (where the seller has delivered the goods) if a declaration of avoidance is not given within a reasonable time (see art 49(2) CISG; for other situations where the right to avoid may be lost under the CISG, see arts 39 and 82). See also art 7.3.2(2) UPICC and 9:303(2) PECL.

[296] For the position that 'special standards' must be applied to determining a fundamental breach under the CISG in the context of the commodities trade, see CISG Advisory Council Opinion (CISG-AC) No 5, 'The Buyer's Right to Avoid the Contract in Case of Nonconforming Goods or Documents', Comment 4.17, available at www.cisgac.com/file/repository/CISG_Advisory_Council_Opinion_No_5.pdf.

[297] Analogy can also conceivably be drawn with an abstract formula in the international instruments (arts 76 CISG, art 7.4.6 UPICC, art 9:507 PECL). If the buyer manages to reasonably resell the goods, delivered by the breaching seller, at a low price, the price obtained in that resale, being

A possible objection to the recoverability of this loss can be that damages for this loss undermine the rules on the loss of the buyer's right to avoid the contract.[298] It can also be argued that sellers should be liable in damages only where they themselves are 'guilty of some degree of culpable complicity in the misdating of the bill of lading',[299] in which case damages should be based on the applicable principles of the law of tort.[300] On balance, it is suggested that, although this type of loss is not expressly provided for in the CISG and other international instruments, the loss of the right to avoid the contract and benefit from the fall in the market price is a real financial loss and there is no reason why it should not be recoverable under the instruments. As this chapter has demonstrated, all types of financial loss are in principle recoverable under the instruments. This position also recognises a documentary breach as an independent ground for claiming damages.[301]

the benefit flowing from the breach (and most likely the mitigation measure) will need to reduce the amount of damages. In *James Finlay & Co, Ltd v NV Kwik Hoo Tong Handel Maatschappij* (n 294), the buyer resold the goods by auction at a loss and was awarded damages as the difference between the price in the contract with the seller and the market price received by the buyer for the goods.

[298] See G Treitel, 'Damages for Breach of a C.I.F. Contract' [1988] LMCLQ 457, 461.

[299] M Bridge (ed), *Benjamin's Sale of Goods*, 10th edn (London, Sweet & Maxwell – Thomson Reuters 2019) [19-214].

[300] Ibid.

[301] That said, the point that documents are a means of selling the goods and the resulting interconnection between the documents and goods must be borne in mind. Suppose that, in a CIF contract, a bill of lading is falsely dated but the goods were in fact shipped within the shipment period (as happened in *Procter & Gamble Philippine Manufacturing Corp v Kurt A Becher GMBH & Co KG* (n 292), where the shipment period was January–February, the goods were in fact shipped in January but the bill of loading bore a February shipment date). It is submitted that in this case, subject to the goods not being 'locked in' the market as result of a documentary breach (see n 292 and the accompanying text), there should be no damages for the lost right to avoid the contract because had the bill of lading stated the true shipment date the buyer would not have been able to reject the documents (because the true date of shipment of the goods is within the contractual shipment period). In contrast, in the situation discussed in the main text (accompanying nn 295 and 297), had the bill of lading stated the true shipment date that date would have most likely rendered the bill of lading non-conforming (as it would have stated a non-contractual shipment date) and the buyer would have been able to reject the documents and avoid the contract on this basis. See further Saidov (n 281) 461–2; for a different view, see C Debattista, *Bill of Lading in Export Trade*, 3rd edn (Haywards Heath, Tottel Publishing, 2009) 235.

Part II

Methods of Limiting Damages

4

Causation[1]

1. GENERAL

THE INTERNATIONAL INSTRUMENTS provide that damages are due only for losses which were caused by the breach of contract. According to art 74 CISG, damages 'consist of a sum equal to the loss … suffered … *as a consequence of the breach*'. Similar provisions are contained in the UPICC and PECL.[2] This requirement can be regarded both as a precondition for liability in damages and as a method of limiting damages.[3] The party in breach cannot be liable for the loss which its breach has not caused and, in this sense, the presence of a causal connection is a necessary precondition for liability in damages. At the same time, causation is a limitation on damages because compensation for losses can be claimed only to the extent that they were caused by the breach.

The reasons for the causation requirement are deeply rooted in our thinking. The notion of causation is a necessity of human thought.[4] One reason is that it is only through this notion that a human being acquires and maintains the sense of him/herself as a separate person. It is also causation which enables a person to think of him/herself as an author of his/her actions capable of making changes in the world.[5] It has been further suggested, in relation to the law of remedies, that the 'whole law of remedies … is based upon the belief that there is uniformity in the sequence of events, in the conduct of men as well as in that of atoms and planets, and that it is possible for men to influence and control the

[1] This chapter is a substantially revised and updated version of D Saidov, 'Causation in Damages: The Convention on Contracts for the International Sale of Goods, the UNIDROIT Principles of International Commercial Contracts, the Principles of European Contract Law' in *Review of the Convention on Contracts for the International Sale of Goods (CISG) 2004–2005* (Munich, Sellier European Law Publishers, 2006) 225.

[2] Article 7.4.2(1) UPICC: 'The aggrieved party is entitled to full compensation for harm sustained *as a result* of the non-performance.' Article 9:501(1) PECL: 'The aggrieved party is entitled to damages for loss *caused* by the other party's non-performance.'

[3] See CT McCormick, *Handbook on the Law of Damages* (St Paul, Minn, West Publishing Co, 1935) 260.

[4] See Lord Wright, 'Notes on Causation and Responsibility in English Law' [1955] *Cambridge L J* 163.

[5] HLA Hart and T Honore, *Causation in the Law*, 2nd edn (Oxford, Clarendon Press, 1985) lxxx–lxxxi.

future as well as to predict it'.[6] It can also be argued that, for many of us, it is fair to hold people liable *only* for the consequences flowing from their own actions[7] (individual, as opposed to collective, responsibility).

Causation is a complex area of law and legal systems differ greatly when it comes to their treatment of causation. These differences are evidenced by the existence of various 'theories' of causation.[8] Causal problems are most acute in tort (delict) or criminal law because the difficult cases on causation mostly concern physical injury or damage. Although the problems of causation arise more rarely in the law of contracts,[9] they may nevertheless pose serious challenges and need to be explored. The purpose of this chapter is to identify such problems insofar as they are relevant to international sales contracts and to explore ways of resolving them.

2. FACTUAL AND LEGAL CAUSATION

Although legal systems differ as to whether the existence of causal connection is a question of fact or of law,[10] drawing a distinction between factual and legal causation seems inevitable.[11] The factual causation inquiry focuses on the history leading to the loss (that is, the chain of events which resulted in the loss) and on the determination of whether the breach was an event in the chain. This inquiry is non-legal and its sole purpose is to provide factual evidence. The legal causation inquiry establishes what legal consequences should be attached to the breach and other events in the chain. This inquiry is not concerned with a history of the loss and is based on value and policy which are questions of law.[12] It determines whether the breach, despite its being one of the conditions of the occurrence of the loss, should be regarded as a 'legal cause'. The legal causation inquiry can only be launched once the facts are established.[13]

To determine whether the breach was an event in the chain leading to the loss (factual causation), the so-called *conditio sine qua non* or 'but for' test is applied

[6] AL Corbin, *Corbin on Contracts* vol 5 (St Paul, Minn, West Publishing Co, 2002) 60.

[7] See Hart and Honore (n 5) 1.

[8] For an excellent analysis of different theories of causation (albeit in the context of tort), see AM Honore, 'Causation and Remoteness of Damage' in K Zweigert and K Drobnig (eds), *International Encyclopedia of Comparative Law*, vol 11, ch 7 (The Hague, Martinus Nijhoff Publishers, 1971).

[9] Hart and Honore (n 5) 308; MI Braginskiy and VV Vitryanskiy, *Contract Law: General Provisions (Dogovornoye pravo: Obshiye polozheniya)* (Statut, Moscow, 1998) 576.

[10] See Honore (n 8) 20–1.

[11] '[It is a] generally accepted notion that, to be a cause of harm in law, the conduct or defined event must at least be a condition … of it' (Honore (n 8) 67).

[12] See Honore (n 8) 21.

[13] The distinction between factual and legal causation is emphasised and relied upon by many commentators (see, eg, C Morris, 'On the Teaching of Legal Cause' (1939) 39 *Columbia L Rev* 1087, 1088–9; EJ Weinrib, 'A Step Forward in Factual Causation' (1975) 38 *MLR* 518).

in most cases.[14] According to this test, a factual cause (condition) of an event is one without which the event would not have occurred. There is much less agreement as to the proper ways of determining which factual causes (conditions) should be treated as legal causes and this is the stage where different theories of causation come into play.

The question arises whether the distinction between factual and legal causes should be the basis for dealing with causation under the instruments. In relation to the CISG, it has been suggested that '[i]t suffices that the breach was a condition of the occurrence of the harmful event (*conditio sine qua non*, 'but for rule') [and that] [i]t is irrelevant whether the damage was caused directly or indirectly by the breach'.[15] One way to interpret this view is to state that the only causal issues that can arise under the instruments are those relating to factual causation and there should be no room for legal causation. Another way to interpret it is to suggest that the 'but for' test should be regarded as comprising both factual and legal tests of causation. Whatever approach to interpreting this view is taken, it follows therefrom that a cause of the loss is one without which the loss would not have occurred and that no other causal inquiry is necessary. This view represents, in essence, the so-called 'equivalence' theory advocated in some legal systems.[16] It has a number of apparent advantages: it relies on the 'but for' test, most often treated as the main test of factual causation; the 'but for' test prevents events which make no difference to the course of events leading up to the loss from being regarded as the cause; the test is relatively simple.[17]

Those commenting on this theory point out that its application may lead to excessive liability and some additional limitations are needed.[18] Its advocates would probably meet this criticism by stating that the instruments leave 'no room for legal theories of causation which limit liability for damage to probable or not entirely remote causal sequences of events, since [they employ] the foreseeability rule … in order to exclude liability for damage which is so remote

[14] This test is not the only test of factual causation. Some commentators pointing out the drawbacks of the test suggest alternative tests of factual causation. The 'but for' test, however, has enjoyed wide acceptance (see Honore (n 8) 67; G Williams, 'Causation in the Law' [1961] *Cambridge L J* 62, 63).

[15] H Stoll, 'Damages: Article 74' in P Schlechtriem (ed), *Commentary on the UN Convention on the International Sale of Goods (CISG)*, 2nd edn (Oxford, OUP, 1998) 558. Some other commentators seem to suggest a similar approach to causation: 'the Convention seeks to place the injured party in the position she would have enjoyed "but for" the breach' (H Bernstein and J Lookofsky, *Understanding the CISG in Europe: A Compact Guide to the 1980 United Nations Convention on Contracts for the International Sale of Goods*, 2nd edn (The Hague, Kluwer Law International, 2003) 139).

[16] 'The equivalence theory is also called the theory of equivalent conditions, the condition theory … and the *conditio sine qua non* theory. According to it every condition in the absence of which the harm would not have occurred in the way in which it did occur (*in concreto*) is a cause of the harm' (Honore (n 8) 33).

[17] Ibid.

[18] Ibid.

as to lie outside the scope of a party's responsibility'.[19] The following discussion will examine whether it is appropriate to confine all causal issues to the 'but for' test and whether the foreseeability rule is capable of dealing with the problems that may be unresolved by the 'but for' test.

3. MULTIPLE SUFFICIENT CAUSATION

On numerous occasions, it has been pointed out that the 'but for' test has its limitations as a test of factual causation in the case of multiple sufficient causation or causal over-determination ('over-determination'). This is a situation where *two or more* events or acts independently result in the consequence in question and each of these events or acts is sufficient *in itself* to bring about this consequence. Because the same consequence would have taken place even if one of the events or acts had not occurred, the 'but for' test does not lead to liability in such cases.

One US case provides an illustration.[20] A manufacturer of leggings concluded a contract with the War Department. The contract provided for liquidated damages for delay in delivery. The manufacturer placed an order with a seller for the supply of webbing necessary for the manufacture of leggings. The seller was late in delivering the webbing and the manufacturer had to pay liquidated damages to the War Department. The manufacturer claimed compensation for this loss and one of the objections raised by the seller was that delay in delivering webbing was not the sole cause of the manufacturer's loss. It claimed that there had been other contributing causes such as 'a landlord's distress and eviction at the buyer's factory, a removal by the [manufacturer] of its plant, a shortage of eyelets necessary to the manufacture of the leggings'.[21] Suppose that those other causes were sufficient in themselves to cause the delay and the loss suffered by the manufacturer. The 'but for' test would lead to the finding that even if the seller had delivered webbing on time, the manufacturer would have suffered the same loss anyway and consequently the seller's breach cannot be said to be the cause of the loss. The foreseeability rule will not resolve the problem because the presence of a causal link is a separate requirement to be met for the seller to be liable. It is also noteworthy that, in the original decision, the foreseeability test was satisfied because the seller had known about the liquidated damages clause in the contract between the manufacturer and the War Department.

[19] Stoll (n 15) 558. This statement relates to art 74 CISG. For a similar view, see M Djordjević, 'Arts 74–77' in S Kröll, L Mistelis and P Viscasillas (eds), *The United Nations Convention on Contracts for the International Sale of Goods*, 2nd edn (München, C.H. Beck and Oxford, Hart, 2018) 961 ('despite common (unwelcome) references of courts to familiar domestic theories of causation, it is the principle of full compensation and principle of recoverability of foreseeable losses that set the guidelines on causation under the CISG').

[20] See *Krauss v Greenbarg* 137 F.2d 569 (1943).

[21] Ibid.

Thus, if we take the view that the 'but for' test is all that is needed for dealing with causal over-determination, the seller would not be liable. Is this a satisfactory result? Before this question is answered, it may be helpful to explore the results that would be achieved if other theories of causation were relied upon. According to one theory, the breach is the cause of the loss if it is a necessary element of a set of conditions sufficient to bring about the loss (the so-called 'NESS' test).[22] The difference between the NESS test and the 'but for' test is that the former is a test of sufficiency and the latter is that of necessity.[23] If the NESS test were applied to our example, both the seller's breach and other events would be regarded as causes because each of them was sufficient to bring about the same loss. Another alternative is to regard the breach as a cause if it was a 'substantial factor' in producing the loss.[24] This test requires that the breaching party be responsible only if its contribution 'was not quantitatively negligible'[25] and it is this test that was applied in the case on which our example was based. The court stated that '[if] a number of factors [were] operating one may so predominate in bringing about the harm as to make the effect produced by others so negligible that they [could not] be considered substantial factors and hence legal causes of the harm produced. In that event liability attache[d], the requisites of legal cause being shown, only to the one responsible for the predominating, or substantial, factor bringing the harm.'[26] What constitutes a substantial factor was defined as the conduct which 'ha[d] such effect in producing the harm as to lead reasonable men to regard it as a cause'.[27] If this theory were applied to our example, the seller's breach would most likely be regarded as a substantial factor and the causal connection between the seller's breach and the loss would probably be established. The main drawback of the 'substantial factor' theory is its irrelevance in the context of causal over-determination. If two or more events and acts are sufficient to produce the same loss, it is difficult to see how each of these acts or events *cannot* be a substantial factor in bringing about the loss.[28]

Returning to the question posed in the previous paragraph, it is submitted that the breaching party should be held liable in cases of causal over-determination. Suppose that two independent suppliers failed to deliver two different but essential materials to the manufacturer who, like the manufacturer in the example above, had to pay liquidated damages to its customer as result. If the 'but for'

[22] See T Honore, 'Causation in the Law', available at plato.stanford.edu/entries/causation-law/; D Hamer, ' "Chance Would Be a Fine Thing": Proof of Causation and Quantum in an Unpredictable World' (1999) 23 *Melbourne U L R* 557, 571–2.

[23] Hamer (n 22) 572.

[24] Honore (n 8) 68–9; Honore (n 22).

[25] Honore (n 8) 69.

[26] *Krauss v Greenbarg* (n 20) 572.

[27] Ibid.

[28] Hart and Honore (n 5) 236, seem to take the same view ('Neither the terminology of "contributory causes" nor that of "substantial factor" is really appropriate in … situations when one of the causes is sufficient without the other, which is also sufficient, to produce the loss complained of').

test is relied upon, the manufacturer will find itself in the situation where, having suffered loss as a consequence of the two suppliers breaching their contracts, it is unable to claim damages against either of them. Because this result would be grossly unfair to the injured party, the 'but for' test has to be rejected. It is suggested that the NESS theory is most appropriate here[29] as it achieves a fair result by enabling the manufacturer to bring a damages claim against the breaching suppliers.[30]

4. HYPOTHETICAL ALTERNATIVE CAUSATION

Another situation where the 'but for' test does not lead to liability is that involving hypothetical alternative causation ('alternative causation'), that is, where the breach produces the loss but the same loss would have occurred even if there had been no breach.[31] The difference between alternative causation and causal over-determination is that an alternative *cause* is *hypothetical* while in the case of over-determination all sufficient causes do *in fact* occur.[32] The reason why the 'but for' test does not lead to liability is that it cannot be said that but for the breach the loss would not have had occurred.

Suppose that two independent suppliers are to deliver two different, but essential, materials for the manufacture of the final product. Suppose further

[29] *Cf Borealis AB v Geogas Trading SA* [2010] EWHC 2789 (Comm), decided under English law, where the seller delivered contaminated butane to the buyer who intended to use it as feedstock in its integrated olefin plant. The seller's breach caused damage to the buyer's plant, equipment and interruption of business. The seller contended that the lost profit, arising from lost production, ought not to be recoverable because there was also an alternative cause leading to the same loss: namely, the buyer having repaired some equipment at its plant. The court held that it was not necessary for the buyer to carry out those repairs at that time, making it clear that the outcome would have been otherwise had those other repairs had to be done at the same time (ibid, [158]–[160]). On this approach, the critical question is whether the buyer has a choice as to when the alternative cause, other than breach, is to take place. Only a negative answer can exempt the breaching party from liability.

[30] The question arises as to how damages should be allocated between the two breaching suppliers. It seems appropriate for the injured party to be allowed to claim damages for the full amount of the loss from either of the suppliers. Suppose the transaction with one supplier is governed by one of the international instruments and the transaction with the second supplier is governed by some other law which uses the 'but for' test. The liability of each supplier is likely to be dealt with separately. The second supplier will be exempt from liability in damages by virtue of the 'but for' test. If the first supplier is then held liable only for a part of the loss, the injured party will not be fully compensated and this result seems unfair to the injured party. Thus, it is submitted that the injured party who claims damages against one supplier for its breach of the contract governed by one of the international instruments should be able to recover the full amount of the loss. If so, the injured party cannot claim damages against the other supplier since it has been fully compensated for the loss (and presumably most legal systems would disallow double recovery). Similarly, if it is shown that the injured party has already recovered damages for the full amount of its loss caused by one supplier's breach of the contract governed by some domestic law, no damages can be claimed against the other supplier for breach of the contract governed by one of the international instruments.

[31] Honore (n 8) 79–81; Hart and Honore (n 5) 249.

[32] Hart and Honore (n 5) 249.

that the second supplier has an obligation to deliver the materials within 20 days after the receipt of the manufacturer's notice of delivery by the first supplier. The first supplier fails to deliver and the manufacturer claims damages for non-delivery. The first supplier presents evidence that even if it had delivered the materials, the second supplier would have failed to deliver and the manufacturer would have suffered the same loss anyway. If it is only the 'but for' test that is relied upon, the manufacturer will not be able to claim damages against the first supplier and will be left uncompensated. To avoid this result, the 'but for' test has to be rejected and the first supplier's breach needs to be recognised as the cause of the loss, both in fact and in law,[33] and a hypothetical alternative cause should be causally irrelevant.[34]

A different approach may be needed where a hypothetical alternative cause is not an unlawful act (such as a breach by the second supplier in the previous example) but a natural event. Suppose that the seller's obligation to deliver the goods consisted in placing the goods on board the ship X. The seller breached the contract by placing the goods on board the ship Y which sank during the voyage. Responding to the buyer's claim for damages for non-delivery, the seller, while recognising its breach, presents evidence that the ship X also sank during the voyage. Therefore, even if it had placed the goods on board the ship X, the buyer would have suffered the same loss anyway. In such cases it may be appropriate not to hold the seller liable because had it performed the contract, the buyer would not have been able to attribute the blame for its loss to anybody's wrongful actions.[35]

5. INTERVENING CAUSE

5.1. General

Problems of causation also arise where some event or act occurs after the breach but before the loss. Where so, the question is whether the breach or the subsequent event/act should be treated as the cause of the loss. If the subsequent

[33] In some cases, it may be unnecessary to reject the 'but for' test as the breaching party may still be held liable on the basis of this test. This may be possible by formulating the consequence of the breach in greater detail (thereby distinguishing it from a consequence which would have flown from a hypothetical alternative cause in terms of time, place, or some other detail of occurrence). But in some cases, real and hypothetical losses can be indistinguishable (see Honore (n 8) 80).

[34] 'A more satisfactory way of explaining how the right conclusion is to be reached is to say that the imaginary subtraction of the alleged causal fact must not be accompanied by the invention of any other imaginary facts in its place, however likely it may be that such a replacement would have occurred in reality' (Williams (n 14) 72).

[35] This view seems implicit in Hart and Honore's statement: '[i]f defendant has wrongfully deprived the plaintiff of an economic opportunity of which, in the alternative, another would *wrongfully* have deprived him he should be liable to pay compensation, because ... plaintiff has a right to any economic advantage which he would enjoy apart from wrongful acts on the part of anyone ...' (Hart and Honore (n 5) 251).

event/act is regarded as such, it is usually referred to as an 'intervening cause' which 'breaks' or 'interrupts' the chain of causation between the breach and the loss. 'Breaking the chain of causation' is a metaphor as 'the sequence of physical events is not interrupted, nor does a mysterious psychological discontinuity take place. The interruption is man-made.'[36] We do so for the purposes of explanation, prediction and imposition of liability.[37] One way of explaining this treatment of causation is that where an intervening event/act is considered much more responsible for the loss than the breach, it is considered unfair to hold the breaching party liable.[38] An intervening cause can be an event, an act of a third party or an act of the injured party. Before each of these situations is addressed, it may be helpful to make a few general remarks.

It has been suggested that our common sense regards as a cause something which interferes in or departs from the *normal or ordinary* course of events. A cause is something which is of abnormal nature. An abnormal factor makes 'a difference' between the loss and the things occurring as usual.[39] If this is true, a subsequent abnormal event will 'break the chain of causation' between the breach and the loss. What is abnormal is relative to the context of the inquiry and the interests and the purposes of the inquirer.[40] Another condition that needs to be met for an event to be regarded as an intervening event is that it must be independent of the breach. If the event would not have occurred but for the breach, it will not break the causal connection.[41]

5.2. Intervening Event and an Act of a Third Party

> Example 1: S agrees to sell to B machinery which S knows is required by B to manufacture goods in its factory. The machinery is due to be delivered on 1 June but S fails to make the delivery. B is losing profit at the rate of £1,000 for each week's delay. This is a normal level of profit for a business of this kind. On 29 June a fire breaks out in B's factory, which is burnt to the ground. On 16 July S delivers the machinery. B would not have been able to put the machinery to use elsewhere during this period.[42]

This example raises the question whether profit lost between 29 June and 16 July was caused by the breach. The answer, it is suggested, should be 'no'. It is clear that even if S had properly performed the contract, B would not have made a profit between 29 June and 16 July. For this reason, it does not seem appropriate

[36] Honore (n 8) 47.
[37] Ibid.
[38] A Burrows, *Remedies for Torts, Breach of Contract and Equitable Wrongs*, 4th edn (Oxford, OUP, 2019) 54.
[39] Hart and Honore (n 5) 29, 34–5.
[40] Ibid, 35–6.
[41] Ibid, 176.
[42] O Lando and H Beale (eds), *Principles of European Contract Law: Parts I and II* prepared by the Commission on European Contract Law (The Hague, Kluwer Law International, 2000) 434.

to regard S's delay in delivering the machinery as causing loss of profit during the said period and the 'but for' test *can* be used to achieve this result.[43]

> Example 2: S failed to load the goods on board a ship on time and the ship left the port later than planned. The ship was caught in a storm and the goods were destroyed. B claims damages for loss suffered as a result of non-delivery. S argues that the loss was not caused by S's failure to deliver on time because the storm broke the chain of causation between S's breach and the loss.

If the loss would have occurred even if there had been no breach, the situation becomes similar to alternative hypothetical causation and, as explained, the preferable solution is not to hold S liable. This result can again be achieved by means of the 'but for' test. Should the position be the same if the ship would not have been caught in a storm had S delivered on time? Before answering this question it should be noted that this situation has arisen in one English case[44] where, as a result of the defendant's (the shipowner's) breach of an obligation to provide a seaworthy ship, the cargo was delayed. Meanwhile, the war between Great Britain and Germany broke out and the British Admiralty prohibited the vessel from proceeding to the destination and ordered her to discharge at Glasgow. As a result, the innocent party had to incur the costs of transshipping the cargo. One question was whether those expenses were caused by the defendant's breach. The court used the foreseeability test, viz whether it was foreseeable to the defendant that the war would break out. It was held that 'the diversion to Glasgow, brought about through the delay in carrying out the contract of carriage ..., is attributable to the default of the owners of the ship, because ... they ought to have foreseen that war might shortly break out and that any prolongation of the voyage might cause the loss of or diversion of the ship'.[45] Thus, the foreseeability test was used in addition to the 'but for' test. In other words, the 'but for' test, as a test of factual causation, was deemed insufficient and was supplemented by an additional criterion of legal causation. This approach seems correct. Sole reliance on the 'but for' test where the breaching party's 'conduct ... merely changes ... the time at which some ... thing arrives at a given place'[46] may lead to liability where a natural intervening event may be much more responsible for the loss. To prevent this result, an additional requirement seems essential[47] and the foreseeability test provides an appropriate and a relevant solution because foreseeability is arguably a feature of our ordinary thought affecting our judgements about causation.[48] Applying this test to our Example 2, it can be argued that where the seller knows (say, on the basis of the

[43] For a similar view, see ibid.
[44] *Monarch Steamship Co Ltd v Karlshamns Oljefabriker (A/B)* [1949] AC 196.
[45] Ibid, 216.
[46] Hart and Honore (n 5) 168.
[47] A similar view seems implicit in ibid.
[48] P Lipton, 'Causation Outside the Law' in H Gross and R Harrison (eds), *Jurisprudence: Cambridge Essays* (Oxford, OUP, 1992) 140.

weather forecast) that if the shipment of cargo is delayed the vessel is likely to be caught in a storm and yet takes the risk and delays the shipment, we are more inclined to state that its breach was the cause of the loss and more reluctant to regard the storm as breaking the chain of causation.

> Example 3: In June S in Paris contracts to sell a Seurat painting to B in Hamburg for FF1 million, the painting to be shipped to B in Hamburg by the end of August. Because of delays on the part of its staff S is unable to arrange shipment earlier than 1 October. On 5 September the French government imposes a ban on the exportation of works of art without a licence, and despite using its best endeavours S is unable to obtain a licence to export the Seurat painting. The value of the painting at the end of August is considered by experts to be FF2 millions.[49]

This is an example involving an intervening act of a third party. The question is whether the ban imposed by the French government should be treated as breaking the chain of causation between delay in delivery and the loss. While relying solely on the 'but for' test would, no doubt, make it easier to deal with this situation, a more complex treatment seems necessary.[50] It cannot be assumed that the mere fact that the loss would not have occurred but for S's delay should necessarily make it liable. Nor can it be assumed that the fact that an act of a third party (such as the governmental ban) was a necessary condition of the occurrence of the loss is in itself sufficient to break the chain of causation between the breach and the loss. A more balanced and arguably fair approach is to apply the 'but for' test in conjunction with some additional requirement and, as argued in relation to Example 2, the foreseeability test (being a fair and workable method for dealing with this situation) is a suitable candidate for this role. If, in Example 3, the chances of an embargo, as determined by the breaching party's foreseeability, were not increased by delay, the breaching party should not be liable. Conversely, if before breaching the contract S foresaw or was in the position to reasonably foresee a possibility of an embargo in case of delay, S should be liable.

Whilst situations such as those in Examples 2 and 3 need to be resolved on the basis of the 'but for' test together with the likelihood/foreseeability test, the desired result can be achieved by means of other theories of causation. It is true that theories of causation 'mostly have little empirical content'[51] and that is why they can be used as a disguise for achieving the desired result.[52] One example is a theory of 'direct/indirect causation' according to which a party is liable only where the loss is a *direct* consequence of the breach.[53] What constitutes an 'indirect consequence' is capable of many interpretations[54] and there seems

[49] The example is given in Lando and Beale (n 42) 435–6.

[50] This approach is taken in ibid ('since but for S's delay in shipping the painting its export would not have been affected by the ban').

[51] Honore (n 8) 66.

[52] For a similar view, see Hart and Honore (n 5) 4.

[53] Honore (n 8) 40.

[54] Ibid, 41–2.

little in the basic statement of the theory to prevent a judge or an arbitrator, who believes that in Examples 2 or 3 the seller should not be liable, from ruling that the loss was an indirect consequence of the breach. The same applies to the 'adequate causation' theory according to which a contingency is a legal cause if it: (1) is a *condition sine qua non* of the loss, and (2) has significantly increased an objective probability of the occurrence of the loss.[55] Whether the breach has significantly increased an objective probability of the loss must be judged from the standpoint of an experienced observer. Knowledge of all the circumstances of which a person of that kind ought to have and of any special knowledge of the breaching party will be implied to such an observer.[56] If, from the standpoint of such an experienced observer, it was likely that the vessel would be caught in a storm or the shipment would be prevented by a government ban in the case of delay, the breaching party would be liable. The approach therefore is very similar to the suggested 'likelihood'/foreseeability test.[57] It is not argued that *all* theories of causation *always* lead to the same result. The point is, rather, that in cases such as those in Examples 2 and 3 more than one theory of causation is potentially able to achieve the desired result.[58]

5.3. Injured Party's Contribution to the Loss

The question of how the issues of liability and causation should be resolved where, after the breach, the injured party's act or omission contributes to the loss is a difficult one. Should such an act break the chain of causation between the breach and the loss or should the risk be allocated in accordance with each party's contribution to the loss? There is no doubt that the injured party's acts or omissions are capable of wholly breaking the causal link,[59] which is a highly

[55] See, eg, Hart and Honore (n 5) 469; GH Treitel, *Remedies for Breach of Contract: A Comparative Account* (Oxford, Clarendon Press, 1988) 163.

[56] Treitel (n 55) 163.

[57] However, the methods used by the two tests are different. For instance, as seen, in Hart and Honore's analysis foreseeability relates to the occurrence of an intervening event. The adequate causation theory refers to the increased probability of the occurrence of the *loss* (not of the intervening event). But as Hart and Honore point out, the probability of the occurrence of an intervening event can sometimes be made relevant by incorporating the event into the description of the loss (see Hart and Honore (n 5) 479).

[58] The focus in this section has been on the problem of whether an event or an act of a third party should break the causal link between the breach and the loss. It can hardly be denied that there may be cases where an event or a third party's act is insufficient to break the chain of causation but has nevertheless contributed to the loss. It is argued, therefore, that a possibility of allocating the loss between the breach and an event/third party's act in accordance with their respective contributions cannot be ruled out. The factors to be relied upon in determining the extent of each contribution are set out below.

[59] 'a voluntary human action ... has a special place in causal inquiries ... because, when the question is how far back a cause shall be traced through a number of intervening causes, such a voluntary action is often regarded both as a limit and also as still the cause even though other later abnormal occurrences have provisionally been recognized as causes' (Hart and Honore (n 5) 42).

fact-sensitive inquiry.[60] In one CISG case,[61] a glass manufacturer received a delivery of defective aluminium hydroxide from the seller and, without a prior examination, mixed it with another material. As a result, defective glass was produced. It was established that 'the defect would have been revealed even by means of simple tests'. Although damages were denied on the ground of the manufacturer's failure to mitigate, the same decision could probably have been reached on the basis of causation by holding that the manufacturer caused its own loss.[62] The critical factor in deciding whether the injured party's actions broke the chain of causation is whether they were reasonable in the circumstances.[63] In the CISG case just mentioned, it was arguably unreasonable for the manufacturer not to inspect the goods because the defects would have been revealed by simple tests and especially because the CISG requires the buyer to examine the goods.[64] Another relevant factor, arguably an aspect of reasonableness, is the injured party's knowledge. The following proposition, whilst made in the context of a domestic legal system, is of general relevance and should equally stand true in the context of the CISG and other instruments:

> 'For the chain of causation to be broken, the claimant need not have knowledge of the legal niceties of the breach of contract; nor ... will the chain of causation only be broken if the claimant has actual knowledge that a breach of contract has occurred – otherwise there would be a premium on ignorance. However, the more the claimant has actual knowledge of the breach, of the dangerousness of the situation which has thus arisen and of the need to take appropriate remedial measures, the greater the likelihood that the chain of causation will be broken. Conversely, the less the claimant knows the more likely it is that only recklessness will suffice to break the chain of causation.'[65]

The conclusion that the injured party's actions/omissions broke the chain of causation must not, it is submitted, be reached lightly because doing so can unjustifiably deprive this party of its valuable right to damages in its entirety.[66] It may be for this reason that some legal systems, such as English law, regard cases where the injured party's conduct breaks the chain of causation as arising in the 'most exceptional circumstances'[67] and do not regard unreasonableness in

[60] See, similarly, *Borealis AB v Geogas Trading SA* (n 29) [104].

[61] Case No 18 U 121/97 Appellate Court Köln (Germany) 21 August 1997 (Aluminium hydroxide), available at cisgw3.law.pace.edu/cases/970821g1.html.

[62] See, eg, *Quinn v Burch Bros (Builders) Ltd* [1966] 2 QB 370; *Beoco Ltd v Alfa Co Ltd* [1995] QB 137.

[63] Hart and Honore (n 5) 144–5, 230.

[64] See art 38 CISG. The argument that the injured party's actions broke the chain of causation between the breach and the loss is even stronger where the injured buyer uses non-conforming goods in its manufacturing process having clear knowledge of the non-conformity (as in Case No 07/03098 Court of Appeals Rennes (France) 27 May 2008, available at cisgw3.law.pace.edu/cases/080527f1.html, where the buyer was held to have failed to mitigate its loss).

[65] *Borealis AB v Geogas Trading SA* (n 29) [46].

[66] As opposed to the decision that the injured party merely contributed to the loss and the loss must be allocated between the parties (on which see the following discussion in the main text).

[67] See *County Ltd v Girozentrale Securities* [1996] 3 All ER 834, 857.

the injured party's conduct in itself sufficient to break the chain of causation.[68] For example, in one case,[69] the buyer was negligent in failing to discover a non-conformity (maximum gross weight) in a motor-home before reselling it to its sub-buyer, despite the vehicle having gone through a pre-delivery check that failed to pick up on the discrepancy in the maximum gross weight.[70] Because there was a strict warranty in the buyer's contract with the seller that was not dependent on the buyer's taking reasonable care to investigate whether the fact, represented in the warranty, was true and because there was nothing to alert the buyer to the possibility of a seller's breach, negligence or unreasonableness in the buyer's conduct did not break the causal chain. Should the same result be reached on these facts under the CISG? It is difficult to answer definitively but because, in contrast with the CISG case[71] noted in the previous paragraph, the buyer *did* carry out an inspection, although not one that picked up on the non-conformity, there may be a stronger case for arguing that a failure to conduct an entirely satisfactory examination did not break the chain of causation. Given the buyer's negligent conduct, a more balanced and optimum treatment may be to apportion the losses between the parties, an issue to which the discussion now turns.

Approaching the injured party's act or omission solely from the perspective of whether it breaks the chain of causation is based on an 'all-or-nothing' view of liability in damages: the breaching party is either fully liable for the loss or not liable at all. It can be argued that there are cases where it is more appropriate to apportion the loss between the parties, as recognised in the UPICC and the PECL. The UPICC provide that '[w]here the harm is due in part to an act or omission of the aggrieved party or to another event for which that party bears the risk, the amount of damages shall be reduced to *the extent that these factors have contributed to the harm*, having regard to the conduct of each of the parties'.[72] Similarly, according to the PECL, '[t]he non-performing party is not liable for loss suffered by the aggrieved party to the *extent* that the aggrieved party *contributed to … [the] effects [of non-performance]*'.[73]

[68] See *Borealis AB v Geogas Trading SA* (n) [45] ('it is difficult to conceive that anything less than unreasonable conduct on the part of the claimant would be capable of breaking the chain of causation. It is, however, also plain that mere unreasonable conduct on a claimant's part will not necessarily do so – for example where the defendant's breach remains an effective cause of the loss, albeit in combination with the claimant's failure to take reasonable precautions in its own interest … By its nature, reckless conduct by the claimant would or would ordinarily break the chain of causation, though there is no rule of law that only recklessness on the part of the claimant will do so').

[69] *Lester John Stacey trading as The New Gailey Caravan/Motorhomes Centre v Autosleeper Group Ltd* [2014] EWCA Civ 1551.

[70] See the finding of the first instance judge: '"Given how I view the Claimant's managerial skills (like his performance in the witness box, poorly), I am not in the least surprised that the his staff registered a vehicle with the DVLA without checking the facts relating to that vehicle or that the undertaking of the pre-delivery checks missed the fact that the maximum permitted axle weight was non-standard."' (cited in ibid, [6]).

[71] Appellate Court Köln (Germany) 21 August 1997 (n 61).

[72] Article 7.4.7 UPICC (emphasis added).

[73] Article 9:504 PECL (emphasis added).

Although the CISG does not contain a similar provision, it contains mechanisms enabling it to recognise the possibility of apportionment. First, it is arguably a logical inference from the causation requirement in art 74 that the part of the loss to which the injured party has contributed cannot be regarded as caused by the breaching party. Second, the mitigation rule can also be interpreted as denying damages which the injured party could have avoided. Finally, art 80 recognises the need for determining the *extent* of the injured party's contribution to the other party's breach and, because the nature of the problem under art 80 is the same as the one here,[74] an 'all-or-nothing' approach is arguably against the spirit of the CISG.

These issues were directly and indirectly at play in a CISG case[75] where the buyer, a food producer, failed to inspect the ground clay, delivered by the seller and containing high levels of dioxin. The buyer used the clay to separate potatoes and then delivered the sorted potatoes, together with the waste peel, to animal feed producers. The court held that both parties were responsible for the damage, resulting from the contamination of the goods, on the basis of a general principle, derived from both arts 77 and 80: namely, that in the case of 'dividable remedies, like damages, the respective party's contribution to the damage has to be reasonably taken into account'.[76] For the reasons stated in the previous paragraph, the decision is, with respect, correct to recognise the possibility of apportioning the loss between both parties. Whilst the decision that the mitigation rule does not cover this scenario is debatable, it is certainly correct that art 80 does not address this situation since the buyer did not contribute to the seller's breach. However, it is submitted that there was no need for the court to resolve the issue by resorting to and constructing a general principle. The same decision could and ought to have been reached on the basis of the causation reasoning. Specifically, the seller ought not to have been liable for the damage to the extent that it had been caused by the buyer's failure to inspect the goods and, upon discovery of contamination, to take further required measures. In other words, the decision ought to have attached due weight to and implemented the causation requirement in art 74.

The position that the loss can and, in appropriate cases, must be apportioned between both parties gives rise to two inter-related difficulties. One relates to the question of how to distinguish between cases where the injured

[74] Article 80 refers to the injured party's contribution to the *breach* and the case under consideration is that of the injured party's contribution to its loss.

[75] Case No VIII ZR 100/11 Supreme Court (Germany) 26 September 2012, available at cisgw3.law.pace.edu/cases/120926g1.html.

[76] Ibid, [33]. The principle, rationalised with reference to the notions of good faith in art 7(1) CISG and the bar on contradictory behaviour, is further formulated in the decision as follows: 'the consequence of the contribution to the damage by the obligee should not be the loss of the claim, but that in case of mutual causing of the damage and dividable remedies like damages the respective contributions to the damage have to be reasonably taken into account in the assessment, weighing and balancing of interests' (ibid, [34]).

party's actions or omissions break the chain of causation and where they merely contribute to the loss. The second question is how the injured party's contribution to the loss can be determined. In some cases, it may be relatively easy to see why and how the loss should be apportioned.[77] Suppose the seller supplied a farmer with a substance designed to be sprayed over the land. The contract contains a clause requiring that several blocks of the land are to be sprayed by the seller and other blocks by the farmer. The parties also have a *strict* obligation to test the substance before using it because if it does not comply with the specified standards, it may adversely affect the soil. The seller delivered a defective substance and none of the parties had taken the trouble to examine it before using. The farmer suffered losses as a result of the soil having been affected by the defective substance. In this case, it seems appropriate to make each party liable for the losses flowing from the blocks for which each party was responsible.

Many cases are likely to be much less straightforward. Consider an example in the Comments on the PECL:

> A leases a computer which under the terms of the contract is to be ready for use in England where the voltage is 240v. The computer supplied is capable of operating on various voltages and, in breach of contract, is actually set for 110v. A prominent sign posted on the screen warns the user to check the voltage setting before use. A ignores this and switches on without checking. The computer is extensively damaged and repairs will cost A £1,500.[78]

The Comments' approach is to split the loss between the parties on a 50/50 basis.[79] Although this (50/50) allocation seems to be based on the Comments' reliance on the notion of fault (discussed below), it is far from clear *why* and *how* fault has led to an equal apportionment of liability. It seems that in many cases of this kind, decisions will depend on courts and tribunals balancing various factors, deemed relevant in the circumstances, and this is why it is very difficult to rationalise such cases. The most that can be done is to identify criteria which can be used to apportion losses between the parties and to provide examples

[77] Both these difficulties were at play in Court of Appeals Rennes (n 64), where being aware of the non-conformity in bra cups, delivered by the seller, the buyer nevertheless used them to manufacture swimming suits. The precise legal basis or reasoning that led the court to award some damages for the cost of processing the bra cups in the course of the manufacturing is unclear. On the one hand, the court held that the buyer had failed to mitigate those costs, which suggests that damages for the costs ought to have been denied altogether since there was no indication of the extent, to which those costs could *not* have been mitigated (the same result could have been achieved on the basis of causation, by holding that the buyer's action broke the chain of causation between the seller's breach and the cost of processing/manufacturing). On the other hand, a relatively small amount of damages for those costs, compared to that claimed, was nevertheless awarded to the buyer. This decision suggests that either the court deemed those costs as partly unavoidable (the mitigation perspective) or the court somehow apportioned that loss between the parties (the causation perspective).

[78] Lando and Beale (n 42) 444.

[79] See ibid.

of the possible interplay between them. The relevant criteria include: (1) causal criteria;[80] (2) gravity of each party's conduct;[81] (3) each party's fault; (4) justice and equity; and (5) the judge's or arbitrator's discretion.[82]

So far as the first criterion is concerned, there are several potentially relevant causal criteria. The theory of adequate causation leads to the determination based on the extent to which each party's contribution increased the probability of the loss.[83] Another criterion flows from a version of the 'efficiency' theory, according to which 'the degree in which a particular condition causes an event may be quantified according to its energetic or efficient quality'.[84] Under this approach, determining each party's contribution is based on 'a quantity of energy' attached to each of the party's actions or omissions.[85] Another criterion which has emerged in cases under the instruments is that of *necessity* of costs incurred by the injured party after the breach. In one CISG case,[86] the seller, who had resold the contract goods after the buyer's failure to pay, claimed, amongst others, damages for the inspection fee it had incurred before reselling the goods. The court dismissed that part of the claim on the ground that the inspection fee was not necessary (presumably, for the purpose of reselling the goods). In another case, the seller's claim for the recovery of costs of sending a person to collect the goods, after the goods had already been shipped back to the seller, was denied on the ground that there was no need for the collection.[87] In yet another case,[88] the buyer's costs incurred prior to the litigation with its sub-buyer were denied because the costs had not arisen 'unavoidably in the

[80] Honore (n 8) 121.

[81] Comment 3 on art 7.4.7 UPICC.

[82] Honore (n 8) 121.

[83] Honore (n 8) 122.

[84] Honore (n 8) 38. According to a less flexible version, 'the cause is a condition to which the highest energy attaches'. This version cannot be relied upon because it will run counter to the provisions of the UPICC and PECL (and the CISG if it is interpreted in the way suggested in this book) which require the extent of the injured party's contribution to the loss to be determined. Even a flexible version of the theory cannot be fully relied upon because, according to Honore, under the flexible version, '[a]ll those whose contributions come above a certain percentage are causes of the harm'. This again implies that if a contribution is below a certain level, it will not be regarded as the cause. This result is not what was intended under the instruments, which recognise the possibility of determining the injured party's contribution to the loss.

[85] For an analysis of the efficiency theory, see ibid, 38–40. The 'equivalence theory' (essentially the 'but for' test) could not be used here because it would allocate each party's contribution on the basis of a 50/50 split, disregarding the possibility of an allocation other than that based on a 50/50 split.

[86] See *China Yituo Group Company v Germany Gerhard Freyso Ltd GmbH and Co KG*, Second Intermediate People's Court (District Court) of Shanghai (China) 22 June 1998, available at cisgw3.law.pace.edu/cases/980622c1.html.

[87] '[T]he Seller sent [a] person for the collection in late August … not long after the fifth group of goods [had been] sent out on 21 August, at a time when there seemed no special necessity [for the] collection. The collection fee sought by the Seller is only a general business fee, and [is] not to be compensated.' (CIETAC 7 November 1996 (Stone products), available at cisgw3.law.pace.edu/cases/961107c1.html).

[88] See Case No P 1997/482 Civil Court Basel (Switzerland) 1 March 2002 (Soyprotein products), available at cisgw3.law.pace.edu/cases/020301s1.html.

sense of sufficient causality' because, by not engaging the breaching seller in the pre-litigation process, the buyer had 'failed to avail itself of any possible support for its case'.

These cases reflect the view that for the costs incurred by the injured party after the breach to be regarded as caused by the breach they must be unavoidable or necessary for dealing with the consequences of the breach. One major consequence of the breach is that the injured party has a 'duty' to avoid or reduce its loss and this duty needs to be exercised in a reasonable manner.[89] That is why there will often be a close connection between what these decisions termed as 'necessity' or 'unavoidability' of costs and the notion of reasonableness. In fact, all these cases can be equally analysed on the basis of whether the innocent party's actions were reasonable. It is therefore suggested that the question whether a cost incurred by the innocent party was caused by the breach is to be answered with reference to whether the cost was reasonable or expedient in the circumstances.

The second criterion leads to the allocation of losses based on the gravity of each party's conduct: 'The more serious a party's failing, the greater will be its contribution to the harm.'[90] This criterion was decisive in the above mentioned CISG case[91] where the buyer failed to examine the ground clay, contaminated with dioxin and used by the buyer to grade potatoes resold (together with the waste peel) to animal feed producers. The decision apportioned the loss on the 50/50 basis, emphasising the similarly grave misconduct on the part of both parties:

> 'When weighing and balancing the respective contributions as required, it is to be taken into account to the disadvantage of [the Seller] that the clay delivered by it not only was non-conforming as described but also that [the Seller] left [the Buyer] in ignorance of the dioxin content known to [the Seller] with the serious consequence of increasing the risk of misuse by [the Buyer]. On the other hand, it has to be considered that [the Buyer] itself failed to take any care with regards to the handling of the clay which was made use of in animal feed although the danger of a dioxin contamination and the risks involved could not have remained unknown to [the Buyer]. Hence, both parties committed similarly serious breaches of duty, independently contributing to the damage, which justifies an equal split of damages.'[92]

The third criterion is based on allocating losses according to each party's fault and, in some legal systems, this criterion is used precisely because of the difficulty of allocating losses on the basis of causal criteria.[93] There are doubts as to whether it is appropriate to use this criterion under the instruments since they

[89] See ch 6.

[90] Comment 3 on art 7.4.7 UPICC.

[91] Supreme Court (Germany) 26 September 2012 (n 75).

[92] Ibid, [36].

[93] See OS Ioffe, *Law of Obligations (Obyazatelstvennoye pravo)* (Leningrad 1975) 140; AP Sergeyev and YK Tolstoy (eds), *Civil Law (Grazhdanskoye Pravo)* (Moscow, Part 1 Prospect Publishing House, 1998) 577.

are generally based on 'strict liability'. If fault is not a precondition for liability in damages, it should not be relevant to determining each party's contribution to the loss. However, one element which characterises the notion of fault may have a role to play. The gravity of breach, as suggested, is likely to be an important criterion of apportioning losses and it is this element which is closely interlinked with the notion of fault.[94] The fourth criterion is based on the notions of justice and equity. While it may have its appeal, it is not conducive to legal certainty and consistency in the application of the international instruments. The fifth criterion is even broader than the previous one because it does not enunciate any value to be protected and simply leaves the matter to the court's or tribunal's discretion.

Interplay between some of these criteria is illustrated by one CISG case[95] where the buyer suffered loss as a result of a breakdown of the machinery delivered by the seller. The contract contained a procedure for determining causes of a breakdown by requiring that first, a bilateral commission between the parties be established to come to an agreement on this matter and if no agreement was reached, each party ought to conduct its own examination of what caused the breakdown. Neither the commission nor the parties themselves managed to identify whether it was the seller's breach or the buyer's failure to follow the instructions that was responsible for the loss. The tribunal stated that:

> due to the fact that the parties [had] failed to determine the cause of the breakdown of the equipment, both of them [had to] suffer a financial burden resulting from that. The greater share of the liability [was] imposed on the Seller since it, as the supplier, had to take into account the specificity of the equipment and should have been more punctilious and demanding in following the provisions stipulated in the contract, in determining the cause of the breakdown of the equipment and in preventing further violations.[96]

Relying on the principles of 'justice and fairness', the tribunal held the seller liable for three-quarters of the loss. The decision is clearly based on the tribunal's perception of what was just and fair in the circumstances and that, in turn, was intertwined with the considerations running along the lines of each party's *fault*. One quarter of the loss was ultimately borne by the buyer because, like the seller, it was not entirely diligent in following the contractual procedure of establishing the cause of the breakdown.[97]

[94] It has been said that '[c]ivil law systems ... distinguish between ordinary (or 'slight') and 'gross' negligence' (Treitel (n 55) 11) and this distinction shows that the two types of fault in those systems depend, to a certain extent, on the gravity of the party's conduct (see D Tallon in CM Bianca and MJ Bonell (eds), *Commentary on the International Sales Law: The 1980 Vienna Sales Convention* (Giuffrè, Milan, 1987) 598).

[95] ICAC No 189/2003, 29 December 2004, available at cisgw3.law.pace.edu/cases/041229r1.html.

[96] ICAC No 189/2003, 29 December 2004, available at cisgw3.law.pace.edu/cases/041229r1.html.

[97] For a somewhat similar approach that fails to explain the precise causal criteria for apportioning the loss between the parties and how exactly the loss was apportioned, see CIETAC 9 January 2008 (Metallic silicon), available at cisgw3.law.pace.edu/cases/080109c1.html ('the non-performance of

6. CAUSATION AND CALCULATION

The role and prominence of the causation requirement in a particular legal system are dependent on whether that legal system prefers the 'concrete' or 'abstract' approach to calculating damages. The former calculates loss with reference to the claimant's *actual* circumstances while the latter calculates damages 'in the abstract' with reference to some fixed formula which usually presumes that an innocent party has acted in a way deemed reasonable. A typical example is the formula, used in the case of non-delivery or non-acceptance, based on the difference between the contract price and the current price at a particular time. This formula does not look at the injured party's *actual* conduct and loss and instead *presumes* that it is possible for this party to make a cover transaction at the current price and that its loss amounts to the difference between the contract price and the current price.[98] In its pure form, the 'abstract' approach to calculation disregards events subsequent to the time fixed in an 'abstract' formula.[99] If the innocent seller, wishing to speculate, waits beyond a reasonable time and only then resells the goods at a price higher than both the contract and the current price, it will, under the 'abstract' approach, be awarded damages for the difference between the contract price and the current price, despite not suffering any actual loss (in fact, by making such a resale, the seller is better off than it would have been had the buyer performed).[100] Thus, benefits made after the time specified in the applicable 'abstract' formula are ignored in calculating damages.[101]

the third installment of goods ... resulted in the termination of the performance of this installment. Both parties should be held responsible for this non-performance. Therefore, the loss arising out of the termination of this installment should be borne jointly by the parties.'). See also ICAC No 97/2002, 6 June 2003, available at cisgw3.law.pace.edu/cases/030606r1.html, where the seller was held liable for two-thirds of the loss, suffered by the buyer due to non-conforming and 'highly sensitive' goods, because the tribunal took the position that: (a) the parties ought to have drafted the contractual provisions on quality specifications, quality control and methods of inspection more robustly; and (b) there were flaws in the way the parties performed the contract, especially in relation to quality control and inspection methods. It is submitted that extending the causation requirement to the pre-contractual stage is unjustifiable and allocates risks in a way that is too unfavourable to the innocent party (see further ch 6, where this case is criticised in the context of the mitigation rule) and therefore the tribunal's reasoning in (a) should not followed). The parties' failure to specify quality specifications sufficiently robustly was relevant to whether there was a lack of conformity in the goods but not to the allocation of damages for breach. Finally, the decision fails to explain the extent to which each of the aspects in (a) and (b) contributed to the buyer's loss.

[98] For a more detailed discussion, see ch 8.

[99] That is, generally the time of avoidance in the case of the international instruments (the CISG also provides that where the contract is avoided after taking over the goods, the current price shall be determined with reference to the time of such taking over (art 76(1) second sentence)) and the time of breach in some common law systems.

[100] See, eg, *AKAS Jamal v Moolla Dawood, Sons & Co* [1916] 1 AC 175; *Campbell Mostyn (Provisions), Ltd v Barnett Trading Company* [1954] 1 Lloyd's Rep 65.

[101] For a similar view, see MG Bridge, 'The Market Rule of Damages Assessment' in D Saidov and R Cunnington (eds), *Contract Damages: Domestic and International Perspectives* (Oxford, Hart Publishing, 2008) 433 ('In its purest, abstract application, the market damages rule pays no regard to the question of factual causation in the award of damages').

If the 'concrete' approach is taken, it can be argued that the seller was only able to gain benefit by reselling the goods *because* the buyer had not performed the contract. It is a corollary of the compensatory principle that any benefits the innocent party obtains *as a result* of the breach must offset losses and the 'concrete' approach requires the seller's resale to be taken into account in calculating damages. The advocates of the 'abstract' approach would, no doubt, object to such a description of the causal relationship between the breach and the seller's benefits by arguing that the benefits were received not as a result of the breach but as a result of the seller's own speculation and risk, which must break the chain of causation between the breach and the benefits. This position is based on the policy of encouraging market speculation by maintaining symmetry: the injured party is to bear fruits of the benefits and risks of losses occurring after the time specified in a particular 'abstract' formula. No such symmetry is likely to be possible under the 'concrete' approach because while the benefits will be taken to offset losses, losses suffered as a result of, for example, the seller reselling after a reasonable period of time (such as storage costs or losses suffered as a result of reselling at a price lower than it would have been had it sold within a reasonable time) will most probably be denied on the ground of the seller's failure to mitigate. This can also be put in terms of causation: by waiting beyond a reasonable time, the seller broke the chain of causation between the buyer's breach and its loss.[102]

The international instruments generally prefer the 'concrete' approach to calculating damages, although they do provide for the 'abstract' approach in certain cases.[103] It follows that those benefits which would not have been received but for the breach must generally be taken to offset losses, even if benefits resulted from the party's speculation on the market.[104]

7. INJURED PARTY'S CONTRIBUTION TO THE OTHER PARTY'S FAILURE TO PERFORM

The injured party's acts or omissions may contribute to the other party's *failure to perform*. All three instruments contain a specific provision designed to deal with this situation. The CISG provides that '[a] party may not rely on a failure of the other party to perform, to the extent that such failure was caused by the first party's act or omission'[105] and similar rules can be found in the UPICC and PECL.[106] This position is usually justified on the basis that

[102] See also ch 6.

[103] For a detailed discussion, see ch 8.

[104] For the discussion of cases where the injured buyer procures goods superior to contract goods, see ch 6.

[105] Art 80 CISG.

[106] Art 7.1.2 UPICC: 'A party may not rely on the non-performance of the other party to the extent that such non-performance was caused by the first party's act or omission or by another event for which the first party bears the risk'. Article 8:101(3) PECL: 'A party may not resort to any

it would be contrary to fairness and good faith to hold the breaching party fully responsible for the actions to which the injured party has contributed.[107] The consequence of this provision is that a party's failure to perform is not regarded as a breach (non-performance) to the extent that it has been caused by the injured party.[108]

The problems of apportionment in this context are very similar to those of apportioning losses where the injured party has contributed to the loss. The only difference is that in the latter situation the injured party contributes to the *loss* whereas in the former it contributes to the defaulting party's *failure to perform*. For this reason, the considerations set out above in relation to cases where the injured party contributes to its own loss are relevant here. This section focuses on two lines of cases that have emerged in the context of the CISG.

The first line of cases concerns the situation where the actions of one party *complicate* the other party's position but do not prevent that party from performing the contract. These are cases where a party has to exercise its judgement and make a choice as to what course to take. Suppose the buyer had given incorrect instructions to the manufacturer and the manufacturer produced non-conforming equipment. Suppose further that the manufacturer was in the position to discover the incorrectness of the instructions and ask the buyer to issue the proper ones. Should the buyer be regarded as *having caused* the manufacturer's failure to produce conforming equipment? The answer depends on whether the manufacturer's conduct was reasonable. If it is reasonable to expect a reasonable person in the manufacturer's position to check the instructions,[109] the buyer should not be regarded as having caused the manufacturer's breach. However, as demonstrated by the CISG cases, the surrounding legal framework and, specifically, rights, obligations of and remedies available to the parties can also be relevant.

In one case,[110] as a result of the buyer's failure to pay for several deliveries, the seller, claiming the payment of outstanding sums, refrained from making

of the remedies set out in Chapter 9 to the extent that its own act caused the other party's non-performance'. Article 9:504 PECL: 'The non-performing party is not liable for loss suffered by the aggrieved party to the extent that the aggrieved party contributed to the non-performance ...'

[107] Lando and Beale (n 42) 359; Comment 1 on art 1.7 UPICC. See also Case No 1 U 280/96 Appellate Court Karlsruhe (Germany) 25 June 1997 (Surface protective film), available at cisgw3.law.pace.edu/cases/970625g1.html; Case No 7 U 1720/94 Appellate Court München (Germany) 8 February 1995 (Automobiles), available at cisgw3.law.pace.edu/cases/950208g1.html.

[108] See Comment 1 on art 7.1.2 UPICC ('[w]hen the article applies, the relevant conduct ... loses the quality of non-performance altogether').

[109] Some of the relevant factors include the parties' expertise, their previous dealings, negotiations and practices and relevant trade usages (see arts 8 and 9 CISG).

[110] Case No 10 O 5423/01 District Court München (Germany) 20 February 2002 (Shoes), available at cisgw3.law.pace.edu/cases/020220g1.html; the decision was affirmed in Case No 10 O 5423/01 Appellate Court München (Germany) 1 July 2002 (Shoes), available at cisgw3.law.pace.edu/cases/020701g1.html.

further deliveries. In principle, the seller was willing and able to deliver. The buyer claimed damages for non-delivery but the court held that the buyer could not rely on the seller's failure to deliver because the buyer itself had caused the seller's failure to perform. In another case,[111] it was held that the seller could not rely on the buyer's failure to open a letter of credit because the seller had failed to perform its obligation to nominate the port of loading. Although it was established that the letter of credit *could* be opened without a port of loading being nominated, the court interpreted the contract as if nominating the port of loading was a condition for the buyer's obligation to open a letter of credit and ruled, based on art 80 CISG, that it was the seller's breach that had caused the buyer's failure to open a letter of credit:

> It is irrelevant whether the opening of a letter of credit would have been possible even without information about the place of loading, because the parties expressly agreed upon the naming of the place of loading by the sellers. Due to this agreement, the sellers had the primary duty to name the place of loading. Only after this act on the part of the sellers did the buyer have the obligation to issue the letter of credit. The non-issuance of the letter of credit, therefore, was caused by an omission of the sellers, and – following Art 80 CISG – the latter cannot rely on the buyer's failure to open the letter of credit.[112]

There are doubts as to whether, in the first case, the buyer's failure to pay could be regarded as the cause of the seller's failure to deliver the goods in the sense of art 80 CISG. The CISG protects the parties like the seller in that case by making available a number of remedies. The seller could, for instance, claim specific performance or, if relevant, avoid the contract (if the breach were fundamental) and claim damages; if the buyer's failure to pay for the previous delivery gave sufficient grounds to conclude that an anticipatory breach would occur, it could suspend performance and/or avoid the contract. But because the seller still had an existing legal obligation, it could not, unless a general right to withhold performance is recognised, simply stop its own performance just because the other party failed to perform and argue that the buyer's failure to perform caused its own non-performance.[113] So far as the express provisions of the CISG are concerned, a breach by one party does not automatically justify

[111] Case No 10 Ob 518/95 Supreme Court (Austria) 6 February 1996 (Propane), available at cisgw3.law.pace.edu/cases/960206a3.html.

[112] Ibid.

[113] For an argument in favour of a general right to withhold performance under the CISG, see, eg, P Schlechtriem, 'Intepretation, Gap-Filling and Further Development of the UN Sales Convention', available at www.cisg.law.pace.edu/cisg/biblio/schlechtriem6.html; P Schlechtriem, 'Subsequent Performance and Delivery Deadlines – Avoidance of CISG Sales Contracts Due to Non-conformity of the Goods' (2006) 18 *Pace Int'l L Rev* 83, 90-93; CISG Advisory Council (CISG-AC) Opinion No. 5, 'The Buyer's Right to Avoid the Contract in Case of Non-Conforming Goods or Documents', available at www.cisg.law.pace.edu/cisg/CISG-AC-op5.html.

the suspension of performance by the other party unless such suspension falls within the scope of art 71[114] or art 58.[115]

The second case also demonstrates that the parties' rights and obligations under the contract and the Convention are relevant to determining whether the seller's omission was the cause of the buyer's failure to perform. If the decision is correct in interpreting the contract as making the seller's nomination of the port of loading a condition for the buyer's obligation to open a letter of credit, it demonstrates that the causal relationship under art 80 CISG can depend on the contractual preconditions for the performance of an obligation. Indeed, if it were the term (express or implied) of the contract that the buyer's obligation to open the letter of credit could *only* be performed after the port had been nominated, the seller's failure to nominate can be said to cause the buyer's failure to open the letter of credit. However, while the decision makes clear that the buyer *could* open the letter of credit without a port being nominated, it is not as clear as to whether the nomination was indeed a contractual *precondition* for the buyer's obligation to open the letter of credit. Considering that the court of lower instance relied on the Convention's provisions on anticipatory breach (the right to suspend performance) to justify the buyer's failure to open the letter of credit, it seems that the court of the final instance, by treating the seller's obligation as 'primary', was similarly looking for a way to justify the buyer's non-performance. If this were the case, this approach might not be entirely satisfactory. It creates uncertainty and encourages passivity by signaling that it may be possible for one party to simply stop its performance as soon as the other party fails to perform. As argued, the Convention provides for a number of remedies and the suspension of performance is expressly authorised only in specified cases.[116] Legal protection is further ensured by other remedies, such as specific performance,[117] setting an additional period of time,[118] avoidance[119]

[114] (1) A party may suspend the performance of his obligations if, after the conclusion of the contract, it becomes apparent that the other party will not perform a substantial part of his obligations as a result of: (a) a serious deficiency in his ability to perform or in his creditworthiness; (b) his conduct in preparing to perform or in performing the contract. [...] (3) A party suspending performance, whether before or after dispatch of the goods, must immediately give notice of the suspension to the other party and must continue with performance if the other party provides adequate assurance of his performance (Art 71 CISG).

[115] 'The seller may make such payment a condition for handing over the goods or documents' (Art 58(1) CISG, second sentence). Although the court in this case relied on Art 58, there are doubts as to its applicability to the case since it seems that the seller refused to deliver the goods because of the buyer's failure to pay for *past* deliveries under *different* contracts (see also D Maskow in Bianca and Bonell (n 94) 423 ('Where successive deliveries are agreed upon, every delivery has to be treated as a separate one ... [T]he seller may not generally withhold delivery because a former delivery has not yet been paid')). See also art 85 CISG.

[116] See art 71 CISG. See also art 58 CISG and n 113 with the accompanying main text.

[117] See arts 46 and 62 CISG.

[118] See arts 47 and 63 CISG.

[119] See arts 49 and 64 CISG.

and damages.[120] It is clear that it is invoking those remedies (whichever is relevant), and not a mere stoppage of its own performance, that is a proper course for the injured party to take. Ceasing to perform its own contract without a legally justifiable reason may put the innocent party in the position where it would commit a breach of contract itself. For these reasons, it is argued that unless there was clear evidence of the parties' intention to treat the seller's obligation as a contractual precondition for the performance of the buyer's obligation, the court chose an unhelpful legal route to protect the buyer.[121]

Another line of CISG cases raises the question whether the fact that the buyer prevented the seller from curing a lack of conformity in the goods could be regarded as causing the seller's delivery of non-conforming goods. In one case,[122] after delivering non-conforming goods the seller offered to deliver new goods in accordance with art 48 CISG. The buyer rejected the offer and the court held that the buyer could not rely on the seller's breach because it 'had hindered the seller's cure of non-conformity'.[123] In another case,[124] although the court did not regard the buyer as having prevented the exercise of the seller's right to cure, the court recognised that it would have been possible for the seller to rely on art 80 if the buyer had thwarted the seller's right to cure.[125] It is suggested that it is correct to interpret art 80 CISG in this way. While the very fact of an offer to cure usually indicates that a breach has already been committed, the seller nevertheless has a *legal right* to cure which, if successfully exercised, will lead to the cessation of the breach. If the buyer prevents the seller from curing a lack of conformity, the seller is prevented from providing proper performance. This broad interpretation of art 80 is in line with its underlying ideas of fairness and good faith: if the seller is legally entitled to

[120] See arts 45, 61 and 74–77 CISG.

[121] A different approach was taken in another CISG case, where the buyer argued that its failure to open a letter of credit was caused by the parties' dispute over the contract price brought about by the seller's attempt to change it. The arbitrator correctly rejected that argument by stating that '[the Buyer] must prove that [the Seller]'s behaviour made the opening of the required letter of credit impossible or almost impossible. The Arbitrator does not find in the file any such evidence. On the contrary, as it has been said, the parties' disagreement on the Fall/Winter season price list did not prevent [the Buyer] from opening a letter of credit on the basis of the first price list. Given that [the Buyer] does not bring evidence that its failure to open the letter of credit was at that time due to an impediment caused by [the Seller], its submission based upon Art. 80 of the CISG shall be rejected' (ICC No 11849, 2003 (Fashion products), available at cisgw3.law.pace.edu/cases/031849i1.html).

[122] See Case No 2 U 31/96 Appellate Court Koblenz (Germany) 31 January 1997 (Acrylic blankets), available at cisgw3.law.pace.edu/cases/970131g1.html.

[123] Ibid.

[124] Case No 271 C 18968/94 Lower Court München (Germany) 23 June 1995 (Tetracycline), available at cisgw3.law.pace.edu/cases/950623g1.html.

[125] 'The buyer's claim for damages is also not excluded by Art 80 CISG, because buyer did not thwart the seller's possibility to remedy the lack of conformity within reasonable time' (ibid).

eliminate the breach and ensure proper performance, it seems unfair to disallow the seller to rely on art 80 if the buyer prevented its right to cure. What needs to be proven is that the requirements of art 48 CISG[126] were met and that the seller would have provided proper performance had the buyer not prevented the exercise of its right to cure.[127]

[126] Article 48(1) CISG: 'Subject to article 49, the seller may, even after the date for delivery, remedy at his own expense any failure to perform his obligations, if he can do so without unreasonable delay and without causing the buyer unreasonable inconvenience or uncertainty of reimbursement by the seller of expenses advanced by the buyer. However, the buyer retains any right to claim damages as provided for in this Convention.'

[127] See also ICAC No 97/2002, 6 June 2003 (n 97) that potentially raises the question whether the buyer's failure to contribute to effective contract drafting in respect of quality specifications and quality control can qualify as the buyer's contribution to the seller's breach. It is submitted that the answer should be 'no' because this issue is only relevant to determining whether there is a lack of conformity in the goods. See further n 97 and ch 6.

5

Foreseeability

1. GENERAL

THE 'FORESEEABILITY' TEST is widely used as a method of limiting damages[1] and it is its popularity amongst legal systems and its perceived suitability to the needs of international commerce which encouraged drafters to introduce the test into the international instruments.[2] According to the CISG, damages 'may not exceed the loss which the party in breach foresaw or ought to have foreseen at the time of the conclusion of the contract, in the light of the facts and matters of which he then knew or ought to have known, as a possible consequence of the breach of contract'.[3] The UPICC also provide that '[t]he non-performing party is liable only for harm which it foresaw or could reasonably have foreseen at the time of the conclusion of the contract as being likely to result from its non-performance'.[4] The PECL contain the following provision: '[t]he non-performing party is liable only for loss which it foresaw or could reasonably have foreseen at the time of conclusion of the contract as a likely result of its non-performance, unless the non-performance was intentional or grossly negligent'.[5] There seems to be an agreement, at least insofar as the CISG is concerned, that it is the injured party who bears the burden of proving foreseeability.[6]

The foreseeability test can be justified on various grounds. First, it is said to rest upon the notion that in determining the desirability of an act, regard is to be

[1] For a CISG case where the foreseeability test is characterised in this way, as opposed to its being a precondition for the breaching party's liability, see Case V No CSK 91/11 Supreme Court (Poland) 8 February 2012, available at cisgw3.law.pace.edu/cases/120208p1.html.

[2] See A Komarov, 'The Limitation of Contract Damages in Domestic Legal Systems and International Instruments' in D Saidov and R Cunnington (eds), *Contract Damages: Domestic and International Perspectives* (Oxford, Hart Publishing, 2008) 250–52.

[3] Article 74 CISG.

[4] Article 7.4.4 UPICC.

[5] Article 9:503 PECL.

[6] See, eg, Case No 3 U 83/98 Appellate Court Bamberg (Germany) 13 January 1999 (Fabric case), available at cisgw3.law.pace.edu/cases/990113g1.html; Case No 7 International Commercial Arbitration Court (ICAC), the Ukrainian Chamber of Commerce, 7 February 2007, available at arb.ucci.org.ua/icac/cases/2006-2010/caseNo7.pdf (in Russian). I Schwenzer, 'Arts. 74–77' in I Schwenzer (ed), *Schlechtriem and Schwenzer Commentary on the UN Convention on the International Sale of Goods (CISG)*, 4th edn (Oxford, OUP, 2016) 1085 (with further references); M Djordjević, 'Arts. 74–77' in S Kröll, L Mistelis and P Viscasillas (eds), *The United Nations Convention on Contracts for the International Sale of Goods*, 2nd edn (München, C.H. Beck and Oxford, Hart, 2018) 970.

had to its foreseeable consequences.[7] This notion is arguably a part of a broader idea that '[t]he commonest person lives according to maxims of prudence wholly founded on foresight of consequences'.[8] The proponents of this view argue that since even outside law people often judge a person's action from the standpoint of whether he/she foresaw the consequences of his/her action, it is natural and fair[9] that the extent of legal liability should also depend on foreseeability by the party of the consequences of his/her actions.[10] The most widely accepted justification of the rule,[11] however, rests on its function of allocating risk in a fair[12] and reasonable[13] manner. The underlying aim is to make it possible for the parties to calculate the risks and their potential liability.[14] If, at the time of the conclusion of the contract, the party foresaw or ought to have foreseen a particular loss, it could have taken it into account and acted accordingly by excluding or reducing its potential liability, procuring insurance, increasing the amount of benefit to be obtained from the contract or even refusing to enter into the contract. This risk allocation function has been viewed as an indication that the foreseeability test is related to the very nature and purpose of the contract[15] and that the breaching party can be liable only to the extent that its liability is within the scope of the contract.[16] Finally, viewed from the perspective of the consequences and incentives to which it gives rise, the foreseeability rule has been justified on the grounds that it encourages commercial activity[17] and promotes economic efficiency. The rule not only enables the parties to manage possible

[7] PS Atiyah, *The Rise and Fall of Freedom of Contract* (Oxford, Clarendon Press, 1979) 432.

[8] JS Mill, 'Sedgwick's Discourse' in JM Robson (ed), *The Collected Works of John Stuart Mill, Volume X, Essays on Ethics, Religion and Society* (London, University of Toronto Press, Routledge and Kegan Paul Ltd, 1969) 63.

[9] 'The principle that does not allow a debtor … to be made liable for the damages resulting from the inexecution of his obligation, above the sum to which he may reasonably have imagined they would amount, being grounded on natural law and equity, we ought to follow' (RJ Pothier, *A Treatise on Obligations, Considered in a Moral and Legal View* (Clark, NJ, The Lawbook Exchange Ltd, 1999) 99–100).

[10] See HLA Hart and T Honore, *Causation in the Law*, 2nd edn (Oxford, Clarendon Press, 1985) 254 stating that '[i]t is not surprising to find that lawyers often stress the importance of foreseeability in relation to problems of responsibility, for even outside law the fact that harm was or was not foreseeable is frequently an important factor in blaming or excusing people for its occurrence'.

[11] There are numerous sources in which this rationale is relied upon (see, eg, P Schlechtriem, *Uniform Sales Law: The UN-Convention on Contracts for the International Sale of Goods* (Vienna, Manz Verlag, 1986) 96).

[12] See Hart and Honore (n 10) 230, stating that foreseeability is a rule which promotes 'a fair balance between the contracting parties'.

[13] See EA Farnsworth, 'Legal Remedies for Breach of Contract' (1970) 70 *Columbia L Rev* 1208.

[14] See, eg, Pothier (n 9) 94; Farnsworth (n 13) 1207; H Bernstein and J Lookofsky, *Understanding the CISG in Europe*, 2nd edn (The Hague, Kluwer Law International, 2003) 140, note 163.

[15] See J Hellner, 'The Limits of Contractual Damages in the Scandinavian Law of Sales' (1966) 10 *Scandinavian L S* 48–9; Comment on art 7.4.4 UPICC.

[16] See A Kramer, 'An Agreement-Centred Approach to Remoteness and Contract Damages' in N Cohen and E McKendrick (eds), *Comparative Remedies for Breach of Contract* (Oxford, Hart Publishing, 2005) 249.

[17] See EW Patterson, 'The Apportionment of Business Risks through Legal Devices' (1924) 24 *Columbia L Rev* 335, 342.

risks, associated with making and performing contracts,[18] but also reduces such risks by protecting the parties from unusual and excessive losses.[19] Its ability to promote economic efficiency can be summarised thus:

> It saves transaction costs in that it represents the usual agreement that most parties would make if they negotiated on the question. It saves the plaintiff the cost of explaining the obvious consequences of breach, of which the defendant knows just as much. It creates an incentive upon the plaintiff to reveal facts peculiarly within the plaintiff's knowledge that will cause the cost of breach to be greater than the defendant would have expected. The defendant, knowing of these peculiar facts, can act accordingly by making a rational allocation of resources to reduce the probability of breach, by refusing to contract, by raising the price, or by excluding liability.[20]

2. THE FORESEEABILITY TEST

2.1. General

In contrast with the common law systems which require that loss be contemplated by both parties,[21] the instruments make clear that it is foreseeability of the breaching party that is relevant.[22] Although this difference is probably of minor practical significance, the instruments' approach is preferable to that of the common law. First, it is more consistent with the 'risk allocation' rationale on the foreseeability rule,[23] based on the assumption of risk by the breaching party.[24] Second, foreseeability of loss is only relevant to the breaching party because 'the plaintiff nearly always knows his own business and circumstances better than the defendant'.[25]

[18] See Komarov (n 2).

[19] See MG Bridge, *The Sale of Goods*, 4th edn (Oxford, OUP, 2019) [12.20] (referring to the view that regards the foreseeability rule 'as consonant with the wishes of the business community that a contracting party should not be the insurer of the other's contractual adventure').

[20] S Waddams, *The Law of Damages*, 4th edn (Toronto, Canada Law Book Inc, 2004) 569 (see this source for references to the relevant law and economics literature).

[21] See *Hadley v Baxendale* (1854) 9 Ex 341, 354.

[22] See art 74 CISG, art 7.4.4 UPICC and art 9:503 PECL.

[23] English law, arguably, went as far as transferring this rationale of the foreseeability rule into a rule in itself. See *Transfield Shipping Inc v Mercator Shipping Inc (The Achilleas)* [2008] UKHL 48 (see, eg, Lord Hope, [30]–[31]: 'The critical question … is whether the parties must be assumed to have contracted with each other on the basis that the [breaching party was] assuming responsibility for the consequences of that event … Assumption of responsibility, which forms the basis of the law of remoteness of damage in contract, is determined by more than what at the time of the contract was reasonably foreseeable.').

[24] See AG Murphey, Jr, 'Consequential Damages in Contracts for the International Sale of Goods and the Legacy of *Hadley*' (1989) 23 *Geo Wash J Int'l L and Economics* 415 (also at www.cisg.law.pace.edu/cisg/biblio/murphey.html).

[25] AL Corbin, *Corbin on Contracts: A Comprehensive Treatise on the Working Rules of Contract Law* vol 5 (St Paul, Minn, West Publishing Co, 2002) 29.

The instruments' foreseeability test is both subjective and objective. The party may be held liable not only for losses which it actually foresaw but also for losses which it 'ought to have foreseen'[26] or 'could reasonably have foreseen'.[27] To make the party liable, it is not necessary to prove that this party *actually* foresaw the loss as long as it was in the position to *reasonably foresee* that loss.[28] There is, at first sight, a difference in the way the instruments formulate the objective standard. The CISG uses the words 'ought to have been foreseen' and they may seem to impose a stricter requirement than that implied by the words 'could reasonably have foreseen' used by the UPICC and the PECL. It is unlikely, however, that this insignificant variation in wording should lead to the Convention being interpreted more restrictively than the UPICC and PECL and this suggestion finds support in the Comments on the two sets of Principles. The Comments on the UPICC state that art 7.4.4 corresponds to art 74 CISG[29] and the Comments on the PECL expressly use the wording used in the CISG.[30]

The question arises whether it is the breaching party itself or a reasonable person in the same circumstances who 'ought to have foreseen' or 'could reasonably have foreseen' the loss. This question may be relevant where some characteristics of the breaching party are different from those attributable to a 'reasonable person'. While in some legal systems it is stressed that it is foreseeability by a *reasonable person* and not of a *party in breach* which is relevant,[31] the wording of art 74 CISG suggests that it is the breaching party itself who ought to have foreseen the loss – 'the loss which the *party in breach* ... ought to have foreseen'.[32] The same can be said about the UPICC and the PECL which

[26] Article 74 CISG. See *Castel Electronics Pty Ltd v Toshiba Singapore Pte Ltd* [2011] FCAFC 55, [318] ('[the breaching seller's] argument is misconceived insofar as it proceeds on the assumption that what "ought to have been foreseen by" [the seller] could only be proved by evidence from [the seller's] employees. When Art 74 speaks of consequences which "ought to have been foreseen" it is speaking of consequences which were, objectively speaking, foreseeable by the breaching party.').

[27] Article 7.4.4 UPICC and art 9:503 PECL.

[28] See, eg, V Knapp, 'Arts 74–77 CISG' in CM Bianca and MJ Bonell (eds), *Commentary on the International Sales Law: The 1980 Vienna Sales Convention* (Milan, Giuffrè, 1987) 541.

[29] See Comment on art 7.4.4 UPICC.

[30] See Comment A on art 9:503 in O Lando and H Beale (eds), *Principles of European Contract Law: Parts I and II* prepared by the Commission on European Contract Law (The Hague, Kluwer Law International, 2000).

[31] 'The debtor cannot escape liability by showing that he personally could foresee less than the reasonable man. This is in fact clear on the face of article 1150, which speaks of damage "which *one* could have foreseen" – not which *he* could have foreseen. The question to be asked is what a reasonable man in the "external circumstances" of the debtor (as opposed to his "internal circumstances", such as intelligence, caution) could have foreseen' (B Nicholas, *The French Law of Contract*, 2nd edn (Oxford, Clarendon Press, 1992) 231).

[32] This provision can be contrasted with the definition of fundamental breach in art 25 CISG, which also uses the foreseeability test. According to art 25, '[b]reach of contract committed by one of the parties is fundamental if it results in such detriment to the other party as substantially to deprive him of what he is entitled to expect under the contract, unless the party in breach did not foresee and *a reasonable person of the same kind in the same circumstances would not have foreseen such a result*'. It can be argued that had the drafters intended to apply the same standard of foreseeability in relation to damages they would have similarly formulated art 74.

state that it is the non-performing party who 'could have reasonably foreseen' the loss.[33] The word 'reasonably' in this context refers to reasonable foreseeability of the *breaching party* and not of a 'reasonable person'.

2.2. Relevant Factors

2.2.1. Knowledge

There are a number of factors to be taken into account when applying the foreseeability test. The first important factor in assessing the breaching party's foreseeability is this party's knowledge. So far as the subjective standard of foreseeability is concerned, a person can only foresee a certain result if it has knowledge of relevant facts and matters enabling it to foresee that result. When it comes to the objective standard of foreseeability, no foreseeability can be implied into a person without considering what knowledge that person had or ought to have had (or could reasonably have had). Knowledge (both actual and implied) is thus an integral part of the foreseeability test, which is expressly recognised in the CISG that refers to foreseeability 'in light of the facts and matters of which [the party] … knew or ought to have known'.[34] Because foreseeability can be both subjective and objective, knowledge can also be of two types: actual and implied.

Actual knowledge of relevant facts is particularly important where the loss is of an unusual kind or of an unusually high extent because if there is nothing extraordinary about its type or extent, the relevant knowledge and foreseeability will, in any event, be implied. Therefore, if a party knows that a breach by the other party is likely to give rise to unusual losses it needs to notify the other party of the likelihood of such losses occurring before or at the time of the conclusion of the contract. Consider the case where the buyer knows that a delay in delivery will cause it to process the goods in a country other than that originally intended and that such a change in location will cause the buyer extra expense. If there is no particular reason why the seller would be expected to know of this consequence,[35] this loss would not be foreseeable to the seller.[36] But actual and implied knowledge have their respective roles to play. The extent of the buyer's lost profits and liability to its sub-buyers may be held foreseeable

[33] Article 7.4.4 UPICC and art 9:503 PECL. In contrast with art 25 CISG, the same standard of foreseeability is used in the definition of fundamental non-performance in art 7.3.1(2) UPICC and art 8:103 PECL.

[34] Article 74 CISG.

[35] This knowledge can be implied to the seller from, for example: the buyer's informing the seller of this potential consequence before or at the time of making the contract; the parties' previous dealings; common knowledge about such a practice of processing the goods; or a relevant trade usage.

[36] Appellate Court Bamberg 13 January 1999 (n 6).

because of the supplier's *actual* knowledge that the buyer is a trader and *implied* knowledge, in the light of the supplier's own business experience, of the usual profit margins received from the sale of the goods in question. In other words, actual knowledge can trigger a further presumption about what the seller is *expected* to know.[37]

The possibility of implying knowledge and foreseeability has led some judges and commentators to argue, no doubt in the interests of uniformity,[38] that certain types of knowledge can generally be implied and certain types of losses can generally be deemed foreseeable. For example, one court stated that where commercial goods were sold to a merchant, a resale 'can always be assumed without any further indications'.[39] Changes in market conditions have also been regarded as part of the knowledge which can generally be implied.[40] The breaching party should be expected to know that the injured party is likely to incur expenses to try to place itself in the position in which it would have been had the contract been properly performed.[41] The following types of loss have also been said to be generally foreseeable: liability to customers or costs of taking the goods back where the goods are sold to a commercial buyer;[42] compensation for missed uses of the goods to be delivered; additional costs for transportation, storage and insurance; the loss of clients resulting from a lack of conformity in the goods.[43]

This approach, it is submitted, is unhelpful. Although the instruments' foreseeability rule allows that the extent of the breaching party's liability be determined by knowledge and foreseeability this party is *presumed* to have had, this does not mean that the rule should be entirely 'de-personalised'. The goals of certainty and uniformity must be balanced against the rationale of the foreseeability rule. As shown, the rule seeks to allocate the risk in a fair and reasonable manner and given the multiplicity of circumstances in which the breaching parties may find themselves, it is unfair to presume that the losses referred to above are necessarily foreseeable. Such a sweeping presumption would negate the very purpose of the foreseeability rule by disregarding a breaching party's

[37] For other examples, see Arbitration Case No 48, 2005 (Ukraine), available at cisgw3.law.pace.edu/cases/050000u5.html ('The Seller *knew* from the very beginning that goods were purchased by the Buyer for further processing and sale of the derived products. Therefore, the Seller *had to realize* that stoppage of supply will cause certain losses for the Buyer' (emphasis added)).

[38] See Schlechtriem (n 11) (stating that '[j]udicial discretion in the assessment of damages can be reduced by standardizing the damages in question …').

[39] Case No 10 Ob 518/95 Supreme Court (Austria) 6 February 1996 (Propane), available at cisgw3.law.pace.edu/cases/960206a3.html.

[40] Case No 2 U 30/77 Appellate Court Hamm (Germany) 23 March 1978 (Brass poles), available at cisgw3.law.pace.edu/cases/780323g1.html (decided on the basis of the ULIS).

[41] See Schwenzer (n 6) 1080.

[42] Ibid, 570.

[43] See F Enderlein and D Maskow, *International Sales Law: United Nations Convention on Contracts for the International Sale of Goods, Convention on the Limitation Period in the International Sale of Goods* (New York, Oceana, 1992) 301.

circumstances. A more balanced approach is to rely on implied knowledge and foreseeability only where they can be reasonably inferred from the particular circumstances. This does not mean that we should refrain from identifying factors and patterns which may lead judges and arbitrators to imply certain types of knowledge. Without being 'set in stone', such factors and patterns can help parties develop reasonable expectations as to how the instruments' foreseeability rule is likely to work in a particular case.

In general, a business person will be presumed to know of the facts and matters which will enable it to foresee the consequences of the breach if such knowledge can be expected of it taking into consideration its commercial experience.[44] Where traders are involved, it is often reasonable to expect the breaching party to know that prices for the goods, particularly in volatile markets, will fluctuate and that the injured party will suffer losses as a result. In one ULIS case,[45] the buyer's refusal to perform put the seller in the position where it had to purchase the goods from the supplier but was unable to find any use for the goods until the time when the price dropped considerably. The court ruled that the seller's loss was foreseeable:

> [The buyer] is a businessperson. Furthermore, the brass material that [the seller] purchased to perform its contract with the buyer is an article which depends on the market. Consequently, considerable fluctuations in price are to be expected. That includes a sudden drop in prices to the depths the seller uses to calculate its losses.[46]

In a CISG case,[47] the delivery of a defective packaging system caused the buyer, amongst other things, to incur additional costs relating to the maintenance of its production facility. The court held that because this loss would be foreseeable 'to any company dealing in implements of manufacture', this loss was foreseeable to the breaching seller as the latter itself was a manufacturer. It may also be the case that the buyer's delay in payment causes the seller to procure credit and, in one case, the cost of doing so was held to have been foreseeable by the buyer.[48]

[44] See Knapp (n 28) 542.

[45] See Appellate Court Hamm, 23 March 1978 (n 40).

[46] See also ICAC No 166/1995, 12 March 1996, available at cisgw3.law.pace.edu/cases/960312r1.html, where the seller's apparently extensive commercial experience was decisive to the tribunal's decision that various types of loss were foreseeable to the seller.

[47] *TeeVee Tunes, Inc v Gerhard Schubert GmbH*, WL 2463537 (SDNY) (No 00 Civ 5189 (RCC)).

[48] See Case No 2 U 1230/91 Appellate Court Koblenz (Germany) 17 September 1993 (Computer chip), available at cisgw3.law.pace.edu/cases/930917g1.html. See also CIETAC 18 April 2003 (Desulfurization reagent), available at cisgw3.law.pace.edu/cases/030418c1.html, where the US buyer's failure to pay caused the Chinese seller the loss of the duty drawback ('duty drawback' seems to refer to a refund of an import duty where the imported goods (or finished products manufactured from them) are subsequently exported from China). The tribunal held that that loss was foreseeable to the buyer because it ought to have known and foreseen 'relevant laws, regulations and policies of the State of the counter party before the international business carried out'. The tribunal reasoned that 'the Buyer, as a businessman in the international trade, [ought to] be prudential [with respect] to its rights and obligations …' and that it was reasonable to expect that it would be aware of Chinese trading policies. While the facts are not set out in sufficient detail to enable drawing the conclusion as to whether the tribunal's decision was correct, its reasoning needs to be treated with caution.

Similarly, in another CISG case,[49] the buyer of mineral water who failed to perform its contractual obligation of providing replacement packaging (bottles, crates and pallets) was treated as having been in the position to foresee that the seller would have to buy replacement packaging to continue with its business operations and to take out a loan for this purpose.[50]

In several cases, besides relying on the breaching party's business experience, courts and tribunals have also relied on some other factors to decide whether it was appropriate to imply knowledge and foreseeability. One such factor was knowledge of the innocent party's business. In one CISG case,[51] the seller knew that the buyer was a car dealer and when its delivery of a non-conforming car made the buyer liable to its customer, the court ordered the seller to compensate the buyer for those damages as they were, in the court's opinion, 'foreseeable'. Where the seller sells a large quantity of the goods and knows that it sells the goods to a wholesaler in a sensitive or highly competitive market, it is likely to be in the position to foresee that the buyer will lose custom, profits and that its reputation and goodwill will be damaged.[52] In some cases, the seller may be held liable for loss of custom and profits even if the breach was trivial so long as the seller knew that the buyer was a trader in a market which is saturated with the type of product delivered by the seller. In a case under the ULIS,[53] the Dutch

The mere fact that a party has entered into a contract with a party from another country is not in itself sufficient to imply knowledge of the intricacies of that country's trading policy and legislation. As argued in the main text, the question of what the breaching party ought to have known and foreseen should be resolved on the basis of the particular circumstances.

[49] Case No T-6/08 Foreign Trade Court, the Serbian Chamber of Commerce (Serbia) 19 October 2009, available at cisgw3.law.pace.edu/cases/091019sb.html.

[50] The seller was awarded damages for the value of replacement packaging and the cost of taking a loan to buy this replacement packaging.

[51] See Case No 22 U 4/96 Appellate Court Köln (Germany) 21 May 1996 (Used car), available at cisgw3.law.pace.edu/cases/960521g1.html.

[52] '[The Sellers] knew that they were delivering to a wholesaler who would resell the meat. The *Atlas*-delivery, furthermore, constituted a large amount, 172 tons, of meat. Therefore, at the time of the conclusion of the contract, [the Sellers] must have been aware that a deficient delivery would cause problems between [the Buyer] and its clients which could not be easily solved by [the Buyer], eg, through a short-time substitute delivery. [The Sellers] also had to take into account that [the Buyer] could lose clients completely in case of a deficient delivery and that it could thereby suffer additional damages' (*EK, L and A v F* Supreme Court (Switzerland) 28 October 1998, available at cisgw3. law. pace.edu/cases/981028s1.html); also *Castel Electronics Pty Ltd v Toshiba Singapore Pte Ltd* (n 26), where the loss of profit margins suffered by the buyer, a distributor, arising from the defects on an 'epidemic' scale in products of a well-known brand (Toshiba), was held foreseeable (see this finding of the first instance judge, accepted by the Federal Court of Australia: 'it was foreseeable at the time of the formation of each of the relevant sales contracts that recurrent failures, recalls and delays in supplying replacements of the 'epidemic' products would have had a repercussive effect in reducing [the buyer's] margins of profit on other "'Toshiba" products.') For cases where loss of custom and damage to reputation and goodwill were not held to be foreseeable in the circumstances (with no sufficient explanation being given), see CIETAC 31 January 2000 (Clothes), available at cisgw3.law. pace.edu/cases/000131c1.html; CIETAC 26 October 1996 (Cotton bath towel), available at cisgw3. law.pace.edu/cases/961026c1.html.

[53] Case No VIII ZR 210/78 Supreme Court (Germany) 24 October 1979 (Cheese), available at cisgw3.law.pace.edu/cases/791024g1.html.

seller who delivered cheese, only 3 per cent of which was found to be defective, was held to be in a position to foresee loss of custom and profits because 'at the time of contract formation both seller and buyer knew that the cheese market in Germany was saturated with Dutch imports so that the threat existed that purchasers such as buyer's customers might change suppliers even for trivially unsatisfactory deliveries other than the defects complained of by buyer'.[54] In a similar vein, where the seller is aware that it sells the goods to be used in the buyer's manufacturing process, it is expected to foresee that non-delivery or the delivery of non-conforming goods is likely to cause the buyer to lose profits from selling the final product.[55]

If the nature of the buyer's business is in itself not indicative of the nature of the loss suffered by the buyer, that loss is unlikely to be foreseeable. For example, if the buyer's business is that of servicing a mining industry it may not necessarily be reasonably foreseeable to the seller, supplying wastewater evaporation devices, that the buyer intended to eventually resell those devices, initially leased to a mining company, to the mining company. Only if this intention to resell was communicated to the seller at the time of concluding the contract with the buyer or if there are specific circumstances that otherwise indicate that the seller ought to have known of such an intention, should this loss be deemed foreseeable.[56] Similarly, it may be that even a short delay in delivering the goods causes the buyer loss of profit on its sub-sale contract because the buyer contracted to deliver the goods to its sub-buyer very shortly after the goods ought to have been delivered by the seller. In this case, the seller's knowledge that the buyer is a trader may not suffice to make this loss of profit foreseeable because the seller also needs to be in the position to know about the buyer's obligation or, at least, intention to resell the goods to its sub-buyer within a very short timeframe.[57]

Where the buyer demands damages for lost profits on its sub-sale contracts, they might not be foreseeable to the seller who had delivered non-conforming goods, if the buyer permitted a wrongful rejection of the goods by its sub-buyers.[58] Where the parties have had a long-standing business relationship,

[54] See, similarly, Case No. 759/2008 Appellate Court Madrid (Spain) 10 March 2009, available at cisgw3.law.pace.edu/cases/090310s1.html, where the buyer's lost profit, arising from its inability to sell non-conforming wine to its customers, was deemed foreseeable to the seller, a wholesaler, who ought to have expected that the addition of benzoic acid to the wine would make it impossible for the buyer to resell the wine.

[55] *TeeVee Tunes, Inc v Gerhard Schubert GmbH* (n 47).

[56] See *Orica Australia Pty Ltd v Aston Evaporative Services, LLC v UE Manufacturing, LLC*, 2015 WL 6172147 (D. Colo. Oct. 21, 2015), 5 ('for Orica to recover lost profits against Aston, it must show that Aston knew or should have known about Orica's plans to resell the Tempest 1600 units to Oaky Creek.').

[57] *Citgo Petroleum Corp v Odfjell Seachem*, 2014 WL 7004049, 8 ('For this delay to be foreseeable, YPF would have needed to understand that Tricon was a reseller, not a company that purchased and used cyclohexane itself, and that Tricon had a short-term deal to resell the product.').

[58] *Re: Siskiyou Evergreen, Inc Debtor*, Case No 602-66975-fra11, unreported, US Bankruptcy Court for the District of Oregon 29 March 2004 (United States), available at cisgw3.law.pace.edu/cases/040329u2.html ('At trial, Barroso conceded that the rejection of the several contracts he had

the breaching seller may be presumed to have been aware of the purpose for which the buyer bought the goods. If, in such a case, the buyer bought the goods for resale, the seller may be presumed to have foreseen that a delay in delivering or non-delivery of the goods would make the buyer liable to its sub-buyers.[59] However, where the nature of the buyer's liability to third parties is unusual, excessive or unjustified, losses flowing therefrom are unlikely to be foreseeable. In one case,[60] the buyer bought materials for use in the construction project it had been commissioned to carry out. As a result of the seller's delay in delivering the goods, the buyer had to pay a contractual penalty to its sub-contractor. The court held that while such penalty clauses 'can be expected to be included in construction contracts', the penalty paid in that case was not foreseeable to the seller because the clause was too disadvantageous[61] to the buyer by requiring it to pay the full amount of the penalty (presumably, deemed excessive in the circumstances) within a short period, considering the large scale of the project. The court, relying on the 'assumption of risk' rationale of the foreseeability rule, stated that the risk that had materialised in that case did not conform to the risk assumed by the seller because the seller 'did not have to reckon with the fact that [the buyer] would forfeit the full contractual penalty with a delay in delivery of two weeks'.[62] Where the breaching seller had no reason to be aware at the time of concluding the contract that the buyer acted as an agent, it is highly unlikely that the buyer's loss of its agency commission would be regarded as a foreseeable loss.[63] Finally, if the law of the seller's country requires the seller to ensure the receipt of payment in a foreign currency in the seller's account at a specified bank within the time prescribed by the law, the payment of a penalty to

with customers in Mexico was wrongful. It follows that the events could not have been foreseen by the seller'). The same result could have been achieved by the mitigation rule: by accepting unjustifiable rejection of the goods by its sub-buyers, the buyer failed to reduce or avoid its loss. For the discussion of the interrelationship between foreseeability and mitigation, see below.

[59] 'Both parties confirmed during the hearings that they had had long-lasting business relations which fact was reflected in numerous contracts. In these circumstances, the [Seller], as a professional participant of the market of this kind of goods, could not have been unaware of the fact that the [Buyer] is not the consumer of the delivered goods and that it distributes them on the internal market of Russia, that naturally includes transshipment (resale) of the purchased goods by the [Buyer] to further customers, as was the case in the relations of the [Buyer] with its customer under Contract No 11-04/KK of 15 April 2004. Equally, having chosen the Russian law as the applicable law, the [Seller] could not have been unaware that failing to perform its obligations to the [Buyer] it will have to recover the loss suffered by the [Buyer] as a result of paying penalties to its contractor in accordance with the rules of Russian civil law' (ICAC No 97/2004, 23 December 2004, available at cisgw3.law.pace.edu/cases/041223r1.html).

[60] Case No 419 O 48/01 District Court Hamburg (Germany) 21 December 2001 (Stones), available at cisgw3.law.pace.edu/cases/011221g1.html.

[61] In fact, the clause was held to be void in accordance with the applicable domestic law.

[62] For other cases, where damages arising from liability to third parties were held unforeseeable (where no satisfactory explanation has been given, however), see Case No 43 O 136/92 District Court Aachen (Germany) 14 May 1993 (Electronic hearing aid), available at cisgw3.law.pace.edu/cases/930514g1.html; CIETAC 7 May 1997 (Horsebean), available at cisgw3.law.pace.edu/cases/970507c1.html.

[63] CIETAC 7 July 1997 (Isobutanol), available at cisgw3.law.pace.edu/ cases/970707c1.html.

state authorities for the seller's non-compliance with this obligation is unlikely to be foreseeable to the buyer unless the buyer was informed about such legislative provisions at the time of contracting.[64]

Another factor that has been relied upon, along with knowledge of the innocent party's business, is knowledge of the nature of the goods. In one case, the tribunal held that the breaching seller should have known that the buyer was a clothing retailer and the goods were seasonal. Therefore, the seller ought to have known and foreseen that 'late delivery would mean that the goods could only be sold [at] reduced price once they were out of season and therefore profits would be lost'.[65] This overview demonstrates that while it is possible to discern a set of factors which may influence the court's or tribunal's decision as to whether to imply certain types of knowledge and foreseeability, the question whether a particular loss was foreseeable must be resolved on a case-by-case basis. The foreseeability rule 'would bear upon the different cases with varying degrees of rigour'.[66]

Another question is whether it is reasonable to presume that the breaching party will always expect the injured party to mitigate its loss and therefore the foreseeable loss is only that which cannot be reasonably avoided or reduced.[67] For example, suppose the seller refuses to deliver the goods at the contract price of £50,000. The buyer intended to resell the goods to its sub-buyer for £80,000 and it is possible for the buyer to purchase replacement goods at the current price of £60,000. Assuming the foreseeability rule refers not only to the type of loss but also to its extent, is it the £30,000 or the £10,000 that is within the seller's foreseeability range? In other words, should the foreseeability rule take into account a reasonably available opportunity to mitigate the loss? It can be argued that it is justifiable to interpret the foreseeability rule in such a way not only because the mitigation rule is a method of limiting damages but also because taking measures of mitigating loss is what reasonable parties often do to protect their own interest.[68] It is submitted, however, that this approach will introduce unnecessary complexity to the foreseeability rule and undermine the mitigation rule as a separate method of limiting damages because its function will be performed by the foreseeability rule. This approach will also place an additional burden on the injured party by requiring it to prove both foreseeability and mitigation. As noted, the burden of proving foreseeability is borne by

[64] Case No A53-11062/16 Arbitration Court Rostov Region (Russia) 7 July 2016, available at ras.arbitr.ru (in Russian); Case No 437/08 Supreme Court (Russian Federation) 14 March 2008, available at www.unilex.info (with reference to the UPICC; the abstract of the decision is available in English).

[65] ICC No 8786, January 1997 (Clothing), available at cisgw3.law.pace.edu/cases/978786i1.html.

[66] Bridge (n 19) [12.23].

[67] The issue was addressed in A Mullis, 'Recoverability of Lost Resale Profit and Compensation Paid to a Sub-Buyer under the Vienna Convention' at the Conference on 'Contract Damages: Domestic and International Perspectives' held in Birmingham, UK, June 2007.

[68] For the 'self-interest' rationale of the mitigation rule, see ch 6.

the injured party while the burden of proof in respect of mitigation is generally borne by the breaching party.[69]

Finally, it should be noted that implied knowledge and foreseeability are dynamic concepts and in applying the foreseeability rule, it needs to be borne in mind that common knowledge, which is the basis for implying knowledge to a given party, changes over time:

> [m]odern business practices (and equipment), accounting methods, and extensive communication of information make more knowledge available to [the] parties. This increased knowledge may make potential amounts of loss easier to compute.[70]

2.2.2. *Other Factors*

Besides knowledge, other factors can influence the court's or tribunal's assessment of whether a particular loss was foreseeable in the circumstances. One such factor is a 'trade usage' and in a ULIS case, the court held that the foreseeability requirement could 'be conclusively met by a showing of trade custom as to foreseeability'.[71] This suggests the possibility that a particular trade usage may categorise certain losses as 'foreseeable' and, where so, it would seem appropriate to rely on the requirements of such a trade usage on the basis of two alternative lines of reasoning. One is to argue that a trade usage forms the background against which the business persons' understandings and expectations arise and a particular usage, as long as it is a true trade usage,[72] can be considered as part of knowledge to be implied. An alternative line of reasoning is that, in such cases, a trade usage already recognises the applicability of the foreseeability rule and it can then be argued that the parties have derogated from the *instruments*' foreseeability rule by implicitly agreeing[73] that it is the foreseeability rule, based on a trade usage, which is applicable.

Another consideration which can influence the interpretation of the foreseeability rule is whether a breach was deliberate or negligent. In fact, the PECL go much further by expressly requiring that, even if the loss was unforeseeable to the breaching party, it is still liable for that loss if its 'non-performance was intentional or grossly negligent'.[74] While no such requirement exists in the CISG and the UPICC, the experience of other legal systems using a similar foreseeability

[69] See ch 6.

[70] Murphey (n 24). For a similar view, see J Lookofsky, *Consequential Damages in Comparative Context: From Breach of Promise to Monetary Remedy in the American, Scandinavian and International Law of Contracts and Sales* (Copenhagen, Danmarks Jurist, 1989) 173.

[71] Supreme Court (Germany) 24 October 1979 (n 53).

[72] See arts 9 CISG, 1.9 UPICC, 1:105 PECL. See further D Saidov, 'Trade Usages in International Sales Law' in D Saidov (ed), *Research Handbook on International and Comparative Law Sale of Goods Law* (Cheltenham, Edward Elgar, 2019).

[73] See arts 6 CISG, 1.5 UPICC, 1:102 PECL.

[74] See art 9:503 PECL.

rule indicates that the assessment of foreseeability may still be influenced by whether the breaching party's breach was deliberate.[75]

A difficult question is whether the foreseeability rule should be concerned with maintaining a proportion between the loss and the amount of benefit received by the breaching party under the contract. For example, if the seller's delivery of defective seeds caused the farmer substantial losses resulting from lost crop, should the seller be liable in full for all the losses suffered by the farmer despite the fact that the price of seeds is incommensurate with the amount of losses? If not, is the foreseeability rule an appropriate tool for limiting damages in such cases? To begin with, it is well known that the foreseeability rule, in its pure form, is often incapable of limiting damages for disproportionate losses[76] as it may well be that such losses were foreseeable: in our example, the farmer may have specifically warned the seller, or the seller with its extensive experience in the agricultural sector could have reasonably expected, that defective seeds were likely to cause substantial losses to the farmer. To address this problem, some legal systems have, on occasions, applied a more restrictive foreseeability rule by holding the breaching party liable for disproportionate losses only where it *accepted* the risk of such losses as a term of the contract.[77] It is suggested that there is no basis for this latter approach (known as the 'tacit agreement rule') in the context of the international instruments. Adopting it would not only lead to non-uniformity in their application,[78] but would also undermine the 'risk allocation' rationale of the foreseeability rule for if, in our example, the seller was in a position to foresee the possibility of the farmer incurring substantial losses, it would be reasonable to expect it to take measures to account for that risk (by charging a higher price, procuring insurance or limiting or excluding its liability). Its failure to do so can, fairly and reasonably, be interpreted as the seller's implied assumption of that risk. However, an outright dismissal of the possibility of disproportionate losses being within the sphere of the foreseeability rule may be too simple an approach. The proportion between the loss and contractual benefit is, it is submitted, a valid concern and in the absence of a specific provision in the instruments to that effect, it should not come as a surprise if the foreseeability rule is used to limit damages in order to reduce the degree of disproportion.[79]

[75] See Bridge (n 19) [12.27].

[76] See Farnsworth (n 13) 1208 ('in cases where the injured party's loss … is greatly out of proportion to the benefit that the party in breach was to have received in return … [foreseeability] does not restrict [liability enough]'); Waddams (n 20) 558 ('the theory that price and liability must be commensurate is a device for restricting liability, and the perceived need for such a device indicates that the rule as announced in *Hadley v Baxendale* is incomplete').

[77] See A Burrows, *Remedies for Torts, Breach of Contract and Equitable Wrongs*, 4th edn (Oxford, OUP, 2019) 98–100.

[78] See Murphey (n 24).

[79] Other tools can be used to deal with this problem, such as: interpreting the contract in such a way as to imply the parties' intention to exclude disproportionate losses; applying the applicable standard of proof in a manner reducing the degree of disproportion; or developing a relevant general principle. Applying the tools of the applicable domestic law (see Bernstein and Lookofsky

Yet another factor which may influence the court's or tribunal's assessment of foreseeability is the degree of detail with which the circumstances of the loss are described. If the circumstances in which the loss has arisen are described in general terms, the likelihood that the loss will be deemed foreseeable will increase;[80] conversely, describing such circumstances in more specific and precise terms may reduce the chances of the loss being foreseeable. If, in the example above, the farmer describes the cause of the loss in a precise technical language, known only to agricultural specialists, the reliance on such a description of the conditions causing no crop to be produced may reduce the chances of the seller being in a position to foresee the loss, unless the seller itself possesses the relevant expertise. In this regard, it is important not to lose sight of the true purpose of the foreseeability rule and not to overemphasise the importance of the description of the *circumstances* giving rise to the loss, as opposed to the *nature and type of the loss itself*. The real concern of the foreseeability rule is the type and nature (as well as the extent) of the loss and as long as they were reasonably foreseeable, this, it is submitted, should be sufficient, even if the party did not have an in-depth understanding of the *circumstances* in which the loss has arisen. To return to our example, if it is reasonable to imply into the seller, having regard to its background and experience, knowledge that the delivery of defective seeds is likely to result in the farmer's inability to produce crop which will result in, say, lost profits and the farmer's liability to third parties, this is sufficient to hold the seller liable for these losses (provided also that the extent of actual losses was within the foreseeable range).[81]

3. FORESEEABILITY OF WHAT?

Legal systems that use the foreseeability rule to limit damages take different positions as to *what* precisely must be foreseen. English law, for example, generally requires that only the *type* of loss be foreseeable while some civil law systems require foreseeability of the type and *extent* of the loss.[82] By simply referring to foreseeability of 'loss' or of 'harm', the international instruments do not make their position clear. The Comments on the UPICC provide that foreseeability in the UPICC 'relates to the nature or type of the harm but not to its extent unless the extent is such as to transform the harm into one of a different kind'.[83]

(n 14) 144), is not, it is submitted, an appropriate route for dealing with this problem because the operation of the remedy of damages is exclusively within the scope of the instruments and domestic rules should not be allowed to interfere.

[80] Waddams (n 20) 562.

[81] For the argument that the rule also requires foreseeability of the extent of the loss, see below. For possible relevance of insurance considerations to the foreseeability rule, see Waddams (n 20) 566–7.

[82] Nicholas (n 31) 231.

[83] Comment on art 7.4.4 UPICC; one commentator supports this view and argues that the same should be the case for the CISG (S Eiselen, 'Remarks on the Manner in which the UNIDROIT Principles of International Commercial Contracts May Be Used to Interpret or Supplement Article 74 of the CISG', available at www.cisg.law.pace.edu/cisg/principles/uni74.html).

Comments on the PECL seem to imply that not only the type but also the extent of the loss are required to be foreseen.[84] There seems to be no particular reason why three very similar provisions of the international instruments should be interpreted differently in relation to this matter. The absence of clarity regarding what needs to be foreseen has far-reaching implications as it will generate not only a non-uniform application of the instruments but also uncertainty as to the injured party's entitlement to, and amount of, compensation. Each of the factors to which foreseeability may potentially refer must be examined.

One factor is the possibility of the occurrence of a loss and it is submitted that this factor must be regarded as foreseeable. Although business persons normally enter into contracts to perform and not to breach them, they must nonetheless be regarded as *always* being in the position to foresee that a breach may occur and that a loss may result therefrom: the possibility of a breach and resulting losses is an integral part of a commercial activity. It can also be argued that damages are an instrument of protecting the party against this risk and the foreseeability rule, being a part of the law of damages, cannot be interpreted in a way which suggests that a business person could *not* foresee the possibility of a breach and the resulting losses. The very existence of the law of damages reflects the recognition of such a possibility.

Some CISG decisions appear to have interpreted the foreseeability rule as requiring foreseeability of *the precise amount* of the loss. In one case,[85] the tribunal denied the buyer's claim for loss of a profit margin on its sub-sale contract because 'the difference between the contract price and the resale price was not foreseeable by [Seller] at the time of the conclusion of the Contract'. Rarely, however, will it be possible for a party to be in the position to foresee the *precise* amount of the loss and the most the breaching party is usually able to foresee at the time of concluding the contract is the type (nature) and extent of the loss. If the rule required foreseeability of the precise amount of the loss, the injured party would in most cases be denied compensation. Such an interpretation would deprive the instruments' remedy of damages of any value.

Furthermore, it is sometimes argued that foreseeability should not be interpreted as referring to the nature (type) of the loss because this would deny damages to those who suffer loss in the amount 'that is fully within reasonable expectation of the party in breach, if that loss was of an unexpected type'.[86] According to this view, the type of loss should be important only where it is indicative of the extent of loss.[87] However, a better approach is to interpret the rule as requiring foreseeability of the type (nature) of the loss as it is a defining

[84] See Illustration 1, Comment A on art 9:503 PECL (Beale and Lando (n 30)).

[85] CIETAC 1 February 2000 (Silicon and manganese alloy), available at cisgw3.law.pace.edu/cases/000201c1.html.

[86] TA Diamond and H Foss, 'Consequential Damages for Commercial Loss: An Alternative to *Hadley v Baxendale*' (1994–1995) 63 *Fordham L Rev* 709.

[87] See ibid.

and integral feature of the notion of loss. It is also suggested that foreseeability of the extent of the loss (which, as argued below, must also be foreseeable) is rarely possible without foreseeability of the type and nature of the loss because translating loss into money is hardly possible without an understanding of the nature or type of the loss. Arguments to the contrary are infrequent and interpreting the rule as requiring foreseeability of the type and nature of the loss is, by and large, uncontroversial and indeed most systems using the foreseeability rule interpret it in this way.[88]

This position, however, is not without difficulty. How are losses to be distinguished from one another? What are the criteria for determining whether the loss that was foreseeable was in fact of the same type as the one actually suffered? The only guidance that the instruments provide is the division between 'loss suffered' and 'loss of profit' and this division is, it is suggested, the necessary starting point. The real difficulty, however, lies at the point where it must be determined whether the loss that was foreseeable and the one which actually occurred fall within the same broad category and are of the same type. For example, are damage to property and losses incurred in mitigation, while both being losses 'actually suffered', of the same type for the purposes of foreseeability? It is suggested that headings under which losses were considered earlier in this book[89] can provide additional guidance: expenditure *wasted* as a result of the breach, additional expenditure *incurred* as a result of the breach, damage to the performance interest, currency losses, damage to reputation and goodwill, loss of profit, loss of a chance and the buyer's loss of the right to avoid the contract on a falling market due to a documentary breach. As is well known, though, no categorisation is ever perfect and an overlap among groupings is inevitable. In attempting to categorise a particular loss, it is important not to get lost in a labyrinth of classifying losses but to keep sight of the 'risk allocation' rationale of the foreseeability rule. Suppose the circumstances clearly indicate that it was foreseeable to the supplier of equipment that the buyer, who services a mining industry, might either lease the equipment or resell it to the mining company. If, as a result of the equipment being non-conforming, the buyer suffers and claims damages for loss of profit,[90] it is submitted that the type of loss (loss of profit) should be deemed foreseeable to the seller regardless of whether this lost profit arose from the buyer's inability to lease or resell the equipment.

The type of loss must be distinguished from its extent which refers to translating the *limits* of the loss into money. The importance and far-reaching implications of requiring the extent of the loss to be foreseeable is illustrated by several CISG cases. One case[91] is where the tribunal interpreted the CISG as

[88] See above.

[89] See ch 3.

[90] This example is partly based on *Orica Australia Pty Ltd v Aston Evaporative Services, LLC v UE Manufacturing, LLC* (n 56).

[91] ICAC No 97/2004, 23 December 2004, available at cisgw3.law.pace.edu/cases/041223r1.html.

not requiring foreseeability of the extent of loss.[92] In this case, the buyer's claim for damages for the penalty it had to pay to its customer was held foreseeable despite the seller's argument that the penalty was excessive. The tribunal held that the amount of the penalty was irrelevant on the ground that 'establishing … the amount of the penalty is entirely a matter to be agreed between the contracting parties … and [it] complies with the freedom of contract principle set forth in the CISG'. The implication of this decision is that as long as the penalty itself was foreseeable, the extent of the loss is irrelevant to the foreseeability rule.[93] This decision can be contrasted with several other decisions where the extent of the loss was deemed relevant. In one case,[94] it was held that although the seller was in a position to foresee that the buyer would have a sub-sale contract and make a profit therefrom, the seller could not reasonably expect that the profit margin exceeded the contract price by 100 per cent. The tribunal did not deny damages altogether but awarded damages for lost profits in the amount of 20 per cent of the original contract price because that profit margin was 'reasonable' (and for that reason, presumably, foreseeable).[95] In another case,[96] the injured buyer who had to take out a loan to make an advance payment was rendered unable to return the loan on time and, as a result, had to pay additional interest on the sum in arrears. The court held that the breaching seller could not foresee the interest rate on the sum in arrears in the buyer's country and instead awarded

[92] See also *Al Hewar Environmental & Public Health Establishment v Southeast Ranch, LLC and Joel Gutierre* (S.D. Fla. 2011), [18] and [20], where the court was seemingly unconcerned with whether the extent of the buyer's losses (loss of a profit margin on a sub-sale and the loss of the guarantee (performance bond) that the buyer was contractually required to provide under its sub-sale contract) was foreseeable to the seller who had failed to deliver the goods.

[93] The same approach appears to have been taken in Case No T-8/09 Foreign Trade Court, the Serbian Chamber of Commerce (Serbia) 15 June 2010, available at cisgw3.law.pace.edu/cases/100615sb.html.

[94] CIETAC 3 June 2003 (Clothes), available at cisgw3.law.pace.edu/cases/030603c1.html.

[95] For a similar case where the same position was taken, see ICAC No 406/1998, 6 June 2000, available at cisgw3.law.pace.edu/cases/000606r1.html ('[Although] the buyer in principle has the right to recover damages for loss of profit … the seller neither knew nor ought to have foreseen that the buyer's loss of profit would be as much as approximately half the price of contract in dispute. Based on this conclusion and also considering the buyer's conduct, the Tribunal considers that the buyer's loss of profit to be compensated should be measured in the amount of 10%. Reaching this conclusion, the Tribunal took into account that the contract had been concluded on CIF terms. Although the contract does not refer to Incoterms, the Tribunal considers it is reasonable and allowed relying on the Incoterms guidelines which reflect the practices of international trade. Regarding the basis of the term CIF, Incoterms 1990 provides that the insurance should cover the price stipulated in the contract plus 10%, ie, a total of 110%. It is commonly known that the mentioned 10% covers the expected profit of the buyer and is the ordinary amount of profit in the practice of international trade'). See also Case No 7 ICAC, the Ukrainian Chamber of Commerce, 7 February 2007 (n 6), where the increase in the current price by 87%, as compared to the contract price, was held unforeseeable to the breaching seller.

[96] Case No 95/3214 District Court of Kuopio (Finland) 5 November 1996 (Butter), available at cisgw3.law.pace.edu/cases/961105f5.html.

damages with reference to the rate which, in the court's opinion, would be foreseeable to the seller.[97]

It is submitted that the instruments should be interpreted as requiring foreseeability of the extent of the loss. First, the 'risk allocation' rationale gives rise to this question: when business persons assume a risk, for what do they assume the risk – the type or the extent of the loss? There is little doubt that it is the financial considerations which underlie business planning and commercial activity and when business persons contemplate losses, they contemplate not only their nature but also the *approximate limits* of their financial liability. If only the type of loss were to be foreseeable, a business person's ultimate consideration would be disregarded and there would always be a danger that foreseeability would lead to liability to the extent which exceeds the boundaries of the assumed risk.[98] The view that foreseeability of the extent of the loss is required thus corresponds both to the way in which business people think and to the 'risk allocation' rationale of the foreseeability rule. Second, restricting foreseeability only to the type of loss is likely to give rise to uncertainty in the international legal environment by making it difficult for parties to estimate the approximate financial limits of their liability if they breach their contracts.[99] This uncertainty can even encourage business persons to exclude the international instruments, which would damage the instruments' unification and harmonisation aspirations. Third, the view that foreseeability refers not only to the type of the loss but also to its extent is supported by the legislative history of the CISG. According to the Report of the First Committee on the 1977 Vienna Draft, a proposal was considered to clarify the wording of what is now art 74 CISG. The proposed version that damages could be claimed for '… loss of such a *nature* which the party in breach could not reasonably have foreseen' was rejected[100] and this seems to evidence the drafters' intention not to restrict foreseeability to the nature or type of the loss. Finally, the wording of art 74 also suggests that the extent of loss is required by the foreseeability test. The phrase that damages '*may not exceed*' the foreseeable loss seems to refer to some *concrete limit*.

[97] 'It has not been shown that K knew the interest rates in Lithuania, namely 7% per month and 0.5% per day interest on arrears, which essentially differs from interest rates in Western Europe. One could not even assume that he should have known it. It is the estimate of the Court, that K should have pre-estimated that the interest loss resulting from not fulfilling the contractual obligations could be about 10% of the sale price, meaning US $8,000' (ibid). For another CISG decision where the extent of loss was deemed relevant to the foreseeability test, see Case No 271 C 18968/94 Lower Court München (Germany) 23 June 1995 (Tetracycline), available at cisgw3.law.pace.edu/cases/950623g1.html.

[98] See, similarly, Schwenzer (n 6) 1079 ('If the extent of the loss is significantly higher than foreseeable, the risk which has materialized differs from the risk which was foreseeable').

[99] *Cf* HG Beale, *Remedies for Breach of Contract* (London, Sweet & Maxwell, 1980) 182).

[100] See H Stoll and G Gruber, 'Arts. 74–77 CISG' in P Schlechtriem and I Schwenzer (eds), *Commentary on the UN Convention on the International Sale of Goods*, 2nd English edn (Oxford, OUP, 2005) 766 note 140.

If only the type of loss were intended to be foreseeable, the wording would have to mean that the recoverable loss is that 'not exceeding the *type* of loss', which would make little sense. Although the latter two arguments are only relevant to the CISG, the first two arguments in themselves suffice to justify interpreting the UPICC[101] and PECL in the same way.

One argument against the view that foreseeability refers to the extent of the loss is that the extent of the loss is a question of quantum or calculation whereas foreseeability is a test 'of remoteness and not one of quantification'.[102] But it is argued that the extent of the loss is not a matter of calculation. The calculation of loss determines the precise amount of the loss;[103] the extent of the loss, in contrast, refers not to the precise amount of the loss but represents a translation of the *limits* of the loss into money or a monetary 'range' within which losses are deemed foreseeable. There is a difficulty of reconciling the position that the extent of loss is required by the foreseeability rule with the fact that the instruments' specific methods of calculating damages[104] are not expressly subject to the foreseeability requirement.[105] One way to reconcile the two is to presume that these calculation methods target *typical* situations which are always foreseeable[106] and to require foreseeability of the extent of the loss in all other situations. This would be consistent with the purpose of these calculation methods of introducing simplicity and clarity when calculating damages.[107]

It is suggested, however, that a better way of interpreting the instruments is to apply the foreseeability rule to the damages claims based on the instruments' damages calculation formulae. First, this would ensure a consistent application of the foreseeability rule to *all* cases. Second, although the the instruments' formulae may well reflect losses which 'arise naturally' and are for that reason usually foreseeable, the cases where the extent of such losses is unforeseeable cannot be ruled out. Suppose the injured seller resells the goods in a reasonable

[101] For a different view, see Comments on the UPICC and Eiselen (n 83) (arguing that the UPICC can be used to interpret the CISG in this respect: 'the Comment [to the UPICC] also makes it clear that the foreseeability relates to "*the nature or type of harm but not to its extent*". This should also be the approach under article 74 of the CISG').

[102] See GH Treitel, *Remedies for Breach of Contract: A Comparative Account* (Oxford, Clarendon Press, 1988) 161 (in relation to the ULIS and the CISG).

[103] As shown, foreseeability does not refer to the precise amount of the loss.

[104] Namely, the difference between the contract price and the price in a substitute transaction (a 'concrete' formula) and the difference between the contract price and the current price (an 'abstract' formula).

[105] Articles 75, 76 CISG, 7.4.5, 7.4.6 UPICC, 9:506, 9:507 PECL. For a detailed discussion, see chs 8 and 9.

[106] See Farnsworth (n 13) 1201 (the losses ' "arising naturally"… are those afforded under the standard formulas based on market price'); Hellner (n 15) 63–4, arguing that the said methods of calculation do not have any connection with foreseeability. See also *Macromex Srl v Globex International Inc*, 2008 WL 1752530 (affirmed in 330 F. App'x 241 (2d Cir. 2009)), upholding the arbitration award of damages for the buyer's loss of profit resulting from the seller's non-delivery of the goods. This loss of profit, determined with reference to the market price of the goods in a place of the intended resale, was deemed foreseeable.

[107] See ch 8.

manner and within a reasonable time on a sharply falling market. As a result, the difference between the contract price and the resale price is exceptionally high. It can be argued that while the buyer was in the position to foresee the possibility of price fluctuations (the type of loss being the difference between the contract price and, depending on the applicable formula, the price in a substitute transaction or the current price), such a drastic fall (extent of the loss) was not foreseeable. Requiring the extent of the difference to be foreseeable would correspond with the rule's purpose of allocating risks in a fair and balanced manner.[108] Finally, although the instruments' formulae do not refer to the foreseeability rule,[109] the suggested approach is not inconsistent with these formulae if they are treated as *specific* methods of calculation and the foreseeability rule is treated as a *general* rule of limiting damages.

4. TIME OF FORESEEABILITY AND DEGREE OF PROBABILITY

Whether a loss was foreseeable is to be assessed with reference to the time of the conclusion of the contract.[110] Although this position has been criticised,[111] the

[108] This approach is taken in a number of CISG cases (see CIETAC 4 February 2002 (Styrene monomer), available at cisgw3.law.pace.edu/cases/020204c1.html; Case No 4 R 219/01k Appellate Court Graz (Austria) 24 January 2002 (Excavator), available at cisgw3.law.pace.edu/cases/020124a3.html (the decision is unusual because the injured seller's resale was considered in the context of art 74 CISG and not art 75); Case No V CSK 63/08 Supreme Court (Poland) 9 October 2008, available at cisgw3.law.pace.edu/cases/081009p1.html (the abstract of this case appears to indicate the court's position that the damages calculated under arts 75 and 76 CISG are subject to the foreseeability rule); Case No 7 ICAC, the Ukrainian Chamber of Commerce, 7 February 2007 (n 6), where the increase of the current price by 87%, as compared with the contract price, was held unforeseeable to the breaching seller).

[109] This argument is relied on in Schwenzer (n 6) 1091–2 to advocate the position contrary to that taken in this book. This commentary argues that applying the foreseeability rule to arts 75 and 76 is 'in contradiction to the express wording of the provision' in arts 75 and 76 (ibid, 1091, 1099). Whilst this view can in principle be taken, there is no express contradiction between the approach in this book and the wording of art 75. As the main text argues, the instruments' formulae, such as those in arts 75 and 76 CISG, are merely specific methods of calculation that should not displace the foreseeability rule in art 74 CISG, which is a general rule of limiting damages applicable to *all* cases, for the reasons set out in the main text. The said commentary also relies on the argument that the breaching party should bear the risk of any exceptional change in prices because the innocent party 'was faithful to the contract' (ibid, 1092). The latter position seems unjustifiable, reflecting the commentary's policy perspective. The foreseeability rule in the CISG and other international instruments is precisely incorporated as one of the instruments' key tools for allocating the risks and losses between the parties. Exceptionally high risks (eg, exceptional price fluctuations) should be allocated between the parties not by interpreting the instruments on the basis of individual policy preferences but on the basis of the instruments' mechanisms, such as the foreseeability test, that are specifically designed for this purpose.

[110] See arts 74 CISG, 7.4.4 UPICC, 9:503 PECL.

[111] It has been said, eg, that '[a] sounder decision can be made nearer the time of performance or breach. The true loss to the party who will be injured by a breach will be, on the average, more apparent the closer in time to the intended breach one tries to predict that loss. Fresher data will be available – a knowledge of prices at a time closer to when performance would be due, for example' (Murphey (n 24), who, however, is in favour of the 'time of making the contract' rule). See also R Samek, 'Relevant Time of Foreseeability of Damages' (1964) 38 *Australian L J* 125.

rule is generally fair. Only the risk assumed by the party at the conclusion of the contract should, as a rule, be of legal significance because the time of making the contract is the only time when the party has an opportunity to protect itself (for example, by raising the price, excluding or limiting liability or procuring insurance). If foreseeability were to be assessed at a time after the contract was concluded, the party would be denied an opportunity for self-protection.[112] This argument can be criticised on the basis that in practice foreseeability of consequences is unlikely to affect the terms of the transaction because '[i]t is normally impracticable to fix a separate rate for every contract'.[113] Whatever the reality may be,[114] the law should not deny the breaching party an opportunity for self-protection. Clarity as to the precise moment in time is also important because negotiations 'leading to the conclusion of the contract may … last a certain period of time'.[115] The time when the contract comes into existence provides the required precision.[116]

However, given the rule's 'assumption of risk' rationale a later time for assessing foreseeability may be more appropriate in some cases. One such case is where after the conclusion of the contract, the parties have agreed to change its terms. It can be argued that, at this stage, a renewed assumption of risk has occurred (at least, insofar as the renegotiated rights and obligations are concerned) because if the potential breaching party has become aware of risks which were not foreseeable at the time of concluding the contract, it now has an opportunity to protect itself.[117] For example, if some time after the contract had been made the parties decided to renegotiate the delivery date and at that time the seller becomes aware that a delay in delivery will cause the buyer to pay an unusually high penalty to a third party, it is appropriate, if this risk materialises, to hold that loss foreseeable by relying on the time when the delivery obligation was renegotiated as long as a reasonable opportunity was available to the seller to protect itself. The instruments' reference to the 'time of the conclusion of the contract' does not necessarily preclude this result because the parties' agreement to change the terms of the contract can be interpreted as reflecting their implied intention to derogate from the provision that foreseeability must be assessed with reference to the time of concluding contract.[118] This result may also be

[112] See statement of a US court in *Patterson v Illinois Cent Ry Co*, 97S.W. 426, 123 Ky 783 (1906) cited in Corbin (n 25) 64. For a CISG case, where the tribunal applied the foreseeability test not just with reference to the time of making the contract but also with reference to a later time of when the invoice was presented contravening, it is submitted, a clear provision in art 74 CISG, see Case No 7 ICAC, the Ukrainian Chamber of Commerce, 7 February 2007 (n 6).

[113] See Atiyah (n 7) 432–3; also Corbin (n 25) 64–5.

[114] See Treitel (n 102) 160, noting the speculative nature of this criticism as well as of the argument that the party can protect itself either at or before the making of the contract.

[115] See Knapp (n 28) 542.

[116] See ibid, 542.

[117] See A Kramer, 'Remoteness: New Problems with the Old Test' in Saidov and Cunnington (n 2) 297–8.

[118] See arts 6 CISG, 1.5 UPICC, 1:102 PECL. So far as the UPICC and PECL are concerned, the only restrictions might be those flowing from mandatory rules in the Principles themselves or

justifiable in some cases involving long-term contracts which often provide that terms such as price, quantity or delivery dates are to be agreed at future points in time.[119] It can be argued that where such contracts are terminable at will, 'a new contract is formed at each and every point in any continuing and terminable relationship'.[120] Thus, if by the time when the parties to a long-term contract are to negotiate a term which was left open for future negotiation, one party becomes aware of risks which it could not foresee at the time of concluding the contract, it may be appropriate to assess the party's foreseeability with reference to the point of such negotiation because it has an opportunity to protect itself at least by terminating the contract. The problem of the date of assessing foreseeability in long-term contracts will rarely arise in practice because 'the parties' assumption of risk will usually be broadly defined for the very reason that the contract is a long-term contract and the parties can be assumed to understand that things will change throughout the life of the contract, and the price and insurance will accordingly be calculated generally and with an eye on the long term'.[121]

So far as the required degree of probability of loss is concerned, the CISG refers to foreseeability of the loss 'as a *possible* consequence of the breach'. This provision is sometimes interpreted as imposing a more extensive liability in comparison with those systems which provide for foreseeability of loss 'as a *probable* result' of the breach.[122] However, the words 'in light of the facts and matters' cut back a potentially extensive liability.[123] The UPICC and the PECL use a more restrictive standard by referring to foreseeability of loss which is 'likely to result from ... non-performance'[124] or which is 'a likely result of ... non-performance'.[125] However, as explained, this difference in wording between the CISG and the two sets of Principles[126] is unlikely to lead to different results in practice.

those emanating from the applicable mandatory domestic, supranational or international law (see arts 1:102, 1:103 PECL; arts 1.5 UPICC and Comment on arts 1.1 and 1.5). The only restriction on party autonomy in the CISG itself is art 12. For the possibility of restrictions, emanating from the applicable mandatory domestic law, in cases where the CISG is 'opted-into', see Schlechtriem (n 11) 35.

[119] For the discussion of long-term contracts, see ch 9.

[120] Kramer (n 117) 301.

[121] Ibid, 302.

[122] *See* JS Ziegel, *Report to the Uniform Law Conference of Canada on Convention on Contracts for the International Sale of Goods*, available at www.cisg.law.pace.edu/cisg/text/ziegel80.html.

[123] See EA Farnsworth, 'Damages and Specific Relief' (1979) 27 *AJCL* 253.

[124] Article 7.4.4 UPICC.

[125] Article 9:503 PECL.

[126] *Cf* J Ramberg, *International Commercial Transactions* ICC Publication 624, 2nd edn (The Netherlands, Kluwer Law International, 2000) 127 ('Semantically there seems to be a difference between the words "possible consequence" and the words "likely to result". To mention a dramatic example one could say that the Third World War hopefully "is not likely to result" but nevertheless "might be possible"').

5. CONCLUDING REMARKS

On a number of occasions, it has been questioned whether the foreseeability rule is an appropriate method of limiting damages. It has been argued, for example, that it is a 'product' of its time and is ill suited to the present age of a 'diverse and complex' economy. It has been suggested that in 'mass-transaction situations a seller cannot plausibly engage in an individualised "contemplation" of the consequences of breach and a subsequent tailoring of a transaction'.[127] More specifically, the period of pre-contractual negotiations, presupposed by the foreseeability rule, 'is far removed from the world of shipping and commodity sales, where transactions are often concluded between substitutes, brokers and ship's agents ... on an expedited and informal basis'.[128] In such conditions, there is little opportunity for extensive negotiations apart from agreeing on the most essential terms. The incentive for disclosing information is also not well suited to the interests of some commercial players such as traders,[129] because possessing information regarding price differentials is '[a]n essential element of middleman entrepreneurship':[130] if the counter-parties possess the relevant information they may prefer to bypass the intermediaries and contract directly with the ultimate buyer or supplier, as the case may be.[131] What can be said in response is that no general rule designed to accommodate a variety of circumstances can be ideally suited to all commercial sectors. If business persons in a particular trade find that the rule is wholly unsuitable to their needs, they can derogate from the unwanted rule.

The rule has also been criticised on the ground that it is inherently imprecise, involving much judicial discretion[132] and giving rise to uncertainty. This point

[127] R Danzig, '*Hadley v Baxendale*: A Study in the Industrialization of the Law' (1975) 4 *JLS* 279–80. The conclusion that foreseeability is a product of historical circumstances in England in the mid-1850s is difficult to support: 'Professor Danzig contends that the decision in *Hadley v Baxendale* was essentially a product of historical circumstances, particularly the peculiar state of industry, law, and the judicial system in England in the mid-1850s. This contention, however, is hard to reconcile with the fact that the principle adopted in *Hadley v Baxendale* also appears in the great French treatise by Pothier ... In view of the differences between mid-1700s France and mid-1800s England, it seems highly unlikely that a principle which appears in both times and places is essentially of the peculiar state of industry, law, and the judicial system in either time or place' (LL Fuller and MA Eisenberg, *Basic Contract Law* (St Paul, Minn, West Group Publishing Co, 1981) 235–6).

[128] MG Bridge, 'The Market Rule of Damages Assessment' in Saidov and Cunnington (n 2) 438.

[129] JT Landa, '*Hadley v Baxendale* and the Expansion of the Middleman Economy' (1987) 16 *JLS* 464 ('[M]arkets with middlemen are characterized by information asymmetry in the producer-middlemen market and the middleman-final consumer market: producer-sellers know only of the prices in their own market and not of the prices in the resale (second) market, while final consumers know of prices in the second market and not of prices in the first market. Only the middleman possesses information on prices in both markets because, in his role or identity as the middleman, he is both a buyer (in the first market) and a seller (in the second market). Price information flowing between the two markets is the result of entrepreneurial activities of middlemen' (ibid, 459)).

[130] Ibid, 465.

[131] See ibid.

[132] See LC Bulow, 'Consequential Damages and the Duty to Mitigate in New York Maritime Arbitrations' (1984) *LMCLQ* 625.

touches upon a perennial dilemma, faced by any legal system, between relying on broad and flexible standards, on the one hand, and specific but precise rules, on the other. The law of damages requires a balanced approach which relies on rules that are sufficiently flexible to accommodate a variety of factual settings and, at the same time, have a discernible content. The foreseeability rule arguably fits this description. It is certainly not true that it 'utterly lacks the descriptive content that allows it to be the principled basis for decision'[133] because it is clear about its underlying considerations and purposes. As demonstrated by this chapter, this rule does not create an unacceptable degree of uncertainty.[134] The foreseeability rule has existed for centuries[135] and is still widely used by many legal systems and the international instruments.[136] This wide acceptance of the foreseeability rule arguably evidences that it is, by and large, an effective method of limiting damages which corresponds to the demands of modern commercial world.

[133] RA Epstein, 'Beyond Foreseeability: Consequential Damages in the Law of Contract' (1989) 18 *JLS* 124.

[134] For empirical research suggesting that broad principles and standards do not necessarily lead to less predictable results than those reached by more detailed rules and are more likely to achieve just and efficient outcomes, see MP Ellinghaus and EW Wright, 'The Common Law of Contracts: Are Broad Principles Better than Detailed Rules? An Empirical Investigation' (2004–2005) 11 *Texas Wesleyan L Rev* 399.

[135] An attempt to introduce foreseeability was first made in Roman law. Much later foreseeability was established as a limitation of damages in art 1150 of the French Civil Code. Since that time, the rule has gained influence in other legal systems, including English law (see, eg, F Ferrari, 'Comparative Ruminations on the Foreseeability of Damages in Contract Law' (1992–1993) 53 *Louisiana L Rev* 1264).

[136] See Treitel (n 102) 150, 152; Beale and Lando (n 30) 441; Komarov (n 2).

6

Mitigation

1. GENERAL

AS IS THE case in some legal systems,[1] the international instruments provide that damages may be reduced to the extent that the loss could have been reduced or mitigated by the injured party. The CISG provides that '[a] party who relies on a breach of contract must take such measures as are reasonable in the circumstances to mitigate the loss, including loss of profit, resulting from the breach. If he fails to take such measures, the party in breach may claim a reduction in the damages in the amount by which the loss should have been mitigated'.[2] According to the UPICC, '[t]he non-performing party is not liable for harm suffered by the aggrieved party to the extent that the harm could have been reduced by the latter party's taking reasonable steps'.[3] Similarly, the PECL provide that '[t]he non-performing party is not liable for loss suffered by the aggrieved party to the extent that the aggrieved party could have reduced the loss by taking reasonable steps'.[4] Although it has been suggested that the rule is self-evident and needs no justification,[5] it is nevertheless helpful to begin this chapter by exploring and articulating its underlying policies and considerations. This inquiry will reveal that the rule's nature is complex and multi-layered, demonstrating that there is often a direct link between the rationale of the rule and its practical application.

The requirement that the innocent party must take reasonable measures to mitigate its loss can be justified on several grounds. First, it is often said to promote economic efficiency[6] and avoidance of waste.[7] For example, where the

[1] For a comparative overview, see, eg, A Komarov, 'The Limitation of Contract Damages in Domestic Legal Systems and International Instruments' in D Saidov and R Cunnington (eds), *Contract Damages: Domestic and International Perspectives* (Oxford, Hart Publishing, 2008) 256–7, 261. For the history of the development of the rule in English law, see PS Atiyah, *The Rise and Fall of Freedom of Contract* (Oxford, Clarendon Press, 1979) 425.

[2] Article 77 CISG.

[3] Article 7.4.8(1) UPICC.

[4] Article 9:505(1) PECL.

[5] A Tunc, *Commentary on the Hague Conventions of the 1st of July 1964 on International Sale of Goods and the Formation of the Contract of Sale*, available at www.cisg.law.pace.edu/cisg/biblio/tunc.html.

[6] See P Linzer, 'On the Amorality of Contract Remedies – Efficiency, Equity, and the Second Restatement' (1981) 81 *Columbia L Rev* 113–14; A Michaud, 'Mitigation of Damage in the Context of Remedies for Breach of Contract' (1984) 15 *Revue Générale de Droit* 300–01. Any argument based

buyer fails to accept the delivery of perishable goods, waste will occur if the seller does not dispose of the goods and the mitigation rule is likely to encourage this seller to do so.[8] Doubts have been expressed as to whether this justification of the mitigation rule is relevant in all cases. It has been argued that 'many typical cases, such as the plaintiff's failure to buy in a rising market, involve no waste of community resources yet the defendant is held not to be liable for a loss that could have been avoided'.[9] It is suggested that even this typical case involves waste in the sense that, but for the mitigation rule, additional costs, such as opportunity costs of using money elsewhere, would have to be incurred. If no mitigation rule had existed, the breaching party would have had to pay a higher amount of damages than it pays with the mitigation rule in force. In other words, if the two situations are compared, different amounts are paid to protect the *very same* expectation/performance interest. The mitigation rule protects the injured party's expectation/performance interest with a lower amount of damages and provides the breaching party with an opportunity to use the remaining money elsewhere.[10] Thus, the economic waste argument can

on economic efficiency faces the difficulty arising from the absence of a single definition of efficiency. One sense in which the term is used is that of avoiding waste and this understanding of the term is relied upon in the main text. Other senses are based on the concepts of Pareto (ie, an allocation of resources which results in no one being worse off and at least one person being better off – see, eg, RA Posner, *Economic Analysis of Law*, 6th edn (New York, Aspen Publishers, 2003) 12–13) and Kaldor-Hicks efficiency (where overall gains outweigh losses – see N Kaldor, 'Welfare Propositions of Economics and Inter-Personal Comparisons of Utility' (1939) 49 *Economics J* 549; JR Hicks, 'The Foundations of Welfare Economics (1939) 49 *Economic J* 696). These notions are not relied upon here for several reasons. First, it is the avoidance of waste argument that is usually put forward to justify the mitigation rule. Second, both Pareto and Kaldor-Hicks notions of efficiency, if applied strictly, would require the assessment of the impact of the allocation of resources on third parties (those other than the contracting parties) and doing so comprehensively is unlikely to be possible. Finally, whether a person is better or worse off is to be judged according to each person's individual conceptions of welfare (see J Coleman (Book Review) 'The Normative Basis of Economic Analysis: A Critical Review of Richard Posner's the Economics of Justice' (1981–1982) 34 *Stanford L Rev* 1105, 1107). The latter two points make it difficult to apply these notions of efficiency properly and draw definitive conclusions as to whether the mitigation rule promotes Pareto or Kaldor-Hicks efficiency.

[7] 'The purpose of the rule on mitigation is to prevent the waste of resources in society, since they are obviously limited' (AT Von Mehren and JR Gordley, *The Civil Law System: An Introduction to the Comparative Study of Law*, 2nd edn (Boston, Little, Brown & Co, 1977) 1115; also GG Letterman, *UNIDROIT's Rules in Practice: Standard International Contracts and Applicable Rules* (The Hague, Kluwer Law International, 2001) 211; H Beale (ed), *Chitty on Contracts*, 33rd edn, vol 1 (London, Sweet & Maxwell, 2019) [26-088]; EA Farnsworth, *Contracts*, 4th edn (New York, Aspen Publishers, 2004) 779; RD Cooter, 'The Best Right Laws: Value Foundations of the Economic Analysis of Law' (1989) 64 *Notre Dame L Rev* 817; CT Wonnell, 'Efficiency and Conservatism' (2001) 80 *Nebraska L Rev* 643, 649).

[8] *Cf* n 111.

[9] S Waddams, *The Law of Damages*, 4th edn (Toronto, Canada Law Book Inc, 2004) 592; similarly, see MG Bridge, 'Mitigation of Damages in Contract and the Meaning of Avoidable Loss' (1989) 105 *LQR* 405.

[10] If money is defined as a claim on community resources (Posner (n 6) 6), it can be said that with the mitigation rule in force the breaching party does not lose an opportunity to exercise its claim on community resources.

generally justify the mitigation rule.[11] There are, however, at least two factors which can hamper the rule's ability to promote efficiency. One relates to the allocation of burden of proof and the extent to which a court or tribunal will enforce the rule.[12] Another factor relates to the operation of the mitigation rule itself: the requirement of reasonableness, built in the rule, may lead to the situation where actions which seemed reasonable at the time of mitigation might in fact result in a failure to mitigate the loss and/or in unexpectedly high costs.[13] The rule's ability to achieve efficient outcomes is subject to these limitations.[14]

The second line of rationalisation of the mitigation rule is based on the ideas of fair dealing and good faith. It has been suggested, for example, that it is not *fair* to hold the breaching party liable for all loss resulting from the breach if the injured party can reasonably avoid or mitigate its loss.[15] Both fair dealing[16] and good faith[17] have been interpreted as requiring the injured party to be, to a certain extent, altruistic[18] by taking into account the other party's interests. So far as the UPICC and PECL are concerned, because they expressly impose a general duty to act in accordance with 'good faith and fair dealing',[19] the mitigation rule

[11] But see below for situations where the mitigation rule can lead to even greater costs than those that would have been incurred had the mitigation rule not existed.

[12] See below.

[13] For a similar view, see MA Eisenberg, 'The Duty to Rescue in Contract Law' (2002–2003) 71 *Fordham L Rev* 647, 659.

[14] It is suggested that economic efficiency is a consideration that is not alien to the international instruments. Generally, it is sometimes said that economic efficiency is particularly important where commercial relations are on foot (see, eg, S Le Pautremat, 'Mitigation of Damage: A French Perspective' (2006) 55 *ICLQ* 206, 213). More specifically, it can be argued that the dominant philosophy underlying modern world trade is that of free trade which is strongly influenced by the theory of comparative advantages, and it is well known that free trade pursues, amongst others, the goal of efficiency (see JH Jackson, WJ Davey, and AO Sykes, Jr, *Legal Problems of International Economic Relations: Cases, Materials and International Regulation of Transnational Economic Relations* (American Casebook Series), 3rd edn (St Paul, Minn, West Publishing Co, 1995) 7–14). There is no doubt that, to a considerable extent, the international instruments are designed to facilitate international trade and promote its underlying philosophy (see Preamble of the CISG; arts 1.7(1) and Comment 1 on art 7.4.8 UPICC; art 1:201 PECL).

[15] See J Cassels, *Remedies: The Law of Damages* (Toronto, Irwin Law, 2000) 339.

[16] See Comment D on art 1:201 PECL (O Lando and H Beale (eds), *Principles of European Contract Law: Parts I and II* (prepared by the Commission on European Contract Law) (The Hague, Kluwer Law International, 2000) 114).

[17] Good faith is a troublesome concept as it has been viewed from several standpoints: as an objective standard synonymous to 'fair dealing' (NE Nedzel, 'A Comparative Study of Good Faith, Fair Dealing, and Precontractual Liability (1997) 12 *Tulane European Civil L Forum* 153); as an objective standard accepted in a particular business community to which parties belong (D Sim, 'The Scope and Application of Good Faith in the Vienna Convention on Contracts for the International Sale of Goods' stating a possibility of such an approach to interpretation of good faith under the CISG, available at www.cisg.law.pace.edu/cisg/biblio/sim1.html#iiib); as a subjective standard as perceived by a particular individual (Comment E on art 1:201 PECL (Lando and Beale (n 16) 114; R Powell, 'Good Faith in Contracts' (1956) 9 *Current Legal Problems* 23). Since the meaning of good faith in the second and third instances depends on a particular community or individual respectively, it is only good faith in the first sense that is able to justify the mitigation rule.

[18] Mitigation is not a wholly altruistic duty, as suggested by C Fried, *Contract as Promise: A Theory of Contractual Obligation* (Cambridge, Mass, Harvard University Press, 1981) 131 (see below).

[19] See art 1.7(1) UPICC and art 1:201 PECL.

can be said to be a specific manifestation of these standards. This view of the mitigation rule is further re-affirmed by the 'duty to cooperate', imposed by the UPICC and PECL,[20] which implies an obligation to take into account to some extent the legitimate interests of the other party, and by art 1:302 PECL, which shows the connection between the mitigation rule and good faith by providing that reasonableness (the notion which underlies the mitigation rule)[21] 'is to be judged by what persons acting in good faith and in the same situation as the parties would consider to be reasonable'.[22] Justifying the mitigation rule in a similar way under the CISG is problematic because it does not expressly provide for general principles of fair dealing and good faith.[23] Nevertheless, the CISG is often viewed as reflecting a general principle of good faith (despite the initial compromise by the drafters to include it only as a standard of interpreting the Convention)[24] and, if this view is taken, the mitigation rule in the CISG can also be justified as a specific manifestation of a general principle of good faith.[25]

The 'duty' to mitigate is not a wholly altruistic duty as it also reflects conduct which is in the interests of the injured party.[26] In many cases, business persons try to reduce or avoid losses where reasonably possible and they often do so not because of their concern for the breaching party's interests, but because they want to mitigate at least some damage done to their financial and commercial interests.[27] For example, it is well known that time is of the essence in commerce

[20] See art 5.1.3 UPICC and art 1:202 PECL.

[21] See below.

[22] T Wilhelmsson, 'Good Faith and the Duty of Disclosure in Commercial Contracting – The Nordic Experience' in R Brownsword, NJ Hird and G Howells (eds), *Good Faith in Contract: Concept and Context* (Aldershot, Ashgate, 1999) 184. See also Comment on art 5.1.3 UPICC, which recognises the link between the duty to cooperate and fair dealing (and good faith). This Commentary also recognises the connection between the duty to cooperate and mitigation.

[23] Good faith is only expressly mentioned as a standard of interpreting the CISG (see art 7(1)).

[24] See, eg, MJ Bonell, 'Art 7 CISG' in CM Bianca and MJ Bonell (eds), *Commentary on the International Sales Law: The 1980 Vienna Sales Convention* (Milan, Giuffrè, 1987) 84; U Magnus, 'General Principles of UN-Sales Law', available at www.cisg.law.pace.edu/cisg/biblio/magnus.html; P Koneru, 'The International Interpretation of the UN Convention on Contracts for the International Sale of Goods: An Approach Based on General Principles' (1997) 6 *Minnesota J Global Trade*, available at www.cisg.law.pace.edu/cisg/biblio/koneru.html; *cf* EA Farnsworth, 'Duties of Good Faith and Fair Dealing under the UNIDROIT Principles, Relevant International Convention, and National Laws' (1995) 3 *Tulane J Intl and Comparative L* 56.

[25] J Klein, 'Good Faith in International Transactions' (1993) 15 *Liverpool L Rev* 131–2; I Schwenzer, 'Arts 74–77', in I Schwenzer (ed), *Schlechtriem and Schwenzer Commentary on the UN Convention on the International Sale of Goods (CISG)*, 4th edn (Oxford, OUP, 2016) 1104 (with detailed further references to sources taking this view); U Magnus, 'Remarks on good faith', available at www.cisg.law.pace.edu/cisg/principles/uni7.html; Case No 7 Ob 301/01t Supreme Court (Austria) 14 January 2002 (Cooling system), available at cisgw3.law.pace.edu/cases/020114a3.html; Case No 10 Ob 518/95 Supreme Court (Austria) 6 February 1996 (Propane), available at cisgw3.law.pace.edu/cases/960206a3.html).

[26] See *DT Ltd v B AG* Commercial Court St Gallen (Switzerland) 3 December 2002 (Sizing machine), available at www.cisg.law.pace.edu/cisg/wais/db/cases2/021203s1.html, stating that the '[seller] has his own self-interest reasons for minimizing any prospective loss and damages to the extent possible'.

[27] For a similar view, see JJ White and RS Summers, *Uniform Commercial Code*, 5th edn (St Paul, Minn, West Publishing Co, 2000) 283.

and an injured seller may want to mitigate its loss as quickly as possible to recover at least some money to be able to invest it in a profitable venture. Otherwise, although it may recover its damages in full at a later date, it may miss an opportunity to make this investment. Similarly, a buyer will often make every reasonable effort to find substitute goods to fulfil its sub-sale at the promised date, thereby avoiding a possible breakdown of commercial relationships, liability and damage to its reputation.[28] Finally, there is no guarantee that the claim for a full recovery of damages will succeed and this, together with the fact that litigation/arbitration may take a long time, may induce the injured party to mitigate to secure at least some money at an early stage. The mitigation rule arguably reflects what many business persons would be doing even if the mitigation rule did not exist. To this extent, the rule reflects a concern for interests of the injured party.[29]

Finally, a few remarks need to be made about the attempts to justify the mitigation rule based on other rules on damages. First, while the conventional position is that the mitigation rule *limits* the protection of the expectation/performance interest,[30] there is a view which regards the mitigation rule as *complementary* to the protection of the expectation/performance interest. It has been argued that mitigation simply adds 'a supplementary policy to those policies justifying protection of the expectation interest and this supplementary policy is that the promisee should not leave it simply to the courts to ensure fulfilment of his expectations, but should rather take it upon himself to adopt other reasonable means to ensure fulfilment of his expectations'.[31] A somewhat similar view is taken in some CISG cases[32] and while it may have its attractions, it seems unlikely that the mitigation rule can be fully justified on this basis. This justification has also been rightly criticised on the ground that '[a] party makes a contract *so that* the other party (backed up by the courts), *and not he himself*, will fulfil his contractual expectation'.[33]

[28] See, eg, *NV Maes Roger v NV Kapa Reynolds*, Appellate Court Gent (Belgium) 10 May 2004, available at cisgw3.law.pace.edu/cases/040510b1.html (where the court, commenting on the buyer's failure to mitigate, stated: 'As Buyer knew that not conducting a cover purchase would severely burden its relationship with its customers and that Buyer could not fulfill its obligations with the delivered plastic film, the damage suffered due to loss of good reputation or as a consequence, that the clientele sustained damages because of missing replacement foil, are attributed to the Buyer and limited to the amount of a possible cover purchase.').

[29] The other side of the same coin is to say that the mitigation rule discourages passivity and instead encourages dynamism, self-reliance, stoicism and responsibility for one's own welfare (see Bridge (n 9) 409–10; Pautremat (n 14)). See also ICC No 8817, December 1997, available at www.unilex.info, decided under the UPICC. According to the abstract of the decision, the arbitrator took the view that the prolonged interruptions in the buyer's manufacturing activity, that initially arose from the seller's non-compliance with its delivery obligations, was partly caused by the buyer's 'inertia'.

[30] See, eg, MB Kelly, 'Living without the Avoidable Consequences Doctrine in Contract Remedies' (1996) 33 *San Diego L Rev* 175, 181.

[31] A Burrows, 'Contract, Tort and Restitution – A Satisfactory Division or Not?' (1983) 99 *LQR* 217.

[32] Supreme Court 14 January 2002 (n 25) ('In the event of non-performance ..., the obligee is generally justified ... to undertake reasonable measures by itself to generate a situation corresponding to proper performance ...').

[33] M Chen-Wishart, *Contract Law*, 2nd edn (Oxford, OUP, 2008) 557.

Second, the mitigation rule is often explained in causal terms by suggesting that a loss that is reasonably avoidable cannot be regarded as caused by the breach.[34] Justifying the mitigation rule on this basis may have far reaching practical implications. For example, if this rationale is adopted, mitigation will become, like causation, a necessary precondition for the right to damages.[35] Demonstrating mitigation would thus become essential for a valid claim for damages to be brought and the injured party will bear the burden of proving mitigation at the same time as it brings its claim. Both results are not in line with an established treatment of the mitigation rule. The rule is generally regarded as a method of *limiting* damages and not as a necessary precondition to the right to claim damages.[36] Further, as shown below, in most cases the initial burden of proof (of a failure to mitigate) is allocated to the breaching party. These reasons[37] are sufficient to downplay the significance of the causation rationale.

2. SCOPE OF THE MITIGATION RULE

Before examining specific mitigation measures, it is helpful to delineate the scope of the mitigation rule. Although the rule is often expressed in terms of a 'duty to mitigate', it is not, strictly speaking, accurate to treat it as such[38] because no liability will be incurred for a failure to mitigate.[39] Mitigation is an act which the injured party should take in its own interest in order not to be precluded from

[34] See *British Westinghouse Electric and Manufacturing Co v Underground Electric Railway Co of London Ltd* [1912] AC 673, 689 (HL); FH Lawson, *Remedies of English Law*, 2nd edn (London, Butterworths, 1980) 66–7; J Smith, *The Law of Contract*, 4th edn (London, Sweet & Maxwell, 2002) 228; A Ogus, *The Law of Damages* (London, Butterworths, 1973) 5; C Schmitthoff, 'The Duty to Mitigate' [1961] *JBL* 363. As shown by Honore, there is nothing extraordinary in regarding a failure to act as a cause (see AM Honore, 'Causation and Remoteness of Damage' in K Zweigert and K Drobnig (eds), *International Encyclopedia of Comparative Law*, vol 11, ch 7 (The Hague, Martinus Nijhoff, 1971) 15).

[35] See E McKendrick, *Goode on Commercial Law*, 5th edn (London, Penguin, 2016) [3.131] ('actual performance of steps in mitigation is not a prerequisite of the claimant's right to recover').

[36] See, eg, Comment 1 on art 7.4.8 UPICC.

[37] For other arguments against this rationale, see MG Bridge, *The Sale of Goods,* 4th edn (Oxford, OUP, 2019) [12.30] ('it seems rather arbitrary to assert that the claimant's disputed loss has only one effective cause, namely his own inanition rather than the preceding breach of contract by the defendant.'); Bridge (n 9) 400–01; similarly, CT McCormick, *Handbook on the Law of Damages* (St Paul, Minn, West Publishing Co, 1935) 128; H McGregor, 'The Role of Mitigation in the Assessment of Damages' in Saidov and Cunnington (n 1) 331.

[38] This point has been made on numerous occasions. In the CISG context, see, eg, Schwenzer (n 25) 1105; V Knapp, 'Arts. 74–77 CISG' in Bianca and Bonell (n 24) 562.

[39] *Cf Castel Electronics Pty Ltd v Toshiba Singapore Pte Ltd* [2011] FCAFC 55, [323]–[324] ('It operates by affording the party in breach "a claim" for a reduction in the damages which will otherwise be payable by that party. Article 77 contemplates that, absent a successful claim by the party in breach for a reduction in "the damages" otherwise payable, the other party will be entitled to recover "the damages". Article 77 thus creates an obligation in one party to mitigate loss and confers a correlative right upon the party in breach to enforce that obligation. The natural and ordinary reading of Art 77 structured as it is, is that the right of enforcement conferred by the second sentence of the Article is an exhaustive statement of the rights of the party in breach.').

recovering damages for the loss which could have been reduced or avoided.[40] Another point relates to the relationship between the mitigation rule and the case where the innocent party itself contributes to its own loss by exacerbating that loss. Suppose the buyer who is aware of the defects in the machinery supplied by the seller uses the machinery and increases its loss by producing defective goods and selling them to its customers.The buyer does not contribute to the seller's breach (supply of defective machinery) but increases its loss due to its own unreasonable behaviour. The question is whether a denial of damages for the loss thus arisen should be based on the buyer's failure to avoid its loss (mitigation) or on the lack of a causal link between the seller's breach and the loss (causation). This is an example of where causation and mitigation are just 'different labels for two sides of the same bottle'[41] and, in principle, either of or both these rules can be used as a legal basis. However, the UPICC and PECL contain a specific provision to this effect[42] which naturally provides the answer to this question. In contrast, the CISG does not contain a similar provision but the same result can be achieved by either the principles of causation (art 74) or mitigation (art 77), or both.[43]

Whether the mitigation requirement applies to the anticipatory breach cases is a challenging question.[44] It is submitted that the mitigation requirement applies to the anticipatory breach cases just as it does to the actual breach cases.[45] There is no doubt that where the contract is avoided for anticipatory breach, the party is entitled to claim damages and this claim, like any other claim for damages, is subject to the mitigation rule. From a policy perspective, it can also be argued that if the instruments are serious about the policies underlying the mitigation rule, they should also be enforced in anticipatory breach cases. Moreover, both the mitigation rule and the anticipatory breach doctrine are often justified on the same basis: namely, with reference to the need to avoid waste and promote economic efficiency.[46] In some cases, applying the

[40] The term a 'duty to mitigate' is used in this book for the sake of convenience.

[41] This phrase is used in McCormick (n 37) 134.

[42] 'Where the harm is due in part to an act or omission of the aggrieved party or to another event for which that party bears the risk, the amount of damages shall be reduced to the extent that these factors have contributed to the harm, having regard to the conduct of each of the parties' (art 7.4.7 UPICC); 'The non-performing party is not liable for loss suffered by the aggrieved party to the extent that the aggrieved party contributed to the non-performance or its effects' (art 9:504 PECL).

[43] As shown in ch 4, the injured party can also contribute to the other party's breach. While the mitigation rule can also, in principle, be relied upon in such cases, it is better not to do so because the instruments contain specific provisions to this effect (arts 80 CISG, 7.1.2 UPICC, 8.101(3) and 9:504 PECL) and that would excessively widen the scope of the mitigation rule.

[44] See NM Galston and H Smit (eds), *International Sales: The United Nations Convention on Contracts for the International Sale of Goods* (New York, Matthew Bender, 1984) 9–41. For a discussion of the doctrine of anticipatory breach and further references, see ch 2.

[45] For a similar position, see Secretariat Commentary on art 73 of the 1978 Draft; Comment A on art 9:505 PECL (Lando and Beale (n 16) 446).

[46] See, eg, D Saidov, 'Anticipatory Non-Performance and Underlying Values of the UNIDROIT Principles' (2006) 11 *Uniform L Rev* 795. The link between the mitigation rule and the anticipatory breach doctrine is further evidenced by the remedy of suspension of performance available under

mitigation rule to the anticipatory breach cases may arguably dictate that the damages be assessed on the basis that the innocent party ought to have avoided the contract.[47] In any case, this result is arguably required by the instruments' general principle of reasonableness.

Another question is whether the duty to mitigate requires the injured party to *discover* a breach, already committed. There is no agreement in CISG cases. In one case, a German seller delivered defective aluminium hydroxide to a French glass manufacturer.[48] Without a prior examination, the buyer mixed the defective aluminium hydroxide with another substance, thereby producing defective glass. The court held that by failing to conduct a prior examination, the buyer had failed to mitigate its loss: had the buyer inspected the goods, 'the defect would have been revealed even by means of simple tests',[49] and the loss would have been either reduced or avoided. The mitigation rule was interpreted more restrictively in another case,[50] where the buyer, a food producer, failed to inspect the ground clay,[51] containing high levels of dioxin and used to separate potatoes which the buyer then sold (together with the waste peel) to animal feed producers. Although the resulting loss was equally apportioned between the buyer and the breaching seller,[52] the mitigation rule was held inapplicable. The court took the view that art 77 'only applies to cases where the party entitled to damages failed to take appropriate measures in order to mitigate the damage caused by the other party's breach or to avoid causing the damage after learning of the potential for damage', noting that there was no knowledge of the buyer of the potential for the occurrence of the damage.[53] It is suggested that the approach in the first case is preferable. The position in the second case is too restrictive because, if adopted, it would exclude most cases of latent or hidden non-conformities in the goods, where buyers can argue that they were not in the

the instruments in the anticipatory breach cases. This remedy performs functions similar to those performed by the mitigation rule (see ibid).

[47] See arts 71 and 72 CISG; arts 7.3.3 and 7.3.4 UPICC; art 9:304 PECL. For a more detailed discussion of this issue and how the mitigation rule operates in the anticipatory breach cases, see ch 9. *Cf* Schwenzer (n 25) 1106.

[48] Case No 18 U 121/97 Appellate Court Köln (Germany) 21 August 1997 (Aluminium hydroxide), available at cisgw3.law.pace.edu/cases/970821g1.html.

[49] Ibid.

[50] Case No VIII ZR 100/11 Supreme Court (Germany) 26 September 2012, available at cisgw3.law.pace.edu/cases/120926g1.html.

[51] The buyer also failed to take other protective measures (see these findings of the Court of Appeal with which the Supreme Court seems to have agreed: 'If [the Buyer] knew about the discovery of high levels of dioxin in clay from German production in 1999 with the consequence of lack of fitness for animal feed production, [the Buyer] would have been responsible to take protective measures against the contamination of not only the food produced but also of the waste destined to be used as animal feed. If [the Buyer] did not know of this possibility, it was nevertheless to blame for not having been informed about the potential danger related to the use of the potato separation clay with help of the generally available sources of information. Especially as a food producer [the Buyer's] product responsibility entailed the obligation to be and remain informed about questions of food safety and disposal and reuse of waste.' (Ibid, [11])).

[52] For a further discussion of this case, see ch 4.

[53] Ibid, [31].

position to know about 'the potential for damage'.[54] It is reasonable to expect buyers to be aware of the potential for hidden non-conformities and to examine the goods to determine whether they are conforming. This argument is more consistent with the requirement of the CISG that the buyer must examine the goods.[55] By taking a clear position regarding the need for the buyer to examine the goods, this argument is also more conducive to legal certainty compared to the position in the second case that requires a fact-specific evaluation of whether the buyer 'learned of the potential for damage'. Thus, unless the examination is prohibitively expensive or otherwise impracticable, it is submitted that the mitigation rule requires buyers to examine the goods to determine whether the seller has breached its obligations relating to conformity of the goods.[56]

Finally, the mitigation rule under the CISG and UPICC is sometimes interpreted in a way that expects the injured party to have exercised a certain level of care when drafting a contract with the seller. In one case,[57] the injured buyer was partly denied damages[58] for the delivery of non-conforming goods on the basis that the buyer as 'a professional participant in the market … did not use due care … when making the contract …'.[59] With the contract goods described as 'highly sensitive',[60] the tribunal expected the buyer to 'insist on setting the clear provisions concerning the quality of the purchased goods and the methods of their inspection'.[61] It is submitted that this approach extends excessively the scope of the mitigation rule. Whilst, as explained, there can be good reasons for the mitigation rule to require the buyer to examine the goods to determine whether there is a lack of conformity, it is argued that the scope of the rule should be confined to the circumstances after the contract is made. The balance of the parties' interests and allocation of risks between them under the instruments will tilt too much against the injured party if the scope of the rule is stretched to the *pre-contractual* stage.[62] From a policy perspective, this approach

[54] As seen from the second case, the court readily adopted that view.

[55] 'The buyer *must* examine the goods, or cause them to be examined …' (art 38 CISG).

[56] The same result in both cases could also have been achieved by the causation reasoning (see ch 4). On a related issue, see also n 112.

[57] ICAC No 97/2002, 6 June 2003, available at cisgw3.law.pace.edu/cases/030606r1.html.

[58] The loss was split between the parties: the seller was held liable for two-thirds of the loss and the buyer was deemed responsible for one third. Although the CISG was applicable and the UPICC were also taken into account, the tribunal relied (incorrectly, it is submitted, because the CISG ought to have governed this matter) on domestic law (art 404(1) of the Russian Federation Civil Code) as the basis for such an allocation of loss.

[59] Ibid.

[60] '[N]otwithstanding the "high sensitivity" of the goods delivered, numerous ways of their [possible] use and the multiple physical influences required for switching on, the parties failed to set in the contract the quality characteristics of the goods to be delivered considering their further use. Nor did the parties set forth the procedure of quality control of the said goods and the methods of such control. The contract also does not contain any references to such technical documentation as the standards set by international organizations and the national standards.' (ibid).

[61] Ibid.

[62] See also the arguments in the next section in favour of a balanced meaning of reasonableness, which also militates against extending the reach of the mitigation rule and increasing a burden on the injured party. For further discussion of this case, see ch 4.

can also: make parties too cautious about entering into contracts, increasing transactions costs; deter parties from entering into contracts; or induce parties to exclude the applicability of the instruments in their contract. All these potential consequences contravene the instruments' unification or harmonisation aspirations and their purpose of promoting international trade.[63]

3. REASONABLE MEASURES

3.1. General

The innocent party is required to take only *reasonable* measures of mitigating loss and what is reasonable depends on the circumstances of a case. In the abstract, several guidelines can be given. The policies underlying the mitigation rule must, it is submitted, influence the meaning of reasonableness. This means that a concern for economic efficiency and avoidance of waste would require the party to take the least costly measures. Fair dealing and good faith would require the innocent party to take the other party's interests into account. At the same time, because the duty to mitigate is not a wholly altruistic duty and reflects a concern for the injured party, the mitigation rule should strike a balance between the legitimate interests of both parties.[64] A guideline flowing from an attempt to strike such a balance is that reasonableness does not require the innocent party to 'conduct itself perfectly',[65] take measures that are unlawful,[66] take considerable risks (financial or otherwise) or damage its reputation.[67] One CISG decision may, at first sight, appear to have held otherwise. In that case,[68] the court found that the German buyer had failed to mitigate its loss as it had only made efforts to make replacement purchases in a region where it operated, without taking into account other suppliers in Germany or abroad.[69] It is submitted, however,

[63] See, eg, the preamble of the CISG.

[64] For a somewhat similar approach to interpreting the CISG, see Case No 4 R 219/01k Appellate Court Graz (Austria) 24 January 2002 (Excavator), available at cisgw3.law.pace.edu/cases/020124a3.html ('The obligation stated in Art 77 CISG is to be interpreted taking into account the competing interests of the parties, as well as commercial customs and the principle of good faith').

[65] *Hewlett-Packard France v Matrox Graphics Inc*, 2020 QCCS 78, [274].

[66] See *Doolim Corp v R Doll, LLC*, 2009 U.S. Dist. LEXIS 45366 (S.D.N.Y. May 28, 2009), [44]–[45], where the seller's resale of the goods, made for the buyer and bearing the buyer's trademark, was deemed reasonable with no infringement of the buyer's trademark rights.

[67] See, similarly, Knapp (n 38) 560; Schwenzer (n 25) 1107; *Hewlett-Packard France v Matrox Graphics Inc* (n 65); *Downs Investments Pty Ltd v Perwaja Steel SDN BHD* [2000] QSC 421 (unfortunately, the court seems to have reached this conclusion not on the basis of the CISG but following the position of the common law). For a similar position in English law, see, eg, *Chitty* (n 7) [26-090].

[68] Case No 3 U 246/97 Appellate Court Celle (Germany) 2 September 1991 (Vacuum cleaners), available at cisgw3.law.pace.edu/cases/910902g1.html.

[69] To illustrate why this decision may be interpreted as requiring the injured party to take considerable risks, it is helpful to recall the English case *Lesters Leather and Skin Co v Home and Overseas Brokers* (1948–49) 82 *Ll L Rep* 202, where the buyer suffered loss as a result of the delivery of defective snakeskins. The seller argued that the buyer ought to have mitigated its loss by having purchased

that a mere possibility of a replacement transaction abroad does not in itself mean that it involves excessive risk and costs. On the contrary, it is reasonable to assume that in international trade replacement transactions often have to be made abroad. What is crucial for determining the reasonableness of a (replacement) transaction is the nature and extent of risks involved if the party goes ahead with that transaction.[70]

3.2. Non-Delivery,[71] Non-Acceptance and Non-Payment

In sales transactions, making a substitute transaction is a typical measure of mitigating loss.[72] Where a buyer fails to pay and take delivery of the goods, a seller can mitigate its loss by reselling the goods[73] and a buyer who does not buy substitute goods after the seller failed to deliver will often have failed to mitigate.[74] For a substitute transaction to be reasonable 'it must have been made in such a manner as is likely to cause a resale to have been made at the highest price reasonably possible in the circumstances or a cover purchase at the lowest price reasonably possible'.[75] This general guideline has been followed in some CISG cases. In one case, after the buyer had breached the contract, the seller resold the goods at a very low price.[76] When the seller claimed the difference

the snakeskins in India. The court held that it was not reasonable for the buyer 'to go hunting the globe to find out where they can get skins' (ibid, 205) and this decision is sometimes interpreted as reflecting the position that reasonableness does not require the innocent party to risk its money too far (J Edelman, S Colton and J Varuhas (eds), *McGregor on Damages*, 20th edn (London, Sweet & Maxwell, 2019) [9-087]).

[70] For measures to be recognised as mitigation, no notice is required to be given to the breaching party, contrary to suggestions in some CISG cases (see ICC No 10274, 1999 (Poultry feed), available at cisgw3.law.pace.edu/cases/990274i1.html; for a more detailed discussion, see ch 8). Contacting the breaching party for assistance in mitigating losses can, however, be a reasonable mitigation measure (see n 140 and the discussion in the text accompanying n 110).

[71] See n 111.

[72] For a detailed discussion of reasonableness of substitute transactions, see ch 8. Before deciding to enter into a replacement transaction, it may sometimes be reasonable for the innocent party to negotiate with the breaching party to persuade it to perform the contract, as happened in *The Rice Corporation v Grain Board of Iraq*, 2008 WL 2115664, where the buyer, the Grain Board of Iraq, refused to take conforming goods delivered on board M/V Alda to the Umm Qasr, Iraq. Following the seller's attempts to persuade the buyer to take the goods, the buyer indicated that it would accept the delivery of the goods from a different vessel. When this was done, the buyer again refused to accept the delivery, resulting in the seller's eventual resale of the goods. In those circumstances, the seller took various measures and correspondingly incurred various costs, such as: demurrage and additional expenses charged by the owners of the M/V Alda and expenses incurred for discharging, storage, segregation, attempted re-shipment, and re-sale fees. All those measures were deemed reasonable mitigation measures and the said costs were recovered. This decision was subsequently overruled on other grounds in *The Rice Corporation v Grain Board of Iraq*, 582 F.Supp.2d 1309.

[73] See *Watkins-Johnson v Islamic Republic of Iran*, Iran-United States Claims Tribunal, Award 370 (429-370-1) 28 July 1989, available at www.cisg.law.pace.edu/cisg/wais/db/cases2/890728i2.html.

[74] See ICAC No 406/1998, 6 June 2000, available at cisgw3.law.pace.edu/cases/000606r1.html.

[75] See Secretariat Commentary on art 71 of the 1978 Draft Convention.

[76] The contract was for the sale of sacks of jute at a price of US$55.90 per 100 bags. The seller made a resale at a price of US$0.30 per sack.

between the contract price and the resale price, the court denied the recovery of that difference on the ground that the resale was not a reasonable substitute transaction.[77]

It is generally accepted that a true substitute transaction must be on terms similar to those in the original contract.[78] In most situations, this will probably be the case because the purpose of the mitigation measures will be closely connected with the purpose for which the contract with a breaching party was concluded. If, for example, the buyer made a contract with the seller in order to make a sub-sale, the buyer will attempt to reduce or avoid potential losses on its sub-sale by making a contract with another seller on similar terms to those in the original contract. Nevertheless, a possibility of mitigating losses by other means cannot be ruled out. It may be reasonable for the innocent party to channel the resources, released as a result of the breach, in a different direction. Suppose that, after the seller's refusal to deliver, the buyer decides to invest the unpaid purchase price in a profitable venture. The returns from this investment may be sufficient to pay damages to the sub-buyer and to be offset against other losses. Although such cases will be rare, the possibility of such measures being reasonable mitigation cannot be ruled out.[79]

While making substitute transactions is a typical mitigation measure, various circumstances may restrict or preclude the injured party's ability to do so.[80] One such circumstance is where the buyer who has already paid the purchase price does not have sufficient financial resources to procure a substitute. Although this concern has been said to reflect an 'unreal conviction',[81] in some CISG cases judges were prepared to take this difficulty into account.[82] A circumstance which can also make it difficult for the injured party to find a substitute transaction is the one involving the delivery of seasonal products. In one such case,[83] the buyer had failed to pay the price for a delivery of shoes. The seller, a shoe manufacturer, attempted to resell the goods but the resale turned out to be impossible because 'all customers were already well supplied and the stocks were still filled from the previous … season'. For this reason, the court held that the seller had not failed to mitigate its loss. In another case,[84] where a clothing manufacturer failed to deliver the goods on time, it was not possible for the buyer to procure

[77] See *Internationale Jute Maatschappij BV v Marín Palomares SL*, Supreme Court (Spain) 28 January 2000, available at cisgw3.law.pace.edu/cases/000128s4.html (for further analysis of this decision, see below).

[78] For a detailed discussion, see ch 8.

[79] See JG MacIntosh and DC Frydenlund, 'An Investment Approach to a Theory of Contract Mitigation' (1987) 37 *University Toronto L J* 115 (arguing, from the standpoint of economic analysis, that there is nothing that would rule out such an interpretation of reasonable mitigation).

[80] Such as where making a substitute transaction is unlawful. See n 66 and the accompanying main text; also ch 8.

[81] See MG Bridge, 'The Market Rule of Damages Assessment' in Saidov and Cunnington (n 1) 443.

[82] See Appellate Court Gent 10 May 2004 (n 28).

[83] See Case No 17 U 146/93 Appellate Court Düsseldorf (Germany) 14 January 1994 (Shoes), available at cisgw3.law.pace.edu/cases/940114g1.html.

[84] ICC No 8786, January 1997 (Clothing), available at cisgw3.law.pace.edu/cases/978786i1.html.

substitute goods (for sale in its retail stores) as they had to be ordered several months in advance, whereas the breach was committed towards the end of the season. It was again held that that the buyer had not failed to mitigate its losses.

Another circumstance preventing the buyer from mitigating its loss by procuring a substitute transaction is where the sub-sale contract requires the delivery of the self-same goods as those in the original contract. In one CISG case,[85] the buyer's sub-sale contract provided for the delivery of the same goods as those in the buyer's contract with the seller in terms of their specifications and place of manufacture (Korea) and, because of the time constraints,[86] that requirement made the buyer unable to procure a substitute to fulfil its sub-sale. Although, strictly speaking, the case does not involve 'self-same' goods, it nevertheless illustrates the same difficulty as the one which the buyer would have faced in the case of 'self-same' goods.[87]

Yet another situation rendering the innocent party unable to mitigate by procuring a substitute is the 'lost volume' situation, where the seller's supply exceeds the demand for the goods. In this case, if the buyer breaches the contract and the seller resells the goods to another buyer, it may be that the seller would have sold the goods to that other buyer even if the first buyer had not breached and a resale is not true a substitute. In one CISG case,[88] the seller agreed to produce a piece of jewellery for the buyer and when the latter failed to pay, the seller claimed damages for the difference between the cost of manufacture and the contract price. The court accepted the claim and dismissed the buyer's objection that the seller had failed to mitigate by means of reselling that piece of jewellery, stating that the objection 'is ineffective as far as the promisee, in performing the substitute transaction, would have lost another similar transaction bringing the same profit as the first transaction'.[89] It seems that several other CISG cases can also be regarded as 'lost volume' cases. Those are cases where the goods were specifically produced or designed for the needs of a particular buyer thereby eliminating any demand for the goods. In one case[90] the fact that the textile manufacturing facility was produced specifically for the buyer's range of products made it virtually impossible for the seller to resell it.[91] In some other cases,[92]

[85] CIETAC 17 October 1996 (Tinplate), available at cisgw3.law.pace.edu/cases/961017c1.html.

[86] '[the] [b]uyer being a Chinese company was unable to find Korean products on the Chinese market within a short time' (ibid).

[87] For a similar case, see CIETAC 29 September 2004 (India rapeseed meal), available at cisgw3.law.pace.edu/cases/040929c1.html (where the tribunal dismissed the seller's argument that the Chinese buyer ought to have procured a substitute delivery of rapeseed meal in its domestic market on the basis that the contract goods were indicated as 'India rapeseed meal').

[88] See Case No 1 Ob 292/99v Supreme Court (Austria) 28 April 2000 (Jewellery), available at cisgw3.law.pace.edu/cases/000428a3.html.

[89] See ibid.

[90] See Commercial Court St Gallen 3 December 2002 (n 26).

[91] The expert's finding was that 'the opportunity to have this machine resold as a whole [was] very improbable' (ibid).

[92] ICAC No 107/2002, 16 February 2004 ('The seller, deprived of the possibility of independently selling the goods produced for the buyer (since according to the conditions of the contract the goods

the impossibility of a seller's resale arose because the goods bore the buyer's trademark, logo or signet. However, the fact that mitigation by means of reselling the goods is not possible does not necessarily mean that mitigation is altogether impossible. For example, it may have been reasonable, in the case of the delivery of jewellery,[93] for the seller to break up the jewellery and sell the precious stones of which it was made. In the case of the specifically designed textile manufacturing facility, the court agreed with the expert's conclusion that the seller's rapid disassembly and re-utilisation of the saleable parts of the machine was 'the most reasonable and prudent solution' in the circumstances.[94]

A substitute transaction is not always an appropriate mitigation measure. In one case,[95] the seller, despite becoming aware after the contract had been concluded that the buyer would not be able to perform, nevertheless ordered the goods (designated for the buyer) from its supplier and then resold them to a third party. The tribunal dismissed the claim for the difference between the contract price and the price in that resale on the ground of the seller's failure to mitigate. The inference seems to be that the seller ought to have refrained from ordering the goods and presumably the damages would then have been the difference between (what would have been) the cost of purchasing the goods from the supplier and the contract price.[96] It is suggested that, to start with, the reasonableness of the seller's conduct ought to have depended on whether the seller could be said to have been in a 'lost volume' situation. If it would *not* have resold the goods to that third party had the buyer *not* breached, ordering from the supplier and then reselling *might* have been a reasonable course of mitigating losses provided that losses resulting from a resale to a third party[97] would be lower than losses resulting from refraining from buying from the supplier.[98] In short, if the seller, before ordering the goods from its supplier, was in the

were marked with buyer's trademark and could not be sold by the seller to a third party without a written consent of the buyer as provided for in … the contract), repeatedly asked the buyer to give this consent …, yet obtained no consent of the kind'); Case No OR.96.0-00-13 Commercial Court Aargau (Switzerland) 26 September 1997 (Cutlery), available at cisgw3.law.pace.edu/cases/970926s1.html (the situation related only to the sale of knives). In one case, the seller managed to resell the goods bearing the buyer's trademark (Case No 7 O 43/01 District Court Göttingen (Germany) 20 September 2002 (Mattresses and bedding accessories), available at cisgw3.law.pace.edu/cases/020920g1.html).

[93] See Supreme Court (Austria) 28 April 2000 (n 88).

[94] See Commercial Court St Gallen 3 December 2002 (n 26) and note a detailed expert's report on the reasonableness of the measures.

[95] CIETAC 29 September 1997 (Aluminium oxide), available at cisgw3.law.pace.edu/cases/970929c1.html.

[96] The decision is curious as the tribunal eventually awarded damages under the 'abstract' formula in art 76 CISG. This highlights the tension between the 'concrete' and 'abstract' approaches to calculating damages. Although the tribunal began with the 'concrete' approach by enquiring what the claimant, in the light of its actual situation, ought to have done, it then suddenly moved away from measuring damages with reference to the claimant's actual circumstances and, instead, relied upon the 'abstract' formula based on hypothetical mitigation (see ch 8).

[97] That is, the difference between the contract price and the price in the resale to a third party together with other possible losses.

[98] That is, the difference between the cost of acquisition and the contract price.

position to estimate and compare losses resulting from a potential resale to a third party, the reasonable mitigation measure ought to have been that which would have resulted in the lower amount of damages.[99] In another CISG case,[100] as a result of the buyer's non-payment for the delivered goods, the parties had concluded an agreement acknowledging the buyer's debt and providing for a payment schedule. When the buyer failed to make a payment and the seller claimed damages, the tribunal dismissed the buyer's argument that the seller had failed to mitigate on the following grounds:

> the Respondent acknowledged its debt in [the] Agreement No 292 of 15 January 2003 and … the Claimant was entitled to expect not only that the Respondent would perform its obligations in good faith and in accordance with the agreed schedule but also to receive the monetary funds necessary for further use in its commercial activity. The Respondent itself by its execution of Agreement No 292 of 15 January 2003 put the Claimant in the position of a contracting party waiting for the performance [where] it could undertake nothing but wait for the Respondent's payments relying on its good faith; yet the Respondent abused [the] Claimant's trust and failed to perform [its] obligation to pay. Taking into consideration the above as well as the fact that the Respondent failed to indicate what exact measures, in its opinion, were not taken by the Claimant in order to mitigate the amount of the loss of profit, the Tribunal rejects Respondent's arguments.[101]

It is sometimes the case that, after the breach, the breaching party offers performing the contract on terms different from those in the original contract. The question arises whether accepting such an offer is a reasonable mitigation measure.[102] In one case,[103] after the conclusion of the contract the buyer offered to purchase the goods at a lower price than the contract price. The seller rejected

[99] This approach flows from the rationale of the mitigation rule. In particular, it ensures the least costly measure, preserving an efficient outcome and a balance between the parties' interests by, on the one hand, protecting the interests of the breaching party and, on the other, only requiring the seller to act to the extent that can be reasonably expected. A similar situation arose in another CISG case (CIETAC 28 May 1999 (Veneer Import), available at cisgw3.law.pace.edu/cases/990528c1.html), where the innocent buyer, after becoming aware that the seller would not be able to deliver the goods, concluded a contract to resell those goods (the situation arose due to the lack of communication between the buyer's internal departments). As a result of the seller's non-delivery, the buyer had to pay damages to its sub-buyer. The tribunal held that no compensation for damages paid to the sub-buyer could be awarded because by entering into the sub-sale contract, the buyer had failed to avoid that loss. This case again illustrates the situation where the mitigation rule and causation are simply two sides of the same coin. The same result could have been achieved (perhaps more easily) on the ground that paying damages to the sub-buyer was of the buyer's own making.

[100] ICAC No 186/2003, 17 June 2004, available at cisgw3.law.pace.edu/cases/040617r1.html.

[101] Ibid; see also ICC No 12111, 3 October 2003, available at www.unilex.info, decided under the UPICC, where the claimant seller, who also committed a breach by delivering non-conforming goods, was denied damages on the basis that it had failed to co-operate with the buyer when the buyer urged the seller to directly contact the buyer's customers to resolve the issues arising from the lack of conformity.

[102] This issue is also dealt with in English law. See, eg, *Payzu Ltd v Saunders* [1919] 2 KB 581 (CA); *Sotiros Shipping Inc v Sameiet Solholt (The Solholt)* [1983] 1 Lloyd's Rep 605 (CA). For an incisive analysis of these cases, see Bridge (n 37) [12.35]–[12.39].

[103] Supreme Court (Spain) 28 January 2000 (n 77).

the offer[104] and resold the goods to a third party at a price lower than both the original contract price and the price in the buyer's offer. The court dismissed the seller's claim for the difference between the contract price and the resale price on the ground that rejecting the buyer's offer had been a failure to mitigate the loss.[105] At first sight, a different result appears to have been reached in another case[106] where it was the seller who was willing to sell the goods at the price higher (US$215.00 per ton) than the contract price (US$190.00 per ton). The buyer rejected the proposal and insisted on the performance at the original contract price. After the seller had failed to deliver, the buyer made a cover purchase from a third party and the tribunal held that the cover purchase was a reasonable mitigation measure and that the buyer was not required to accept the seller's offer. However, the decisions do not necessarily reflect different approaches to the interpretation of reasonableness of mitigation. It is argued that what is critical in these types of case is whether accepting the offer would lead to the injured party surrendering its right to damages and avoidance of the contract.[107] If so, then accepting the breaching party's offer cannot be a reasonable measure to mitigate loss. This would be grossly unfair to the injured party and would, no doubt, contravene the mitigation rule's aim of striking a fair balance between the legitimate interests of both parties. If accepting the offer does not lead to the injured party surrendering of its right to avoid the contract and claim damages for the difference between the original contract price and the

[104] The seller did not strictly speaking reject the offer as it agreed to accept it subject to the 'buyer's payment on the issuance of a letter of credit drawn on a prestigious Dutch bank to cover the purchase price that buyer offered'. However, the Court itself treated that condition as a rejection taking into account that 'the commercial relationship that had existed between the parties since 1988 was without incidents concerning the payment of the supplied merchandise'. In addition, 'in the substitute sale no special guarantees of the payment of the price were demanded; [the] seller simply made payment conditional "after receipt of the invoice"'.

[105] In a very similar case (CIETAC 1 March 1999 (Canned mandarin oranges), available at cisgw3.law.pace.edu/cases/990301c1.html), the tribunal also refused to award the difference between the contract price and the resale price and instead awarded the difference between the contract price and the price determined with reference to *both* the average price (in Germany) and the price offered by the buyer (based on the Chinese market price). This decision reflects a curious mixture of both the 'abstract' and 'concrete' approaches to assessing damages: assuming that accepting the buyer's offer was a reasonable course of action, the 'concrete' method in its pure form would have dictated awarding the difference between the contract price and the price in the buyer's offer. The tribunal, however, did not consider the price in the buyer's offer as decisive but merely as a helpful factor in determining what seemed to the tribunal as a 'reasonable price' on which it eventually relied. This approach is unfortunate because, as argued below, the CISG expresses a preference for the 'concrete' measure, which is in harmony with the mitigation rule. What the tribunal ought to have done was to calculate damages on the basis of what ought to have been a reasonable mitigation measure in the light of the claimant's circumstances.

[106] ICC Case No 6281, 1989 (Steel bars), available at cisgw3.law.pace.edu/cases/ 896281i1.html. Although the case itself was governed by Yugoslav law, when the tribunal dealt with the issues of mitigation it also considered what the position would have been under the CISG.

[107] Such surrender can occur where accepting the breaching party's offer leads to a modification of the existing contract, as opposed to making a new contract, with no undertaking by the breaching party to compensate for the difference between the original and the renegotiated price.

newly accepted price, there is no reason why accepting the offer should not be a reasonable mitigation measure. The decisions referred to in this paragraph do not make clear whether these considerations were at play, making it difficult to assess whether the results in those cases are correct.[108]

Finally, in some countries, a breach of contract will entail an innocent party paying a penalty to state authorities. For example, where the seller's domestic law requires it to sell foreign currency received from its international transactions to the state, it may have to pay a penalty for not doing so if the buyer fails to pay the contract price. In some such cases, the applicable domestic law provided that the penalty would *not* be imposed if the seller brought a claim against the buyer within a specified period and, where the sellers had failed to do so, damages for the payment of the penalty were denied on the ground of the seller's failure to mitigate that loss.[109] The innocent buyer may also find itself in the position of paying a penalty to state authorities but such a situation is likely to arise not as a result of currency regulations, but due to some other legislative requirements. In one case,[110] the buyer had to pay a penalty to customs authorities as a result of the seller's failure to deliver the goods. Having established that the payment of the penalty was caused by non-delivery, the tribunal implied that the buyer had not failed to mitigate that loss because it had, on several occasions, warned the seller that a failure to deliver would entail the penalty. Since in this case the penalty requirement emanated from a different type of legislation than that in earlier cases of non-payment, there is no reason to suppose that there was a similar provision enabling the buyer to avoid its loss by bringing a claim against the seller within a prescribed period.

3.3. Non-Conforming Goods and Delay in Performance

Various mitigation measures may have to be taken where non-conforming goods are delivered but accepted by the buyer or where there is a delay in performing the contract. To identify a reasonable mitigation measure, the purpose for which the party entered into the contract with the breaching party may be relevant.

[108] The decisions in some other CISG cases can be criticised for failing to properly address the breaching parties' argument that the innocent parties had failed to reduce losses because they ignored the breaching parties' proposals (see CIETAC 30 October 1991 (Roll aluminium and aluminium parts), available at cisgw3.law.pace.edu/cases/911030c1.html; Case No 95/3214 District Court of Kuopio (Finland) 5 November 1996 (Butter), available at cisgw3.law.pace.edu/cases/961105f5.html).

[109] Arbitration 9 July 1999 (Ukraine) (Metal production goods), available at cisgw3. law.pace.edu/cases/990709u5.html ('If the Seller had not delayed presenting the Tribunal with the demand for the recovery from the Buyer of the debt for the goods until the expiration of 90 days since the date of customs clearance of the goods, Seller would not have incurred these damages'); Arbitration 27 October 2004 (Ukraine) (Lavatory paper), available at cisgw3.law.pace.edu/cases/041027u5.html; Arbitration 10 May 1999 (Ukraine) (Sunflower seeds meal), available at cisgw3.law.pace.edu/cases/990510u5.html.

[110] ICAC No 85/2002, 26 June 2003, available at cisgw3.law.pace.edu/cases/030626r1.html.

Where the buyer accepts non-conforming goods[111] bought either for resale or for its own use,[112] it may be worth attempting to cure a lack of conformity where reasonably possible. If the buyer intended to resell the goods, remedying the lack of conformity may bring the goods into their conforming state enabling the buyer to resell them as planned.[113] Where the seller is the supplier of non-conforming goods, the seller may itself offer remedying the non-conformity and the question then is whether accepting this offer is a reasonable mitigation measure. The answer depends on whether the proposed cure will enable the buyer to fulfil its purpose of reselling the goods as planned, considering such inter-related factors as: whether accepting the seller's proposed cure will cause the buyer unreasonable inconvenience or unreasonable expense;[114] the time by which the buyer planned or was required to deliver the goods to its sub-buyer or customer; whether the proposed cure is expected to be effective and final in the sense of providing an effective resolution.

The latter set of factors was relevant in a case[115] where the seller delivered defective graphic cards installed in the computers that the buyer sold to its customers. The court rightly held that accepting a technical solution proposed by the seller was not a reasonable mitigation measure because that solution was no more than a 'temporary fix' which did not 'prevent the failure from reoccurring after approximately two weeks'.[116] The court further held that the buyer

[111] Where the buyer decides to reject non-conforming goods and (typically) avoid the contract, the scenario becomes equivalent to that of non-delivery of the goods and the considerations examined in the previous section become relevant. See also Case No. 759/2008 Appellate Court Madrid (Spain) 10 March 2009, available at cisgw3.law.pace.edu/cases/090310s4.html, where a non-conformity in the goods (wine) was deemed to have rendered the goods non-tradeable and the court appears to have suggested that the destruction of the wine would have been a more reasonable measure of dealing with the goods (provided it was less expensive) than shipping them back to the seller, as the buyer in fact did (which was deemed unnecessary, with the buyer's claims for damages for the cost of such shipment rejected).

[112] Where the buyer uses contract goods in its manufacturing/production process in the knowledge that they are non-conforming, that is likely to constitute a failure to mitigate. In Case No 07/03098 Court of Appeals Rennes (France) 27 May 2008, available at cisgw3.law.pace.edu/cases/080527f1.html, the buyer, a manufacturer of swimming suits, continued to use non-conforming bra cups, delivered by the seller, despite its knowledge of the non-conformity. The court rightly held that the buyer had failed to mitigate its loss: 'Given that the [Buyer] had already contacted Mr. P on 26 September when 860 pairs of cups had been processed in Tunisia, but nevertheless, the [Buyer] did not decide to stop the processing until three days later, when already 1,800 pairs of cups had been processed, and given that a production line of bathing suits produces 1,200 bathing suits within three days … a non-conformity like the poor adhesion between "the covering fabric and the whole piece" and its debonding during the mechanical handling requires a very quick reaction. The three-day period can therefore not be considered as sufficiently short, wherefrom follows that the [Seller]'s request for the application of Art. 77 is well founded' (this case is further discussed in chs 4 and 8). For the discussion of whether the mitigation rule requires the buyer to examine the goods to determine whether they are conforming, see the paragraph accompanying nn 49 and 56.

[113] CIETAC 31 January 2000 (Clothes), available at cisgw3.law.pace.edu/ cases/000131c1.html.

[114] Analogy can be drawn with the preconditions to the seller's right to cure under the CISG in arts 34, 37 and 48.

[115] *Hewlett-Packard France v Matrox Graphics Inc* (n 65).

[116] Ibid, [268].

was not required to accept another technical solution proposed by the seller. In addition to finding that none of those two proposed solutions provided a final resolution to the problem, the court highlighted two other factors that seem to show that the seller's proposal was not an effective and a commercially viable solution. One was that the (second) proposed solution did not pass the buyer's internal validation tests. Second, both proposed solutions would require ceasing the replacement of the graphic cards, whereas the buyer's customers insisted on having the graphic cards replaced.[117] Finally, when a viable technical solution had been developed jointly by the parties and accepted by the buyer in October 1999, the question was whether the buyer failed to mitigate its loss by 'pushing its use' and implementing it only in March and April 2000.[118] The court's decision, giving a negative answer, appears well aligned with the nature of the mitigation rule which, as explained, does not require an innocent party to act perfectly or run the risk of damaging its reputation:

> 'Even if [the buyer] could have acted sooner and put an end more quickly to replacing cards, it was not obliged to conduct itself perfectly with a view to saving money for [the seller]. It was entitled to reasonably satisfy its customers' needs, or even desires, to avoid as much as possible any long-term impact on its reputation resulting from the defect affecting [the seller's] graphic cards. In the Court's view, the preponderance of proof establishes that [the buyer] acted reasonably and did not fail to mitigate its damages.'[119]

If the goods were bought for the buyer's own use, curing them may likewise enable the buyer to use them as intended.[120] Provided that costs of cure are reasonable in the circumstances,[121] damages for such costs are often an appropriate compensation.[122] The mitigation rule appears to have been interpreted

[117] Ibid, [270]–[271].

[118] Ibid, [273].

[119] Ibid, [274]. Another example of a commercially oriented interpretation of reasonableness, showing that courts do not expect perfect conduct from the injured buyer, who received non-conforming goods, can be found in *Castel Electronics Pty Ltd v Toshiba Singapore Pte Ltd* (n 39). In this case, the buyer, an Australian-based distributor of electrical products, claimed damages arising from defects, that were said to have reached 'epidemic' proportions, in products of a well-known brand (Toshiba) supplied by the seller. The first instance judge found (and the Federal Court of Australia appears to have accepted this finding) that the buyer's decision to continue to supply these products to the market (in the light of the seller's repeated representations that the defects had been rectified) was found to be a reasonable mitigation measure: 'I do not regard decisions by [the buyer] to launch the 'epidemic' products … on the Australian wholesale market as prompted by anything other than a desire to keep faith with its retailers and protect the reputation of the 'Toshiba' brand. [The buyer's] endeavours in this respect, although largely unsuccessful, were reasonably seen as likely to mitigate the damage flowing from the breaches which I have found [the seller] to have committed of the successive sales contracts' (ibid, [329]).

[120] ICC No 8740, October 1996 (Russian coal), available at cisgw3.law.pace.edu/cases/968740i1.html may be relevant.

[121] This stems from both the mitigation rule and a general principle of reasonableness underlying the international instruments.

[122] This again demonstrates the connection between the mitigation rule and the calculation of damages. For a more extensive discussion of the 'cost of cure' method of calculating damages, see ch 8.

in one case,[123] where the CISG was inapplicable but Art 77 CISG was nevertheless engaged with,[124] as far as requiring the buyer of an electro-erosion machine, delivered in a non-conforming state, to lease another machine (so that the buyer's business operations are not interrupted) whilst attempting to cure the non-conformity in the machine delivered by the seller.[125] Whilst the decision contains little factual information, it is suggested that, as a general matter, this interpretation of the mitigation rule appears too stringent and harsh on innocent buyers. As explained, the reasonableness criterion, underlying the mitigation rule, means that innocent parties are not required to take measures that entail considerable burdens or risks, financial and otherwise. Interpreting Art 77 CISG as requiring the innocent buyer to bear the cost of cure *and* the cost of leasing or acquiring another machine imposes an excessive financial and commercial (in terms of an investment of time and effort) burden, going well beyond the reasonableness threshold. This interpretative approach is difficult to justify, unless the circumstances are such that: the magnitude of potential losses caused by the delay in the buyer's business operations is too high compared to the cost of cure *and* leasing or acquiring another machine; it is reasonable to attempt to cure the non-conforming goods; and the cost of leasing another machine is not substantial in the light of the buyer's financial position and the fact that the buyer is already incurring the cost of cure.

If cure is not possible or reasonable, the buyer may still have to make full use of the goods on hand[126] and one way of doing so is to sell them at a reduced price.[127] In fact, in some cases reselling the goods may be the only way

[123] Case No 70025609579 Appellate Court Rio Grande do Sul (Brazil) 20 May 2009, available at cisgw3.law.pace.edu/cases/090520b5.html.

[124] 'the Court invoked art. 77 of the CISG and its reception in Brazilian Restatement of Law no. 169 …, ascertaining that the party who relies on a breach must take measures to reduce the loss' (ibid).

[125] In this case, the buyer was found to have failed to mitigate and denied damages for both its loss of profit and the cost cure that the buyer had incurred. This decision can also be conceivably interpreted as implying that the buyer ought to have rejected the non-conforming machine and then presumably avoided the contract with the seller, extricating itself from its contractual obligations, to make it easier to enter into a new contract for another machine. If so, it highlights the controversial question of whether the mitigation rule requires an innocent party to reject the goods and avoid the contract. Although the wording of art 77 suggests that the mitigation rule applies only to the remedy of damages, it can be argued that the mitigation rule can require an innocent party to reject the goods and avoid the contract. First, similar to what has been suggested above in the context of anticipatory breach, the policy rationale of the mitigation rule points in favour of such an interpretation (see further ch 9). Secondly, even outside the policy argument, it can be contended that rejecting non-conforming goods and avoiding the contract can be measures that, if taken, will ultimately avoid or reduce losses and for this reason can be required under art 77. A counter-argument to the latter point is that, under this interpretation, the remedy of avoidance (and the rejection of the goods, if it is a separate remedy under the CISG) becomes subsumed under and dictated by, becoming secondary to, a specific rule on the remedy of damages.

[126] See CIETAC 5 July 1993 (Copperized steel tubes), available at cisgw3.law.pace.edu/cases/930705c1.html ('in order to prevent the loss from spreading, the Buyer is responsible for making full use of usable copperized steel tubes').

[127] CIETAC 29 March 1999 (Flanges) available at cisgw3.law.pace.edu/ cases/990329c1.html.

of mitigating the loss. In one CISG case[128] where non-conforming goods of a seasonal nature were delivered, the buyer argued that it had requested the seller to remedy the defects but received no response. As the end of the sale season was approaching and the storage fees were increasing (causing financial difficulties), the buyer again contacted the seller requesting the latter to collect the goods. The buyer finally suggested that because it could not afford to incur the cost of returning the goods itself, it had no choice but to resell the goods at a reduced price. The tribunal rightly accepted that the buyer's conduct was in accordance with its duty to mitigate. Where goods bought for use in the manufacturing process are delivered late, it may be reasonable to find a replacement for the period of delay, particularly if a timely commencement of manufacturing is of the essence.[129] Provided that the cost of such a replacement is reasonable, the buyer's conduct is likely to be a reasonable way of mitigating loss and the costs of replacement become, at the same time, an appropriate method of calculating damages for the delay. It may also be reasonable for the buyer to use the goods from its existing stock to execute its plans during the period of delay.[130]

Another question concerns the extent to which an innocent buyer is entitled and/or required to take measures to avoid the loss before the damage manifests itself or occurs. In the above-mentioned case,[131] involving a delivery of defective graphic cards installed in the buyer's computers, the buyer took preventive measures by repairing the graphic cards even in those computers that have not yet failed. Those measures were rightly deemed reasonable, with the buyer having been awarded damages for the cost of those preventive measures, because the issue of which, and when, particular graphic cards would fail was entirely unpredictable.[132]

Finally, can the mitigation rule be interpreted so as to require the injured buyer to attempt to renegotiate the terms of the contract with its sub-buyer? In one CISG case,[133] the buyer claimed compensation for damages paid to its sub-buyer for delay in delivering the goods which in turn had been caused by the seller's failure to deliver on time. The tribunal held that the buyer had failed to mitigate that loss for several reasons. First, the buyer ought to have asked its sub-buyer about the possibility of changing the terms of the contract so as to extend the delivery date. Second, the buyer ought to have suggested compensation for being released from its obligations under the sub-sales contract, as provided for in art 409 of the Russian Civil Code[134] (applicable as domestic law). Third, the

[128] CIETAC 26 October 1996 (Cotton bath towels), available at cisgw3.law.pace.edu/cases/961026c1.html.

[129] See Supreme Court Austria, 14 January 2002 (n 25).

[130] See ICC No 8740 (n 120).

[131] *Hewlett-Packard France v Matrox Graphics Inc* (n 65).

[132] [154]–[155]. This case is further discussed in ch 8.

[133] ICAC No 97/2004, 23 December 2004, available atcisgw3.law.pace.edu/cases/041223r1.html.

[134] According to art 409, parties can agree that an obligation can be terminated in exchange for compensation (payment of money, transfer of property, etc).

buyer ought to have proposed, with reference to art 333 of the Russian Civil Code,[135] to reduce the amount of penalty on the grounds that it was excessive. It may be helpful to address each of these grounds in turn.

So far as the first ground is concerned, if the tribunal's approach were correct and to be followed, this would mean that in *every* case of delay in delivery, a buyer would have to attempt to renegotiate its sub-sales contract or, otherwise, face the reduction in its damages claim for the compensation paid to its sub-buyer. It is suggested that buyers cannot be expected to attempt to renegotiate their sub-sale contracts every time they face a damages claim by sub-buyers due to the sellers' delay in delivering the goods. By expecting too much of the injured party, the tribunal's approach disturbs the balance between the parties' legitimate interests which the mitigation rule is designed to strike.[136] The same criticism applies to the second and third grounds which, it is submitted, unjustifiably extend the boundaries of the mitigation rule and place an excessive burden on the injured party.[137] The third ground is also flawed in another respect. While there is little doubt that legal treatment of liquidated damages clauses is outside the CISG, art 333 of the Russian Civil Code merely provides for the power of the *court* to reduce the amount of liquidated damages where they are 'incommensurate to the consequences of the breach of an obligation'. The effect of this provision is to provide the buyer with a right to challenge, by bringing a legal action, the amount in a liquidated damages clause in its sub-sale contract. It follows, from the tribunal's reliance on this provision, that the injured party ought to have tried to negotiate the reduction of liquidated damages by referring to art 333 as the basis of a possible legal action. If the tribunal's real concern related to a possibly excessive liquidated damages claim, an appropriate way of ensuring that the burden of paying an unusually high amount is not placed on the breaching party ought to have been the foreseeability, and not the mitigation, rule.[138]

The argument that the mitigation rule does not require the injured party to attempt to renegotiate the terms of its sub-sale contract is advanced only as a *general* proposition. Because the meaning of reasonableness ultimately rests on the facts, a possibility of *exceptional* cases where renegotiating the sub-sale contract may be a reasonable measure of mitigating loss cannot be ruled out.[139]

[135] According to art 333, if the amount of liquidated damages due for payment is evidently incommensurate to the consequences of the breach of an obligation, the court has the power to reduce it.

[136] For an approach that lies at the opposite end of the 'allocation of risk' spectrum, see ICC No 13009, 2006, available at www.unilex.info, decided under the UPICC, where the buyer was not deemed to have failed to mitigate under art 7.4.8 UPICC when it joined its sub-buyer in the proceedings against the seller. According to the abstract of the decision, doing so was a 'common judicial practice'.

[137] As regards the third ground, this argument is relevant if the tribunal's decision is interpreted as requiring the injured party to actually bring a claim to reduce the amount of liquidated damages. The injured party cannot be expected to bring such a claim every time it faces a liquidated damages claim by its sub-buyer.

[138] As argued, the foreseeability rule relates to both the type and the extent of the loss (see ch 5).

[139] For a somewhat analogous situation involving the seller's loss arising from the delay in payment by the buyer, see Case No A53-11062/16 Arbitration Court Rostov Region (Russia) 7 July 2016, available at ras.arbitr.ru (in Russian). The seller was required by the currency regulations in its country

It may be, for example, that the sub-buyer unequivocally expresses its willingness, in the light of a long-standing business relationship or as a gesture of goodwill, to extend the delivery date or reduce the amount of liquidated damages. Where so, it may be reasonable to expect the buyer to renegotiate the sub-sale contract.[140]

4. MITIGATION AND EVENTS SUBSEQUENT TO THE BREACH

There is a close connection between the mitigation rule and the calculation of damages. For example, as seen above, a reasonable measure aimed at mitigating loss often provides a basis for calculating damages.[141] It is possible to go further by suggesting that the mitigation rule cannot be separated from the issues of calculation and nowhere is this more evident than in the context of the dilemma between the so-called 'concrete' and 'abstract' approaches to calculating damages.[142] The relationship between the two is that of reciprocal influence.[143] On the one hand, the mitigation rule influences the specific methods the law adopts to calculating damages. Thus, the instruments' 'concrete' formula[144] – the difference between the contract price and the price in a substitute transaction – reflects a typical measure of mitigating loss. The instruments' 'abstract' formula[145] – the difference between the contract price and the current

to ensure the receipt of payment in a foreign currency on its account in a specified bank within the prescribed time. Due to the buyer's failure to pay on time, the seller could not comply with this obligation and had to pay a penalty to state authorities. The seller was held to have failed to mitigate this loss because the seller had not exercised its right under the law to request an extension of the time at which the foreign currency payment ought to have been deposited (similarly, Case No A53-11062/2016 Arbitration Court North Caucasus Region (Russia) 1 December 2016, available at ras.arbitr.ru (in Russian); Case No 6 International Commercial Arbitration Court (ICAC), the Ukrainian Chamber of Commerce, 27 December 2006), available at arb.ucci.org.ua/icac/cases/2006-2010/caseNo6.pdf (in Russian).

[140] A possible range of measures to mitigate loss is wider than that addressed in this book. Other examples of reasonable mitigation, provided by the CISG cases, include: expediting the shipment (*Delchi Carrier SpA v Rotorex Corporation* 1994 WL 4955787), contacting the breaching party to receive information which could help mitigate losses (ICAC No 54/1999, 24 January 2000, available at cisgw3.law.pace.edu/cases/000124r1.html), hiring an attorney in the breaching party's country (Case No 31 C 534/94 Lower Court Alsfeld (Germany) 12 May 1995 (Flagstone tiles), available at cisgw3.law.pace.edu/cases/950512g1.html; Case No A56-23325/2015 Arbitration Court St Petersburg and Leningrad Region (Russia) 27 March 2019, available at ras.arbitr.ru (in Russian)), paying fees for storing the goods that cannot be shipped from the seller's country due to the seller's failure to perform its obligation to provide the required export documents and reaching a settlement with the storage company and the shipping agent to prevent further costs that would arise due to the detention of the goods (Case No A56-23325/2015 Arbitration Court St Petersburg and Leningrad Region (Russia) 27 March 2019, available at ras.arbitr.ru (in Russian)).

[141] Examples include making a substitute transaction or incurring costs of cure (see above).

[142] For an extensive discussion of these approaches to calculation, see ch 8.

[143] This discussion is partly based on D Saidov and R Cunnington, 'Current Themes in the Law of Contract Damages: Introductory Remarks' in Saidov and Cunnington (n 1) 21.

[144] See arts 75 CISG, 7.4.5 UPICC and 9:506 PECL.

[145] See arts 76 CISG, 7.4.6 UPICC and 9:507 PECL.

price – also incorporates the mitigation rule because hypothetical mitigation is incorporated into this 'abstract' formula. On the other hand, the role and functioning of the mitigation rule depend on whether a particular legal system prefers the 'concrete' or 'abstract' approach to calculating damages. For instance, by estimating damages as the difference between the contract price and the price in a substitute transaction, the instruments' concrete formula is based on the injured party's *actual* conduct. A true application of the mitigation rule likewise requires an assessment of the party's *actual* conduct and this is why the mitigation rule is in perfect harmony with the 'concrete' approach. In contrast, the instruments' 'abstract' formula causes the mitigation rule to lose its 'identity' and because mitigation is 'built into' this formula it 'does not expressly appear as a separate issue'.[146] For this reason, those legal systems which generally prefer the 'abstract' approach do not let the events occurring subsequent to the breach influence the calculation of damages. For instance, some common law systems presume that the innocent party ought to have mitigated at the time of the breach[147] (or soon thereafter) and consequently any gains or losses made after that time are generally ignored when damages are calculated. It is not surprising, therefore, that where the 'abstract' approach is the starting point, the injured party may often find itself either under- or over-compensated.[148]

The instruments generally prefer the 'concrete' approach to calculating damages and the mitigation rule should not lose its identity.[149] However, the instruments also provide for the possibility of using an 'abstract' formula, which creates tension between that formula and the mitigation rule. Although, as argued in a later chapter, the mitigation rule should have priority, it is hoped that such cases will be rare and in fact the instruments' 'abstract' formula can successfully complement the mitigation rule.[150] Because the 'concrete' approach and the mitigation rule are the starting point for the international instruments, benefits received and losses made subsequent to the breach and avoidance[151] are to be taken into account. This explains, for example, why in a CISG case[152] where the buyer who lost an opportunity to resell the goods because of the seller's breach and delayed reselling the goods in an attempt to speculate on market prices was denied the recovery of storage costs. The tribunal held that the buyer ought to have resold the goods in good time. Although a similar result would probably have been achieved in the common law systems adhering to the

[146] See McGregor (n 37).

[147] See, eg, ss 50(3) and 51(3) of the UK Sale of Goods Act 1979.

[148] A number of considerations have been put forward to justify such results (for a detailed discussion, see ch 8).

[149] See, however, the discussion in ch 8 where in a number of CISG cases judges and arbitrators preferred the 'abstract' measure and did not attach sufficient weight to the mitigation rule.

[150] For a detailed discussion and analysis, see ch 8.

[151] In contrast with some common law systems, the instruments' 'abstract' formula refers not to the time of breach but to the time of avoidance of the contract (and, in case of the CISG where the goods were taken over, to the time of such taking over).

[152] CIETAC 30 March 1999 (Electric heaters), available at cisgw3.law. pace.edu/cases/990330c3.html.

'abstract' measure, this would not have been so on the ground of the buyer's failure to mitigate by reselling the goods but because the buyer would have been presumed to have mitigated at the time of the breach (or shortly thereafter), ignoring any losses or gains occurring after that time. One reason underlying this approach is that speculation is in fact encouraged. The buyer's conduct after the time when it had reasonable opportunity to mitigate is its own speculation. This policy is ensured by maintaining a symmetrical position: because the party chooses to speculate, it should do so at its own risk and it is only fair that losses and gains should not be taken into account in calculating damages.[153] Hence, storage costs incurred by the buyer after the time it could have resold the goods would have been at the buyer's risk.

The instruments' preference for the 'concrete' approach is probably not as conducive to speculation as some common law regimes.[154] Nor can symmetry be thus maintained: while the buyer, in this case, will have to *bear the risks* of its speculation (by being denied damages for its storage costs), it will *not enjoy the fruits* of its speculation by retaining any gains it may make by reselling them at a higher price than the one it would have received had it resold in good time because gains will have to offset any losses the buyer may have suffered (such as profit margin on a lost sub-sale or storage costs that would have been incurred even if the buyer had resold the goods in good time). It can be argued, however, that discouraging speculation and a lack of symmetry are not good reasons for derogating from the 'concrete' measure because the latter is more in line with the fundamental compensatory purpose of damages: namely, achieving, as much as possible, a *true* compensation for the *actual* loss.[155]

The question of the extent to which benefits gained subsequent to the breach are to be taken into account also arises where after the breach the injured party enters into a transaction more favourable to itself than the original contract. This may occur, for example, where the buyer after the seller's breach purchases goods of higher quality than those under the original contract and makes a greater profit than it would have made otherwise.[156] It may even be the case that profits thus received outweigh all losses the buyer may have initially suffered

[153] See, eg, *AKAS Jamal v Moolla Dawood, Sons & Co* [1916] 1 AC 175; *Campbell Mostyn (Provisions) Ltd v Barnett Trading Company* [1954] 1 Lloyd's Rep 65.

[154] A legal regime strictly adhering to the 'concrete' measure can be criticised on the ground that it encourages artificial transactions by forcing the injured parties, like the buyer in the case above (see n 152 and accompanying text), to resell the goods only to buy them immediately afterwards to enable themselves to continue to speculate (see SM Waddams, 'The Date for the Assessment of Damages' (1981) 97 *LQR* 445, 447).

[155] For a similar argument in the context of the common law, see D McLauchlan, 'Expectation Damages: Avoided Loss, Offsetting Gains and Subsequent Events' in Saidov and Cunnington (n 1).

[156] For a CISG case where the seller argued that, as a result of its breach, the buyer bought better goods than those which the seller had failed to deliver, see Case No 411 O 199/02 District Court Hamburg (Germany) 26 November 2003 (Phtalic anhydride), available at cisgw3.law. pace.edu/cases/031126g1.html. For an English case on this point, see *British Westinghouse Electric and Manufacturing Co Ltd v Underground Electric Railways Co of London Ltd* (n 34) 690.

as a result of the breach (for example, the costs of returning the goods and the difference between the contract price and the price at which the goods of higher quality were bought). If so, is this buyer entitled to damages? From the perspective of the 'concrete' approach, the actual situation in which the buyer eventually found itself as a result of the breach cannot be ignored and, because no loss is suffered, no damages are due to the buyer. Because of the instruments' preference for the 'concrete' approach, benefits which would not have been received but for the breach must be taken into account in calculating damages.

It can be argued that the question of whether benefits actually flow from the breach is a difficult one. English law, for example, draws the distinction between benefits arising from a breach and mitigation, on the one hand, and those which are independent of breach and mitigation, on the other. While the former are taken into account because they form 'part of a continuous dealing with the situation' arising from the original transaction, the latter are considered disconnected from that transaction and for this reason are to be ignored.[157] Although it is not always clear how the line is to be drawn between the two types of case, the distinction is sometimes justified on the ground that benefits are to be regarded as disconnected from the breach, mitigation and the original contract where the innocent party does *more* than it is required by the duty to mitigate.[158] This position once again reflects reluctance to take into consideration what is deemed to be the party's *own speculation*. Any benefits or risks flowing from such speculation are to be ignored and the breaching party is considered to have nothing to do with the injured party's speculation as it is a matter peculiar to the injured party's circumstances. It is evident that this treatment reflects the 'abstract' approach to damages. While this approach has a number of benefits,[159] it is not generally in line[160] with the instruments' preference for the 'concrete' approach.[161]

5. THE RECOVERABILITY OF COSTS INCURRED IN MITIGATING LOSS

In taking measures to mitigate loss, the innocent party will often incur various costs, such as costs arising from finding and concluding a substitute transaction,

[157] *British Westinghouse Electric and Manufacturing Co Ltd v Underground Electric Railways Co of London Ltd* (n 34) 690.

[158] See McGregor (n 37).

[159] See ch 8.

[160] Within the common law itself, the soundness of this distinction is sometimes strongly doubted. See McLauchlan (n 154) ('Attempting to formulate a general principle to be applied in determining whether a post-breach gain constitutes a relevant compensating advantage, as opposed to a mere collateral benefit, is hazardous, especially given … the multifarious range of factual circumstances that come before the courts'); see also an overview in Saidov and Cunnington (n 143) 22.

[161] However, as shown in ch 8, the 'abstract' approach is not entirely alien to the instruments and on a number of occasions judges and arbitrators applying the CISG preferred to rely on the 'abstract' measure.

curing a lack of conformity in the goods, attempting to return the goods, etc.[162] Subject to such costs being reasonable,[163] they are recoverable under the international instruments. Under the CISG, they are recoverable as 'loss suffered as a consequence of the breach'[164] and the UPICC and PECL contain a specific provision to this effect.[165] Although the recoverability of costs incurred in mitigating loss may seem self-evident, it may be helpful to articulate a rationale for this position. First, the principles of full compensation and the protection of the expectation/performance interest dictate the recoverability of such costs for if they were truly aimed at mitigating loss, they would not have been incurred had there been no breach. In other words, their recoverability is necessary to place the party in the position in which it would have been had the contract been performed. Second, it has been argued that '[i]nasmuch as the law denies recovery for losses that can be avoided by reasonable effort and expense, justice requires that the risk incident to such effort should be carried by the party whose wrongful conduct makes them necessary'.[166] A related argument is that the recoverability of costs incurred in mitigation provides an appropriate incentive to the innocent party to mitigate by ensuring that it will not be worse off as a result of mitigation.

6. BURDEN OF PROOF

The position taken in a vast majority of the CISG cases is that the breaching party bears the burden of proving, by establishing relevant facts and presenting evidence,[167] that the injured party failed to mitigate its loss.[168] Placing this

[162] See also n 72.

[163] For a more detailed discussion of the reasonableness of costs, see the discussion on costs of cure in ch 8.

[164] See Knapp (n 38) 561.

[165] See art 7.4.8(2) UPICC ('The aggrieved party is entitled to recover any expenses reasonably incurred in attempting to reduce the harm.'); art 9:505(2) PECL ('The aggrieved party is entitled to recover any expenses reasonably incurred in attempting to reduce the loss.').

[166] AL Corbin, *Corbin on Contracts*, vol 5 (St Paul, Minn, West Publishing Co, 2002) 237.

[167] Article 77 CISG seems to support this result by providing that 'the party in breach *may claim* a reduction in the damages'. The relevant provisions of the UPICC and PECL (arts 7.4.8(1) UPICC and 9:505(1) PECL) formulate the mitigation rule in stronger terms by stating that the injured party 'is not liable' for the loss which could have been reasonably avoided. Although this formulation may appear to treat the mitigation rule as a necessary precondition for the right to claim damages, it is suggested that the Principles' provisions should not be so interpreted. There is no good reason for deviating from a widely accepted treatment of the mitigation rule as merely a method of limiting damages and an established practice, as evidenced by CISG cases, of placing the initial burden of proof on the breaching party (see also the discussion above in relation to the possibility of justifying the mitigation rule by reference to the principle of causation).

[168] See Supreme Court Austria (n 25); *Treibacher Industrie, AG v TDY Industries Inc* 464 F.3d 1235 [11th Cir 2006]; ICC No 8574, September 1996 (Metal concentrate), available at cisgw3.law.pace.edu/cases/968574i1.html; see further other cases referred to below.

burden on the breaching party was rationalised in one case with reference to 'commercial commonsense': 'It would be distinctly surprising if the onus of proof cast upon the party in breach by the second sentence of Art 77 could be cast off by that party simply asserting non-compliance by the innocent party with the obligation created by the first sentence of the Article.'[169] This burden has also been interpreted as requiring the breaching party to refer to *specific* measures the injured party ought to have taken[170] and the amount by which the injured party's damages claim should be reduced;[171] but, if the injured party has in fact taken some measures, the breaching party must prove that they were not reasonable mitigation measures by showing specific alternative courses of action that ought to have been taken.[172] For example, if the seller argues that an alleged cover purchase was made at too high a price, it must prove that cheaper substitutes were reasonably available to the buyer.[173]

While generally recognising the breaching party's burden of proof, the decisions are less uniform when it comes to the consequences of the breaching party's failure to meet that burden. In some cases, a presumption has immediately been drawn that the injured party *had not* failed to mitigate its loss.[174] In some other cases, the injured party has received a less favourable treatment. In one case,[175] despite the expert's report that procuring a substitute was not possible in several parts of the buyer's country (Germany), the court ruled that because it might have been possible to procure a substitute in other parts of the country or abroad, damages ought to be reduced. The court's view of the role of allocating burden of proof was expressed thus:

> The buyer purchased from a Dutch seller in the present case, therefore offers from foreign countries, at least from all of Germany, should have been considered. It is decisive that the buyer does not offer any explanation regarding its efforts to instigate a substitute purchase. It is true that the burden of proof for a failure to mitigate damages is on the creditor, that is, the seller in the present dispute … But the onus of proof is irrelevant because the buyer was at least obliged to submit which offers for a substitute transaction it obtained and from which companies. The legal consequence of Art 77 CISG is solely a reduction in the amount by which the loss should have been mitigated. However, as the buyer's submissions are overall incomplete, the Court cannot determine the extent of the damages, so that a set-off with a claim for loss of profit is also unjustified for these reasons.

[169] *Castel Electronics Pty Ltd v Toshiba Singapore Pte Ltd* (n 39) [325].

[170] See, eg, ICAC No 186/2003 (n 100); see also cases referred to in n 172.

[171] *Hewlett-Packard France v Matrox Graphics Inc* (n 65) [264] ('the CISG stipulates at Article 77 that it is the defendant vendor who has the burden to prove a failure to mitigate damages as well as the amount by which the claim should be reduced as a result.').

[172] See, eg, Supreme Court Austria, 6 February 1996 (n 25); *Treibacher Industrie AG v TDY Industries Inc* (n 168); ICC No 8574 (n 168).

[173] See Case No 1 U 167/95 Appellate Court Hamburg (Germany) 28 February 1997 (Iron molybdenum), available at cisgw3.law.pace.edu/cases/970228gl.html.

[174] *Treibacher Industrie AG v TDY Industries Inc* (n 168).

[175] See Appellate Court Celle, 2 September 1998 (n 68).

It is possible therefore that even where judges recognise that it is the breaching party who bears the burden of proof (and where it fails to do so), the injured party may still be required to provide evidence of taking measures to mitigate its loss.[176] Finally, in some other cases, judges and arbitrators appear to have taken the initiative in establishing whether the injured party had mitigated its loss.[177] Although the latter two approaches may be seen as undermining the purpose of allocating burden of proof (ie, establishing a true state of affairs by placing a responsibility for doing so on the parties themselves), it is probably inevitable that such approaches will be taken from time to time. As pointed out on many occasions,[178] legal systems differ insofar as judicial approaches to taking evidence are concerned and this difference is probably reflective of a broader difference between judicial cultures. Some systems are strictly adversarial, while some others are characterised by greater involvement of judges in the course of proceedings (eg, taking of witness testimony and appointing and examining experts). The interpretation and enforcement of the mitigation rule will depend on the applicable procedural rules and a broader judicial culture within which a particular dispute is considered.

[176] For a somewhat similar approach, see ICAC No 97/2004 (n 133). From a practical perspective, such an approach may be sensible since, as noted in one CISG case (Commercial Court St Gallen (n 26), the injured party is usually in a better position than the breaching party to identify the most reasonable measures that it is able to take. In that case, the court seems to have gone so far as to suggest that art 77 CISG requires the injured party to disclose any relevant facts relating to its measures to mitigate losses; there is, however, no support for such an interpretation in art 77 CISG. Such an interpretation would only be possible if the burden of proof were placed on the injured party and, as shown, this has not been the case in a vast majority of CISG decisions. The case also illustrates that the applicable procedural rules may impose on the injured party a duty to assist the court in providing evidence.

[177] See Supreme Court Austria (n 25); ICAC No 71/1999, 2 February 2000, available at www.cisg.law.pace.edu/cisg/wais/db/cases2/000202r1.html; ICAC No 385/1998, 18 October 1999, available at www.cisg.law.pace.edu/cisg/wais/db/cases2/991018r1.html.

[178] See, eg, H Kötz, 'Civil Justice Systems in Europe and the United States' (2003) 13 *Duke J Comparative Int'l L* 61; The Rt Hon Lord Mance, *The Common Law and Europe: Differences of Style or Substance and Do They Matter?* (Holdsworth Club Presidential Address delivered in Birmingham Law School on 24 November 2006, published by Holdsworth Club of the University of Birmingham, 2007).

Part III

Proof of Loss and Calculation of Damages

7

Standards of Proving Loss and Determining the Amount of Damages[1]

1. GENERAL

TO BE AWARDED damages, the innocent party must prove that it has suffered loss and legal systems often require that loss be proven with a particular degree of precision or certainty.[2] This requirement is also regarded as another method of limiting damages because compensation is generally awarded only to the extent that losses have been proven with the required degree of certainty.[3] Of the three instruments, only the UPICC contain an express requirement with respect to the degree of certainty with which loss must be proven by stating that '[c]ompensation is due only for harm, including future harm, that is established with a reasonable degree of certainty'.[4] The UPICC also contain two other mechanisms dealing with uncertainty in proving losses. Article 7.4.3(2) provides that '[c]ompensation may be due for the loss of a chance in proportion to the probability of its occurrence' and if 'the amount of damages cannot be established with a sufficient degree of certainty, the assessment is at the discretion of the court'.[5] The CISG and the PECL contain no analogous provisions. This chapter will begin by examining these provisions of the UPICC. The remaining part of the chapter will explore the question whether similar standards can be developed under the CISG and PECL.

[1] This chapter is a substantially revised and updated version of D Saidov, 'Standards of Proving Loss and Determining the Amount of Damages' (2006) 22 *J Contract L* 1.

[2] See GH Treitel, *Remedies for Breach of Contract: A Comparative Account* (Oxford, Clarendon Press, 1988) 192.

[3] See, eg, EA Farnsworth, 'Legal Remedies for Breach of Contract' (1970) 70 *Columbia L Rev* 1145, 1213 ('[the requirement of certainty] further diminishes the protection that the law affords the promisee's expectation').

[4] Article 7.4.3(1) UPICC.

[5] Article 7.4.3(3) UPICC.

2. THE STANDARD OF 'REASONABLE CERTAINTY'

2.1. General

As noted, the UPICC require that losses be proven with 'a reasonable degree of certainty' and this standard can be justified on the basis of the notion of reasonableness. Generally, the standard of proof refers to how much needs to be shown and to the level of precision which must flow from the presented evidence to prove the alleged loss. It is widely recognised that absolute certainty in proving losses cannot be required because the nature of some losses often prevent the injured party from presenting evidence which would prove the alleged losses with absolute certainty.[6] For this reason, the standard is based on the idea that the innocent party must prove its loss only with such a degree of precision which can be *reasonably* expected of the party taking into account the nature of the loss and other relevant circumstances. If reasonableness is a general principle underlying the UPICC, it can even be argued that the standard of 'reasonable certainty' is its specific manifestation.[7]

The first question is whether this standard refers to the fact and/or amount of loss and before this question can be answered it has to be asked whether a distinction between the fact and amount of loss needs to be drawn at all. It has been suggested that the distinction is 'meaningless for nearly all practical purposes'[8] because:

> 'the fact of loss' and 'the amount of loss' are in effect different terms for the same thing, since proof of the amount of loss with a reasonable degree of certainty conclusively establishes the fact of loss, and, conversely, the only way to prove the fact of loss would seem to be by proving with reasonable degree of certainty at least a minimum amount of loss. It thus would seem that an attempted distinction between these two is of no real significance.[9]

Indeed, in many cases proving the fact of loss will necessarily involve proving its amount and proving the amount will naturally establish the fact of loss. However, this will not always be the case because it is possible for the innocent party to establish the fact of loss without proving its amount. This may happen, for example, in cases involving loss of reputation or loss of profit due to the

[6] For example, proving lost profits may involve guesswork in relation to hypothetical future or past events and the occurrence of such events will depend on different contingencies, such as economic conditions, prices, consumer preferences, etc.

[7] For the view justifying 'the standard of certainty' as a means of allocating the risk between the parties, see CT McCormick, *Handbook on the Law of Damages* (St Paul, Minn, West Publishing Co, 1935) 105; MD Weisman and Clements, 'Protecting Reasonable Expectations: Proof of Lost Profits for New Business' (1991) 76 *Massachusetts L Rev* 186, 196).

[8] See AF Halaby, 'No Summary Judgement for You! One State's (Unjustified) Treatment of Contract Claims for Lost Profits' [1998] *U Miami Business L Rev* 57, 61–62.

[9] See Note, 'Damages – Loss of Profits Caused by Breach of Contract – Proof of Certainty' (1932–1933) 17 *Minnesota L Rev* 194, 196.

interruption or destruction of a newly established business[10] where the court or tribunal may be convinced, in the light of economic conditions surrounding the business and the party's commercial experience, that despite a failure to prove the monetary value of the loss the party has lost profits. This situation may also arise in the context of costs incurred as a result of the breach. In one CISG case, although a party failed to prove the amount of the expenses it had incurred due to the breach, the court took the view that the party had nevertheless suffered some loss.[11] Similarly, in a case where the UPICC were applied, the panel stated that '[i]n many of the Claims the Claimants' documentary or other evidence established that an alleged loss had, in fact, occurred. But the evidence was insufficient in those Claims to demonstrate with a reasonable degree of certainty the amount of the loss'.[12] Thus, because the distinction between the fact and amount of the loss needs to be drawn, it is submitted the standard of 'reasonable certainty' applies to both the fact and amount of the loss.[13]

Like any other standard based on reasonableness, this rule is not capable of being precisely defined[14] and its meaning can only be determined in the context of the particular facts. The UPICC refer to the applicability of the standard to 'harm'[15] and since no particular type of harm or loss is specified, it follows that any type of recoverable loss must be proven with 'reasonable certainty'.[16] The amount and types of the required evidence are those which can be reasonably expected of the injured party taking into account the nature of the alleged loss and all the relevant circumstances.

It is probably true that, in general, it is more difficult to prove 'loss of profit' (*lucrum cessans*) than 'loss suffered' (*damnum emergens*). Proving lost profit often involves inquiry into a hypothetical future or past: in trying to prove its loss of volume the seller may argue that had the buyer bought the goods it would

[10] See DL Goetz, KL Moore, DE Perry, DS Raab, and JS Ross, 'Article Two Warranties in Commercial Transactions: An Update' (1987) 72 *Cornell L Rev* 1159, 1247–1249.

[11] Case No T 171/95 District Court Saane (Switzerland) 20 February 1997 (Spirits), available at cisgw3.law.pace.edu/cases/970220s1.html.

[12] United Nations Compensation Commission, Panel of the Commissioners, Panel F1, Recommendation S/AC.26, 23 September 1997, available at www.unilex.info.

[13] For the discussion of the question whether the practice of US courts of flexibly applying the standard to the fact and amount of loss (ie, sometimes applying the standard to both aspects of the loss and sometimes applying the standard only to the fact of the loss) is appropriate in the context of the instruments, see Saidov (n 1) 11–13.

[14] 'What is a "reasonable estimate" and what is "reasonable certainty"? No answer that is even "reasonably" definite can be made to such questions, in the abstract and unrelated to a specific set of facts … [I]n any living case, the "reasonableness" of anything must be determined by one or more specific living men whose judgment must necessarily depend upon their mental power, their own specific education and life experience, and their emotional characteristics and background' (AL Corbin, *Corbin on Contracts: A Comprehensive Treatise on the Working Rules of Contract Law* Vol 5 (St Paul, Minn, West Publishing Co, 2002) 107).

[15] See art 7.4.3(1) UPICC.

[16] The same is generally the case in the US law: 'The requirement with respect the certainty of proof is the same when the plaintiff is asking damages to reimburse his pecuniary losses as when he is asking damages to make up for gains prevented' (Corbin (n 14) 113).

have sold more than it in fact did and the possibility of selling more goods will be linked either to hypothetical past or hypothetical future; where the buyer claims lost profits as a result of the breach of a long-term contract, it may be difficult in the absence of specific sub-sale contracts to establish what profit margins, if any, the buyer would have received had there been no breach; the owner of a new manufacturing business may have difficulty proving lost profits it would have earned from reselling the final product had the seller delivered the goods or delivered conforming goods.[17] In all these cases, whether loss has been suffered will depend on a number of factors, such as future prices, relevant economic conditions, behaviour of third parties, etc. Because we do not possess perfect knowledge,[18] proving lost profits with 'reasonable certainty' can be difficult. In contrast, losses falling into the category of 'loss suffered' (the diminution in the party's existing assets and financial situation)[19] involve fewer problems of proof because the party often has records of costs incurred as a result of the breach.[20]

2.2. Proving 'Loss Suffered'

The buyer's liability to its sub-buyers arising from the seller's breach can be sufficiently established by presenting a settlement agreement or the sub-sale contract containing a relevant liquidated damages clause,[21] together with a receipt of the payment issued by the sub-buyer.[22] Invoices are often accepted by courts and tribunals as sufficient evidence of the expenses incurred as a result of the breach.[23] Documents issued by relevant organisations can also provide evidence

[17] See *Topp Paper Company LLC v ETI Converting Equipment*, 2013 WL 12101111 (S.D. Fla. 2013), where the seller delivered non-functioning machines (used for producing labelling) to the buyer, who was new to the labelling business ('Topp's proposal to calculate lost-profit damages by "comparing the difference between Topp's projected income, as set forth in its 2009 through 2011 income projections, and its actual income,"... does not provide an adequate basis to assess lost profits with a reasonable degree of certainty ... Topp's projections are not based on Topp's existing business record because the labeling business was a new one for Topp. Nor does Topp offer evidence to allow comparison of Topp's business with other businesses that have been in existence for some time and are "closely comparable.').

[18] See S Waddams, *The Law of Damages*, 4th edn (Toronto, Canada Law Book Inc, 2004) 517.

[19] See ch 3.

[20] This is not always the case. It may be easier to prove lost profits than 'loss suffered' where, for instance, the buyer presents its sub-sale contract. In contrast, it may be difficult to prove its costs, caused by the breach, if such costs will be incurred in the future.

[21] In one CISG case, a mere presentation of sub-sale contracts with no evidence of the actual payment of damages to sub-buyers was insufficient to establish the loss (see CIETAC 7 July 1997 (Isobutanol), available at cisgw3.law.pace.edu/cases/ 970707c1.html).

[22] See CIETAC 7 April 1999 (PVC Suspension), available at cisgw3.law.pace.edu/cases/990407c1.html.

[23] See Case No. 7 O 147/94 District Court Paderborn (Germany) 25 June 1996 (Granulated plastic), available at cisgw3.law.pace.edu/cases/960625g1.html; ICC No 7585, 1992 (Foamed board machinery), available at cisgw3.law.pace.edu/cases/927585i1.html; ICC No 7531, 1994 (Scaffold fittings), available at www.cisg.law.pace.edu/cisg/wais/db/cases2/947531i1.html; ICAC No 166/1995, 12 March 1996, available at cisgw3.law.pace.edu/cases/960312r1.html.

of the costs incurred. For instance, a bank's report can verify that the buyer has incurred costs in opening a letter of credit or an auditing company's report can certify some other expenditure made.[24] Where the buyer had to pay a penalty to customs authorities as a result of the seller's breach, the presentation of the decision issued by the authorities together with payment orders was held sufficient to prove that loss.[25] Experts' reports have also been accepted as evidence of cost of curing a non-conformity.[26] Where the seller incurred storage charges as a result of the buyer's failure to accept the delivery on time, invoices issued by storage companies or receipts for the payment of storage fees were accepted as sufficient evidence of this loss.[27] Where the seller had to procure replacement packaging as a consequence of the buyer's breach of its contractual obligation to provide replacement packaging for the mineral water, delivered by the seller, the price lists of companies supplying packaging were accepted as evidence of the value of replacement packaging.[28] Damage to reputation/goodwill[29] may be proven on the basis of records demonstrating the difference between the volume of sales and profits made before and after the loss,[30] testimony of competent witnesses,[31] the dependence of the buyer's business on contract goods,[32] testimony by former customers and other witnesses indicating that business was

[24] See ICAC No 166/1995 (n 23).

[25] ICAC No 85/2002, 26 June 2003, available at cisgw3.law.pace.edu/cases/030626r1.html.

[26] See Case No. 3 O 196/01 District Court Köln (Germany) 25 March 2003 (Racing carts), available at cisgw3.law.pace.edu/cases/030325g1.html; see also *Srl RC v BVBA RT* Appellate Court Antwerp (Belgium) 27 June 2001, available at cisgw3.law.pace.edu/cases/010627b1.html (where the 'abstract' calculation of damages for non-conforming goods, provided by an expert, was relied upon).

[27] See Case No 438/2013 Supreme Court (Spain) 1 July 2013, available at cisgw3.law.pace.edu/cases/130701s4.html; CIETAC 30 December 2002 (Manganese), available at cisgw3.law. pace.edu/cases/021230c1.html.

[28] Case No T-6/08 Foreign Trade Court, the Serbian Chamber of Commerce (Serbia) 19 October 2009, available at cisgw3.law.pace.edu/cases/091019sb.html.

[29] See D Saidov, 'Damages to Business Reputation and Goodwill under the Vienna Sales Convention' in D Saidov and R Cunnington (eds), *Contract Damages: Domestic and International Perspectives* (2008, Hart Publishing, Oxford) 403–5.

[30] See ICC No 3880, 27 September 1983 in S Jarvin and Y Derains, *Collection of ICC Arbitral Awards 1974–1985: Recueil Des Sentences Arbitrales De La CCI* (The Hague, Kluwer Law International, 1990) 161; Tampere Court of First Instance (Finland) 17 January 1997 (Canned food), available at cisgw3.law.pace.edu/cases/970117f5.html; see also *NV Maes Roger v NV Kapa Reynolds* Appellate Court Gent (Belgium) 10 May 2004, available at cisgw3.law.pace.edu/ cases/040510b1.html (where the lower instance found that the buyer 'could not realize sales and the quality problem led to cancelled or dismissed business relationships with the [b]uyer'. However, this finding was rejected by the Appellate Court).

[31] *Barrett Co v Panther Rubber Mfg Co* 24 F.2d 329, 337 (C.A.1 1928) ('The testimony of competent witnesses shows that the reputation of its product was high with jobbing trade …'); *Delano Growers' Cooperative Winery v Supreme Wine Co, Inc* 473 N.E.2d 1066, 1076 ('Supreme presented testimony of its former officers to support the evidence that Delano caused the injury to Supreme's business reputation'); *Simpson v Restructure Petroleum Marketing Services* 830 So.2d 480, 486 (La. App. 2 Cir., 2002).

[32] Tampere Court of First Instance, 17 January 1997 (n 30) ('the business activities of [the buyer] rested on the shoulders of Diamante products'); *Barrett Co v Panther Rubber* (n 31).

discontinued because of defective goods.[33] An example of how damage to reputation can be demonstrated is provided by one US case where the buyer, whom the court found to have had an 'excellent reputation' in the industry before the breach, claimed that its reputation had been damaged. One piece of evidence related to the fact that one customer after becoming aware of the buyer's problems required the buyer to procure a performance bond before it would proceed with the project.[34]

2.3. Proving Loss of Profit

The difficulty of satisfying the standard of 'reasonable certainty' in proving lost profits may depend on a capacity and a situation in which the injured party has acted.[35] It has been suggested, for example, that the problem of proving lost profits rarely arises where the seller is not in a lost volume situation (ie where its ability to supply does not exceed demand for the goods)[36] because its losses depend on either the resale (a 'concrete' formula) or the current (an 'abstract' formula) price.[37] Once the hurdle of establishing the relevant price is overcome,[38] loss of profit can be easily established with 'reasonable certainty' because it can be calculated as the difference between the contract price and the resale[39] or current/market price.[40] There are cases, however, where neither the 'concrete' nor the 'abstract' formulae fully eliminate the problem of proving lost profits. Suppose the seller intended to invest the purchase price into a potentially profitable venture shortly after the due date for payment. If damages under the 'concrete' or 'abstract' formulae are awarded later than the time when the seller could have made an investment, the seller can argue that the damages awarded do not compensate it fully for lost profit it would have received otherwise: while it was compensated for the loss of its 'profit margin', the award does not take into

[33] Tampere Court of First Instance, 17 January 1997 (n 30); *Sol-O-Lite Laminating Corp v Thos W Allen* 223 Or. 80, 353 P.2d 843 ('Four customers who had done business with defendant ... testified concerning their receipt of the defective material and how they had reduced or terminated their dealings because of it'); *Davidson v Barclays Bank* [1940] 1 All ER 316, 324.

[34] *Marvin Lumber and Cedar Company, Marvin Windows of Tennessee, Inc v PPG Industries, Inc* 401 F.3d 901, 913 (C.A.8 (Minn.), 2005).

[35] See EA Farnsworth, *Contracts*, 4th edn (New York, Aspen Publishers, 2004) 801–03; Comment, 'Lost Profits as Contract Damages: Problems of Proof and Limitations on Recovery' (1955–1956) 65 *Yale L J* 992, 1000–15.

[36] See Farnsworth (n 35) 801.

[37] See ibid.

[38] See ch 8.

[39] In one CISG case, the resale contract price was proven by presenting a resale contract, supported by a witness statement of the buyer in the resale transaction (see ICC No 10274, 1999 (Poultry feed), available at cisgw3.law.pace.edu/cases/990274i1.html).

[40] See arts 75, 76 CISG, 7.4.5, 7.4.6 UPICC, 9:506, 9:507 PECL. For a detailed discussion of these methods of calculation, see ch 8.

account lost profit it *could* have earned had an investment been made.[41] Where so, the seller's burden of proving its lost profit is not fully discharged by meeting the requirements of either the 'concrete' or 'abstract' formula (whichever is applicable) because it must also prove that it would have made an investment and gained an additional profit.[42]

It is more difficult to meet the 'reasonable certainty' requirement where the seller's capacity to supply exceeds the demand for the goods and where, as a result of the buyer's breach, it has sold fewer goods than it would have sold otherwise ('lost volume'). Even if it resells the goods to a third party, it can argue that this transaction would have been made even if the buyer had performed. As discussed, the seller will have to prove that: its capacity exceeds the demand for the goods; even if the buyer had performed the contract, it would have been able to sell more goods than it did due to the breach; and the additional sale would have been profitable.[43]

It has been argued that few difficulties of proving loss arise in the case of a buyer who buys a fixed quantity of goods for prompt delivery because the 'concrete' and 'abstract' methods of calculation reduce the difficulty of proof.[44] At this point, it is relevant to note that, in contrast with the injured seller, these calculation methods compensate the buyer not for loss of profit but for the non-receipt of the goods: the difference between the contract price and either the re-purchase or current price compensates the buyer for the higher amount of money it had (or would have) to pay to purchase substitute goods. This compensation is usually sufficient to fully compensate the buyer because it now has the goods on hand (or is in the position to purchase them) and can make the planned profit. The only difficulties of proof the buyer will face are those

[41] As explained in ch 8, to avoid double compensation it must be taken into account that the margin received from the buyer was, in the sense, the 'price' the seller would have paid to make a profit on the investment.

[42] The buyer's late payment can cause the seller an inflationary or an exchange rate loss (see further chs 3 and 9). In both cases, because the seller receives a lower amount than what would have been received but for the breach, it suffers (in a non-losing contract) loss of its profit margin built into the contract price. For a CISG case, taking the position that is easy to prove exchange rate losses in modern conditions, see Case No C1 08 45 Higher Cantonal Court Valais (Switzerland) 28 January 2009, available at cisgw3.law.pace.edu/cases/090128s1.html ('The creditor must submit evidence regarding the allegation that if the debtor had paid in time it would have immediately converted the sum of money into the legal currency at its domicile or place of business and, therefore, it could have avoided further devaluation of the currency used for the payment. Submitting this evidence is easy because if the creditor can show a loss due to the conversion into the legal currency at its domicile or place of business, the judge presumes this damage; and the debtor can still submit evidence to rebut this presumption of fact … Nowadays, the conversion rate of currencies is a commonly known fact, which does not need to be submitted or evidenced. It can be checked on the Internet, in official publications and in the written press; thus, it is accessible to everybody … In addition, the Internet allows fast access to the applicable exchange rates on a specific date; therefore, it is not necessary to obtain a bank statement or a copy of the written press on the specific date').

[43] See ch 3.

[44] Farnsworth (n 35) 801.

relating to proving a cover purchase[45] or the current price.[46] But in some cases, despite having obtained substitute goods, the buyer may still suffer loss of profit. Suppose that the need to make a cover purchase has caused delay in reselling the goods and the buyer now has to reduce the resale price because the goods were seasonal. To prove its loss of profit, the buyer will need to demonstrate that had the seller performed the contract, it would have been able to sell the goods at a higher price and, if so, an original sub-sale contract and evidence of an arrangement whereby the sub-buyer accepted the goods at reduced prices may be sufficient to prove the buyer's loss of profit.

The buyer may also suffer loss of profit where it accepts non-conforming goods and manages to resell them at a lower price than initially planned. Resale contracts, bills of lading, and tax invoices have been accepted by some tribunals as sufficient evidence of such a resale.[47] Similarly, it may be that because the goods were needed for resale at a specific time, the buyer had to reduce the price to persuade the sub-buyers to accept a late delivery. In one such case involving the sale of shoes, the court stated that the buyer ought to have provided:

> a detailed account of which consignment of shoes she had firmly sold at what price, to which customers and, with which stipulated times of delivery; further, at what point in time she received the shoes from the [seller] and forwarded them to her customers. Finally, [the buyer] would have had to submit that her customers were entitled under their contracts to refuse acceptance of the goods based on late delivery.[48]

In another case[49] where the buyer, a distributor of electric products based in Australia, alleged that the decline in sales of its computers had been caused by the defective graphic cards, delivered by the seller and installed in the buyer's computers, the court awarded damages for the loss of the buyer's profit margin.[50]

[45] See Case No. 21 O 703/01(028) District Court Braunschweig (Germany) 30 July 2001 (Metal), available at cisgw3.law.pace.edu/cases/010730g1.html (where the buyer proved a substitute transaction by presenting a number of documents, including a contract with the buyer's subsidiary for the purchase of substitute goods, 'packing list' certifying that the goods had been packed and were ready for shipment to the destination, invoices, transportation documents and certificates of the receipt of the goods at the destination); Case No. 411 O 199/02 District Court Hamburg (Germany) 26 November 2003 (Phtalic anhydride), available at cisgw3.law.pace.edu/cases/031126g1.html ('The fact that in the sales contract … with Company H the date given is the 29th of March 2003 is readily consistent with the submission of the Buyer that this contract was signed on 2 April 2002 – after the additional period of time (*Nachfrist*) given to the Seller had expired. The shipment dates of the bills of lading … do not conflict with the substitute purchase having been concluded on 2 April 2002, since according to the submission of the Buyer it was a purchase of goods already on water. Even if it might appear unusual that the conditions of a "Local Letter of Credit" did not allow a ninety-day period and fell considerably short of the payment goal of ninety days agreed upon for the substitute purchase, the court does not doubt the truthfulness of the substitute purchase in its overall evaluation.').

[46] See ch 8.

[47] CIETAC 7 April 1999 (n 22).

[48] Case No. 7b O 142/75 District Court Münster (Germany) 24 May 1977 (Shoes), available at www.cisg.law.pace.edu/cisg/wais/db/cases2/770524g1.html (decided on the basis of the ULIS).

[49] *Castel Electronics Pty Ltd v Toshiba Singapore Pte Ltd* [2011] FCAFC 55.

[50] See also Case No 4A_440/2009 Supreme Court (Switzerland) 17 December 2009, available at cisgw3.law.pace.edu/cases/091217s1.html, where (on the basis of domestic rules on evidence and

The court relied on expert evidence and the buyer's 'product sales inventory reports' (PSI) to ascertain the appropriate lost profit margin to be awarded in the light of the state of the Australian market of electronic appliances ('brown goods'):

> 'the decline in sales was partly attributable to the contraction of the Australian brown goods market from 2003 and increased competition between participants in that market, all of which attributed to greater discount by wholesalers. The primary judge was entitled to rely upon the [expert] evidence … and the evidence contained in the PSI reports from 2003 onwards … Those reports provided telling evidence of the state of the market during that period independent of [the buyer's] problem with the defective products … His Honour was right in our opinion to conclude as an estimate that [the buyer's] margins on its other Toshiba products would have averaged 20% in each of the financial years ended 2005, 2006 and 2007.'[51]

The buyer-manufacturer may similarly suffer a loss of profit as a result of receiving non-conforming goods, which may prevent the buyer from making and selling the final products as intended. In one such case,[52] where the seller delivered non-functional machines that the buyer bought to make quality labels, the court accepted the testimony from the buyer's employees together with invoices, contracts and orders cancelled by the buyer's customers as sufficient evidence of the loss of profit the buyer would have made on those contracts had there been no breach:

> 'This is not a situation where the damages would be speculative since [the buyer] actually had clients who had placed orders for labels with [the buyer]. Thus, to the extent that [the buyer] seeks to establish its lost profits by relying on this type of evidence, [the buyer] satisfies the requirement that its lost profits be ascertainable within a reasonable degree of certainty.'[53]

Finally, proving lost profit with 'reasonable certainty' can be especially difficult in long-term contracts where resolving the question whether the buyer has suffered loss of profit involves an inquiry into various factors (often unknown at the time of proceedings) including: future price levels[54] and demand for the goods, quantity of the goods to be sold, the buyer's ability to resell the goods, state of competition in a relevant trade sector, etc. One helpful way of

proof) the buyer, a retail seller of watches, failed to prove its loss profit because it had not presented 'the retail contracts the performance of which was the reason why the order was placed with [the Seller], in order to establish accurately the exact retail prices' (ibid, [4]). This was the decision of the court of first instance with which the Supreme Court appears to have agreed but which also held that the lost profit claim failed due to the buyer's failure to mitigate under art 77 CISG.

[51] Ibid, [265]–[267].

[52] *Topp Paper Company LLC v ETI Converting Equipment* (n 17).

[53] Ibid, 14.

[54] See CIETAC 19 January 2003 (Ferrochrome), available at cisgw3.law.pace.edu/cases/030119c1.html ('The Buyer submitted its internal production cost calculation schedule and three sales invoices … The Arbitration Tribunal holds that [the] internal production cost calculation schedule is for its internal use only; the Buyer did not provide the relevant contract and the market price of the same kind to sustain the sales price which it alleged.').

determining loss with 'reasonable certainty' can be to examine the buyer's past business experience.[55] If the conditions in which the buyer made profits in the past are similar to the present conditions and to those reasonably expected to surround the buyer's business in the future, a reasonable estimation of loss can be made based on the buyer's past dealings. This approach is already evident in international arbitration practice. In a case where a UK importer had brought a claim against a Hungarian export company for non-delivery, the tribunal stated that the 'estimation of a loss of profit is mainly based on expectation of the future. In this context the Tribunal has to start taking into account the history of developments in the past'.[56] The injured buyer can argue that its business has grown in comparison with the volume in its previous dealings and it is entitled to higher profits than those received in the past. In such a case, the buyer will have to present strong evidence to support this argument and 'mere commercial optimism'[57] is unlikely to be sufficient. For example, in another arbitration case (governed by Lebanese law) where a Lebanese distributor claimed damages for breach of contract against a Western European car manufacturer, the tribunal stated that:

> the Lebanese distributor had claimed as damages ... 3 years of lost profit based on the profit in 1961, and alternatively, based on the average of the last 3 years. Although it was not contested that the sales of the claimant had gone up, the automotive sales market was too uncertain to apply the first alternative.[58]

Having regard to comparable businesses is another factor which can help determine lost profits with 'reasonable certainty'. If there are businesses with a similar commercial activity that operate under similar circumstances, evidence relating to the profitability of such businesses may shed light on what the party's future profits would have been had the contract been performed.[59] A state of competition in the relevant trade sector can also provide some guidance because if the claimant would have faced fierce competition in selling the goods if the contract

[55] See, eg, McCormick (n 7) 107; Corbin (n 14) 126; Note, 'The Requirement of Certainty in the Proof of Lost Profits' (1950) 64 *Harv L Rev* 317, 319). The same can apply to determining the seller's lost profits (see Case BZ.2007.55 Appellate Court St. Gallen (Switzerland) 13 May 2008, available at cisgw3.law.pace.edu/cases/080513s1.html, where the seller's lost profit was determined on the basis of the seller's account of its profit margin in the previous year to that in which the seller claimed damages).

[56] ICC No 5418, 1987 (see *Collection of ICC Arbitral Awards 1986–1990: Recueil des Sentences Arbitrales de la CCI 1986–1990* (compiled by S Jarvin, Y Derains, and JJ Arnaldez) (The Hague, Kluwer Academic Publishers Group, 1994) 131.

[57] This statement was made in ibid, 132.

[58] ICC No 1250, May 1964 (see *Collection of ICC Arbitral Awards 1974–1985: Recueil des Sentences Arbitrales de la CCI* (compiled by S Jarvin and Y Derains) (Kluwer Law International, The Hague 1990) 32).

[59] See *Topp Paper Company LLC v ETI Converting Equipment* (n 17), where damages for the buyer's loss of profit, calculated with reference to the buyer's projected profits, were denied partly because the buyer failed to provide evidence of comparison of the buyer's business with established and 'closely comparable' businesses; *Ginza Pte Ltd v Vista Corporation Pty Ltd* [2003] WASC 11

had been performed, this fact would demonstrate potential difficulties the party would have encountered in selling the goods. At the same time, the party's past business experience could demonstrate that it has successfully withstood the competition.[60]

3. JUDICIAL DISCRETION

The UPICC confer the power on a court to assess damages at its own discretion where losses cannot be established with the required degree of certainty.[61] The Comments on the UPICC explain that this provision has been introduced to empower the court 'to make an equitable quantification of the harm sustained' as opposed to 'refus[ing] any compensation or award[ing] nominal damages'.[62] The main difficulty is the uncertainty this provision generates regarding the circumstances in which courts and tribunals will exercise their discretion. It is submitted that a threshold for invoking this provision must be high. Courts and tribunals must be convinced that the injured party has indeed suffered the alleged loss. They must also ensure that all reasonably available evidence has been presented and that their discretion is exercised within the confines of such evidence. This suggestion is in line with the way the UPICC have thus far been interpreted. In one case,[63] the tribunal was convinced that some loss had been suffered despite the fact that damages fell 'into the category of damages which may normally not be established ... in an arithmetically satisfactory manner'. In another case,[64] the tribunal expressly stated that the claimant had suffered some loss despite its failure to prove it with 'reasonable certainty'. The tribunal stated that 'in exercising such discretion, the Panel took into account the level and type of evidence that should reasonably be required of a Claimant given the overall circumstances at the time of the loss'.[65] In yet another case, the tribunal explained that:

> This discretion in the assessment of damages operates ... within the confines of a scrupulous examination of the evidence presented by the Parties. The Tribunal continues

(where the court specifically asked a counsel of one of the parties about whether any assessment of comparable businesses had been carried out (for the purposing of assessing damage to goodwill)).

[60] See Note (n 55) 321.

[61] 'Where the amount of damages cannot be established with a sufficient degree of certainty, the assessment is at the discretion of the court' (art 7.4.3(3) UPICC). See Arbitration Tribunal of the City of Panama, 24 February 2001, available at www.unilex.info, where the tribunal, acting as *amiable comopositeur*, could not ascertain the precise amount of damages and made an 'equitable quantification' based on this provision of the UPICC (the abstract of this decision is available in English).

[62] Comment 2 on art 7.4.3 UPICC.

[63] See ICC No 5835, June 1996, available at www.unilex.info.

[64] See United Nations Compensation Commission (n 12) (see also accompanying text).

[65] Ibid. In a similar vein, see ICC No 10422, 2001, available at www.unilex.info, where in the absence of the calculation of the distributor's lost net profit margin, the tribunal exercised its discretion under art 7.4.3(3) UPICC but having regard to the value of the goods the distributor bought from the breaching supplier and the number of sales achieved by the distributor.

to operate within a frame defined by the law, and specifically must avoid acting as an amiable compositeur (which powers the present Tribunal does not have).[66]

4. STANDARDS OF PROVING LOSSES AND DETERMINING THE AMOUNT OF DAMAGES UNDER THE CISG

4.1. General

In contrast with the UPICC, the CISG is silent as to the standards of proving loss and determining the amount of damages.[67] To decide whether a particular matter should be dealt with by the CISG, it needs to be determined whether this matter is governed by the Convention and, if so, whether there is any relevant general principle which can resolve it.[68] If the matter is not governed by the Convention or if no relevant general principle can be found, the matter will be dealt with by the law applicable by virtue of private international law.[69] These guidelines have been insufficient to achieve anything even remotely reminiscent of uniformity and the discussion of the CISG, in cases and scholarly writings, reveals different approaches to dealing with the issues of standards of proving losses and determining the amount of damages among which the following can be identified.

4.1.1. The Matter is a Procedural Issue Outside the CISG

Article 4 CISG provides that the Convention governs only the issues of formation of contracts and substantive law[70] and the matters of procedural law are often treated as being outside the CISG.[71] Whether the standards of proving loss and determining the amount of damages are a matter of substantive or procedural law may be of some importance to deciding whether it is a matter governed by the Convention. Thus, it has been argued that because the issue of certainty with which losses need to be proven is a matter of procedural law, it

[66] ICC No 9950, June 2001, available at www.unilex.info.

[67] See Commercial Court Zürich (Switzerland) 10 February 1999 (Art books), available at cisgw3.law.pace.edu/cases/990210s1.html ('The CISG does not determine which degree of certainty is necessary for a judge to form his or her profit hypothesis'); Case No HG 970238.1 District Court Saane (Switzerland) 20 February 1997 (Spirits), available at cisgw3.law.pace.edu/cases/970220s1.html ('CISG does not provide any principle regarding damages whose exact figure is not verifiable').

[68] Article 7(2) CISG.

[69] Ibid.

[70] See art 4 CISG ('This Convention governs only the formation of the contract of sale and the rights and obligations of the seller and the buyer arising from such a contract'). See Case No VIII ZR 121/98 Federal Supreme Court (Germany) 24 March 1999 (Vine wax), available at cisgw3.law.pace.edu/cases/990324g1.html; *FCF SA v Adriafil Commerciale Srl* Supreme Court (Switzerland) 15 September 2000, available at cisgw3.law.pace.edu/cases/000915s1.html.

[71] See Federal Supreme Court (Germany) 24 March 1999 (n 70); Supreme Court (Switzerland) 15 September 2000 (n 70).

is beyond the scope of the CISG and needs to be dealt with on the basis of the applicable law.[72] This approach was taken in several CISG cases.[73] In one case, for example, the court stated, with reference to s 54 of the Swiss Code on Civil Procedure, that '[s]ubmissions must be clear, complete and definite'.[74] In another case, the court relied on the domestic civil procedural rules according to which 'any contention of a party is sufficiently substantiated, if … it is detailed to such an extent that a court is in a position to take evidence on that allegation'.[75] In some other cases, courts exercised their discretion in determining the amount of damages derived from domestic procedural rules and, it is submitted, these cases can be regarded as examples of where determining the amount of damages was regarded as a matter of domestic procedural law. For instance, in several cases judges and arbitrators relied on s 287 of the German Code of Civil Procedure which granted the power to evaluate damages.[76] A similar approach was taken in another case where the tribunal stated that:

> the arbitrator fixes the … amount of damages at his discretion … The legal basis for such a discretionary determination of the amount of damages is sec. 273 of the Austrian Code of Civil Procedure, which is also applicable within the scope of the CISG.[77]

[72] See J Lookofsky, *Consequential Damages in Comparative Context: From Breach of Promise to Monetary Remedy in the American, Scandinavian and International Law of Contracts and Sales* (Danmarks Jurist, Copenhagen 1989) 283, note 158; H Bernstein and J Lookofsky, *Understanding the CISG in Europe: A Compact Guide to the 1980 United Nations Convention on Contracts for the International Sale of Goods*, 2nd edn (The Hague, Kluwer Law International, 2003) 144; EC Schneider, 'Consequential Damages in the International Sale of Goods: Analysis of Two Decisions', available at www.cisg.law.pace.edu/cisg/wais/db/articles/schnedr2.html.

[73] Case No A98/126 District Court Sissach (Switzerland) 5 November 1998 (Summer cloth collection), available at cisgw3.law.pace.edu/cases/981105s1.html; Appellate Court St. Gallen (Switzerland) (n 55).

[74] See Commercial Court Zürich, 10 February 1999 (n 67). Although this standard was not stated in the part of the decision (para 2(d)) which dealt with damages, it seems that it was the standard the court had in mind when it held (para 3.1(b)) that 'the [buyer]'s submissions regarding the damage … do not come close to a sufficient substantiation'.

[75] *DT Ltd v B AG* Commercial Court St. Gallen (Switzerland) 3 December 2002 (reference was made to § 56 of Swiss Code on Civil Procedure), available at cisgw3.law.pace.edu/cases/021203s1.html. See also District Court Sissach (Switzerland) 5 November 1998 (n 73) ('law of evidence is determined by the *lex fori*, as the law of evidence belongs to the procedural law. Therefore, each Court applies its own law of evidence'); Case No. CI 04 162 Appellate Court Valais/Wallis (Switzerland) 21 February 2005 (CNC machine), available at cisgw3.law.pace.edu/cases/050221s1.html; Case No 32 O 508/04 District Court Bayreuth (Germany) 10 December 2004 (Tiles), available at cisgw3.law.pace.edu/cases/041210g1.html; Hamburg Arbitration, Partial award of 21 March 1996 (Chinese goods), available at cisgw3.law.pace.edu/cases/960321g1.html.

[76] See Case No. 5 O 543/88 District Court Hamburg (Germany) 26 September 1990 (Textiles), available at cisgw3.law.pace.edu/cases/900926g1.html; Hamburg Chamber of Commerce, Partial award of 21 March 1996 ('National law, including the tribunal's power to evaluate [damages], laid down in Sect. 287 ZPO, applies to determination of damages'); ICC No 8611/HV/JK, 23 January 1997 (Industrial equipment), available at cisgw3.law.pace.edu/ cases/978611i1.html ('the arbitrator must be free to judge the damages following his own convictions on the basis of the known data and on the assumption of a normal course of business (see Art. 287 of the German Civil Procedural Code)').

[77] Vienna Arbitration SCH-4318, 15 June 1994 (Rolled metal sheets), available at cisgw3.law.pace.edu/cases/940615a4.html.

Judicial discretion may exist not only within the framework of rules governing the extent of recoverable damages but also *as a substitute for such rules*[78] and the latter category of cases seems to be precisely of this nature (that is, where judicial discretion is, in a sense, a legal standard for determining the amount of damages).

4.1.2. Not All Procedural Issues are Outside the CISG

It is also possible to take a more flexible approach by not regarding every procedural issue as being outside the CISG. As one commentator suggests, 'the CISG may indirectly govern procedural matters'.[79] This suggestion finds support in the CISG cases touching upon the allocation of burden of proof – an issue often treated as procedural and viewed, by the majority of courts and commentators, as governed by the CISG.[80] Therefore, it may still be possible for standards of proving losses and determining the amount of damages to fall within the Convention's scope even if they are regarded as a procedural issue.[81] If so, the next step is to find a general principle capable of establishing a relevant standard. Otherwise the applicable standard will have to be found in the law applicable by virtue of the rules of private international law.[82]

4.1.3. The Standards of Proving Loss and Determining the Amount of Damages are a Matter of Substantive Law

Even if procedural issues are outside the CISG, the standards of proving loss and determining the amount of damages may still be within its scope if they are treated as a matter of substantive law. Although they may appear to be a procedural issue, the distinction between procedural and substantive law is not clear-cut for 'there exists no systematic abstract criterion that would enable a given case to be classified unequivocally and rationally as being either of a "procedural" or a "substantive" nature'.[83] It is also worth noting that standard of proving loss is regarded as part of the substantive law by such well known

[78] See Treitel (n 2) 174.

[79] P Schlechtriem, 'Arts. 1–6 CISG' in P Schlechtriem and I Schwenzer (eds), *Commentary on the UN Convention on the International Sale of Goods (CISG)*, 2nd (English) edn (Oxford, OUP, 2005) 72.

[80] See, eg, *Rheinland Versicherungen v Srl Atlarex and Allianz Subalpine SpA* District Court Vigevano (Italy) 12 July 2000, available at cisgw3.law.pace.edu/cases/000712i3.html; Commercial Court Zürich (Switzerland) 10 February 1999 (n 67); I Schwenzer and P Hachem, 'The Scope of the CISG Provisions on Damages' in Saidov and Cunnington (n 29) 98; A Mullis, 'Twenty-Five Years On – The United Kingdom, Damages and the Vienna Sales Convention' (2007) 71 Rabels Zeitschrift für ausländisches und internationales Privatrecht 35, 48; M Djordjević, 'Arts 74–77' in S Kröll, L Mistelis and P Viscasillas (eds), *The United Nations Convention on Contracts for the International Sale of Goods*, 2nd edn(München, C.H. Beck and Oxford, Hart, 2018) 962–4.

[81] On the relativity of the distinction between substance and procedure, see the next paragraph and n 111.

[82] Article 7(2) CISG.

[83] See CG Orlandi, 'Procedural Law Issues and Law Conventions' (2000) 5 *Uniform L Rev* 23, available at www.cisg.law.pace.edu/cisg/biblio/orlandi.html (with further reference).

restatements of contract law as the UPICC[84] and US Restatement (Second) of Contracts.[85] On this basis, it can be argued that even if the CISG does not govern the issues of procedural law, one way of bringing the issue of the standards of proving loss and determining the amount of damages into the Convention's scope is to argue that it is a matter of substantive law[86] and to find a general principle capable of developing the relevant standard.

4.1.4. The CISG Governs the Issue of Proving Loss and Contains Relevant Requirements

In a number of the CISG cases, the Convention appears to be interpreted as containing a specific standard of proof. In one case, the court stated that '[u]nder Art. 74 CISG, the [buyer] would have to exactly calculate her damage'.[87] In another case, the CISG was interpreted as requiring that damages be calculated 'precisely'.[88] One court stated that '[a] damages claim according to Art. 74 CISG … necessitates a specific ascertainment of damage'.[89] Similarly, one tribunal held that under the CISG the claimant 'must substantiate and strictly prove the existence and exact amount of its damage'.[90] Two comments need to be made. First, this approach to interpreting the CISG may be welcomed by those who believe that there is no fundamental objection to the 'creative development of the Convention's written rules [as] it is justified by the need to promote uniformity of interpretation'.[91] However, these decisions can be criticised for failing to demonstrate how judges and arbitrators arrived at their conclusions. Nowhere does the CISG mention such standards and it is suggested that this approach is dangerous because, if followed, it will encourage courts and tribunals to read into the CISG the rules which it simply does not contain. Second, the meaning of

[84] See art 7.4.3(1).

[85] See § 352 ('Damages are not recoverable for loss beyond an amount that the evidence permits to be established with reasonable certainty.').

[86] Regarding the standards of proving loss and determining the amount of damages as a matter of substantive law does not guarantee that courts and tribunals will inevitably view the issue as falling within the Convention because they can still regard it as falling outside its scope. This approach seems to be taken in a CISG case decided by a US court. The court stated that '[i]n conformity with *the common law*, to recover a claim for lost profit under UNCCISG, a party must provide the finder of fact with sufficient evidence to estimate the amount of damages with reasonable certainty' (*Delchi Carrier SpA v Rotorex Corporation* 1994 WL 495787 (emphasis added)); see also *ECEM European Chemical Marketing B.V. v. The Purolite Company* (E.D. Pa. Jan. 29, 2010), where the US court relied on the 'reasonable certainty' standard under the law of the state of Pennsylvania.

[87] Case No 3 U 246/97 Appellate Court Celle (Germany) 2 September 1998 (Vacuum cleaners), available at cisgw3.law.pace.edu/cases/980902g1.html.

[88] See Case No 22 U 4/96 Appellate Court Köln (Germany) 21 May 1996 (Used car), available at cisgw3.law.pace.edu/cases/960521g1.html.

[89] Case No 10 O 5423/01 District Court München (Germany) 20 February 2002 (Shoes), available at cisgw3.law.pace.edu/cases/020220g1.html.

[90] ICC No 9187, June 1999 (Coke), available at cisgw3.law.pace.edu/ cases/999187i1.html.

[91] R Herber, 'Preamble and Arts. 1–7 CISG' in P Schlechtriem (ed) *Commentary on the UN Convention on the International Sale of Goods (CISG)*, 2nd edn (in translation) (Oxford, Clarendon Press, 1998) 65–66.

such standards as 'precise', 'exact' or 'specific' ascertainment of damages is not clear. Are they, for example, similar to the 'reasonable certainty' standard in the UPICC or do they require proving loss with mathematical precision and absolute certainty? If the latter is the case, these standards can be criticised because, as is well recognised by different legal systems[92] and some CISG cases,[93] it is rarely possible for losses to be proven with mathematical precision. Imposing such a high standard of proof is likely to diminish the level of protection damages afford to the injured party and possibly deter business persons from applying the CISG, impeding the Convention's unification aspirations.

4.1.5. Relying on Non-National Sources of Law

In some CISG cases, the amount of damages was determined *ex aequo et bono*.[94] The concept of *ex aequo et bono* is generally understood as '[a]ccording what is equitable and good'.[95] In the context of international law, it has been said that '[a] decision-maker … who is authorized to decide *ex aequo et bono* is not bound by legal rules and instead follow equitable principles'.[96] One commentator also refers to several definitions of *ex aequo et bono* given in legal literature:

> 'The power to decide ex aequo et bono … is generally considered as an authorization to act contra legem, to depart from the law, to change the law, to accept a claim not recognized by the law or to reject a claim based on the law.' To decide ex aequo et bono is to seek a 'resolution … that is equitable, minimizes harm to either party, and enables potential adversaries to maintain a valuable commercial relationship; the role of such an arbitrator is said … to be that of an amiable compositeur.' 'The amiable compositeur is in fact a judge, but one who enjoys greater flexibility in adopting a solution … even though from a strictly legal point of view [the solution] may not be … correct.'[97]

Deciding matters *ex aequo et bono* is not a rare phenomenon in international commercial arbitration (and sometimes even features in the decisions of national courts as the cases above demonstrate).[98] It is submitted that the CISG would

[92] See, eg, Treitel (n 2) 192 ('[m]ost systems of law impose some requirement as to "certainty" of damage, but the requirement is not in any of them regarded as an absolute one').

[93] 'The Court has a certain discretion in awarding damages, and that is certainly no less true in relation to the full compensation principle envisaged by Article 74 CISG … [Ma]thematical precision is certainly not required under the CISG' (*Hewlett-Packard France v Matrox Graphics Inc*, 2020 QCCS 78, [248]).

[94] District Court Hasselt (Belgium) 18 October 1995, available at www.unilex.info); *Vital Berry Marketing NV v Dira-Frost NV* District Court Hasselt (Belgium) 2 May 1995, available at cisgw3.law.pace.edu/cases/950502b1.html; *Steinbock-Bjonustan EHF v NV Duma* District Court Kortrijk (Belgium) 4 June 2004, available at www.cisg.law.pace.edu/cisg/wais/db/cases2/040604b1.html; *JM Smithuis Pre Pain v Bakkershuis* Commercial Court Hasselt (Belgium) 20 September 2005, available at cisgw3.law.pace.edu/cases/050920b1.html.

[95] See BA Garner (ed), *Black's Law Dictionary*, 7th edn (St Paul, Minn, West Publishing Co, 1999) 581.

[96] See ibid, 581.

[97] PJ McConnaughay, 'Rethinking the Role of Law and Contracts in East-West Commercial Relationships' (2001) 41 *Virginia J Intl L* 470, with further references.

[98] See also Case No 295401/HA ZA 07-2802 District Court Rotterdam (Netherlands) 15 October 2008, available at cisgw3.law.pace.edu/cases/081015n2.html ('the district court will award ex aequo et bono an amount of €904,00 for non legal costs.').

only allow determining damages on this basis where the parties agreed on such a determination in their contract, derogating from the Convention's rules on damages,[99] or if the matter of proving loss and determining damages fell outside the Convention (or if there were no relevant general principle) and the applicable rules allowed damages to be thus fixed.[100]

4.1.6. *Judicial Discretion not Based on Any Legal Principle*

Courts and tribunals sometimes exercise their discretion in fixing damages without relying on any legal basis. For example, in one case (governed by Hungarian law) the tribunal stated that in 'international arbitration cases the tribunal is not bound by specific rules for the taking of evidence provided that both parties were allowed to present their case'.[101] A similar approach appears to feature in some other cases where the arbitrators' award of damages was explained in terms of the amount being 'sufficiently proven',[102] 'plausible and trustworthy',[103] 'proven to [the tribunal's] satisfaction'[104] or 'appropriate'[105] with no reference to any legal standard. There are many CISG cases where similar statements are made. For example, determining the amount of damages has been discussed in terms of being 'reasonable',[106] 'sufficiently proved'[107] or supported by 'sufficient evidence'[108] or substantiated 'in detail';[109] and, once again, these statements do not seem to be based on any legal standard. If the standard of proving losses and determining the amount of damages is a matter governed and capable of being resolved by the CISG this approach cannot be correct. It is only where the matter is outside the CISG, that courts and tribunals *may* have a power to do so.[110]

[99] See art 6 CISG.

[100] See, eg, art 21(3) of the Rules of Arbitration of the International Chamber of Commerce 2017 ('The arbitral tribunal shall assume the powers of an *amiable compositeur* or decide *ex aequo et bono* only if the parties have agreed to give it such powers'); art 22.4 of the LCIA Arbitration Rules 2020 ('The Arbitral Tribunal shall only apply to the merits of the dispute principles deriving from "ex aequo et bono", "amiable composition" or "honourable engagement" where the parties have so agreed in writing.'). For the discussion of possible reliance on some other non-domestic sources of law, see Saidov (n 1) 60–63.

[101] ICCNo 5418 (n 56) 134).

[102] See ICC No 6076, 1989 (see ibid, 246).

[103] See ICC No 5294, 22 February 1988 (see ibid, 188).

[104] See ICC No 3572, 1982 (see ibid, 163).

[105] See ICC No 6829, 1992 (see *Collection of ICC Arbitral Awards 1991–1995: Recueil des Sentences Arbitrales de la CCI 1991–1995* (compiled by JJ Arnaldez, Y Derains, and D Hascher (The Hague, Kluwer Academic Law Publishers, 1997) 282).

[106] See Case No 95/3214 District Court of Kuopio (Finland) 5 November 1996 (Butter), available at cisgw3.law.pace.edu/cases/961105f5.html; post-1989 CIETAC (Cloth wind coats), available at cisgw3.law.pace.edu/cases/900000c1.html.

[107] See CIETAC 1995, available at www.unilex.info; *SA P v AWS* Tribunal de Commerce Namur (Belgium) 15 January 2002, available at cisgw3.law.pace.edu/cases/020115b1.html.

[108] See Case No 7 O 43/01 District Court Göttingen (Germany) 20 September 2002 (Mattresses and bedding accessories), available at cisgw3.law.pace.edu/cases/020920g1.html.

[109] See Case No 12 U 62/97 Appellate Court Hamburg (Germany) 5 October 1998 (Circuit boards), available at cisgw3.law.pace.edu/cases/981005g1.html.

[110] For further discussion, see Saidov (n 1) 65–67.

4.2. The Matter is Governed and Capable of being Resolved by the CISG

In the light of this non-uniform treatment, it is submitted that a standard of proof is a matter governed by the CISG.[111] First, art 74 CISG undoubtedly requires the injured party to prove its loss. Second, the issue of proving loss and determining the amount of damages is an integral part of the *exercise* of the right to damages. This right is expressly governed by the Convention and if determining a relevant standard of proof were a matter outside the Convention's scope, not only would the *exercise* of the right to damages *under the CISG* be non-uniform but the implementation of policies underlying the law of damages would also be undermined. The CISG contains a relevant general principle of reasonableness[112] capable of developing an appropriate standard of proof. It is submitted that because it is often not possible for the injured party to prove its losses with absolute precision what should be required is that loss be proven only with such a degree of precision which can be *reasonably* expected of this party in the circumstances. In other words, the party must prove its losses with a 'reasonable degree of certainty'.[113] Because the CISG is capable of developing this standard, it is unnecessary to use the 'reasonable certainty' standard in art 7.4.3 UPICC to supplement the CISG. Nevertheless, the UPICC can help formulate this standard under the CISG with precision.[114]

[111] This position is now increasingly accepted. See CISG Advisory Council (CISG-AC) No. 6 'Calculation of Damages under CISG Article 74', available at www.cisg.law.pace.edu/cisg/CISG-AC-op6.html, Rule 2; Schwenzer and Hachem (n 80) 99; Mullis (n 80) 49; J Gotanda, 'Using the UNIDROIT Principles to Fill Gaps in the CISG' in Saidov and Cunnington (n 29) 119. For a contrary position in cases, see Supreme Court (Switzerland) 17 December 2009 (n 50). It is also correct that given the relativity of the distinction between substantive and procedural law, how the issue of standard of proof can be categorised from the perspective of this distinction, should be irrelevant to the question whether a standard of proof is governed by the CISG. See further in I Schwenzer and P Hachem, 'Arts 1–6', and I Schwenzer, 'Arts 74–77' in I Schwenzer (ed), *Schlechtriem and Schwenzer Commentary on the UN Convention on the International Sale of Goods (CISG)*, 4th edn (Oxford, OUP, 2016) 75–6, 85 and 1085.

[112] See, eg, AH Kritzer, 'Reasonableness', available at www.cisg.law.pace.edu/cisg/text/reason.html#schl (with further references).

[113] See, similarly, CISG-AC No. 6 (n 111) Rule 2; Djordjević (n 80) 964–6 (seemingly in favour of this position).

[114] See J Gotanda, 'Using the UNIDROIT Principles to Fill Gaps in the CISG' in Saidov and Cunnington (n 29) 120. The position under the PECL is not entirely clear. The official comments on the PECL acknowledge that the European legal systems 'generally require a sufficient degree of 'certainty' of loss in order to award damages' (O Lando and H Beale (eds), *Principles of European Contract Law: Parts I and II*, prepared by the Commission on European Contract Law (The Hague, Kluwer Law International, 2000) 442). How should this statement be interpreted? Was it the drafters' intention to leave the matter to domestic law otherwise applicable or were the PECL intended to cover the issue of standard of proof precisely because it would be a common feature of European legal systems that losses need to be proven with a 'sufficient degree of certainty'? In principle, it would seem that the analysis presented above in relation to the CISG can be equally applicable to the PECL (see arts 1:106, 1:302; see also comments on art 1:302 explaining that various provisions of the PECL are based on the notion of reasonableness).

5. LOSS OF A CHANCE AND JUDICIAL DISCRETION

As shown, the UPICC contain some other mechanisms for dealing with uncertainty of losses such as the possibility of claiming damages for loss of a chance and exercising judicial discretion. It has been argued in an earlier chapter that loss of a chance is recoverable under both the CISG and the PECL for two reasons.[115] First, there are good reasons for treating a chance as an important 'asset' in commercial transactions which should be afforded legal protection. The second reason is based on the recognition that loss of a chance is also a standard of proving losses. From this perspective, this book has argued that loss of a chance should be recoverable to prevent an 'all-or-nothing' result in awarding damages, striking a fair balance between both parties' interests. The UPICC carry this policy much further by allowing damages to be assessed at the discretion of the court where the injured party cannot prove its loss with sufficient certainty and/or its lost chance to profit. Can the interpretation of the CISG and PECL be stretched that far? As some CISG cases demonstrate,[116] this is what judges and arbitrators sometimes do where they feel that fairness dictates that despite the injured party's inability to prove losses, it should be awarded some compensation. It is suggested that the approach of the UPICC reflects a particular policy choice that arguably tilts the balance too much in favour of the party claiming damages *and* generates considerable legal uncertainty given that, based entirely on judicial discretion, it can make a potential damages award entirely unpredictable. In the absence of a specific provision to indicate such a distinct policy choice, it is submitted that the CISG and PECL should not be interpreted as if they contain a similar mechanism and, to this extent, should be treated as based on a different allocation of risks and striking a different balance between the parties to those in the UPICC.[117] This position is also more conducive to certainty in the international legal environment and the instruments' uniform application.

[115] See ch 3.

[116] See District Court Saane, 20 February 1997 (n 67) (where although the exact amount of damages could not be established, the court was persuaded that the seller had suffered some loss); CIETAC 5 February 1996 (Peanut), available at cisgw3.law.pace.edu/cases/960205c1.html ('the Arbitration Tribunal deems that the Buyer's claim for a price difference … and interest on this amount is not supported by sufficient evidence and should not be accepted. However, considering that … the Seller's failure to deliver the goods deprived the Buyer of its expectation for making a profit … [t]he Arbitration Tribunal deems that a reasonable sum for compensation is 1/3 of the price difference claimed by the Buyer'); CIETAC 27 April 2000 (Wool), available at cisgw3.law.pace.edu/cases/000427c1.html ('the Arbitration Tribunal holds that based on principles of equity, the Buyer shall compensate certain amount to the Seller, and US $10,000 would be reasonable.'); for an example of an approach where a tribunal simply split losses on what presumably seemed equitable to the tribunal, see CIETAC 31 December 1996 (High carbon tool steel), available at cisgw3.law.pace.edu/cases/961231c2.html.

[117] A different position is taken in this edition of this book in respect of this question, compared to the view expressed in the first edition.

8

Calculation of Damages (Part I)

1. GENERAL

ONCE IT IS known for what losses damages need to be awarded, those losses need to be translated into money.[1] Labels used to describe this process are many and include such terms as 'quantum', 'quantification', 'measure', 'assessment' and 'calculation'.[2] This chapter examines various methods of translating losses into money which can be used under the international instruments. Before examining the specific methods of calculating damages, it is helpful to outline a general structure of the instruments' damages provisions insofar as it is relevant to the issue of calculation. The structure of all three instruments is very similar, as they all provide two specific formulae for calculating damages in cases where the contract has been avoided[3] (terminated).[4] The two formulae are well known to legal systems. The first formula can be used where the injured party concludes a transaction in substitution of the breached contract and it is based on the difference between the price in the original contract and the price in the substitute contract.[5] This formula is an instance of the so-called 'concrete' approach to calculating damages that requires the examination of the claimant's *actual* circumstances. In contrast, the second formula is an instance of the so-called 'abstract' approach to calculating damages that is detached from the claimant's actual circumstances. It is based on the presumption that the claimant's damages consist of the difference between the original contract price and the 'current price'.[6] All other losses, not covered by these formulae or arising where the contract has not been avoided/terminated, are to be compensated under the instruments' general provisions on damages which provide for the principle of *full compensation* and, whether implicitly or expressly, pursue the purpose of putting the injured party in the position in which it would have been had the contract been properly performed.[7] Although these general

[1] GH Treitel, *Remedies for Breach of Contract: A Comparative Account* (Oxford, Clarendon Press, 1988) 105.

[2] E Peel, *Treitel – The Law of Contract*, 15th edn (London, Thomson–Sweet & Maxwell, 2020) 1137.

[3] The term used by the CISG.

[4] The term used by the UPICC and PECL.

[5] See arts 75 CISG, 7.4.5 UPICC and 9:506 PECL.

[6] See arts 76 CISG, 7.4.6 UPICC and 9:507 PECL.

[7] See arts 74 CISG, 7.4.2 UPICC and 9:502 PECL. For further discussion, see ch 2.

provisions do not contain any specific method of calculation, there is no doubt that various calculation methods can be used under these provisions so long as they are in line with the principle of full compensation and protect the party's 'expectation/ performance' or 'positive' interest. Finally, in contrast with the CISG and PECL, the UPICC provide guidance on how to calculate damages for loss of a chance.[8]

This chapter generally tracks the structure of the instruments' provisions. First, it will address the methods of calculating damages where the contract has been avoided; and second, the issue of calculating damages will be dealt with in the context of different types of breach where the contract has not been avoided. The remaining issues relating to the calculation of damages will be examined in the next chapter.[9]

2. CALCULATION: THE AVOIDANCE OF THE CONTRACT

2.1. 'Concrete' Method of Calculation

2.1.1. General

According to the CISG, '[i]f the contract is avoided and if, in a reasonable manner and within a reasonable time after avoidance, the buyer has bought goods in replacement or the seller has resold the goods, the party claiming damages may recover the difference between the contract price and the price in the substitute transaction as well as any further damages recoverable under article 74'.[10] The corresponding provisions of the UPICC[11] and PECL[12] are similar. However, because the two sets of Principles are also applicable to transactions other than sales transactions, their provisions make a broad reference to a 'replacement'[13] and 'substitute'[14] transactions. As noted, this method of calculation looks at the claimant's *actual* conduct and situation and reflects the 'concrete' approach to calculating damages. This method of assessment is known to many legal systems[15] and is sometimes used as the basis for a contractual damages calculation

[8] See art 7.4.3(2) UPICC.

[9] See ch 9.

[10] Article 75 CISG.

[11] 'Where the aggrieved party has terminated the contract and has made a replacement transaction within a reasonable time and in a reasonable manner it may recover the difference between the contract price and the price of the replacement transaction as well as damages for any further harm.' (art 7.4.5 UPICC).

[12] 'Where the aggrieved party has terminated the contract and has made a substitute transaction within a reasonable time and in a reasonable manner, it may recover the difference between the contract price and the price of the substitute transaction as well as damages for any further loss so far as these are recoverable under this Section.' (art 9:506 PECL).

[13] See art 7.4.5 UPICC.

[14] See art 9:506 PECL.

[15] See Notes on Article 9:506 PECL in O Lando and H Beale (eds), *Principles of European Contract Law: Parts I and II*, prepared by the Commission on European Contract Law (The Hague,

clause.[16] It can perhaps be justified on the basis that it reflects what parties often do in practice.[17] It may often be in the injured party's interest[18] to conclude a replacement transaction after avoiding the contract with the breaching party to enable itself to proceed with the arrangements planned in connection with the contract with the breaching party (eg, sub-sale). This 'concrete' method of calculation is also closely linked with a duty to mitigate because concluding a replacement transaction is often a typical measure of mitigating losses.[19] This rule of concrete assessment has been praised for introducing a degree of simplicity, clarity and certainty into the law of damages.[20] The praise is probably due to the rule's ability to alleviate, in many cases, the difficulty of proving and assessing damages because making a reasonable substitute transaction within a reasonable time often fixes the injured party's damages[21] (with further losses being recoverable under a general provision on damages).

Damages assessed under this 'concrete' formula compensate the *seller* for the *profit margin* it expected to receive from the sale of goods. If upon non-acceptance by the buyer, the seller resells (in a reasonable manner and within a reasonable time) the goods at a lower price than that in the contract with the buyer, the difference between the contract price and the price in the resale compensates the seller for a decreased profit margin (if any).[22] However, so far as the buyer is concerned, this 'concrete'[23] formula leads not to an award of lost profit,[24] but to damages for not having received the goods at an agreed price. The buyer can have two kinds of expectation – the expectation of receiving the

Kluwer Law International, 2000) 448; F Enderlein and D Maskow, *International Sales Law: United Nations Convention on Contracts for the International Sale of Goods; Convention on the Limitation Period in the International Sale of Goods* (NY, Oceana, 1992) 303.

[16] See CIETAC 20 January 1993 (Ferrosilicon), available at cisgw3. law.pace.edu/cases/930120c1.html.

[17] See Secretariat Commentary on Article 71 of the 1978 Draft, para 3.

[18] V Knapp, 'Arts. 74–77 CISG' in CM Bianca and MJ Bonell (eds), *Commentary on the International Sales Law: The 1980 Vienna Sales Convention* (Milan, Giuffrè, 1987) 548–49.

[19] For a similar view, see, eg, P Schlechtriem, *Uniform Sales Law: The UN-Convention on Contracts for the International Sale of Goods* (Vienna, Manz Verlag, 1986) 97; CISG Advisory Council (CISG-AC) Opinion No. 8, 'Calculation of Damages under CISG Articles 75 and 76', available at www.cisgac.com/file/repository/CISG_AC_Opinion_8_English.pdf, Comment 2.1.2. For a 'self-interest' rationale of the mitigation rule, see ch 6.

[20] See also n 133.

[21] See JO Honnold, *Uniform Law for International Sales under the 1980 United Nations Convention*, 3rd edn (Deventer, Kluwer Law International, 1999) 448–49.

[22] See *Sunrise Foods international Inc v Ryan Hinton Inc*, 2019 WL 3755499 (D Idaho, 2019), where the court rightly rejected the damages claim by the seller, who resold to a third party the quantity of corn not accepted and paid for by the breaching buyer, for an alleged profit margin on the basis that the contract price already incorporated the seller's profit margin; ICC No 7585, 1992 (Foamed board machinery), available at cisgw3.law.pace.edu/cases/927585i1.html.

[23] The same point applies to the 'abstract' measure in arts 76 CISG, 7.4.6 UPICC and 9:507 PECL.

[24] See CIETAC 30 July 1996, where both parties incorrectly referred to the 'concrete' assessment as a method of calculating lost profits (Ferro-molybdenum alloy), available at cisgw3.law.pace.edu/cases/960730c2.html; see also Arbitration No 48, 2005 (Ukraine), available at cisgw3.law.pace.edu/cases/050000u5.html (where the tribunal incorrectly viewed damages under art 76 CISG as compensating the buyer for lost profits).

subject-matter and the expectation of putting it to some profitable use. The former is what the instruments' 'concrete' formula protects.[25]

2.1.2. *The 'Concrete' Formula: Preconditions and Application*

The preconditions for using this 'concrete' formula are as follows. First, all three instruments expressly provide that their provisions are to be used where the contract is avoided[26] and where a substitute contract is made after avoidance.[27] It is usually the avoidance of the contract which makes clear that the contract will no longer be performed and it is only the avoidance that discharges the parties from their contractual obligations, setting them on course to procure a substitute.[28] Second, this method of calculation can be used if the innocent party has *in fact* concluded a substitute transaction and, for this reason, a CISG case where the tribunal awarded damages in accordance with this method where the buyer was yet to procure a substitute[29] was not correctly decided. Third, a transaction made after avoiding the contract with a breaching party must truly aim at *replacing* the original contract. To perform this function a substitute transaction needs to be connected to the original contract and be able to secure the injured party's interest in the performance of the original contract.[30] These are general guidelines and the real challenge is to define what constitutes 'a substitute' in the particular circumstances.

For instance, can the manufacturer, after rejecting the seller's delivery, use the goods purchased earlier to fulfil orders which were initially planned to be fulfilled by means of the goods to be delivered by the seller? In a CISG case based on similar facts,[31] the court stated that previously ordered goods could not be considered substitute goods. The reason is most likely based on the fact that the buyer was in a lost volume situation where the demand for the goods exceeded the buyer's ability to supply. Given that the true purpose of the goods ordered previously was to satisfy orders *in addition* to those that the seller's delivery was intended to fulfil, they were not truly a replacement sale. By using them to meet the demand for one set of orders the buyer lost an opportunity to satisfy other additional orders it would have realised had there been no breach. A true

[25] See Treitel (n 1) 123.

[26] For the discussion of whether this method of calculating damages can be used where the contract has not been avoided, see below.

[27] See arts 75 CISG, 7.4.5 UPICC and 9:506. See also I Schwenzer, 'Arts 74–77' in I Schwenzer (ed), *Schlechtriem and Schwenzer Commentary on the UN Convention on the International Sale of Goods (CISG)*, 4th edn (Oxford, OUP, 2016) 1087–95.

[28] Ibid. It is, of course, possible for a party to procure a substitute without avoiding the contract. However, an innocent party may often not want to do so as long as there is a possibility that the other party will still perform the contract (because, eg, it does not need two sets of similar goods or does not have financial resources to buy similar goods twice). The course of action which provides this party with the greatest legal security and freedom to act is to avoid the contract.

[29] CIETAC 30 October 1991 (Roll aluminium and aluminium parts), available at cisgw3.law.pace.edu/cases/911030c1.html.

[30] See Schwenzer (n 27) 1087–8.

[31] *Delchi Carrier SpA v Rotorex Corp* 1994 WL 495787.

replacement transaction is therefore one that does not leave a party in the position in which it loses an additional unit of profit.

What if the same question arises under similar facts but without any loss of volume? Suppose the buyer has goods in stock which it had bought before concluding the contract with the seller or before the seller breached the contract. Suppose further that after avoiding the contract with the seller, the buyer uses the goods from its stock to fulfil orders which the seller's goods were intended to fulfil. Should the buyer be entitled, under this 'concrete' formula, to claim the difference between the price of previously ordered goods and the price under its contract with the seller? On the one hand, it can be argued that this should not be possible. First, if a true replacement transaction must be concluded with an intention to substitute an original transaction,[32] it can hardly be argued that previously purchased goods were bought with an intention to replace the contract with breaching party. Second, it will be recalled that one of the preconditions for the instruments' 'concrete' formula is that a replacement be made *after* avoiding the contract. Consequently, where goods were bought before the avoidance of the contract with a breaching party, such a purchase cannot be within the scope of this 'concrete' formula.

On the other hand, it can be suggested that the international instruments do not require (at least expressly) a substitute transaction to be accompanied by an intention to replace the original contract. To qualify as a substitute, a transaction needs to be able to perform the *function* of replacing the contract with the breaching party regardless of whether this was the claimant's intention at the time of making that transaction. It can also be proposed that because the instruments require a substitute transaction to be made in a reasonable manner, it is the *reasonableness* of using that transaction as a substitute for the original contract that should be decisive. The same argument can be used to address the point concerning the time of avoidance. It can be argued that it may be reasonable for a party to use the goods from its stock as a substitute even before the contract is avoided. It has been suggested that there may be cases where it is certain that the promisor will not perform the contract (because, for example, it has clearly stated so) and it would be contrary to good faith for a breaching party to argue that the innocent party ought to have sent a notice of avoidance before making a substitute contract.[33]

It is submitted that, in the interests of clarity, certainty and uniformity in the application of the international instruments, it is better not to deviate from the express wording of the instruments' provisions and to interpret a substitute only as a transaction occurring after avoidance. This is not to say that,

[32] B Borisova, 'Commentary on the Manner in which the UNIDROIT Principles May Be Used to Interpret or Supplement Article 75 of the CISG', available at www.cisg.law.pace.edu/ cisg/principles/uni75.html.

[33] See H Stoll and G Gruber in P Schlechtriem and I Schwenzer (eds), *Commentary on the UN Convention on the International Sale of Goods (CISG)*, 2nd (English) edn (Oxford, OUP, 2005) 776. The most recent edition takes a different view, similar to that in this book (see Schwenzer (n 27) 1089).

where goods were bought before avoidance, damages cannot be calculated as the difference between the price in that transaction and the original contract because, as argued below, this method of calculation should be possible under the instruments' general provisions on damages.[34] This means, however, that the provisions expressly providing for the instruments' 'concrete' formula[35] are restricted to cases where a substitute occurred after avoidance, which removes cases involving 'previously ordered goods' from the scope of these provisions.

The case of previously ordered goods raises a more general question of whether there must be some connection between an original contract and an alleged substitute. It seems that some connection must exist between the two but this connection need only be established to demonstrate that an alleged substitute was indeed a replacement for the original contract. The question to be asked should be whether an alleged substitute was made *because* the original contract failed to materialise and whether this alleged substitute transaction would have been made if the original contract had been performed. Various factors can be relevant to showing this connection.

One is the similarity of terms which normally points in favour of the existence of this connection. In one case, the seller failed to deliver 39,200 kg of de-stoned frozen cherries and the buyer's purchase of exactly the same quantity of the goods of the same description was rightly deemed to be the buyer's replacement transaction.[36] In a case[37] involving a sale of iron-molybdenum, the court took into account the similarity of terms in both contracts and the period of time within which an alleged substitute had been made. The court held that an alleged cover transaction which involved the purchase of approximately 17–20 tonnes of goods with 60 per cent concentration of molybdenum was similar to the originally agreed delivery of approximately 18 tonnes with minimum 64 per cent concentration of molybdenum. The fact that an alleged substitute had been made within two weeks after the seller's refusal to deliver led the court to state that 'the connection in time between the two contracts [was] so close that reasonable doubts concerning the contract's designation as a cover transaction [were] not present'.[38] A different result was reached in another case[39] where the tribunal ruled that an alleged substitute was not a replacement contract simply because an alleged substitute was under the CIF terms as opposed to C&F terms in the original contract and the due date for delivery was later than in the original contract. It is suggested that these grounds *in themselves* do not necessarily constitute a sufficient basis for not recognising an alleged substitute as a

[34] See arts 74 CISG, 7.4.2 UPICC and 9:502 PECL.
[35] Articles 75 CISG, 7.4.5 UPICC and 9:506 PECL.
[36] Case No A56-108602/2017 Arbitration Court St Petersburg and Leningrad Region (Russia) 7 August 2018, available at ras.arbitr.ru (in Russian).
[37] Case No 1 U 167/95 Appellate Court Hamburg (Germany) 28 February 1997 (Iron molybdenum), available at cisgw3.law.pace.edu/cases/970228g1.html.
[38] Ibid.
[39] CIETAC 18 April 1995 (Clothes), available at cisgw3.law.pace.edu/ cases/950418c1.html.

replacement because, as discussed below, a substitute contract does not always have to be made on terms identical to those in the original contract. For the result in this case to be justifiable, additional factors ought to have been invoked to demonstrate that the differences relating to the delivery terms reflected a lack of causal connection between the original contract and the alleged substitute.[40] A claimant's conduct subsequent to the alleged substitute can also be relevant to deciding whether there is a connection between the two transactions. For instance, if the buyer demands the delivery of the very same goods from the same seller after the alleged substitute has taken place, this fact may indicate that the alleged cover was not a substitute for the original contract.[41] Sometimes tribunals take into consideration the purpose for which an injured party has entered into the contract with the breaching party and determine whether an alleged substitute would be able to fulfil that purpose. In one case, the tribunal having identified the differences concerning a number of contract terms (name, specification, country of origin, manufacturing date, quantity of the goods and delivery dates) in the alleged substitute and the buyer's sub-sale contract, held that the alleged substitute was not a true replacement.[42]

One well-known difficulty of establishing a connection between an alleged substitute and the original contract arises where the injured party is involved in a continuous trading in similar goods.[43] This situation often occurs in the commodities trade, where 'merchants conduct their buying and selling activities across a broad front'.[44] Where so, it may be difficult or even impossible to ascertain whether an alleged substitute has been made to replace the contract with a breaching party or whether this transaction is just another transaction concluded in the usual course of business. One way that may alleviate the injured party's burden of proof is for this party to send a notice,[45] whether in conjunction with the notice of avoidance[46] or independently, informing the breaching party of its intention to make a substitute transaction. But it is suggested that sending such a notice should not necessarily be regarded as sufficient proof that an alleged substitute was a replacement transaction. Given that an injured party has an incentive to identify a transaction most beneficial to its financial interests (in the sense that a seller, for example, has an incentive to identify a resale with

[40] One such factor could be the buyer's sub-sale contract the terms of which corresponded to the terms of the original contract. For the discussion of this factor, see below.

[41] See CIETAC 11 February 2000 (Silicon metal), available at cisgw3.law.pace.edu/cases/000211c1.html.

[42] See CIETAC 30 November 1997 (Canned oranges), available at cisgw3.law.pace.edu/cases/971130c1.html.

[43] This situation may have arisen in Case No 7 U 2959/04 Appellate Court München (Germany) 15 September 2004 (Furniture leather), available at cisgw3.law.pace.edu/cases/040915g2.html.

[44] MG Bridge, *The Sale of Goods*, 4th edn (Oxford, OUP, 2019) [12.47].

[45] Schwenzer (n 27) 1088; JS Ziegel, 'The Remedial Provisions in the Vienna Sales Convention: Some Common Law Perspectives' in N Galston and J Smit (eds), *International Sales: The United Nations Convention on Contracts for the International Sale of Goods* (NY, Matthew Bender, 1984) 9–39.

[46] See arts 26 CISG, 7.3.2 UPICC and 9:303 PECL.

the lowest price),[47] care is required to ensure that an alleged substitute can be reasonably treated as a replacement.

There is no agreement as to what the appropriate course of action is where it is impossible to establish a true substitute transaction. While some sources suggest that this 'concrete' formula should not be used and the insruments' 'abstract' formula should be used instead,[48] others argue that '[t]he fact that any of a number of transactions may have been the substitute transaction does not amount to the conclusion that there was no substitute transaction'[49] and it is sufficient to point to several of those transactions as long they can perform the function of replacing the broken contract.[50] So, how 'concrete' should the instruments' 'concrete' formula be? Is it necessary for a claimant to identify one specific transaction as an actual substitute or is it sufficient, where no actual substitute can be established, to point to any transaction(s) which can be viewed as a reasonable substitute? It is suggested that to preserve clarity and relative simplicity of this 'concrete' formula, it is better to treat it as requiring that a specific transaction has *actually* been made to replace the broken contract. As explained, to meet this requirement it must be established that the alleged substitute was made because of the failure of the original contract to materialise and because it would not have been made had the original contract been performed.[51]

The next precondition for using the 'concrete' formula is that a replacement transaction be carried out in a 'reasonable manner'. This requirement further informs the definition of a 'substitute transaction'. In general terms, a replacement procured in a 'reasonable manner' is a transaction based on conduct expected of a prudent, careful and reasonable business person.[52] Making a substitute transaction in a reasonable manner is closely linked with the notion of good faith[53] and it is arguable that the reasonableness of a transaction is to be judged from the standpoint of good faith. More specifically, in the context of sales transactions a reasonable manner means the seller's resale at the

[47] See JJ White and RS Summers, *Uniform Commercial Code*, 5th edn (St Paul, Minn, West Publishing Co, 2000) 266.

[48] Secretariat Commentary on Article 72 of the 1978 Draft, para 2.

[49] J Yovel, 'Comparison between Provisions of the CISG (Measurement of Damages when Contract Avoided: Article 76) and the Counterpart Provisions of the PECL (Article 9:507)', available at www.cisg.law.pace.edu/cisg/text/peclcomp76.html.

[50] Ibid.

[51] *Cf* CISG-AC No 8 (n 19) Comment 2.3.4 ('Identifying a single transaction as a substitute may be difficult for an aggrieved party that often deals in contracts similar to the avoided one. Such a party has several options, including identifying a substitute transaction prior to engaging in it, choosing the first transaction after avoidance as the substitute, or proceeding abstractly under Article 76.').

[52] See ICC No 10274, 1999 (Poultry feed), available at cisgw3.law.pace.edu/ cases/990274i1.html; ICC No 8128, 1995 (Chemical fertiliser), available at cisgw3.law.pace.edu/cases/958128i1.html.

[53] '[R]easonableness is to be judged by what persons acting in good faith and in the same situation as the parties would consider to be reasonable …' (art 1:302 PECL). Good faith may also come into play if we recall the link between the 'concrete' formula and mitigation and a good faith rationale of the mitigation rule (see ch 6).

highest price reasonably possible or the buyer's re-purchase at the lowest price reasonably possible.[54] It is also arguable that if the price in an actual substitute transaction is extremely unfavourable to the innocent party[55] as a result of, say, drastic fluctuations in the market price (that is, if in the case of the innocent seller the resale price is extremely low and in the case of the innocent buyer the price of purchasing replacement goods is extremely high), entering into such a replacement transaction may fall outside the 'reasonable manner' requirement.[56] Given that this 'concrete' formula is closely linked with a duty to mitigate, the suggested interpretation is well aligned with and arguably flows from the position[57] that the mitigation rule does not require the innocent party to take measures that entail severe financial consequences[58] or risks.[59] This interpretation is further in line with an earlier argument[60] that the recovery of the amount produced by this formula should be subject to the foreseeability test.[61] Further, just as the reasonableness criterion underlying the mitigation rule does not require 'perfect conduct',[62] so does the 'reasonable manner' criterion not require the innocent party to 'exhaust all possible avenues of research prior to engaging in a resale or cover purchase'.[63] Finally, it goes without saying that a replacement transaction can only be made in a reasonable manner if entering into it is lawful. For instance, if the seller has manufactured the goods which bear the buyer's trademark and which were wrongly not accepted and paid for

[54] Secretariat Commentary on Article 71 of the 1978 Draft, para 4. See Arbitration Court St Petersburg and Leningrad Region 7 August 2018 (n 36), where the seller failed to deliver 19,800 kg of frozen cherries (at the price of €1.50 per kg) and the buyer's purchase of the same quantity of frozen cherries in its replacement transaction at the price of €2.20 per kg was deemed reasonable.

[55] See Case No A63-5945/2017 Arbitration Court, Stavropol Region (Russia) 16 November 2017, available at ras.arbitr.ru (in Russian), where the buyer, whilst having attempted to enter into a replacement transaction, eventually did not do so in order to avoid a loss that would otherwise arise because of a substantial rise in the market price.

[56] Unless entering into such a replacement transaction avoids an even higher loss, such as where a manufacturer/producer is in urgent need of replacement goods to maintain its manufacture/production.

[57] See ch 6.

[58] See Case No A53-1781/2018 The Fifteenth Arbitration Appellate Court Rostov-on-Don (Russia) 3 July 2018, available at ras.arbitr.ru (in Russian), where following the seller's non-delivery of steel the buyer did not enter into a replacement transaction because of the sharp rise in the current/market price of steel and the lack of financial resources, especially because the buyer had made an advance payment to the seller that had not been returned to the buyer.

[59] Proving damages often carries a risk for innocent parties, such as that of a failure to meet the proof or evidentiary requirements. This risk becomes greater if innocent parties think that the 'reasonable manner' criterion covers drastic price fluctuations.

[60] See ch 5.

[61] The suggested interpretation of the 'reasonable manner' criterion and the earlier argument, that the foreseeability test should be applicable to the instruments' 'concrete' and 'abstract' formulae, provide safeguards for one and the same set of objectives: namely, that the breaching party should not be liable in damages for the unusually high price difference; nor is entering into such a replacement transaction a reasonable measure and is likely to contravene the innocent party's interests.

[62] See ch 6.

[63] CISG-AC No 8 (n 19), Comment 2.3.1.

by the buyer, reselling them can only be reasonable if doing so does not infringe on the buyer's trademark rights.[64]

In practice, judges and arbitrators often take into account the market price to determine whether a substitute transaction was made in a reasonable manner (and this is the point where there is little difference between the instruments' 'concrete' and 'abstract' formulae).[65] If the price in a buyer's substitute transaction is lower than the market price, it is very likely that this substitute is reasonable.[66] The same most probably applies to cases where the price in a substitute transaction corresponds to the market price.[67] But in some cases it may be that despite the price in the seller's substitute transaction being lower than the market price, the substitute transaction is still reasonable. For instance, in one case the tribunal held that it was reasonable for a price in a substitute transaction to be slightly lower than the market price where, as a result of the buyer's refusal to accept goods, the 'goods became backlogged at the port and were at a disadvantageous position to be resold'.[68]

The existence/absence of more favourable alternatives is also relevant to determining whether the price in a substitute transaction is reasonable and, in one case,[69] the burden of demonstrating such alternatives was placed on the breaching party. Thus, a German court dismissed the breaching seller's argument that the buyer could have obtained a cheaper substitute because the seller had failed to sufficiently demonstrate 'where and at what possible lower price the buyer at the relevant point [in] time could have bought cheaper goods'.[70] In another case,[71] the seller's resale at a 20 per cent discount as compared to the original price was deemed reasonable after it had unsuccessfully tried to resell the goods at a better price for two months.

The next question is whether, to be a reasonable substitute, a replacement transaction needs to be on the same terms as those in the original transaction and whether goods need to correspond to the original contract in terms of description, quality and quantity. Because the purpose of making a substitute

[64] See *Doolim Corp v R Doll, LLC*, 2009 U.S. Dist. LEXIS 45366 (S.D.N.Y. May 28, 2009), [44]–[45], where on similar facts the court declared that the seller could resell the goods with the buyer's trademark because, based on the US law, the seller would have 'an implied license to trademarked goods' to mitigate its damages. For the relevance of a 'black market' for determining the current price, see nn 205–207 and the accompanying main text.

[65] See, eg, Case No A53-32531/2016 Arbitration Court Rostov Region (Russia) 2 February 2018, available at ras.arbitr.ru (in Russian).

[66] See CIETAC 10 June 2002 (Rapeseed dregs), available at cisgw3.law. pace.edu/cases/020610c1.html; 10 August 2000 (Silicon metal), available at cisgw3.law.pace.edu/ cases/000810c1.html.

[67] See *Downs Investments Pty Ltd v Perwaja Steel SDN BHD* [2000] QSC 421; CIETAC 4 September 1996 (Natural rubber), available at cisgw3.law.pace.edu/cases/ 960904c1.html; ICC No 10329, 2000 (Industrial product), available at cisgw3. law.pace.edu/cases/000329i1.html.

[68] CIETAC 4 June 1999 (Industrial raw material), available at cisgw3. law.pace.edu/cases/990604c1.html.

[69] Case No 411 O 199/02 District Court Hamburg (Germany) 26 November 2003 (Phtalic anhydride), available at cisgw3.law.pace.edu/cases/031126g1.html.

[70] Ibid.

[71] ICC No 10274 (n 52).

transaction is to replace the original contract, a substitute contract generally needs to be on similar terms to those in the original contract.[72] Nevertheless, it is also widely accepted that the terms of a substitute transaction need not be *identical* to those of the original contract.[73] This position stems from the notion of reasonableness which only requires that a replacement be a *reasonable* substitute;[74] but it should be tempered by a guideline that a transaction cannot be a substitute if it 'is so different from the original contract in value or kind as not to be a reasonable substitute'.[75] Despite these guidelines, it is difficult to draw a clear line between the types and extent of differences which are and are not acceptable in the light of the reasonableness criterion. Considering specific situations provides further guidance.

Where a substitute transaction involves goods which are not identical to those in the original contract, it may have been made in a reasonable manner if substitute goods are of the same technical specification.[76] Even if they are not, they may still be treated as a reasonable replacement if the difference in specifications is 'slight', 'minor' or 'unimportant'.[77] In rare circumstances, it may perhaps be possible for a reasonable substitute to involve goods *substantially different* from those under the original contract, if the latter were unique and if finding substantially different goods was the only reasonable option to replace the contract goods.[78] The purpose for which an injured party had made the original contract is often indicative of whether a substitute has been made in a reasonable manner. In one case,[79] the tribunal dismissed the breaching seller's argument that the buyer ought to have procured a substitute on the ground that the contract between the buyer and its sub-buyer provided for the goods to be

[72] See Borisova (n 32); ICC No 8128 (n 52) ('The first condition is that goods in replacement are of the same type and quality'). For cases where it was possible for an injured buyer to enter into replacement transactions on the same terms, see: Arbitration Court St Petersburg and Leningrad Region 7 August 2018 (n 36), where the buyer purchased in its replacement transaction the same quantity of the same goods as in the contract with the breaching seller (39,200 kg of de-stoned frozen cherries); Case No 4A_440/2009 Supreme Court (Switzerland) 17 December 2009, available at cisgw3.law.pace.edu/cases/091217s1.html ('[the Buyer] had the opportunity to purchase watches of the same model as [the Seller] refused to deliver in breach of its obligations, through the retailer that was awarded exclusivity in the Ukraine.').

[73] See Secretariat Commentary on Article 71 of the 1978 Draft, para 4; CISG-AC No 8 (n 19) Comment 2.3.4; Case No 3K-3-230/2013 Supreme Court (Lithuania), available at www.unilex.info (with reference to art 7.4.5. UPICC; the abstract of the decision is available in English) See also Comment 2 to § 2-712 UCC.

[74] See Secretariat Commentary on Article 71 of the 1978 Draft, para 4.

[75] See Comment B on Article 9:506 PECL and illustration 2 in Lando and Beale (n 15) 448.

[76] See District Court Hamburg 26 November 2003 (n 69).

[77] ICC No 8128 (n 52) (where the specifications of substitute chemical fertilisers differed from those under the original contract in terms 'purity and water content').

[78] See Case No 419 O 48/01 District Court Hamburg (Germany) 21 December 2001 (Stones), available at cisgw3.law.pace.edu/cases/011221g1.html. Although the preconditions for applying art 75 CISG were not met in this case, it provides an illustration where apparently unique goods (natural stone) were involved and where the buyer argued that it had to find some other material to use in its construction works.

[79] CIETAC 17 October 1996 (Tinplate), available at cisgw3.law.pace.edu/cases/961017c1.html.

produced in Korea and it would have been unreasonable for the buyer to procure goods made in some other country.[80]

A well-known difficulty of determining whether a substitute is made in a reasonable manner arises where an injured buyer acquires goods superior to contract goods. In the abstract, it is impossible to state whether procuring superior goods constitutes a reasonable substitute. If identical or similar goods are reasonably available at a lower price than that of superior goods, then purchasing superior goods is unlikely to be a reasonable substitute. If superior goods were the only ones reasonably available to the buyer, purchasing them might be a reasonable replacement. Where so, the benefit arising from using superior goods, which the buyer would not have had if the seller had performed the contract, must be taken into account. This means that the amount of damages calculated under the instruments' 'concrete' formula must be reduced by the amount reflecting the value of such benefits.[81]

Sometimes contracts allow a breaching party to perform in alternative ways and, if so, the question is how the requirement of making a substitute transaction 'in a reasonable manner' should be interpreted. If the breaching seller had an option to deliver between 8 and 10 tonnes of potatoes, should the buyer be allowed to claim the difference between the price of 10 tonnes of potatoes it has bought in replacement and the contract price for the same quantity? The question may be important because, assuming the overall price in both contracts did not vary depending on the quantity purchased, the greater the quantity the higher the difference will be between the contract price and the price in a substitute transaction. Although in some cases it may be possible to determine the precise quantity the seller would have delivered had it performed the contract, in many cases this will not be possible. A workable solution can be to adopt a presumption regarding what the breaching party would have done. It is relevant to note that some common law systems assume that the breaching party would have performed the contract in the way which is least burdensome to itself. For instance, if, in our example, delivering the minimum quantity is the least burdensome way of performing, it will be assumed that the seller would deliver 8 tonnes of potatoes and the buyer's substitute needs to be a replacement for that quantity.[82] It is suggested that a similar approach should be taken under

[80] No goods of Korean origin were reasonably available to the buyer due to time limitations. For a similar CISG case, see CIETAC 29 September 2004 (India rapeseed meal), available at cisgw3.law.pace.edu/cases/040929c1.html, where the tribunal dismissed the seller's argument that the Chinese buyer ought to have procured a substitute delivery of rapeseed meal in its domestic market on the basis that the contract goods were indicated as 'India rapeseed meal'.

[81] For a similar view in the context of the UCC, see White and Summers (n 47) 209.

[82] See, eg, Peel (n 2) 1029; S Waddams, *The Law of Damages*, 4th edn (Toronto, Canada Law Book Inc, 2004) 536–37. For a similar approach in a CISG case involving art 76 CISG, see Arbitration No 48 (n 24) (see further the discussion on long-term contracts in ch 9). See also CIETAC 4 February 2002 (Styrene monomer), available at cisgw3.law.pace.edu/cases/ 020204c1.html, where the injured seller, who had an option of delivering '+/– 5%' of the specified quantity, resold 5% less than that quantity and where this resale was found to be reasonable.

the international instruments. First, injured parties need certainty as to what is considered reasonable in such circumstances and establishing a presumption provides clear guidance. Second, given that most traders are driven by self-interest and commercial rationality, a presumption that a breaching party would have acted in the way, which is least burdensome or most beneficial to itself, seems a fair and reasonable one to draw.

The next question is whether this should be an irrebuttable presumption or whether it should be possible for the injured party to rebut it. While this presumption *itself* will rarely be untrue, disagreements may arise as to what would have been the conduct which is most beneficial or least burdensome to the breaching party. The common law, for example, assumes that the seller in our example would have always been better off by selling the minimum permissible quantity (ie, 8 tonnes of potatoes) and this assumption, it is submitted, cannot be true in *all* situations for it may well be that the seller would have expected the market prices to fall, in which case it might have deemed beneficial to sell the maximum quantity before the expected market fall.[83] Because the presumption that the breaching party would have acted in the way most beneficial/least burdensome to itself *and* the question of *what precisely* such actions would have been are inter-connected,[84] it is better for a drawn presumption, together with a court's view of what specific action the breaching party would have taken, to be rebuttable. It would be unfair and contrary to the compensatory purpose of damages to deprive the injured party of an opportunity to present evidence as to what the breaching party's conduct would have been.

Another situation giving rise to the question whether a substitute is reasonable is where an injured party makes a substitute transaction with its affiliate, subsidiary or parent company. One court decision seems to imply that purchasing substitute goods from a subsidiary company does not in itself prevent a transaction from being a reasonable substitute and it is suggested that this is the correct approach.[85] Although making a substitute transaction with an affiliate may in some cases be a factor raising suspicions as to its reasonableness, the decisive question is whether this transaction has been concluded in a reasonable manner.

[83] See Peel (n 2) 1029.

[84] This is so because the presumption *in itself* that the breaching party would have acted in the most beneficial/least burdensome way does not resolve the matter and the answer to the question of what *precisely* such conduct would have been is necessary.

[85] Case No 21 O 703/01(028) District Court Braunschweig (Germany) 30 July 2001 (Metal), available at cisgw3.law.pace.edu/cases/010730g1.html. Another decision appears to imply a contrary position (see CIETAC 30 April 1997 (Molybdenum alloy), available at cisgw3.law.pace.edu/cases/970430c1.html). A similar approach to the one suggested in this book was taken in an arbitration case governed by the UCC. In that case, the innocent buyer made a cover purchase from its parent company holding 100% interest in the buyer. The tribunal stated that it 'would not go so far as to say that no transaction between parent and wholly owned subsidiary can ever constitute a reasonable purchase … [and that] a purchase from an affiliate may in some circumstances be used to establish cover' (ICC No 6955, 1993 in JJ Arnaldez, Y Derains and D Hascher, *Collection of ICC Arbitral Awards, 1991–1995: Recueil des Sentences Arbitrales de la CCI* (The Hague, Kluwer Law International, 1997) 267, 296).

To prevent an injured party from abusing the situation at the expense of the breaching party (for example, if the seller sells the goods to its subsidiary at an unusually low price), the market price for the goods can be a reference point for what is a reasonable price[86] and the question whether reasonable alternatives were available to the injured party needs to be explored.

Finally, it may be that the breaching party offers performing the contract on terms different from those initially agreed. For instance, a breaching buyer may propose to buy the goods at a lower price than that in the contract. It is submitted that in this case there is no reason why the seller's resale to the breaching buyer cannot be regarded as a reasonable substitute[87] provided that there was no other option reasonably available to the seller of reselling to a third party at a higher price than that offered by the buyer. In fact, in one case,[88] rejecting the breaching buyer's offer and reselling at an even lower price than the one offered by the buyer was considered a failure to mitigate. The seller's claim for the difference between the contract price and the resale price was dismissed and the award of damages was based on the difference between the contract price and the price offered by the buyer.[89] However, it is suggested that the reasonableness of a replacement transaction must not be dictated solely by the price difference as there may be other relevant considerations. Suppose a seller who had already delivered an instalment of non-conforming goods, in respect of which the buyer complained to the seller, offered the buyer a new instalment at a price lower than the price in a replacement transaction which the buyer concluded, having rejected the seller's offer. In these circumstances, despite a higher price a replacement transaction may well have been entered into in a 'reasonable manner' if the buyer has justifiably lost confidence in the seller's ability to deliver conforming goods.[90]

[86] See ICC No 6955 (n 85), where the tribunal stated that establishing that a cover purchase from a parent company was reasonable 'would seem to require either a showing that the purchase would have been a reasonable one in the market place or that the price charged was no more than the reasonable costs of the parent in producing the product'.

[87] Provided that accepting the buyer's offer is not interpreted as renegotiating the original contract and waiving the seller's right to damages.

[88] *Internationale Jute Maatschappij BV v Marín Palomares SL* Supreme Court (Spain) 28 January 2000, available at cisgw3.law.pace.edu/cases/000128s4.html. For the discussion of the issue of whether accepting a breaching party's offer can be a reasonable mitigation measure, see ch 6.

[89] It seems that this was also a 'concrete' method of calculating damages, albeit different from the one provided for in art 75 CISG, because it was based on the claimant's *actual* circumstances. This decision raises the question whether art 76 ought to have been used instead or whether art 76 is simply an alternative measure. If the buyer's offer reflected the current price at the time, there would be little difference between the court's method of calculation and an 'abstract' formula in art 76. But if there were a substantial difference between them, the question would be important. If the buyer's offer contained a higher price than the current price, it can be argued that the formula in art 76 would overcompensate the seller because had it acted reasonably by accepting the buyer's offer, its damages would have been lower. The question emphasises a dilemma between whether the instruments should give priority to the 'concrete' approach and mitigation in the light of the claimant's actual circumstances or whether, in cases such this, art 76 based on hypothetical mitigation should be available as an alternative. This question will be returned to below.

[90] This scenario is similar to Case No 07/03098 Court of Appeals Rennes (France) 27 May 2008, available at cisgw3.law.pace.edu/cases/080527f1.html, where the factor, noted in the main text, was

The final precondition under this 'concrete' formula is that a substitute transaction must be made *within a reasonable time* after avoidance.[91] What is a reasonable time depends on the circumstances. Nevertheless, there seems to be a rather uniform trend concerning the maximum period which can be considered reasonable. Several months (usually 2–3 months) have been the longest period that judges and arbitrators have thus far been prepared to regard as reasonable[92] and, on several occasions,[93] it has been stated that the period of six months was outside a reasonable period of time.[94] The relevant factors include the nature and characteristics of the goods, the purpose for which the original contract was made and the availability/absence of markets. Avoidance can only become effective if the notice of avoidance has been given by the party avoiding the contract[95] and there is a concern that because the injured party is able to control the time of avoidance, there is a risk that it may engage in speculation at the breaching party's expense. For example, an innocent buyer who still keeps the goods may decide not to avoid the contract at once to see whether the market price is going to rise.[96] If its speculation proves unsuccessful and the market price persistently falls, the difference between the contract price and the price in a late substitute transaction will be higher than what it would have been had the contract been avoided earlier. It has been correctly suggested that such speculation at the breaching party's expense can be countered by the mitigation rule which can

unfortunately not taken into account by the court. The decision appears to focus on the price difference and the delivery period in the replacement transaction and in the terms of the seller's offer being the same.

[91] See arts 75 CISG, 7.4.5 UPICC and 9:506 PECL.

[92] See *GmbH Lothringer Gunther Grosshandelsgesellschaft für Bauelemente und Holzwerkstoffe v NV Fepco International* Appellate Court Antwerp (Belgium) 24 April 2006, available at cisgw3.law.pace.edu/cases/060424b1.html; *Downs Investments v Perwaja Steel* (n 67); Case No 17 U 146/93 Appellate Court Düsseldorf (Germany) 14 January 1994 (Shoes), available at cisgw3.law.pace.edu/cases/940114g1.html.

[93] Appellate Court Antwerp 24 April 2006 (n 92); *NV Van Heygen Staal v GmbH Stahl und Metalhandel Klockner* Appellate Court Gent (Belgium) 20 October 2004, available at cisgw3.law.pace.edu/cases/041020b1.html.

[94] In other cases, 'reasonable time' ranged from several days to several weeks: *R GmbH v O AG* District Court Zug (Switzerland) 12 December 2002 cisgw3.law.pace.edu/cases/021212s1.html (2 days); CIETAC 18 August 1997 (Vitamin), available at cisgw3.law.pace.edu/cases/970818c1.html (5 days); *Treibacher Industrie, AG v TDY Industries, Inc* US District Court [Alabama] 464 F.3d 1235 (17 days). Where a replacement transaction is concluded on the same day as the day of avoidance, it is made within a reasonable time (see CIETAC 4 February 2002 (n 82)).

[95] There is no agreement, as far as the CISG is concerned, as to whether a notice of avoidance (art 26) becomes effective upon dispatch or upon receipt by the breaching party (for a brief overview of different positions and for the argument that a notice of avoidance becomes effective upon receipt by the breaching party, see P Schlechtriem, 'Effectiveness and Binding Nature of Declarations (Notices, Requests or Other Communications) under Part II and Part III of the CISG' (1995) Cornell Review of the Convention on Contracts for the International Sale of Goods 95 (also available at www.cisg.law.pace.edu/cisg/biblio/schlecht.html). Under the UPICC and PECL, a notice of termination becomes effective upon receipt by the breaching party (see art 1.10 and Comment 4 on Article 7.3.2 UPICC and art 1:303 and Comment on Article 4:112 PECL).

[96] If so, the buyer is likely to prefer not to avoid the contract and to keep the goods.

arguably require that an earlier date at which the injured party ought to have avoided the contract should be taken as the reference date.[97]

Finally, in contrast with § 2-706 UCC[98] and contrary to suggestions by some tribunals,[99] the international instruments do not require an injured party to provide the breaching party with a notice of its intention to make a substitute transaction.[100] As noted, such a notice may in some cases help alleviate the burden of establishing a substitute transaction. More generally, the notice requirement takes account of the breaching party's interests since it has a direct interest in being informed about the other party's course of action. The injured party's decision to make a substitute contract will often affect the breaching party's practical decisions[101] and if a substitute transaction materialises, it is likely to affect the breaching party's legal position.[102] Therefore, because a notice appears to be in both parties' interests, it is advisable that an innocent party inform the other party, either together with a notice of avoidance or separately, of its intention to make a substitute transaction.[103]

2.1.3. *The Difference between the Contract Price and the Price in the Substitute Contract*

The amount of damages to be awarded under the instruments' 'concrete' formula is calculated as the difference between the contract price and the price in a transaction deemed to be a true substitute. The only issue to be borne in mind in performing this straightforward exercise is that it may be necessary to

[97] See P Schlechtriem, 'Damages, Avoidance of the Contract and Performance Interest under the CISG', available at www.cisg-online.ch/cisg/Schlechtriem_Damages_Avoidance.pdf. It can, of course, be argued that there is nothing wrong in an innocent party's speculating at the market. What cannot be allowed, though, is for this speculation to occur at the breaching party's expense. This seems to be the general attitude of English sales law and, to balance these two considerations, an 'abstract' formula is adopted as a general measure with any speculation being, at the same time, *at the risk* and *for the benefit* of the innocent party. The situation where the mitigation principle dictates that the injured party ought to have avoided the contract earlier, the question arises whether the next step is to rely on an 'abstract' formula with its presumed mitigation rationale or whether the 'concrete' assessment (difference between the contract price and the price that would have been paid/received had the contract been avoided at the time required by the mitigation rule) should be used. This question will be addressed below.

[98] § 2-706 UCC requires that where the resale is a 'private sale', the 'seller must give the buyer reasonable notification of his intention to resell'.

[99] CIETAC 31 December 1996 (High carbon tool steel), available at cisgw3.law.pace.edu/cases/961231c2.html (the tribunal seems to have gone as far as to suggest that the injured seller ought to have consulted the buyer regarding the resale price).

[100] The absence of such a requirement is confirmed in several decisions (see ICC No 10274 (n 52); ICC No 6281, 26 August 1989 (Steel bars), available at cisgw3.law.pace.edu/cases/896281i1.html).

[101] Communicating an innocent party's intention to make a substitute transaction may give rise to a breaching party's expectation that a claim for damages will soon be brought, which may, in turn, induce the breaching party to make preparations (such as hiring a lawyer) for defending the claim.

[102] For example, if a substitute transaction meets the preconditions described above, it is likely to predetermine the amount of damages the breaching party is likely to pay.

[103] For cases where such notice was given see District Court Hamburg 26 November 2003 (n 69); ICC No 10274 (n 52).

adjust one of the two prices. The terms of a substitute transaction may not be identical to those in the original contract and adjustments may be necessary to make the two prices comparable. One example is where a substitute transaction is made on different trade terms. In one case,[104] the original contract was made under CFR terms while the buyer's substitute was concluded on FOB terms. Because the FOB price did not take account of freight, the tribunal added the amount of freight to the price of the substitute contract and only then did it subtract the contract price from the adjusted price of the substitute transaction. The same result can be achieved if the amount of freight is subtracted from the CFR price.[105] Another example involves a country which imposed value added tax (VAT) on domestic sales and therefore the sales price would include the amount of VAT while 'export sales' prices would not. In that case,[106] after the buyer had breached its 'export' contract (the price of which did not include VAT), the seller resold the goods to a domestic buyer (at a VAT-inclusive price). To make the two prices comparable the tribunal deducted the amount of the VAT from the resale price.

Yet another more difficult case of adjustment is where one transaction is made on 'cash' terms while the other is on 'credit' terms. Suppose the buyer failed to buy the goods for, say, £54,000 payable in semi-annual instalments over a three-year period and the seller resold them for £35,000 on 'cash' terms. It is not correct simply to calculate the difference between the two prices and award damages of £19,000 because the present value of £54,000 payable over six instalments is likely to be less than £54,000 payable at once.[107] First, the maximum amount the seller will be receiving per year is £18,000 and therefore taking £54,000 as the reference price and assuming that this is the amount the seller will receive at once gives the seller a windfall. Second, with time the value of money tends to decrease. Therefore, the correct award of damages will require discounting and determining the present value of £54,000.

2.1.4. Relationship with Other Losses

The international instruments provide that besides damages for the difference between the contract price and the price in a substitute transaction, an injured party can also recover damages for any further loss.[108] The latter can include a great variety of losses. The seller may claim damages for costs of storage, care and maintenance of the goods incurred between the buyer's breach and the

[104] See CIETAC 15 November 1996 (Oxytetrecycline), available at cisgw3.law.pace.edu/cases/96 1115c1.html.

[105] For another case of the adjustment of price involving art 75 CISG, see CIETAC 8 November 2002 (Canned asparagus), available at cisgw3.law.pace.edu/cases/021108c1.html.

[106] See CIETAC 16 August 1996 (Dioctyl phthalate), available at cisgw3.law.pace.edu/cases/9608 16c1.html.

[107] See White and Summers (n 47) 267 (main text and note 6).

[108] See arts 75 CISG, 7.4.5 UPICC and 9:506 PECL.

seller's resale.[109] The injured seller may also claim interest on any loan it had to take out as a result of not getting the price on the expected date. The buyer, in turn, may incur costs of hiring a broker to find a substitute and/or may have to pay damages to its sub-buyer for a delay in delivery.

Care is required to ensure that further damages do not overcompensate the innocent party. It has been correctly held that where damages are awarded under the 'concrete' formula, the buyer cannot claim additional damages for loss of profit it would have earned on the sub-sale because a substitute transaction provides the buyer with the goods to perform its sub-sale contract and earn that profit.[110] Similarly, the seller cannot claim damages for a profit margin it expected to receive from the original sale together with damages for the difference between the contract price and the price in a substitute resale as this would constitute a double recovery.[111] Nevertheless, the injured party may claim damages caused by the delay between the due date for performance under the original contract and the date of the performance under a substitute transaction. For example, if the buyer buys the goods to use them in its manufacturing business, it may suffer loss of profit due to a halt in the manufacture until substitute goods are bought. In this case, it is appropriate to award both damages under the 'concrete' formula *and* loss of profit caused by the delay.[112]

2.1.5. Burden of Proof

Assuming that burden of proof is a matter governed by the international instruments, the injured party bears the burden of proving that the preconditions under the instruments' 'concrete' formula have been met. Specifically, the injured party needs to prove that it has avoided the contract and made a substitute transaction in a reasonable manner and within a reasonable time. If the breaching party claims that one or more of the preconditions have not been met, it bears

[109] See Case 438/2013 Supreme Court (Spain) 1 July 2013, available at cisgw3.law.pace.edu/cases/130701s4.html (storage costs); Case 2007Gahap97810 Seoul Central District Court (The Republic of Korea) 19 December 2008, available at cisgw3.law.pace.edu/cases/081219k3.html (costs of storage of crude oil).

[110] See CIETAC 10 October 1996 (Petroleum coke), available at cisgw3.law. pace.edu/cases/961010c1.html; Case No 12 HKO 4174/99 District Court München (Germany) 6 April 2000 (Furniture), available at cisgw3.law.pace.edu/cases/000406g1.html. See also the discussion below in relation to damages for non-conforming goods.

[111] See CIETAC 16 August 1996 (n 108).

[112] See Case No 1 Kfh O 32/95 District Court Ellwangen (Germany) 21 August 1995 (Spanish paprika), available at cisgw3.law.pace.edu/cases/950821g2.html. The seller may also suffer loss of profit or loss of a chance to profit if it has lost an opportunity to invest part of the price as result of the buyer's non-payment. In this case, damages under the 'concrete' formula cannot be awarded fully together with damages for loss of profit or loss of a chance to profit because had the contract been performed part of the profit margin from selling the goods would have been a payment for further opportunity to profit. Therefore, if damages for loss of profit/loss of a chance are awarded, the amount of the planned investment needs to be subtracted from damages calculated under the instruments' 'concrete' formula.

the burden of proving that assertion. For example, if the breaching seller claims that a substitute transaction has not been concluded in a reasonable manner, it may have to prove that goods at lower prices were reasonably available to the buyer. A failure to do so is likely to lead to the award of the difference between the contract price and the price in a substitute transaction.[113]

2.2. 'Abstract' Method of Calculation

2.2.1. *General*

The other method of calculation, expressly provided for in the instruments in cases where the contract is avoided, compensates for the difference between the contract price and the 'current' price. Article 76(1) CISG provides that '[i]f the contract is avoided and there is a current price for the goods, the party claiming damages may, if he has not made a purchase or resale under art 75, recover the difference between the price fixed by the contract and the current price at the time of avoidance as well as any further damages recoverable under art 74. If, however, the party claiming damages has avoided the contract after taking over the goods, the current price at the time of such taking over shall be applied instead of the current price at the time of avoidance'. The wording of the corresponding provisions of the UPICC and PECL is similar.[114] However, because the two sets of Principles cover not only sales transactions but also other transactions, they do not refer to the current price of the 'goods' but to the price of the 'performance contracted for'.[115] The provision analogous to the second sentence of art 76(1) CISG is also absent from the UPICC and PECL.

This method is well known to domestic legal systems.[116] It is an instance of the so-called 'abstract' approach to calculation that does not examine the claimant's particular circumstances.[117] This 'depersonalised'[118] formula simply

[113] See ICAC No 155/1994, 16 March 1995, available at cisgw3.law.pace.edu/cases/ 950316r1.html; District Court Hamburg 26 November 2003 (n 69) ('The seller did not sufficiently submit where and at what possible lower price the buyer at the relevant point of time could have bought cheaper goods').

[114] Article 7.4.6 UPICC: 'Where the aggrieved party has terminated the contract and has not made a replacement transaction but there is a current price for the performance contracted for, it may recover the difference between the contract price and the price current at the time the contract is terminated as well as damages for any further harm'. Article 9:507 PECL: 'Where the aggrieved party has terminated the contract and has not made a substitute transaction but there is a current price for the performance contracted for, it may recover the difference between the contract price and the price current at the time the contract is terminated as well as damages for any further loss so far as these are recoverable under this Section'.

[115] See ibid.

[116] Lando and Beale (n 15) 449.

[117] 'the market-price rule is founded on an abstraction. It is concerned not with the factual situation of the claimant buyer but with the position of the notional, reasonable buyer, who is hypothesized as locked into remedial action on a single, statutorily defined date' (E McKendrick, *Goode on Commercial Law*, 5th edn (London, Penguin, 2016) [14.62]).

[118] See EA Farnsworth, 'Legal Remedies for Breach of Contract' (1970) 70 *Columbia L Rev* 1145, 1198.

presumes that it is possible for an injured party to make a substitute transaction at the current price as soon as it has freed itself from the original contract.[119] In this sense, the formula presumes mitigation.[120] At the same time, there may be tension between this 'abstract' formula and the mitigation rule. Being preoccupied with a hypothetical transaction, the former is not concerned, as the mitigation rule would be, with the claimant's *actual* conduct. It is also well known that an 'abstract' formula can lead to over- or under-compensation.[121] For example, suppose the buyer who planned to resell ontract goods to a sub-buyer manages to reach a settlement with the latter and avoid liability for non-delivery caused by the seller's non-delivery. Suppose further that the contract price was £50,000 and the price in a sub-sale was £60,000. If the current price (at the time of avoidance) was £70,000, the 'abstract' formula would award the buyer £20,000 instead of £10,000 (£60,000 – £50,000) representing the buyer's actual loss of profit. Conversely, if the current price fell to £40,000, the 'abstract' formula would lead to no damages since the current price is lower than the contract price. In this case, the buyer is arguably under-compensated because it has still suffered loss of profit of £10,000. Similar considerations may arise where the buyer, *after* the expiration of a reasonable time (as required by the 'concrete' formula), purchases goods at a price lower than the current price at the time of avoidance. In this case, damages under the 'abstract' formula will most likely over-compensate the buyer. How can such results be justified in the light of the compensatory purpose of damages?

First, in English sales law where the 'abstract' method of calculation is the main presumptive rule of calculating damages, it is often said that the arrangements the injured party has made with third parties (sub-sale or cover purchase) is a circumstance 'peculiar to the injured party' with which the breaching party 'has nothing to do' and that 'it does not lie in the breaching party's mouth' to say that the injured party is over-compensated.[122] Second, it can be argued[123] that the law should not worry about over-compensating the injured party because if an 'abstract' formula is not used, it is the breaching party who keeps the advantage of market movements.[124] From this perspective, an 'abstract' formula can be viewed as a kind of gain-based measure aimed at preventing a breaching party's unjust enrichment.[125] Third, it has been argued that over-compensation can be

[119] See, eg, Case No 19 U 97/91 Appellate Court Hamm (Germany) 22 September 1992 (Frozen bacon), available at cisgw3.law.pace.edu/cases/920922g1.html ('This provision relies upon the idea that obligor is entitled to conduct [a] cover transaction at the market price').

[120] *Cf* McKendrick (n 117) [14.61]–[14.62].

[121] See, eg, Bridge (n 44) [12.83]; White and Summers (n 47) 212–13.

[122] See, eg, *Rodocanachi, Sons & Co v Milburn Brothers* (1886) 18 QBD 67; *John Neil Mouat v Betts Motors Ltd* [1959] AC 71.

[123] D Simon and GA Novack, 'Limiting the Buyer's Market Damages to Lost Profits: A Challenge to the Enforceability of Market Contracts' (1978–1979) 92 *Harv L Rev* 1395, 1396, 1403.

[124] If we take the very first example in the previous paragraph of the main text, it can be argued that if the innocent buyer is not overcompensated by a £20,000 award, the breaching seller will effectively benefit as a result of its own breach.

[125] Simon and Novack (n 123), 1403; Yovel (n 49).

justified because what the injured party loses is an *opportunity* to make a profit from market movements and it is an opportunity which a breaching party keeps to itself by breaching the contract.[126] It has been further suggested that this opportunity 'has the value assigned by the market, which weighs the chance of winning or losing and arrives at a quantification of those chances in the form of the market price'[127] and, for this reason, 'market damages represent the true value of the market opportunity denied to the plaintiff'.[128] Fourth, in relation to cases where a party delays finding a substitute in order to observe market movements, it can be contended that there is nothing wrong in speculating. The 'abstract' approach maintains symmetry by giving the party the fruits of its speculation (thereby encouraging speculation) and, at the same time, forcing it to bear the risk of unsuccessful speculation. This way, speculation does not occur at the breaching party's expense. Fifth, if the mitigation rule were to set a limit on the recovery of damages, it would encourage 'artificial transactions' in the sense that an injured seller, for example, wishing to speculate on a rising market would sell the goods to reduce its loss, as required by the mitigation rule, and then would immediately repurchase them.[129] The law, it has been argued, should not encourage such artificial transactions.[130] The 'abstract' approach to calculating damages is also said to be the most practical approach because it does not pretend to 'search for the elusive goal of perfect compensation' and, in contrast with the 'concrete' assessment, does not involve the complexity and high costs associated with the inquiry into the claimant's particular circumstances.[131] It has been further suggested that an 'abstract' formula can be viewed as a kind of statutory liquidated damages clause which may encourage performance and deter breaches.[132] Finally, probably the most important justification is that an 'abstract' formula has the advantage of simplicity and certainty since, by referring to a hypothetical transaction, it avoids the complexity, uncertainty and time required to examine the claimant's circumstances. With this in mind, it can be contended that the 'abstract' assessment is much better suited than its 'concrete' counterpart to those sectors of trade where certainty regarding parties' legal positions and speed are of utmost importance.[133] It is the kind of

[126] Ibid 1419; RE Scott, 'The Case for Market Damages: Revisiting the Lost Profits Puzzle' (1990) 57 *University Chicago L Rev* 1155, 1169.

[127] Simon and Novack (n 123) 1419.

[128] Ibid, 1420.

[129] See S Waddams, 'The Date for the Assessment of Damages' (1981) 97 *LQR* 445, 447. To some extent, this point can be countered by arguing that the upshot of the mitigation rule is that the recovery is, in any event, limited to the amount of *avoidable loss* and that it is not necessary for an injured party to *actually* mitigate its loss since whether the seller makes an artificial sale and then repurchases the goods is of no significance (apart from additional mitigation costs) because the amount of recovery is likely to be the same in both cases.

[130] Ibid, 447.

[131] Waddams (n 82) 29–30.

[132] EA Peters, 'Remedies for Breach of Contract Relating to the Sale of Goods Under the Uniform Commercial Code: A Roadmap for Article Two' (1963–1964) 73 *Yale L J* 199, 259.

[133] '[A] punctilious insistence upon standards and time is much more justifiable in the case of commodities traders active on a broad front who engage in the complex managerial process of

'rough justice'[134] rather than the goal of perfect compensation that some traders would arguably prefer. It may also be claimed that avoiding the complexity and length of time, associated with examining the claimant's circumstances, may be more appropriate for the efficient administration of justice.[135]

2.2.2. Relationship between 'Concrete' and 'Abstract' Measures

For some legal systems, the starting point is the 'abstract' measure[136] while some other systems seem to allow an injured party to select between the 'concrete' and 'abstract' measures.[137] The international instruments show their preference for the 'concrete' measure by stipulating that the difference between the contract price and the current price can be claimed where no substitute transaction has been made.[138] In other words, the 'concrete' measure has precedence over the 'abstract' measure and if the injured party has made a replacement transaction which meets the requirements of the instruments' 'concrete' formula, damages must be calculated 'concretely'.[139] Despite the drafters' intention to introduce certainty by means of this hierarchical structure,[140] the answer to the question of how relentless the instruments are in their commitment to the 'concrete' measure remains uncertain. Besides the important consideration of certainty, this question is also significant because the answer to it will demonstrate whether: the argument that, in comparison with some domestic systems the instruments (the CISG in particular) are less well suited to certain trade sectors, is justifiable; and that the instruments can reap the benefits associated with the 'abstract'

stitching together their various purchase and resale commitments' (MG Bridge, 'The Evolution of Modern Sales Law' [1991] LMCLQ 52, 59); 'Certainty and speed is a virtue of futures trading, uncertainty a possible recipe for disaster. Time is money in the market area …' (S Fisher and M Hains, 'Futures Market Law and Practice and the Vienna Sales Convention' [1993] LMCLQ 531, 555). See also MG Bridge, 'Uniformity and Diversity in the Law of International Sale' (2003) 15 *Pace Int'l L Rev* 55, 67; and, most recently, A Tettenborn, 'Abstract Damages in International Sale Contracts – When should They be Available?' in D Saidov (ed), *Research Handbook on International and Comparative Sale of Goods Law* (Cheltenham, Edward Elgar, 2019).

[134] CT McCormick, *Handbook on the Law of Damages* (St Paul, Minn, West Publishing Co, 1935) 184–5.

[135] See MG Bridge, 'The Market Rule of Damages Assessment' in D Saidov and R Cunnington, *Contract Damages: Domestic and International Perspectives* (Oxford, Hart Publishing, 2008) 446 ('A perfect sense of justice in the application of rules of damages assessment is at odds with the efficient administration of justice').

[136] See ss 50(3) and 51(3) of the English Sale of Goods Act.

[137] See §§ 2-706, 2-708, 2-712 and 2-713 UCC.

[138] See arts 76 CISG, 7.4.6 UPICC and 9:507 PECL.

[139] See CISG-AC No 8 (n 19) Comment 4.1.2; Ziegel (n 45) 9–39. See also B Nicholas, 'Vienna Convention on International Sales Law' (1989) 105 *LQR* 201, 230 (expressing regret regarding the precedence of art 75 over art 76 CISG where the injured seller resells at a price higher than the current price and points out that the result of the 'concrete' formula in art 75 debarring the use of art 76 is harsh because the breaching buyer is allowed to keep the benefit of a good bargain made by the seller. This position echoes the approach of English sales law which generally favours the 'abstract' measure and highlights the existing tension stemming from the choice and relationship between the 'concrete' and 'abstract' measures).

[140] See Honnold (n 21) 452.

assessment. To answer this question, the relationship between the instruments' 'concrete' and 'abstract' formulae needs to be explored.

It is usually recommended that the abstract formula be used where: the innocent party fails to conclude a substitute transaction; the requirements of the 'concrete' formula are not met; or it is impossible to determine which transaction is a replacement for the breached contract.[141] The latter situation has been addressed above and it is suggested that where it is impossible to establish an actual replacement transaction, it is justifiable to resort to the instruments' 'abstract' formula. The first two situations, however, raise a difficult issue of the relationship between the instruments' 'abstract' formula and the mitigation rule. The innocent party's failure to make a replacement transaction or conclude a transaction in a reasonable manner or within a reasonable time will often constitute a failure to mitigate. Should the abstract formula *alone* be applied with the mitigation rule disregarded or should the amount of avoidable loss set the ceiling for recovery? It can be argued that the 'abstract' formula already presumes mitigation because it is based on a *hypothetical* substitute transaction. But at the same time damages produced by the 'abstract' formula can conflict with the mitigation rule because by looking at a hypothetical transaction, it is not concerned with whether the injured party has *actually* taken steps to mitigate its loss. Several CISG cases show that where the requirements of art 75 are not met, judges and arbitrators often resort to art 76 with no or little regard to the mitigation rule.[142] In many cases, this approach may be justifiable because the 'abstract' measure is based on a hypothetical substitute with reference to the 'current/market' price, which reflects a typical mitigation measure.[143]

[141] See, eg, JS Sutton, 'Measuring Damages under the United Nations Convention on the International Sale of Goods' (1989) 50 *Ohio State LJ* 737 (also at www.cisg.law.pace.edu/cisg/biblio/sutton.html).

[142] See Supreme Court (Spain) 1 July 2013 (n 109), where in respect of the part of the goods, which the buyer failed to accept and pay for, the court awarded the seller damages under art 76 without examining whether the seller could have mitigated that loss by, for example, reselling the goods (as the seller did in respect of the other part of the goods); CIETAC 29 September 1997 (Aluminium oxide), available at cisgw3.law.pace.edu/cases/970929c1.html, where although the tribunal found that the seller had failed to mitigate by purchasing the goods from its supplier despite there having been no indications that the buyer would be able to perform the contract, the tribunal did not calculate damages on the basis of how the seller ought to have mitigated (which, presumably, would have been refraining from purchasing the goods from its supplier with the result that damages would be for the loss of the profit margin). Instead, the tribunal relied on the 'abstract' formula in art 76; CIETAC 1 March 1999 (Canned mandarin oranges), available at cisgw3.law.pace.edu/cases/990301c1.html (discussed below – see note 148 and accompanying paragraph in the main text); Case Nos 1 U 143/95 and 410 O 21/95 Appellate Court Hamburg (Germany) 4 July 1997 (Tomato concentrate), available at cisgw3.law.pace. edu/cases/970704g1.html ('As the buyer does not claim to have bought goods in replacement and there is a current price for the goods at issue, the buyer is entitled to recover the difference between the price fixed by the contract and the (higher) current price at the time of avoidance according to Art. 76(1) CISG') and Case No A3 1997 61 District Court Zug 21 (Switzerland) October 1999 (PVC and other synthetic materials), available at cisgw3.law.pace.edu/cases/991021s1.html, which seem to demonstrate how easy the courts find it to dispense with the mitigation inquiry and resort to art 76 CISG; see also CIETAC 30 July 1996 (Molybdenum iron), available at cisgw3.law.pace.edu/cases/960730c1.html and CIETAC 30 July 1996 (n 24).

[143] See Arbitration No 48, 2005 (n 24); similarly, CISG-AC No 8 (n 19) Comment 2.4.3.

However, the mitigation rule may lead to results different from those flowing from the 'abstract' formula.

Take the seller who rejected the breaching buyer's offer to purchase the goods at a price higher than contracted for and resold them at a price lower than that offered by the buyer. The mitigation rule (a part of the 'concrete' approach to calculating damages) may disallow the recovery exceeding the difference between the contract price and the price offered by the buyer. From the perspective of the mitigation rule, if the price offered by the buyer is higher than the current price, the 'abstract' formula (the difference between the contract price and the current price) over-compensates the seller because had it acted reasonably by accepting the buyer's offer, its damages would have been lower.[144] Another example is where the seller, after the buyer's failure to accept the goods, delays avoiding the contract to see whether the market price is going to rise. If this speculation proves unsuccessful because the market falls and the seller eventually avoids the contract and resells the goods, the mitigation rule may require damages to be assessed as if the contract were avoided earlier when the price was higher. The instruments' 'abstract' formula would give the seller the difference between the contract price and the current price at the time of avoidance and this difference is higher than the amount produced by the mitigation rule.[145]

The instruments' position is unclear as to whether their 'abstract' formula alone should be applied with the mitigate rule disregarded or whether the amount of avoidable loss should set the ceiling for recovery. On the one hand, they seem to allow resort to the 'abstract' measure whenever the replacement transaction is not made or where an alleged substitute is not made in a reasonable manner or within a reasonable time.[146] The availability of the 'abstract' formula in such cases, seemingly *as of right*, suggests that the question whether the party has actually mitigated its loss can be ignored, especially because their 'abstract' formula already presumes hypothetical mitigation. On the other hand, the mitigation rule is presented by the instruments as a rule of *general application* which suggests that damages cannot exceed the amount of avoidable loss. According to this approach, the amount of reasonably avoidable loss sets the ceiling for recovery in *all* cases including those where the instruments' 'abstract' formula is used. How should this tension be resolved? It is submitted that it cannot be resolved without restricting the scope or diminishing the role of either the instruments' 'abstract' formula or the mitigation rule. There are strong arguments supporting both approaches and it is not easy to resolve this difficulty.

[144] For the discussion of a CISG case based on similar facts, see note 148 below and an accompanying paragraph in the main text.

[145] This situation may rarely arise, however, because avoidance of the contract should generally be effective only if exercised within a reasonable period of time and this means that the exercise of the right to avoid is aligned with the mitigation rule. See further n 169 and the accompanying main text.

[146] This position is taken in CISG-AC No 8 (n 19) in its Rule 2.4 ('In the event that the aggrieved party's substitute transaction was unreasonable, damages may be calculated according to Article 76 or Article 74.').

To support the use of the instruments' 'abstract' formula, it can be said that if the mitigation rule sets the ceiling for recovery in *all* cases, this will, in cases similar to the above examples, deprive the instruments' 'abstract' formula of its purpose. Allowing the mitigation rule to interfere with a rule already based on 'hypothetical mitigation' would be anomalous. Since the instruments provide for the instruments' 'abstract' formula, it seems reasonable to infer that the instruments were intended to incorporate its underlying policies.[147] One such policy is to promote simplicity and certainty in calculating damages by dispensing with the need to examine the claimant's particular circumstances and hence to apply the mitigation rule. In short, the abstract formula does not presuppose the application of the mitigation rule. This approach is taken in one CISG case[148] where the breaching buyer offered to purchase the goods (the contract price of which was \$12.20 per box) at the price of \$11.40 per box of the goods. The seller rejected the offer and resold the goods for \$7.79 per box. The tribunal determined that a reasonable current/market price was \$10.40 per box and awarded the difference between the contract price (\$12.20) and the current/market price (\$12.20–10.40 = \$1.80). This decision demonstrates the tribunal's preference for the abstract measure that disregards the mitigation rule which, if applied, would have most likely dictated accepting the buyer's offer to purchase at \$11.40 per box because that would have resulted in the lowest amount of damages (\$12.20–11.40 = \$0.80).

To support the priority of the mitigation rule, it can be argued that the mitigation rule, being a rule of general application, cannot be ignored and consequently damages must not exceed the amount of avoidable loss.[149] The instruments generally favour the calculation of damages in accordance with the claimant's *actual* situation by giving precedence to a 'concrete' formula and by pursuing the purpose of putting the party in the position in which it would have been had the contract been properly performed. The mitigation rule should also override the 'abstract' measure[150] because, as explained, it is in harmony with the 'concrete' measure. For these reasons, it is suggested that the latter position is to be preferred in cases similar to the examples above.[151] This means that the

[147] See above for other policies underlying the 'abstract' approach to calculating damages.

[148] CIETAC 1 March 1999 (n 142).

[149] With respect to some of the examples above, it can also be argued that ignoring the mitigation rule would allow an innocent party to engage in speculation and arguably be over-compensated.

[150] This approach appears to be taken in Supreme Court (Switzerland) 17 December 2009 (n 72), arising from the seller's failure to deliver the goods, where the buyer was denied damages for its lost profit (the difference between the contract price and the retail price at which the buyer would have resold the goods). Without resorting to art 76 CISG, the court held that the damages of the injured buyer, who failed to mitigate its loss by entering into a replacement transaction, were limited by the difference between the contract price and the price that the seller in that replacement transaction would have charged the buyer. See also Case No 7 International Commercial Arbitration Court (ICAC), the Ukrainian Chamber of Commerce, 7 February 2007, available at arb.ucci.org.ua/icac/cases/2006-2010/caseNo7.pdf (in Russian).

[151] A potentially difficult relationship between the instruments' 'abstract' formula and the mitigation rule results, it is suggested, from the drafters' failure to clarify this relationship. By stipulating

scope of the 'abstract' measure needs to be restricted where it is evident that, in the light of the mitigation rule, its application would result in a windfall.[152]

Nevertheless, it is hoped that such cases will be rare and some CISG cases demonstrate that the 'abstract' formula in art 76 often complements the mitigation rule. In several cases, where the seller's resale did not meet the requirements of art 75, it was held that the seller ought to have mitigated its loss by reselling at the current market price and consequently damages were calculated in accordance with art 76.[153] In one case, the tribunal held that the injured buyer ought to have mitigated its loss by procuring substitute goods at the market price and calculated damages according to the Convention's 'abstract' formula.[154] In a similar vein, art 76 can, as noted,[155] be used to complement the 'concrete' formula in art 75, which is a specific instance of the mitigation rule.[156] For example, where the price in a replacement transaction is in line with the current/market price, the courts and tribunals are likely to take a position that a replacement transaction was made in a 'reasonable manner'.[157]

This book's suggestion that the mitigation rule should set the ceiling for recovery where the 'abstract' measure produces a windfall may not be in line with a number of the CISG cases that are favourable to the use of the 'abstract' measure. Some cases reveal that some courts and tribunals are not particularly concerned about the relationship between the 'abstract' measure and the mitigation rule and resort to the former paying little or no attention to the latter.[158] This attitude probably stems from the relative simplicity and convenience of using the 'abstract' approach in practice. The remaining cases relating to situations where the contract was avoided and touching upon the relationship between arts 75 and 76 also reveal an attitude favouring the 'abstract' measure. In one case,[159] the 'concrete' and 'abstract' formulae in arts 75 and 76 respectively were treated as alternatives. The court stated that '[t]he [s]eller may choose between reselling

the possibility of relying on the 'abstract' formula, the drafters ought to have foreseen the potential conflict with the duty to mitigate.

[152] A similar approach seems to be taken in the context of art 76, in the case of anticipatory breach, in P Schlechtriem, 'Calculation of Damages in the Event of Anticipatory Brach under the CISG', available at www.cisg-online.ch/cisg/FS%20Hellner.pdf 1, 11, 13–14. As a matter of principle, CISG-AC No 8 (n 19) also rightly takes the position that the application of art 76 (or of art 75) CISG must not result in a windfall (see Rule 1.3 and Comment 1.3.1).

[153] Arbitration, June 1999 (China) (Peanut kernel), available at cisgw3.law.pace.edu/cases/990600c1.html ('[The] [s]eller should take reasonable measures to resell the goods at the current market price to mitigate its loss. [The] [s]eller's reasonable and direct loss of profits should be the difference between the contract price and the current market price.'); Appellate Court Hamm 22 September 1992 (n 119).

[154] Arbitration No 48, 2005 (n 24).

[155] See the main text accompanying nn 66 and 67.

[156] See the main text accompanying n 19.

[157] See Arbitration Court Rostov Region (n 65), where this was so held, with all other terms in the replacement transaction having been similar to those of the contract with the breaching seller.

[158] See note 142.

[159] Case No 4 R 219/01k Appellate Court Graz (Austria) 24 January 2002 (Excavator), available at cisgw3.law.pace.edu/cases/020124a3.html.

the goods and recovering the difference between the contract price and the price in the substitute transaction following Art. 75, or, without reselling the goods, [Seller] may recover the difference between the contract price and the current price at the time of the avoidance, Art. 76(1)'.[160] Although this interpretation clearly contravenes the structure of these CISG provisions (which only allows resorting to art 76 if art 75 cannot be applied), it reflects a desire to confer a higher standing on the 'abstract' formula in art 76 than it actually has. In some other more extreme cases, arbitrators appear to have treated the 'abstract' measure in art 76 as a starting point.[161] In one case,[162] where the seller partly failed to deliver the goods (and partly delivered non-conforming goods) bought for resale, the tribunal awarded the buyer the difference between the contract price and 'the average market price' without even considering whether the buyer had attempted to find a replacement in accordance with arts 75 and 77.[163] In another case,[164] the tribunal carefully considered whether art 76 could be applied and only after concluding that it could not did it resort to art 75.[165] It is difficult to justify this approach considering the Convention's express requirement to apply its 'concrete' formula first.

2.2.3. *The Instruments' 'Abstract' Formula: Preconditions and Application*

The first condition for using their 'abstract' formula is that the instruments' 'concrete' formula is inapplicable. The second precondition is that the contract has been avoided.[166] This provision potentially enables the injured party to engage in a speculative delay in avoiding the contract at the breaching party's expense.[167] This danger can be countered by the rules on the avoidance of the contract. Under the UPICC and PECL, the injured party loses the right to avoid the contract unless it does so within a reasonable time.[168] So far as the CISG is

[160] Ibid. The same approach is taken in: *Doolim Corp v R Doll, LLC* (n 64) [42]; The Fifteenth Arbitration Appellate Court Rostov-on-Don 3 July 2018 (n 58).

[161] Effectively taking an approach similar to that of English sales law.

[162] ICAC No 175/2003, 28 May 2004, available at www.cisg.law.pace.edu/cases/040528r1.html.

[163] The tribunal did not ignore the mitigation rule completely by noting that insuring the goods allowed the buyer to reduce the loss. The duty to mitigate, however, was not considered to determine whether the buyer ought to have found a replacement to fulfil its sub-sale.

[164] ICC No 8740, October 1996 (Russian coal), available at cisgw3.law.pace.edu/cases/968740i1.html (see the buyer's third counterclaim).

[165] For another case with a similar approach, see Case No 18-40 "K" Arbitration Court of Moscow City (Russia) 3 April 1995 (Russian coal), available at cisgw3.law.pace.edu/cases/950403r1.html.

[166] The original proposal in the 1978 Draft Convention referred to the current price 'at the time he first had the right to declare the contract avoided' (see art 72(1) of the 1978 Draft Convention, available at www.cisg.law.pace.edu/cisg/1978draft.html). However, some of the delegates took the view that since it might be difficult to establish the precise moment when the contract could first be declared avoided, the provision was too elastic and uncertain and potentially created room for a great deal of litigation. The provision referring to the time of avoidance was therefore considered to be more certain (see deliberations at the 10th Plenary Meeting of the 1980 Vienna Diplomatic Conference, available at www.cisg.law.pace.edu/cisg/plenarycommittee/summary10.html).

[167] See examples above.

[168] See arts 7.3.2 UPICC (and Comment 3 thereon) and 9:303 PECL.

concerned, the same limitation is expressly imposed in specified cases only[169] and it is not clear whether it is applicable in other cases.[170] There is a possibility therefore that in cases other than those specified in the CISG, the 'reasonable time' limitation may not be applicable and, to that extent, the rules of avoidance under the CISG may not be able to counter the injured party's speculation.[171] In any event, as argued above, the problem of speculation can be tackled by the mitigation rule. In addition, a specific mechanism of countering the problem of speculative delay in avoiding the contract can be found in the CISG,[172] which provides that if the party has avoided the contract after 'taking over the goods, the current price at the time of such taking over shall be applied instead of the current price at the time of avoidance'.[173] Consequently, where the party has taken over the goods, it will not be able to engage in speculation by delaying the time of avoidance.

The provision on 'taking over of the goods' has been criticised. First, the injured party may find itself in the position where it is not yet aware of the breach at the time where the goods were taken over.[174] This may be the case, for example, where there is a hidden defect in the goods which could not reasonably have been discovered at that time.[175] Assessing damages with reference to the current price at the time of taking over in such cases has been said to cause prejudice to the buyer[176] and it is further submitted that such an assessment is not entirely in line with the rationale underlying the Convention's 'abstract' formula. The formula arguably implies that a party is in the position to make a hypothetical replacement transaction and the party would not see the need for a replacement unless it is aware of the breach. For this reason, it would appear that awareness of the breach is a necessary assumption underlying this 'abstract' formula.[177]

[169] See arts 49(2) and 64(2)(b) CISG.

[170] For the view that this limitation should apply to all cases and not just those specified in the CISG, see, eg, J Yovel, 'Buyer's Right to Avoid the Contract: Comparison between Provisions of the CISG (Article 49) and the Counterpart Provisions of the PECL (Articles 9:301, 9:303 and 8:106)', available at www.cisg.law.pace.edu/cisg/text/peclcomp49.html#jyvii.

[171] See Treitel (n 1) 119 (assuming that the reasonable time limitation under the CISG is applicable to all cases).

[172] Knapp (n 18) 555; Comment (b) on Article 76 in J Ziegel and C Samson, *Report to the Uniform Law Conference of Canada on Convention on Contracts for the International Sale of Goods* (1981), available at www.cisg.law.pace.edu/cisg/wais/db/articles/english2.html.

[173] Article 76(1) CISG.

[174] See Treitel (n 1) 119; Schlechtriem (n 19) 97.

[175] See Treitel (n 1) 119.

[176] See ibid.

[177] It is recognised that the injured party's awareness of the breach is an assumption underlying an 'abstract' formula in English sales law (see ibid, 117). It is interesting to pose the question whether the approach of English law, which generally determines the market price as at the date of the breach, is more in line with the rationale underlying an 'abstract' formula than the approach of the international instruments because the date of breach or the period shortly thereafter are considered to be the time when the injured party would find a replacement. The 'breach date' rule is in absolute harmony with the policy of encouraging speculation as all benefits and losses after that date are generally ignored in assessing damages. The 'time of avoidance' rule also encourages speculation but, in the absence of the rules on avoidance and mitigation, speculation would occur at the

Second, this provision is partial in operation as it is generally applicable only to the buyer.[178] This means that the CISG contains an asymmetry by placing greater emphasis on, and providing for an additional means of countering the danger of speculation, in the case of an injured buyer without any justification.

These concerns can be alleviated by the following. The provision on 'taking over of the goods' is not relevant in many cases, such as those where goods are not delivered.[179] Similarly, the situation where the injured party may not be aware of the breach at the time of taking over will arise only in some, but not all, cases and the first concern applies to such cases only. It is submitted, however, that in such cases the Convention's 'abstract' formula should be inapplicable. The formula assumes that the injured party is able (in this case, at the time of taking over) to find a hypothetical replacement and, as noted, the party will not see the need to do so unless it is aware of the breach. Since the concern stems from the party's unawareness of the breach, the assumption underlying the formula is not present.

The next precondition under the instruments' 'abstract' formula is that there must be a 'current price' for the goods. The CISG provides that 'the current price is the price prevailing at the place where delivery of the goods should have been made or, if there is no current price at that place, the price at such other place as serves as a reasonable substitute, making due allowance for differences in the cost of transporting the goods'.[180] It can also be defined as 'the price generally charged for such goods sold under comparable circumstances in the trade concerned'.[181] A similar definition is contained in the UPICC that provide that the 'current price' 'is the price generally charged for goods delivered or services rendered in comparable circumstances at the place where the contract should have been performed or, if there is no current price at that place, the current price at such other place that appears reasonable to take as a reference'.[182] Despite these guidelines, the CISG cases demonstrate that the greatest difficulty with applying this 'abstract' formula stems precisely from the need to determine the 'current price'.

In capitalist economic systems, the current price is usually understood to mean the 'market price',[183] that is, the price at which the goods can be sold or bought at

expense of the breaching party. In this sense, the approach of English sales law arguably leads to more symmetrical and fair results. The time of taking over of the goods is clearly intended to counter speculation and is therefore based on a different policy than that underlying the 'abstract' measure with reference to the 'breach date' rule. The question would have been important had the 'abstract' formula constituted a *prima facie* measure of damages under the international instruments as, in that case, it would have played a primary role in the assessment of damages.

[178] See Treitel (n 1) 119. See also Honnold (n 21) 451 ('sellers seldom avoid the contract *after* taking over the goods').

[179] See Ziegel and Samson (n 172).

[180] Article 76(2) CISG.

[181] CISG-AC No 8 (n 19) Rule 4.3.

[182] Article 7.4.6(2) UPICC. PECL do not contain a similar provision.

[183] See Nicholas (n 139) note 30; DWM Waters, 'The Concept of Market in the Sale of Goods' (1958) 36 *The Canadian Bar Rev* 360, 365 ('there appears to have been no contention in the courts against at least regarding the words 'market or current' as identical in meaning).

the relevant market. However, the current price can in principle be a price other than the market price[184] and for this reason the two cannot be treated as always having an identical meaning. Nevertheless, because in most cases the current price will be derived from the market price, it is necessary to explore the notion of a market, so that a market price can be ascertained.[185] The term 'market' does not have a precise meaning.[186] In English sales law, the term 'available market' means 'that the situation in the particular trade in the particular area was such that the particular goods could freely be sold'[187] and the market price is to be fixed by the laws of supply and demand.[188] In other words, the 'market' is not 'confined to sales and purchases at a particular place set aside for the bringing together of seller[s] and buyers but extends to any situation in which goods are dealt in as fungibles at prices fluctuating according to supply and demand'.[189] There is no reason why these guidelines cannot be used to determine whether a market exists for the purposes of the instruments' 'abstract' formula. In fact, a somewhat similar approach is taken in a CISG case[190] where it was stated that a market should provide an objective basis for determining the value of goods and that this objective basis was 'formulated by the existence of a variety of suppliers and a variety of consumers seeking similar goods and purchasing them for a current value determined on the basis of supply and demand'. According to another CISG case, a market implies that there are 'regular business transactions for goods of the same type'.[191] It is also widely accepted that in modern economic conditions markets do not necessarily imply a physical location and should, as noted, be understood as a 'situation in a particular trade' or 'a particular level of trade'.[192]

It is also relevant to note that in English sales law a market is generally said to exist where it can absorb all goods by 'would-be sellers' and has the capacity to supply (meet the demand of) all 'would-be buyers'.[193] This position is not taken to its extreme. In one case[194] involving the sale of 15,000 tons of lard, it was held

[184] This seems to be the position of Comment 2 on Article 7.4.6 UPICC ('[The current price] will often, but not necessarily, be the price on an organised market. Evidence of the current price may be obtained from professional organisations, chambers of commerce, etc.').

[185] See, however, Waters (n 183) 385–6 (arguing, in the context of the common law, against gearing the 'market price' to the meaning of 'market' on that basis that 'with the widening of the economic horizon and trade levels, evidence of 'market prices' is increasingly drawn from more remote sources, for example, foreign exchanges and a variety of publications' and that '[s]ometimes prices will be quoted when in fact buyers or sellers are nowhere to be found'. However, what this commentator really advocates is the extension of the notion of the 'market price' and this seems to be the approach taken by the international instruments which do not confine their 'abstract' formula to the 'market price' and instead refer to the presumably broader notion of the 'current price').

[186] McKendrick (n 117) [14.52].

[187] *Thompson (WL) v Robinson (Gunmakers)* [1955] Ch 177, 187.

[188] *Charter v Sullivan* [1957] 2 QB 117, 128.

[189] McKendrick (n 117).

[190] ICC No 8740, October 1996 (n 164).

[191] Appellate Court München 15 September 2004 (n 43).

[192] See *Heskell v Continental Express Ltd* [1950] 1 All ER 1033, 1056.

[193] See *Thompson (WL) v Robinson (Gunmakers)* (n 187); M Bridge (ed), *Benjamin's Sale of Goods*, 10th edn (London, Thomson–Sweet & Maxwell, 2019) [17-005].

[194] *Garnac Grain Co Inc v HMF Faure & Fairclough Ltd* [1968] AC 1130, 1138.

that where it was possible for the injured party to buy smaller quantities (up to 2,000 tons at time) over a period of time, a market could be said to exist. It is submitted that a similar approach to the notion of a 'market' should be taken under the instruments. Since the rationale of their 'abstract' formula is based on the injured party's being in the position to make a hypothetical substitute transaction, it seems to follow that a market should generally be able to absorb all of the seller's goods or meet the entire demand of the injured buyer.[195] At the same time, this approach does recognise that a market may exist where not all goods can be available at once (the reverse being that not all goods can be absorbed at once) so long as it is reasonable for the injured party to satisfy its interest by going into that market in the light of its business situation.

In short, the meaning of a market can be defined with reference to the following characteristics. First, although it is impossible to state the number of potential buyers and sellers, there must be a 'sufficiency'[196] of buyers and sellers to constitute a market. Second, the market should provide a means of putting potential buyers and sellers in touch with each other.[197] Third, there must be a certain degree of activity[198] or regularity of transactions. Fourth, a market must be one for similar or comparable goods.[199] Fifth, markets do not necessarily imply a physical location. Finally, a market generally exists where all goods can be absorbed or the entire demand can be met by it. But where the injured party's needs cannot be met at once, there may still be a market if it provides an opportunity for this party to satisfy its needs over a period of time and it is reasonable for it to do so.

It is likely that the absence of one (and, certainly, of more than one) of the aforementioned characteristics points to there being no market for the goods. For example, in one CISG case[200] involving the contract for the supply of coal, it was found that coal had a variety of specifications and its value was dependent on the particular needs of each customer. For these reasons, there was no objective basis for establishing the market price. It is suggested that the tribunal's inability to find a market for coal can be primarily explained by the absence of the third characteristic feature, that is, the lack of the necessary degree of activity or regularity of transactions.[201] The dependence of the value of coal on

[195] This point is at the core why the 'abstract' formula is inapplicable to the lost volume situation. Where the seller's supply exceeds the demand for the goods, there is no market for the goods because it is not able to absorb the seller's goods. To reverse this point, had there been a market for the seller's goods, a lost volume situation would not have arisen.

[196] See Bridge (n 44) [12.72].

[197] See the main text accompanying note 189; Bridge (n 44) [12.72].

[198] See Bridge (n 44) [12.72].

[199] Some judges and arbitrators applying the CISG seem to take a flexible approach by relying upon similar goods where identical goods cannot be found (see the quote from the ICC No 8740, October 1996 (n 164); see also cases discussed below). Article 7.4.6(2) UPICC also reflects a degree of flexibility in this respect by defining the current price as 'the price generally charged for goods delivered or services rendered in *comparable* circumstances' (emphasis added).

[200] ICC No 8740, October 1996 (n 164).

[201] The decision implies that a market must consist of 'many purchasers and sellers actively engaged in *regular* trading' (ibid (emphasis added)).

a variety of specifications and the particular needs of a customer rendered coal a 'specialised' type of goods and some goods 'can be specialized to the point of insufficient activity to evidence a market'.[202] It is suggested that it is this latter statement that best explains the decision in that case.

Despite the said general characteristics of a market, difficulties may arise regarding the appropriateness of using a particular market in specific circumstances. One such situation is where the seller breaches a forward contract and no forward market exists for the goods. Can the buyer rely on a spot market to determine the current price?[203] It is suggested that this should be possible as long as such a hypothetical transaction can be deemed a reasonable substitute given the buyer's business situation and what the buyer intended to do with the goods. The problem of the comparability of prices should not be acute because prices in these markets ('physical' markets), albeit not necessarily identical, would generally reflect a similar price movement.[204] Another situation is where the only market available is the so-called 'black market'[205] and the question is whether such a market can be used as the basis for determining the current price. The position in some common law systems is that, in principle, the market price can be derived from a 'black market'[206] and the same can be argued in the context of the international instruments so long as in the circumstances this market provides a sound basis for determining the current price. A critical factor is whether it is reasonable to expect the injured party to make a hypothetical cover in the black market. If procuring a cover in the black market is unlawful, doing so cannot be reasonable.[207]

Turning to other considerations relating to the current price, the Convention's starting point is that the current price is the price 'at the place where delivery of the goods should have been made',[208] whereas the UPICC (being also applicable to contracts other than sales) refer to the place 'where the contract should have been performed'.[209] The seller's delivery obligation is set out in art 31 of the CISG[210] and the provision referring to the current price at the place of

[202] See Bridge (n 44) [12.72]. This position was followed in English law in *Hughes v Pendragon Sabre Ltd (t/a Porsche Centre Bolton)* [2016] EWCA Civ 18, [36].

[203] There are numerous sources setting out the types and definitions of markets (see, eg, *Gebruder Metelmann GmbH & Co KG v NBR (London) Ltd* [1984] 1 Lloyd's Rep 614 (sugar markets); McKendrick (n 117) [4.24]–[4.34]; for a helpful collection of materials with further comments, see P Todd, *International Trade Law* (London, Thomson–Sweet & Maxwell, 2003) 16–49).

[204] Because the prices in physical and futures markets reflect similar price movements (see, eg, *Gebruder Metelmann GmbH & Co KG v NBR (London) Ltd* (n 203)), the same can probably be said in relation to spot and forward prices (both being in a physical market).

[205] A black market has been defined as one where 'the goods are bought and sold surreptitiously' (*Benjamin* (n 193) [16-071]).

[206] See *John Neil Mouat v Betts Motors Ltd* (n 122).

[207] See similarly *Benjamin* (n 193) [16-071].

[208] Article 76(2).

[209] Article 7.4.6(2).

[210] 'If the seller is not bound to deliver the goods at any other particular place, his obligation to deliver consists: (a) if the contract of sale involves carriage of the goods – in handing the goods over to the first carrier for transmission to the buyer; (b) if, in cases not within the preceding subparagraph, the contract relates to specific goods, or unidentified goods to be drawn from a specific stock

delivery has been criticised because it may not be suitable for the injured buyer. The application of art 31 will often lead to the market in the seller's country[211] and it may be practically difficult for the buyer to prove the market price in that country.[212] Relying on the price at the place of the arrival of the goods can be more appropriate for the buyer[213] and it has been suggested that to resolve this difficulty art 76(2) CISG might need to be interpreted flexibly.[214] There is a danger, however, that flexibility is only achievable by contravening the text of art 76(2). It is, of course, possible to hold that there is no current price in the seller's country and then to rely on the current price in the buyer's country on the basis that the latter is the place that 'serves as a reasonable substitute', as required by art 76(2). But this may not always be the case as the current price in the seller's country may well exist. In such cases, a court or tribunal can either try to find a justification for holding that there is no current price at the place of delivery in order not to deviate from art 76(2) or simply ignore its wording and rely on the price in the buyer's country. This latter approach appears to have been taken in one CISG case,[215] where the injured buyer who had its place of business in Russia claimed damages under the Convention's 'abstract' formula relying on the current price in the Russian market. The tribunal readily accepted the buyer's argument without paying attention to art 76(2), which requires, in the first instance, the current price at the place of delivery to be determined.[216] This approach must not be followed because the Convention's express requirement as to the use of the current price at the place of delivery cannot be ignored.[217]

or to be manufactured or produced, and at the time of the conclusion of the contract the parties knew that the goods were at, or were to be manufactured or produced at, a particular place – in placing the goods at the buyer's disposal at that place; (c) in other cases – in placing the goods at the buyer's disposal at the place where the seller had his place of business at the time of the conclusion of the contract.' (art 31 CISG).

[211] Each of the three places listed in art 31 will often be in the seller's country (see note 210).

[212] See Honnold (n 21) 452.

[213] Ziegel and Samson (n 172) ('I prefer the test in UCC 2-713(2) viz "the place for tender (of the goods) or, in cases of rejection after arrival or revocation of acceptance, as of the place of arrival"').

[214] Ibid.

[215] See ICAC No 175/2003, 28 May 2004 (n 162). A similar approach may have been taken in Arbitration No 48, 2005 (n 24), where the tribunal relied on the market price on the Ukrainian market (the buyer's place of business). This statement would be true if the place of delivery were a place other than Ukraine and it is not clear from the decision what the place of delivery was.

[216] This statement is true if the place of delivery were the place other than the buyer's country. This seems to have been the case because the contract was on 'CPT' ('Carriage Paid To ...') terms according to which the seller's delivery obligation consists of delivery into the custody of the carrier (or to the first carrier if there are subsequent carriers) for transporting the goods to the destination (see J Ramberg, *ICC Guide to Incoterms 2000: Understanding and Practical Use* (Paris, ICC Publishing SA, 1999) 125). However, at the same time the decision refers to the contractual provision requiring the seller to deliver the goods to the place of destination. If, on the true construction of the contract, the seller undertook to deliver to the place of destination, then the criticism of the case becomes irrelevant.

[217] At first sight, this approach seems to be taken in CIETAC-Shenzhen Arbitration 18 April 1991 (Silicate iron), available at cisgw3.law.pace.edu/cases/910418c1.html, where the US buyer claimed damages under art 76 CISG relying on the market price in the US while the place of delivery was a Chinese port. The tribunal dismissed the buyer's argument and relied on the current price in the Chinese market but it did so not because of the Convention's express requirement to this effect but

The next question is how the Convention's requirement, that the current price must be determined at the place of delivery of the goods, should be interpreted in the context of a particular contractual trade term, such as FOB or CIF. A challenge that these trade terms present is that they require sellers to deliver not just goods but also documents.[218] More so, in the context of some trade sectors, such as the 'commodities trade', the goods are traded for the purpose of speculation, with traders being parties to 'strings' or 'chains'. The goods are often bought and sold in transit[219] and, with documents used as 'symbols' of the goods,[220] the seller's 'delivery' obligations may consist primarily in the delivery of documents since the seller may have purchased the goods afloat that had already been shipped by another seller in the chain. It is suggested that, where so, and the seller is a mere intermerdiary in a string who has not shipped the goods, the meaningful interpretation of art 76(2) CISG is that 'delivery of the goods' should be understood to mean the delivery of documents representing the goods. The place of delivery of the goods should, in this context, mean the place of the delivery of documents.[221]

More difficult is the case where an FOB or CIF seller is required to ship the goods itself because the seller's 'delivery' obligations concern both the goods and documents. Where the places of shipment of the goods and of the delivery of documents are different, which of them is appropriate under art 76(2) CISG? Given the express reference in art 76(2) to the place of the delivery of the *goods* and the need for clarity and the Convention's uniform application, it is best to rely on the place of delivery of the goods,[222] not documents.[223] However, art 76(2) is arguably based on the rationale that it is possible for the innocent

for other unrelated reasons (the reason being that the current price in the Chinese market reflected more accurately the delivery conditions of the contract). It is submitted that although the result is correct so far as art 76(2) CISG is concerned, the proper legal basis for reaching this result ought to have been art 76(2) itself.

[218] See 'FOB-Free on Board' (A1, A6) and 'CIF-Cost, Insurance and Freight' (A1, A5 and A6) in *Incoterms 2020 by the International Chamber of Commerce (ICC): ICC Rules for the Use of Domestic and International Trade Terms* (Paris, International Chamber of Commerce (ICC) 2019) 106, 108, 126,128.

[219] In contrast with English law, the trade of goods in transit is possible under the FOB term under INCOTERMS (see n 225).

[220] For the discussion of functions of documents and further references, see ch 3.

[221] See further D Saidov, 'The Present State of Damages under the CISG: A Critical Assessment' (2019) 13 *Vindobona J Int'l Commercial L Arbitration* 197, 209–1. See also in English law *C Sharpe & Co Ltd v Nosawa & Co* [1917] 2 KB 814.

[222] See CIETAC 9 January 2008 (Metallic silicon), available at cisgw3.law.pace.edu/cases/080109c1.html, involving the contract on the following terms: 'FOB Huangpu (Guangzhou), Shanghai, or Tianjin (at the [Buyer]'s option)'. The current price was determined on the basis of the average of FOB prices at a 'Chinese port' without, however, specifying whether the average of FOB prices was determined in the context of a particular port or whether it was determined with reference to other potentially relevant ports (the buyer failed to prove that it had nominated the port of shipment). See also ICC No 8502, November 1996, available at www.unilex.info, where the meaning and place of delivery (Ho Chi Minh City) was also rightly interpreted with reference to the contractual FOB term ('FOB Ho Chi Minh City port').

[223] Ibid, 210–1.

party to make a hypothetical replacement transaction at the current price at the place of delivery of the goods. This means that if the innocent party can prove that there was no such possibility, this provision in art 76(2) should be inapplicable and the alternative provision in it, discussed in the next paragraph, should be applicable. Finally, both FOB and CIF terms, as defined by INCOTERMS 2020,[224] give a seller an option of either shipping the goods itself or procuring them in transit.[225] With this in mind and if the contract does not specify the mode of delivery, it is suggested that the interpretation of art 76(2) should depend on the choice the seller makes. If the sellers ships the goods itself, the position proposed in this paragraph should be taken. If the seller does not ship the goods and purchases them in transit, the solution advocated in the previous paragraph should be adopted.

The CISG further provides that where there is no current price at the place of delivery of the goods, 'the price at such other place as serves as a reasonable substitute, making due allowance for differences in the cost of transporting the goods'[226] should be used. Similarly, the UPICC provide that if no current price exists at the place where the contract should have been performed, 'the current price at such other place that appears reasonable to take as a reference'[227] should be used. What is a 'reasonable substitute' or a 'place that appears reasonable … as a reference' cannot be defined precisely. In general terms, reasonableness of substitution must be determined 'from the point of view of an average merchant, in light of the justifiable interests of both parties'.[228] The substitute place is reasonable if it offers comparable conditions. This place is sometimes the one which is physically most proximate.[229]

The reported CISG cases in which this issue has arisen were not, at least expressly, concerned with balancing the parties' interests. Nor did they appear to search for the place physically most proximate. Instead, it is striking that in all these cases the arbitrators preferred to rely on what they called the

[224] The meaning of trade terms is, of course, not confined to INCOTERMS. The contract may, eg, specify a trade term and subject their interpretation to another legal regime. For a fuller discussion of this issue, see D Saidov, 'Trade Usages in International Sales Law' in D Saidov (ed), *Research Handbook on International and Comparative Law Sale of Goods Law* (Cheltenham, Edward Elgar, 2019) 96–131.

[225] FOB A2 in *Incoterms 2020* (n 218) 106: 'The seller must deliver the goods either by placing them on board the vessel nominated by the buyer at the loading point, if any, indicated by the buyer at the named port of shipment or by procuring the goods so delivered' (the position is different in English law where an FOB seller must ship the goods itself; see, eg, *Esteve Trading Corporation v Agropec International (The Golden Rio)* [1990] 2 Lloyd's Rep 273). CIF A2 in *Incoterms 2020* (n 218 126: 'The seller must deliver the goods either by placing them on board the vessel or by procuring the goods so delivered.' Typically, it is CIF and CFR terms that are associated with the sale of goods in transit (see, eg, J Ramberg, *International Commercial Transactions*, 3rd edn (Stockholm, ICC – Norstedts Juridik, 2004) 98 ('CFR- and CIF-terms … are commonly used for sale of goods in transit')).

[226] Article 76(2).

[227] Article 7.4.6(2).

[228] Knapp (n 18) 556.

[229] CISG-AC No 8 (n 19) Comment 4.5.2.

'international market price'. In doing so, they all took care to ensure that the international market price was fixed in accordance with the conditions comparable to the terms of the original contract. In one case,[230] where the FOB contract was avoided in April 1997, the international FOB market price in April 1997 was taken as a reasonable substitute price. In another case,[231] where the contract was for No. 2 copper scrap, 'the fair international market price for No. 2 scrap copper' was taken as the basis for the Convention's 'abstract' formula, ensuring that the substitute price related to the goods of precisely the same technical specifications.[232] In yet another case,[233] the tribunal appeared to fix the international market price on 'CIF Rotterdam' terms as it was expressly pointed out that the original contract price included freight to Rotterdam.[234]

Is the reliance on the international market price appropriate? In the age of globalised markets, the existence of and reliance on international market prices can hardly be surprising and there is evidence of substantial reliance on such prices in other areas of law.[235] It is suggested therefore that so long as they can be duly proven, such prices should be used under the instruments' 'abstract' formula.[236] If international market prices truly exist and can be validly ascertained, they will alleviate the difficulty of ascertaining the current price. They may also render the issues of a 'physical location' of a market, and consequently the provisions concerning the 'place of delivery' and 'reasonable substitutes' in arts 76(2) CISG and 7.4.6(2) UPICC less important and relevant. The existence of an international market price may, however, create a false sense of irrelevance of the need for comparability to the original contract. As partly seen from the cases discussed in the previous paragraph, either an international market price for the goods which are identical or comparable to those under the original contract

[230] See CIETAC 25 December 1998 (Basic pig iron), available at cisgw3. law.pace.edu/cases/981225c2.html.

[231] See CIETAC 12 January 1996 (Scrap copper), available at cisgw3.law.pace.edu/cases/960112c1.html.

[232] The case can be criticised for taking the position that the current price must be the price at the time of the delivery of the goods which is incorrect as the CISG provides that the relevant time is that of the avoidance of the contract (see ibid).

[233] See CIETAC 2 May 1996 ("FeMo" alloy), available at cisgw3.law.pace.edu/cases/960502c1.html.

[234] This seems to imply the tribunal's awareness of the necessity to adjust the international market price in accordance with the terms of the contract to make the two prices comparable. However, no mention was made of an insurance charge which is also a part of the CIF price.

[235] This author has come across petroleum contracts in which the determination of value of petroleum was based on 'international market prices' (for an overview of different types of upstream petroleum contract referring to international market prices, see, eg, Z Gao, *International Petroleum Contracts: Current Trends and New Directions* (London, Graham & Trotman, 1994) 129, 182; for the discussion of the nature and structure of oil markets, see EE Smith, JS Dzienkowski, JS Lowe, OL Anderson and GB Conine, *International Petroleum Transactions*, 2nd edn (Denver, Rocky Mountain Mineral Law Foundation, 2000) 749–60).

[236] See CIETAC 29 September 2004 (n 80) ('The Arbitration Tribunal notes that India rapeseed meal is not popular goods purchased internationally, and has no international price quote').

will need to be found or an international market price will constitute a general yardstick to be adjusted to approximate the terms of the original contract.[237]

Under the CISG, if there has been no taking over of the goods or if the contract has been avoided before such taking over, the current price must be determined as of the time of the avoidance of the contract.[238] It is suggested that this requirement needs to be interpreted with a reasonable degree of flexibility. As mentioned, the rationale underlying this 'abstract' formula is that an injured party is in the position to make a hypothetical transaction as soon as the contract is avoided. However, it is not always possible for an injured party to find a substitute precisely on the date of avoidance and it seems fair that a reasonable period after the avoidance of the contract should still be regarded as meeting the requirements of this 'abstract' formula. For example, in some cases where the current price could not be established at the time of avoidance, arbitrators treated the current price several days after that time as acceptable under art 76 CISG.[239] Similarly, if there are several prices available on different dates, all within a reasonable period after avoidance, it may be best,[240] given the date of avoidance is already departed from, to even out those prices (as opposed to selecting only one) to rely on a balanced or average price throughout this period.

So far as the CISG is concerned, the current (or, where appropriate, market) price needs to relate to the goods of the same description and quantity as those in the contract.[241] The UPICC appear to take a somewhat flexible approach by referring to the current price for goods delivered 'in comparable circumstances'.[242] The question is: how similar should the description of the goods, for which current/market price is available, be under the instruments' 'abstract' formula? The CISG cases demonstrate that arbitrators generally try to ensure that the description of the goods, the current price of which is relied upon, is as similar as possible to that of contract goods. One case[243] involved the sale of 20 tons of ferro-molybdenum (60 per cent molybdenum content), 'CFR Pusan', with goods being loaded in a specified port in China. The buyer alleged

[237] *Soinco v NKAP* Zurich Arbitration (Switzerland) 31 May 1996, available at cisgw3.law.pace.edu/cases/960531s1.html ('the world market price cannot be simply taken to be the [London Metal Exchange] price … [and] the necessary adjustments to reflect transportation and other costs free Hungarian border [had to be made]').

[238] See arts 76(1) CISG, 7.4.6(1) UPICC and 9:507 PECL.

[239] See CIETAC 20 January 1993 (n 16); CIETAC-Shenzhen 18 April 1991 (n 217). There are cases in which arbitrators appear to have taken too flexible an approach by not determining the date of the avoidance of the contract and taking the current price nearest to (and preceding) the contractual time of delivery as the basis (CIETAC 23 April 1995 (Australian raw wool), available at cisgw3.law. pace.edu/cases/950423c1.html; CIETAC 11 February 2000 (n 41)). It is argued that by failing to determine the date of avoidance and to examine whether the current price was available at that date, the arbitrators failed to comply with the requirement of art 76(1).

[240] For this approach in English law, see *Somasteel SARL v Coresteel DMCC* [2015] EWHC 1234 (Comm), [50]–[51], where the buyer relied on the price most favourable to it but the court preferred to even out other available prices that were close to the relevant time.

[241] See Secretariat Commentary on Article 72 of the 1978 Draft.

[242] Article 7.4.6(2) UPICC.

[243] See CIETAC 30 July 1996 (n 24).

that it had made a substitute re-purchase of 20 tons ferro-molybdenum with 60 per cent of molybdenum content on 'CFR Rotterdam' terms. The tribunal refused to recognise that transaction as a substitute and instead relied on the Convention's 'abstract' formula by adopting, as a starting point, the price in the buyer's alleged substitute transaction and then subtracting from it the difference between the freight rates to Rotterdam and Pusan (the difference being US $89,000). In another case,[244] involving the sale of 'no-name' vacuum cleaners, as opposed to branded ones, it was held that there was no market for 'no-name' vacuum cleaners and art 76 CISG was not applied.

An arguably more lenient approach is taken in some other CISG cases. In one case, the seller from China agreed to sell to the buyer from Luxemburg 500 tons of silicon and manganese alloy, 'CFR Rotterdam', delivery period September-October 1998. In awarding the injured buyer damages under art 76 CISG (with the contract avoided on 30 October 1998), the tribunal relied, as a starting point, on the 'FOB Rotterdam' price (loading being in the main port in China) for the goods of better quality.[245] The tribunal then made two adjustments to that price. First, it was held that the price of the goods of superior quality would exceed that of contract goods by approximately 15 per cent and to make the current price comparable to the contract price, it had to be reduced by the said percentage. Second, because the contract price was the 'CFR Rotterdam' price, the freight rate from the stipulated loading port to Rotterdam had to be added to the 'FOB' price. This decision demonstrates that arbitrators are prepared to be flexible in interpreting the 'current price' by making necessary adjustments to the price of the goods, the description of which differs from that in the original contract.[246] This approach should generally be welcomed as it is not always possible to find the current price for the goods of identical description.[247]

The capacity in which the injured party has acted under the contract can be relevant to determining the current price. If it is the seller, the 'selling' current/market price is relevant and vice versa, if the injured party is the buyer, it is the 'buying' current/market price that is relevant.[248] Although the difference between the two is usually insignificant, there may be cases where this difference is considerable.[249] In the same vein, it may need to be determined whether

[244] See Case No 3 U 246/97 Appellate Court Celle (Germany) 2 September 1998 (Vacuum cleaners), available at cisgw3.law.pace.edu/cases/980902g1.html.

[245] The silicon content was above 17% and manganese content was above 65% while, according to the contract, the goods were to contain 14% silicon and 60% manganese.

[246] For other CISG cases involving adjustments of prices, see CIETAC 24 April 1997 (Oxidised aluminium), available at cisgw3.law.pace.edu/cases/970424c1.html; CIETAC 29 September 1997 (n 142); CIETAC 11 February 2000 (n 41). Since those decisions do not clearly state the date when the contract was avoided, it is difficult to say whether the adjustment of an FOB price to a CIF/CFR price or vice versa was correct in the circumstances.

[247] But see in English law *Esteve Trading Corporation v Agropec International (The Golden Rio)* (n 225), discussed in the first edition of this book.

[248] *Benjamin* (n 193) [16-072]; Waters (n 183) 378.

[249] See *Kwei Tek Chao v British Traders and Shippers Ltd* [1954] 2 QB 459, 497–8.

the contract price was a wholesale or a retail price as there is often a noticeable difference between the two.[250]

It must be emphasised that a relentless drive to ensure the strict comparability of prices may create a dangerous and arguably unfair situation where no current prices are found to exist, rendering the claimant unable to claim damages under the instruments' 'abstract' formula. It is submitted that ultimately the crucial consideration should be this: which hypothetical transaction is a reasonable replacement[251] given the injured party's circumstances, including the purpose for which it made the contract and the business environment and trade sector in which it operates? It may be that there is no wholesale market for the goods and a hypothetical cover at a retail market is the only option. If so, it may be justifiable to take a retail price as the basis for the current price.[252] The problem of too strong an emphasis on the comparability of prices can also be avoided by exercising a reasonable degree of flexibility, as has been done in a number of cases,[253] by means of adjusting prices and/or looking at comparable goods and transactions.

Determining the current price is a question of fact.[254] The current price must be 'reliably verifiable'.[255] The nature of evidence that needs to be presented to prove the current price is likely to depend on the location and/or type of the market. The evidence of the current price can be provided, for example, by the relevant professional organisations and chambers of commerce.[256] There are cases where the current price was derived from an offer by a third party to sell the same goods as those under the contract and on similar terms[257] or from the price the seller received by reselling contract goods.[258] In the same vein, it seems

[250] *Heskell v Continental Express Ltd* (n 173) ('Retail prices differ largely from wholesale prices'). For a CISG case, where the wholesale current price was relied upon, see ICAC No 175/2003, 28 May 2004 (n 162).

[251] See, similarly, CISG-AC No 8 (n 19) Rule 4.5(b).

[252] For a similar position in English law, see *Benjamin* (n 193) [16-072].

[253] Some such cases have been addressed above. For other cases, see the discussion below and the following section on 'Burden of proof'.

[254] See Waters (n 183) 384.

[255] Yovel (n 49).

[256] See Comment 2 on Article 7.4.6 UPICC. That said, Comment 4.3.1 of CISG-AC No 8 (n 19) rightly states that '[t]he requirement that a current price exists does not mandate that there be an official or unofficial market quotation for the goods in question'.

[257] See CIETAC-Shenzhen 18 April 1991 (n 217); CIETAC 20 January 1993 (n 16); Arbitration Court Rostov Region 2 February 2018 (n 65).

[258] CIETAC 26 June 2003 (Alumina), available at cisgw3.law.pace.edu/cases/030626c1.html. But see Case No V CSK 63/08 Supreme Court (Poland) 9 October 2008, available at cisgw3.law.pace.edu/cases/081009p1.html, where the court took the position, according to the abstract of this case, that examples of individual transactions were not enough to establish the current price under art 76. *Cf Glencore Energy UK Ltd v Cirrus Oil Services Ltd* [2014] EWHC 87 (Comm) (decided under English law), involving Ebok crude oil from a relatively new field in Nigeria that was sold as a blend of oil from various wells or reservoirs within the Ebok field. In those circumstances, where there were no publicly reported figures on the market price of Ebok crude oil, the court chose to rely on reports, based on the seller's market intelligence, of similar transactions made in a market (not involving the contracting parties) as evidence of the market price.

that an offer by a third party to buy the goods from the buyer or the price in its sub-sale contract (or previous sales by the buyer of similar goods to third parties)[259] may provide a basis for determining the current price.[260] The terms of the original contract may also provide an indication of the current price. For example, in one case,[261] the tribunal determined the current price on the basis of the amount of refund, set by the contract, to be provided by the seller if there is a shortage of delivery. However, none of these approaches to establishing the current price can be of universal application. Whether a particular price is indicative of the current price must be decided in the particular context. Other sources of evidence[262] of the current price may include prices quoted on exchanges,[263] surveys carried out by an independent company with a view to determining the current price,[264] opinions of experts[265] or traders[266] regarding the existence and level of the current price, market intelligence,[267] specialised industry,[268] trade sector, or financial publications.[269]

In emphasising the need for *flexibility* in fixing the current price, arbitrators often exercise their discretion, and when fixing the current price they rely on prices which appeared to them as 'practical', 'feasible', 'reasonable'[270] or 'fair'[271] in the circumstances. The desire to be flexible has occasionally spilled over to the final determination of damages under art 76 CISG. In one case, the

[259] See ICAC No 175/2003, 28 May 2004 (n 162).

[260] J Edelman, S Colton, J Varuhas (eds), *McGregor on Damages*, 20th edn (London, Sweet & Maxwell, 2019) [25-064]. But see Supreme Court (Poland) 9 October 2008 (n 258).

[261] See ICAC No 133/1994, 19 December 1995, available at cisgw3.law.pace.edu/cases/951219r1.html.

[262] The applicable rules on the admissibility of evidence impact on what can be brought as evidence in a particular case.

[263] See Supreme Court (Spain) 1 July 2013 (n 109) (the market price of feed wheat was determined based on the data provided by the Barcelona Corn Exchange); also CIETAC 12 January 1996 (n 231) (where, it seems, the reference was intended to be to a specialised commodity exchange). Art 76 CISG does not require the existence of official or unofficial market quotations but 'the lack of such quotations raises the question whether there is a 'current price' for the goods' (para 6 of the Secretariat Commentary on Article 72 of the 1978 Draft).

[264] ICAC No 133/1994, 19 December 1995 (n 261); Arbitration Court Rostov Region 2 February 2018 (n 65).

[265] Appellate Court München 15 September 2004 (n 43).

[266] See Waters (n 183) 384.

[267] See *Glencore Energy UK Ltd v Cirrus Oil Services Ltd* (n 258), where the court relied on market intelligence disclosed by the seller. Despite treating it as 'hearsay' the court stated that in reality the situation was 'little different from the basis upon which experts usually opine – namely on reported prices for deals done' (ibid, [86]).

[268] Such as S&P Global Platts (on which see also n 359) in the case of such products as oil, gas, coal and metals (www.spglobal.com/platts/en) or Metal Expert in the case of iron and steel industry (metalexpert.com/en/index.html). Both these sources were relied on, amongst others, to determine the current price of metal products in Arbitration Court Rostov Region 2 February 2018 (n 65); see also The Fifteenth Arbitration Appellate Court Rostov-on-Don (n 58).

[269] See CIETAC 24 April 1997 (n 246); CIETAC 29 September 2004 (n 80); Waters (n 183) 384.

[270] See CIETAC 18 August 1997 (n 94); CIETAC 25 October 1994 (High tensile steel bar), available at cisgw3.law.pace.edu/cases/941025c1.html.

[271] See CIETAC 12 January 1996 (n 231); CIETAC 24 April 1997 (n 246).

tribunal, having determined the difference between the contract price and the market price, further reduced the amount thus obtained by 10 per cent due to 'the price cut-off tendency on the markets for these goods in Ukraine'.[272] This decision is not easily justifiable because under art 76 CISG, the difference between the current and contract prices ought to have fixed the final award of damages (unless there were further losses recoverable under art 74). If there was a widespread tendency to reduce the 'market price', the tribunal ought to have incorporated the level of the reduction into the determination of the current price, whilst achieving the same result.[273]

2.2.4. *Burden of Proof*

The injured party bears the burden of proving the preconditions under the instruments' 'abstract' formula.[274] It must prove that: the contract has been avoided; a substitute transaction meeting the requirements of the 'concrete' formula has not been made; there exists a current price at the relevant time and place.[275] The breaching party has the burden of rebutting the claims thus raised.[276] Sometimes the tribunals do not strictly allocate the burden of proof in this manner. For instance, in one case[277] the tribunal requested *both* parties to submit evidence regarding the existence of the current price. It is suggested that this approach contravenes the proper allocation of burden of proof (assuming it is a matter governed by the instruments).[278]

In some CISG cases where the injured party (or both parties, as was the case in the case just referred to) failed to establish the current price, the tribunals took the initiative by determining the current price themselves.[279] Although this

[272] Arbitration No 48, 2005 (n 24).

[273] The decision also leaves room for different interpretations. One way to interpret it is to argue that because there was a widespread tendency in the Ukrainian market to reduce what the tribunal called the market price, then perhaps the tribunal did not determine the market price correctly and it is the *reduced amount* which was the true market price at the time. Another interpretation is to view the decision as having correctly decided the level of the *market* price and then to argue that the *current* price was actually lower than the market price because of the tendency to reduce the market price.

[274] This is, of course, subject to the issue of burden of proof being governed by the international instruments.

[275] See *Novia Handelsgesellschaft mbH v AS Maseko* Tallinn Circuit Court (Estonia) 19 February 2004, available at cisgw3.law.pace.edu/cases/040219e3.html; ICAC No 133/1994, 19 December 1995 (n 261).

[276] Burden of proof can be understood in two senses. 'In its broadest sense, 'burden of proof' refers to the ultimate establishment of the truth of the basic proposition ... In its narrow sense, [it] refers to a party's obligation to go forward with the evidence to rebut the other party's initial or prima facie proof ... The basic distinction is that, in its broadest sense, burden of proof always rests on the same party, while the burden of going forward with the evidence changes from party to party throughout the trial' (RR Anderson, 'Incidental and Consequential Damages' (1987) 7 *J L Commerce* 327, 393–4).

[277] See CIETAC 30 June 1999 (Peppermint oil), available at cisgw3.law.pace.edu/cases/990630c1.html.

[278] See ch 1.

[279] See ibid; ICAC No 133/1994, 19 December 1995 (n 261).

approach could be applauded for its flexibility and the tribunal's determination to fix the current price where possible, it can undermine, to some extent, the purpose of the allocation of burden of proof – that is, its being a mechanism of dealing with uncertainty by raising/rebutting presumptions based on the evidence presented by the *parties*. If this approach is followed, it may be the case that despite the injured party's inability to prove its claim for damages by failing to establish the current price, a court/tribunal might itself fix the current price and help that party succeed.[280] Whether a court/tribunal is able to pursue the matter on its own initiative is often addressed by the applicable rules of procedure[281] and for this reason non-uniform treatment of claims for damages (generally and under the instruments' 'abstract' formula in particular) is to be expected.

2.2.5. *Relationship with Other Losses*

The instruments provide that in addition to damages under the 'abstract' formula, the injured party may recover damages for any further losses.[282] These losses may include various additional costs the injured party has incurred or will incur as a result of the breach. For instance, the seller may incur extra costs of storage and maintenance of the rejected goods or the buyer may incur liability to its sub-buyers due to the seller's breach. Courts/tribunals need to ensure that damages for further losses do not over-compensate the injured party. The buyer cannot, as a rule, claim damages for the lost profit margin on a sub-sale together with damages under the 'abstract' formula because the latter implies that the buyer is *in the position* to purchase the goods to fulfil its commitments.[283] It is where a necessary delay between the time of breach and the date for determining the current price causes the buyer loss of profit (stoppage in the manufacturing process) that the buyer can claim damages for lost profits for the period of delay.

Some commentators seem to suggest that the injured buyer *can* claim damages for the lost profit margin it expected to receive on a sub-sale if it exceeds damages under the 'abstract' formula.[284] It is contended that this position is not well founded. If the buyer is able to prove that it would have earned a higher level profit margin and if it has not made a replacement transaction (which often constitutes a failure mitigate), then it has a choice: either to claim

[280] Such an approach can, of course, also favour the breaching party.

[281] See, eg, arts 43 and 44 of the CIETAC Arbitration Rules 2015, available at www.cietac.org/Uploads/201904/5cc129286b1c3.pdf. For a CISG case where the court emphasised its *inability*, according to the applicable procedural rules, to collect evidence on its own initiative to determine the current price under art 76 CISG, see Tallinn Circuit Court 19 February 2004 (n 275).

[282] See arts 76(1) CISG, 7.4.6(1) UPICC and 9:507 PECL.

[283] For a CISG case where the buyer was thus over-compensated, see CIETAC 30 November 1997 (n 42).

[284] See Knapp (n 18) 554.

damages 'abstractly' or 'concretely'.[285] Under the latter approach, damages may be awarded, subject to the duty to mitigate, for the loss of the *actual* profit margin the buyer would have made on a sub-sale (that is, the difference between the contract and *sub-sale* prices) and this award precludes a claim based on the instruments' 'abstract' formula.[286] However, if this 'abstract' formula (the difference between the contract and *current* prices) is relied upon, it is argued that a further loss in the amount by which the expected actual profit margin exceeds damages under the 'abstract' formula cannot be claimed. Although the relevant provisions suggest that *any further loss*, including loss of profit, can be claimed, the award of the expected profit margin on a sub-sale, together with damages under the 'abstract' formula, goes against the rationale and considerations underlying the 'abstract' formula. First, as noted, it implies that the buyer can buy a replacement and fulfil its sub-sale contract, earning its profit margin. Second, numerous policy considerations[287] justify the 'abstract' approach as *an alternative* and not as a supplement to, the 'concrete' approach to calculating damages.[288] In a similar vein, in relation to the seller the instruments' 'abstract' formula implies that it is able to resell the goods and earn a profit margin. But there may be cases where due to not receiving the payment on time, the seller has lost an investment opportunity. In this case, a claim for loss of profit (or loss of a chance to profit) along with damages under the instruments' 'abstract' formula may be justifiable if it is taken into account that, had the contract been performed, a part of the profit margin that the seller would have received from selling the goods would have been directed towards making an investment.

2.2.6. *Cases where the Instruments' 'Abstract' Formula is Inapplicable*

The instruments' 'abstract' formula is not applicable where at least one of its preconditions is not met and/or where at least one of its underlying assumptions is not present. The formula's central assumption is that the injured party is in the position to make a hypothetical replacement transaction and where this is not the case, the formula becomes irrelevant. One example of where that

[285] There is no reason why the injured party should not have this choice under the international instruments. The instruments' provisions cannot be interpreted as *requiring* the party to rely on their 'abstract' formula where no replacement transaction is made (the only hierarchy established is that between arts 75 and 76 CISG, 7.4.5 and 7.4.6 UPICC, 9:506 and 9:507 PECL).

[286] See ICAC No 160/1997, 5 March 1998, available at cisgw3.law.pace.edu/cases/ 980305r2.html ('[the] buyer's claim for the award of the price difference between the current market price and the price fixed by the contract between the parties, claimed with reference to Art. 76 of the CISG, was rejected by the Tribunal. The Tribunal's conclusion … was based on the position that the lost profit, which is to be compensated to the buyer, should be calculated based on the difference between the price for the goods as fixed in the contract between [the] buyer and the third party, and the price for the goods as fixed in the contract between [the] buyer and [the] seller, and thus, … lost profit of the buyer is fully compensated for.'

[287] See above.

[288] A similar position seems to be taken in the Secretariat Commentary on the 1978 Draft Convention (stating that art 72 (a counterpart of art 76 CISG) 'sets forth an alternative means of measuring damages where the contract has been avoided but no substitute transaction was entered into').

assumption is not present, even where there is a market for the goods, is where the injured buyer's sub-sale contract requires the delivery of 'self-same' goods as those in the contract with the seller.[289] In an already-mentioned CISG case,[290] the buyer's sub-sale contract provided for the delivery of the same goods as those in the buyer's contract with the seller in terms of their specifications and place of manufacture (Korea) and, because of the time constraints,[291] that requirement made the buyer unable to procure a substitute to fulfil its sub-sale. Although the situation does not strictly speaking involve self-same goods, it highlights the same difficulty faced by a buyer in the case of 'self-same' goods which renders the buyer unable to procure a substitute.[292] Another case analogous to that of 'self-same goods' concerns commodities traders[293] buying and selling in 'strings'. Suppose such a buyer re-sells the goods, bought from the breaching seller, to its sub-buyer under a CIF contract that requires the buyer to give notice of appropriation[294] (specifying, say, the vessel's name, the date of the bill of lading, the goods shipped and their quantity).[295] If, under the law governing the sub-sale contract, the effect of giving such notice to its sub-buyer[296] is that the buyer becomes bound to deliver the particular goods specified in the notice,[297] it is highly unlikely that there will be a market where *this* buyer can hypothetically buy replacement goods to fulfill its obligations under the sub-sale contract.

Another instance where the injured party is not in the position to make a replacement transaction is a lost volume situation, whether it is a lost volume seller or buyer-seller. One way to explain this is to state that even if the injured party may seem to be in the position to make a hypothetical transaction, that would be a transaction which it would have made in any event and it cannot be a replacement for the original contract. Another explanation is that where supply exceeds demand (lost volume seller) or where demand exceeds supply (lost volume buyer-seller), there is no market in which the seller can sell or the

[289] For the discussion in the context of English law, see McKendrick (n 117) [14.56]–[14.60].

[290] CIETAC 17 October 1996 (n 79).

[291] '[The] [b]uyer being a Chinese company was unable to find Korean products on the Chinese market within a short time' (ibid).

[292] For a similar case, see CIETAC 29 September 2004 (n 80).

[293] On which see further the paragraphs in the main text accompanying nn 218 and 225 and ch 3.

[294] See also CIF A10 in *Incoterms 2020* (n 218): 'The seller must notify the buyer that the goods have been delivered in accordance with A2 [reproduced in n 225]. The seller must give the buyer any notice required to to enable the buyer to receive the goods'. For some remarks, in a CISG case, on the seller's duty to appropriate the goods in a contract on CIF terms, treated by the tribunal as an international trade usage/custom, see CIETAC 21 May 1999 (Excavator), available at cisgw3.law.pace.edu/cases/990521c1.html.

[295] See, eg, The Grain and Feed Trade Association (GAFTA) Contract No. 100 (Contract for Shipment of Feedingstuffs in Bulk Tale Quale – CIF/CIFFO/C&F/C&FFO TERMS), art 11(a): 'Notice of appropriation shall state the vessel's name, the presumed weight shipped, and the date or the presumed date of the bill of lading.'

[296] The commercial purpose of the notice is to inform the buyer of the goods that were allocated as those to be delivered under the contract with the seller and to enable the buyer to put in place the discharging/receipt or resale arrangements.

[297] As is the case in English law (see, eg, *Re R and H Hall Ltd & WH Pim (Jnr) and Co's Arbitration* (1928) 33 Com Cas 24, HL).

buyer-seller can buy in order to resell the goods. Had there been an available market for the goods, a lost volume situation would not have arisen in the first place. Where the instruments' 'abstract' formula is not applicable, damages may still be claimed under a general provision on damages.[298]

3. NON-CONFORMING GOODS

3.1. General

The next situation to consider is where the seller delivers non-conforming goods[299] which: are accepted by the buyer; or *have* to be accepted because the buyer fails to avoid the contract or does not have the right to avoid. The difference between this case and those discussed previously is that, here, the buyer does not avoid the contract and has non-conforming goods on hand. Because the buyer has received the goods, it would not normally seek to find a substitute. That is why the formulae referring to prices in an actual or hypothetical replacement transaction are irrelevant. In contrast with some domestic legal regimes,[300] the international instruments do not contain a specific provision relating to the calculation of damages in the case of non-conforming goods. The legal basis for awarding damages in such a case is the instruments' general provisions on damages.[301]

3.2. Concrete v Abstract Calculation

The dilemma between the 'concrete' and 'abstract' calculation equally arises in cases of non-conforming goods. Suppose the seller delivers non-conforming goods bought for resale and the buyer manages to persuade its sub-buyers to accept the non-conforming goods without any price reduction and without any liability to the sub-buyers. Under the 'concrete' approach, no damages are due to the buyer because it has suffered no loss. The goods, despite the non-conformity,

[298] See, similarly, CISG-AC No 8 (n 19) Comment 6.4.

[299] Article 35(1) and (2) CISG: '(1) The seller must deliver goods which are of the quantity, quality and description required by the contract and which are contained or packaged in the manner required by the contract. (2) Except where the parties have agreed otherwise, the goods do not conform with the contract unless they: (a) are fit for the purposes for which goods of the same description would ordinarily be used; (b) are fit for any particular purpose expressly or impliedly made known to the seller at the time of the conclusion of the contract, except where the circumstances show that the buyer did not rely, or that it was unreasonable for him to rely, on the seller's skill and judgement; (c) possess the qualities of goods which the seller has held out to the buyer as a sample or model; (d) are contained or packaged in the manner usual for such goods or, where there is no such manner, in a manner adequate to preserve and protect the goods.'

[300] See, eg, § 2-714 UCC and s 53(2) and (3) SGA.

[301] Articles 74 CISG, 7.4.2 UPICC and 9:501 PECL.

were resold as planned and the buyer earned the same profit it would have earned had the goods been conforming. The 'abstract' approach may lead to a different result. If, for example, the difference between the (market) value of conforming goods and those actually delivered is relied upon as a specific means to calculate damages 'abstractly' and if there is a difference between these two values, the buyer would be entitled to damages for this difference. This would be so, despite the buyer having suffered no actual loss[302] and some legal systems prefer the latter result.[303]

The position of the international instruments is not entirely clear and it is suggested that the structure the instruments adopt to cases where the contract has been avoided can be used by analogy in cases of non-conforming goods. This would mean that the 'abstract' approach should be limited to those cases where the 'concrete' calculation cannot be applied and, in any event, the mitigation rule should set the ceiling for recovery. Applying this approach to the example in the previous paragraph, the 'concrete' approach would lead to no recovery as the claimant has suffered no *actual* loss and it can also be argued that persuading the sub-buyers to accept the goods on the same terms without incurring any liability was a reasonable mitigation measure which avoided the loss. In short, it is suggested that the instruments should generally be interpreted as expressing a preference for the 'concrete' measure coupled with the mitigation rule, which is in harmony with the 'concrete' approach.

The differences between the 'concrete' and 'abstract' approaches should not be exaggerated. These differences seem to be largely confined to the types of case noted above and in most cases the two approaches converge. This convergence can be seen even in legal regimes which generally prefer the 'abstract' approach. For example, damages for breach of warranty in English sales law are prima facie measured by 'the difference between the value of the goods at the time of delivery to the buyer and the value they would have had if they had fulfilled the warranty'.[304] It may often be the case that there is no market price for non-conforming goods[305] and so the difference between the two values can be derived

[302] There is an argument that the buyer, in these cases, does suffer losses, such as an injury to its reputation or loss arising from having paid too high a price corresponding to superior goods contracted for and not to the inferior goods delivered (see Bridge (n 135)). But it cannot be assumed that such losses will always arise. Even where, say, the buyer in fact suffers damage to its reputation, it cannot be assumed that this loss necessarily corresponds to damages produced by the 'abstract' approach. For these reasons, this argument on its own cannot fully justify the 'abstract' approach to calculating damages for non-conforming goods.

[303] See *Slater v Hoyle & Smith* [1920] 2 KB 11.

[304] Section 53(3) SGA.

[305] See *Benjamin* (n 193) [17-052] ('normally, there is no market in the ordinary sense for damaged or defective goods'). It must be borne in mind, however, that the goods may be non-conforming because they do not comply, say, with the particular contractual requirements but may not be 'defective', in which case there may well be a market for them. See, eg, *Septo Trading Inc v Tintrade Ltd* [2020] EWHC 1795 (Comm), [75] ('In the present case the fuel oil was not damaged or defective but had a specification which did not comply with the contract of sale and purchase. The specification was an industry standard, ISO 8127, and further blending was required to make it acceptable to bunker fuel buyers.').

from the costs *actually* incurred by the injured party to bring the goods into their conforming state,[306] or the value of non-conforming goods may be determined based on the price for which they were *actually* resold by the buyer.[307] Thus, considerations relating to the injured party's actual situation often enter into the 'abstract' measure.

3.3. Specific Methods of Calculation

3.3.1. Buyer's Resale

Buyers often resell non-conforming goods at reduced prices and in several cases the amount by which a profit margin on sub-sale had been reduced was awarded as damages.[308] The buyers have also been awarded lost profits even where no resale of non-conforming goods had taken place. In one CISG case, where the seller failed to supply a conforming packaging production system, the buyer was awarded damages for profits it would have earned from the orders that would have materialised had the goods been conforming.[309] The buyer may also suffer loss of custom[310] as a result of the delivery of non-conforming goods and in some CISG cases it was deemed appropriate to award such damages.[311]

3.3.2. Cost of Cure

Where buyers cure a lack of conformity in the goods, the costs of doing so are a convenient and accurate measure of the loss suffered as a result of non-conforming goods. In principle, this method can be used not only where an

[306] See McKendrick (n 117) [14.41].

[307] See *McGregor on Damages* (n 260) [25-065] ('The price at which the buyer has resold the defective goods may be taken as evidence of their value where this is difficult to assess. Such evidence can play a more important part here than in other situations since, where goods are defective, it is likely that there will be no market for them.').

[308] Case No 3 U 83/98 Appellate Court Bamberg (Germany) 13 January 1999 (Fabric), available at cisgw3.law.pace.edu/cases/990113g1.html ('As a result of the deviation in colour and texture, the buyer had to offer its customer a reduction in price of 10% … [and] [t]he seller is obliged to reimburse the buyer for this loss of profit under Art. 74 CISG'); CIETAC 4 November 2002 (Beech log), available at cisgw3.law.pace.edu/cases/021104c1.html; CIETAC 11 April 1997 (Silicon metal), available at cisgw3.law.pace.edu/cases/970411c1.html. See also CIETAC 26 November 1998 (Leather gloves), available at cisgw3.law.pace.edu/cases/981126c1.html (where, although there was no award of damages for non-conforming goods, a similar result was achieved by the tribunal recognising that the buyer's resale at a 30% discount was reasonable and ordering the buyer to pay only 70% of the contract price).

[309] See *TeeVee Tunes Inc et al v Gerhard Schubert GmbH* not reported in F.Supp.2d 2006, WL 2463537 (SDNY) (No. 00 Civ 5189 (RCC) (the issue of mitigation was not addressed).

[310] See ch 3 for the argument that it is not entirely accurate to treat loss of custom as a separate head of loss and that it is loss of profit, flowing from loss of custom, that best describes this loss.

[311] See *EK, L & A v F* Supreme Court (Switzerland) 28 October 1998, available at cisgw3.law.pace.edu/cases/981028s1.html.

injured party has *actually* incurred costs of cure[312] but also with reference to hypothetical costs.[313] In contrast with the previous method of calculation which compensates for the loss in the amount of the profit margin, the 'cost of cure' measure compensates for the loss in the reduction in the value of the goods. Loss of profit, either based on the loss of a profit margin on sub-sale or on the reduced volume of production and sales, cannot usually be claimed in addition to damages based on the 'cost of cure' measure because cure brings the goods into their conforming state, which then enables the buyer to earn profits as planned. However, if cure causes delay or stoppage in the manufacturing process resulting in loss of profit which would not have occurred had the goods been conforming, damages for this loss of profit should be recoverable along with costs of cure. It may also be that, acting reasonably, the buyer initially attempts to cure a lack of conformity, but in the end cure proves partly or wholly ineffective, resulting in the loss of existing (and/or potential) customers. Where so, it is appropriate for the buyer to be awarded damages for the cost of cure *and* loss of profit, resulting from the customers rejecting the goods in relation to which cure proved ineffective and/or from the loss of customers who decide not to do business with the buyer in the future.[314]

Costs of cure must be truly necessary and directed at curing the non-conformity. The mitigation rule and arguably a general principle (idea) of reasonableness, underlying the international instruments, require that costs of cure be reasonable. In some legal systems, the requirement of reasonableness has been said to necessitate an assessment of: whether the innocent party has effected cure or intends to do so; the innocent party's conduct subsequent to the breach; and whether there is a proportion between the cost of cure, the contract price, the benefit already received by the injured party and the benefit to be obtained from cure.[315] It is submitted that there is no reason why these factors should not be relevant to assessing the reasonableness of cure under the international instruments. There are signs that judges and arbitrators applying the CISG have already approached the 'cost of cure' measure in the same manner. Thus, the requirement of costs being necessary or appropriate for effecting cure is expressly mentioned in several decisions. In one case involving the delivery

[312] Case No 25 O 99/09 District Court Stuttgart (Germany) 29 October 2009, available at cisgw3.law.pace.edu/cases/091029g1.html, where the buyer was awarded the cost it incurred to cure a lack of conformity in the artificial turf supplied by the seller for use in the indoor golf course.

[313] See CIETAC 21 May 2006 (Diesel generator), available at cisgw3.law.pace.edu/cases/060521c1.html, where the buyer did not in fact affect cure and where reasonable costs of cure were awarded on the assumption that that amount would be used by the buyer to cure the non-conformity in the future; for the discussion of the recoverability of future losses, see ch 3.

[314] See *Castel Electronics Pty Ltd v Toshiba Singapore Pte Ltd* [2011] FCAFC 55, where the buyer was rightly awarded damages for the lost profit margin (arising from the overall decline in sales of the buyer's computers caused by the seller's delivery of defective graphic cards installed in those computers) and the cost of employing additional staff who dealt with customer complaints and rectified or attempted to rectify the defects.

[315] See Peel (n 2) 1014–15.

of defective racing cars, the court referred to the need of costs of repair being 'usual and appropriate for corrective actions performed by a specialist workshop'[316] and, in another case, the tribunal made clear that the costs of making defective coal usable had to be 'necessary'.[317] The cost of cure can be reasonable even where cure is affected and the cost of doing so is incurred before a lack of conformity manifests itself. In a case[318] where the installation of defective graphic cards, delivered by the seller, in the computers that the buyer sold to customers worldwide led the buyer to take preventive measures by repairing the graphic cards even in those computers that have not (yet) failed. Those measures were deemed reasonable because the failure of the graphic cards was entirely unpredictable, both in relation to which of them would fail and when they would fail.[319] The seller's argument that such preventive repairs should not be recoverable was rejected as 'unrealistic and unacceptable, especially considering that even [the seller] itself conducted such repairs'.[320]

The requirement that costs be directly related to curing the non-conformity has also emerged. In one CISG case,[321] non-conformity caused the buyer to 'double pass' the materials through the non-conforming equipment to ensure that a conforming product was manufactured. The buyer claimed damages for, as the court put it, additional 'variable overhead' costs and costs of labour incurred in executing the 'double passing'. To calculate these costs, the buyer took the annual depreciation and repair costs for its entire plant, computed an hourly overhead rate on that basis, and then applied that rate to the 'double passing' process. The court correctly denied such calculation on the basis that it was not 'accurate to attribute the same proportionate cost of repairs to [the equipment in question] as is attributable to [the buyer's] other machinery'.[322] It was also found to be inappropriate to apply the 'overall depreciation figure', determined with reference to the buyer's other machinery, to the equipment delivered by the seller.[323]

Some decisions reflect a concern that the costs of cure should not be excessive. In one case[324] involving the delivery of defective clothes, the costs of remedying the defects incurred by a German buyer were found to be in line with 'the average labor fee in Germany' and this conclusion was also confirmed by 'an audit report

[316] Case No 3 O 196/01 District Court Köln (Germany) 25 March 2003 (Racing carts), available at cisgw3.law.pace.edu/cases/030325g1.html.

[317] ICC No 8740, October 1996 (n 164).

[318] *Hewlett-Packard France v Matrox Graphics Inc*, 2020 QCCS 78.

[319] Ibid, [154].

[320] Ibid, [155].

[321] *Mansonville Plastics (BC) Ltd v Kurtz GmbH* 2003 BCSC 1298.

[322] Ibid.

[323] '[I]t does not seem appropriate to apply the same rate of depreciation to an old machine such as the continuous pre-expander as is applied to new equipment' (ibid).

[324] CIETAC 31 January 2000 (Clothes), available at cisgw3.law.pace.edu/cases/000131c1.html. See also District Court Köln 25 March 2003 (n 316) where the expert's view of the reasonableness of the costs was accepted by the court.

issued by an independent auditor'. In another case, the importance of maintaining the proportion between the cost of cure, on the one hand, and the contract price and the benefit to be received from cure, on the other, is also expressly emphasised.[325] Finally, if cure results in bringing the goods into a better state than that in which they would have been had they been conforming,[326] this level of improvement must be taken into account to reduce damages. This follows both from the compensatory purpose of damages[327] and the 'concrete' approach to calculation.

3.3.3. Difference in Value

Damages for the delivery of non-conforming goods can also be measured by the difference between the value of non-conforming goods actually delivered and the value of conforming goods that ought to have been delivered under contract (the 'difference' formula). As noted, this 'difference' formula can be seen as a primary vehicle for implementing the 'abstract' approach to damages. Although it has been argued that it is the 'concrete' approach that is generally favoured by the international instruments,[328] the 'difference' formula can still be applied where neither of the first two methods is applicable.[329] This may be the case, for example, where the buyer is unable to prove its lost profits *and* where the goods are incapable of cure. Like the 'cost of cure' measure, the 'difference' formula compensates not for loss of profit but for the reduction in the value of the goods.[330] Because this compensation can be said to restore, in monetary terms, the injured party to the position of having conforming goods and because the value of an asset generally takes account of future profits to be made from that asset, awarding loss of profit in addition to damages under this 'difference'

[325] See Case No 7 Ob 301/01t Supreme Court (Austria) 14 January 2002 (Cooling system), available at cisgw3.law.pace.edu/cases/020114a3.html (see particularly the decision of the court of the second instance). For a well-known English contract law case dealing, among others, with the question of maintaining a proportion between the cost of cure and the contract price and the benefit to be received from cure, see *Ruxley Electronics and Construction Ltd v Forsyth* [1996] AC 344 (HL).

[326] See Waddams (n 82) 129–32.

[327] See art 7.4.2(1) UPICC, which requires 'any gain to the aggrieved party resulting from its avoidance of cost or harm' to be taken into account.

[328] See Case No 6 R 160/05z Appellate Court Linz (Austria) 23 January 2006 (Auto), available at cisgw3.law.pace.edu/cases/060123a3.html, where the decision implies that the 'abstract' measure in cases of non-conforming goods is available as of right under the CISG ('In cases where the contract is upheld and the seller delivers defective goods, the buyer is entitled to claim the reduction in value as a non-performance loss. The reduction in value is formed by the difference between the value of the goods in a condition that would conform to the contract and the actual value of the delivered defective goods' (with reference to commentators)).

[329] This is not to say that the 'cost of cure' measure cannot be used as a means of taking the 'abstract' approach because the essence of the 'abstract' approach is simply to rely on a fixed formula 'in the abstract' with little regard to the claimant's actual circumstances. The 'cost of cure' measure can be used as such a formula in the same way as the 'difference' formula.

[330] As noted, the 'cost of cure' measure is sometimes viewed as a specific means of determining the difference between the value of conforming goods and those actually delivered (see ICC No 8740, October 1996 (n 164)).

formula constitutes a double recovery.[331] However, if a claim for loss of profit is confined to a particular period which does not cover the entire working life of goods,[332] damages under the 'difference' formula can be awarded for the period for which lost profits are *not* claimed.[333] In such a case, when applying the 'difference' formula, the depreciation of the goods needs to be taken into account.[334]

The 'difference' formula requires determining the value of both conforming and non-conforming goods and it is likely that in most cases it is the market price which provides a reference point. Difficulties arise where there is no relevant market price, particularly in the case of non-conforming goods.[335] As noted, in such cases the price the buyer obtained from reselling non-conforming goods may provide an indication of their value. It has also been suggested above that costs of cure can evidence the difference between the value of conforming goods and the value of non-conforming goods. Where this has not been possible, the tribunals have simply awarded a price allowance usually based on a rate which seemed reasonable to them in the circumstances.[336]

The question of what point in time is relevant for determining these two values remains unresolved. It has been suggested that if an analogy is drawn with the instruments' abstract formula, such as that in arts 76 CISG, 7.4.6 UPICC and 9:507 PECL, which refers to the 'current price' at the time of avoidance/termination,[337] the time of breach is irrelevant.[338] It has also been argued

[331] See, eg, Waddams (n 82) 82–83; RL Dunn, *Recovery of Damages for Lost Profits*, 6th edn (Alameda CA, Lawpress, 2006) 566; KM Kolaski and M Kuga, 'Measuring Commercial Damages via Lost Profits or Loss of Business Value: Are these Measures Redundant or Distinguishable?' (1998–1999) 18 *J L Commerce* 1.

[332] In principle damages can be claimed for the entire working life of the goods. However, this is not always possible. For example, in one CISG case where damages (albeit not lost profits) were calculated with reference to the entire working life, the court stated that although the equipment 'may have a 20-year life span, it does not necessarily follow that [the buyer] will keep using it for the full 20-year period. It could become functionally obsolete or uneconomic in a shorter period, much in the same fashion as personal computers become obsolete even though they are still able to perform to their initial specifications. There are numerous other contingencies which may cause [the buyer] to cease operating the equipment prior to 2017' (*Mansonville Plastics (BC) Ltd v Kurtz GmbH* (n 321).

[333] This was the claim brought in the English case *Cullinane v British 'Rema' Manufacturing Co Ltd.* [1954] 1 QB 292, which was not upheld by the court. For the discussion of this widely criticised case, see McKendrick (n 117) [14.47]–[14.49].

[334] See the text accompanying notes 321–322.

[335] See n 305.

[336] See CIETAC 29 May 1996 (Handicrafts), available at cisgw3.law.pace.edu/cases/960529c1.html; CIETAC 8 August 1996 (Diaper machine), available at cisgw3.law.pace.edu/cases/960808c1.html (although it is not entirely clear, the tribunal may have relied upon the remedy of the reduction of the price); CIETAC 5 July 1993 (Copperised steel tubes), available at cisgw3.law.pace.edu/cases/930705c1.html. The same approach is reported to have been taken in the context of English sales law, see Bridge (n 44) [12.120] ('Experienced trade umpires will often award a price allowance, though the method of calculation is not commonly stated.').

[337] This is subject to the special case under the CISG, where the goods have been taken over, at the time of such taking over (see art 76(1)).

[338] See S Eiselen, 'Remarks on the Manner in which the UNIDROIT Principles of International Commercial Contracts May Be Used to Interpret or Supplement Article 74 of the CISG', available at www.cisg.law.pace.edu/cisg/principles/uni74.html.

that '[t]he further forward the moment for determination is extended, the more accurately the exact extent of the foreseeable damages may be determined'.[339] For these reasons, either the time the action is lodged or the time of judgment have been suggested as the more appropriate points in time and of the two, it is the time of judgment that is usually preferred.[340] It is submitted, however, that there are stronger arguments in favour of earlier points in time, such as the time of delivery, the time when the buyer takes over the goods or when the buyer discovers or ought to discover a lack of conformity. First, calculating damages with reference to either of these points in time creates greater certainty because the amount of damages can then be determined long before the legal proceedings, whereas the time of judgment is an uncertain date in the future. Secondly, these times are closer to the time of the occurrence of the loss, which consists in having non-conforming goods on hand and that occurs when the goods are delivered to or are taken over by the buyer.

Thirdly, the suggested approach creates greater synergy with the mitigation rule. If the difference in value between conforming and non-conforming goods is determined with reference to abstract/hypothetical costs of cure,[341] such costs must be 'reasonable', as explained above. The reasonableness of those costs, in turn, should be determined in accordance with the time when a reasonable person in the buyer's position can be expected to cure. In most cases, the buyer can be expected to cure soon after the goods are delivered, taken over or after it ought to become aware of a lack of conformity. In those legal systems, which use this 'difference' formula, the date of delivery is sometimes justified on the basis that the buyer can immediately resell the goods on the market after that time.[342] The idea of mitigation is again built into this rationale. If this is how the 'difference' formula can also be rationalised, at least in part, under the international instruments, such rationale also supports an earlier date: where it is reasonable to expect the buyer to resell non-conforming goods and where the buyer has not done so or is unable to prove that it has done so, the date of delivery or the date when the buyer ought to become aware of a lack of conformity are generally appropriate points in time.

Finally, art 76 CISG envisages the possibility of relying on the current price at the time of the buyer taking over the goods to prevent the buyer's speculation by delaying avoidance in order to get a higher difference in damages. A date of judgment can similarly induce the buyer to speculate on the market by delaying or protracting legal proceedings to push the calculation date further. Art 76 CISG arguably reflects the Convention's concern about the innocent party's speculation and, if so, one of the earlier mentioned dates is preferable

[339] S Eiselen, 'Unresolved Damages Issues of the CISG: A Comparative Analysis' (2005) 38 *Comparative Int'l L J Southern Africa* 36.

[340] See ibid.

[341] See the paragraph in the main text accompanying nn 313 and 314 and n 330.

[342] See *Benjamin* (n 193) [17-053].

because of their ability to counter such speculation. Which of the suggested three dates is to be taken as a reference point must be decided based on what the mitigation rule dictates in the circumstances.

3.4. Non-Conforming Goods, the Meaning of 'Loss' and the 'Performance Interest'

The case of non-conforming goods may raise the difficult question regarding the *meaning* of loss. It has already been seen that the same question arises when a particular legal regime has to make a choice between the 'concrete' and 'abstract' methods of calculation. It seems, however, that in the case of non-conforming goods the problem of the meaning of 'loss' extends beyond the framework of the dilemma between the 'concrete' and 'abstract' approaches. The problem arises where, at first sight, the delivery of non-conforming goods does not appear to result in noticeable adverse financial consequences for the innocent party. A few examples can illustrate the problem.

One example (1) is where a company conscious of human rights buys goods from a seller under the contractual condition that no child labour will be used in manufacturing the goods and is prepared to pay twice the amount of the market price to ensure that the condition is complied with.[343] Suppose further that the seller breached the contract by employing children in manufacturing the goods but this does not change the tangible properties of the goods and the buyer can fulfil its business plans with no loss in profits. Another example (2) is where a professional photographer orders a car of a particular colour, paying extra to ensure compliance, but a car of a different colour is delivered.[344] Despite a breach, the market price of the car actually delivered is higher than that of the one ordered.

In these examples, although a breach of contract has clearly occurred, it is not immediately clear whether the buyers can be said to have suffered any loss and, if so, how that loss can be described and measured. It is submitted that the complexity of this problem cannot be fully revealed and adequately analysed from the perspective of the dilemma between the 'concrete' and 'abstract' approaches to calculation.[345] The inability of the 'abstract' approach (the difference between the (market) value of conforming and non-conforming goods) to rationalise the meaning of loss in such cases is demonstrated by its failure to produce consistent results: while there will be no damages in example 2, damages may be due in example 1 if there is a market price for both goods

[343] I Schwenzer and P Hachem, 'The Scope of the CISG Provisions on Damages' in Saidov and Cunnington (n 135) 94.

[344] Ibid.

[345] See also ch 3.

manufactured with and without child labour.[346] The 'concrete' approach, in turn, will only lead to the recoverability of such losses if, in the first place, the law is prepared to award damages based on the 'subjective value' the party has placed on the performance (non-economic interest). Thus, although the role of the performance interest in calculating damages is connected with the choice between the 'abstract' and 'concrete' approaches (for they can still be used to help place an appropriate monetary value),[347] it is nevertheless an independent issue requiring separate treatment.[348]

As suggested earlier,[349] the cases where damage to the performance interest can potentially be a recoverable head of loss include those where a party places a subjective or non-economic value on the performance. In calculating damages for this loss the emphasis is placed not so much on the economic consequences of the breach as on the subject-matter of the bargain, the innocent party's right to performance and the other party's duty to perform:[350] the innocent party did not receive the performance to which it was entitled and, in such cases, 'the scope of losses to be compensated has to reflect the very purpose of the duty that has been breached'.[351] The difficulties of proving and measuring such losses are not insurmountable. One way to prove and place a monetary value on this loss is for a court or tribunal to 'ask itself, hypothetically, if the parties had agreed on a liquidated damages clause, whether … it would have included compensation for non-pecuniary benefits'.[352] If so, the amount stipulated by such a hypothetical clause can provide an estimate of the loss. It can also be argued that because the buyers in both examples paid an additional price to ensure compliance with the contractual terms, calculating damages with reference to that additional price is a sound measure because it reflects precisely the value the injured party placed on the performance. In example 1, it may also be possible to calculate damages with reference to the relevant market because there may be different market prices for goods manufactured with and without child labour.[353] In example 2, losses can also be calculated on the 'cost of cure' basis (corrective paintwork) and such a measure can be both 'concrete' (if the works have *actually* been done) and 'abstract' (with reference to costs which are reasonable to carry out

[346] *Cf* C Hawes, 'Damages for Defective Goods' (2005) 121 *LQR* 389. For further examples, see ch 3 and D Saidov and R Cunnington, 'Current Themes in the Law of Contract Damages: Introductory Remarks' in Saidov and Cunnington (n 135) 25–6.

[347] See below.

[348] See Saidov and Cunnington (n 346) 135.

[349] See ch 3.

[350] Schwenzer and Hachem (n 343).

[351] Ibid.

[352] A Ogus, 'The Economic Basis of Damages for Breach of Contract: Inducement and Expectation' in Saidov and Cunnington (n 135).

[353] 'Today there are … markets for products manufactured under inhumane conditions, as opposed to markets for products produced in compliance with basic human rights, or products that are fairly traded' (Schwenzer and Hachem (n 343)).

such works).[354] In some cases, damages can even be calculated, subject to the requirements proposed earlier,[355] with reference to gains made by the breaching party as a consequence of its breach. For instance, in example 1 damages may have to be calculated with reference to the savings made by the breaching manufacturer as a result of using child labour.[356]

4. DELAY IN DELIVERY

Where the seller delivers the goods late and the buyer accepts the delivery without avoiding the contract, there again arises the need to make a choice between the 'concrete' and 'abstract' measures.[357] This book has argued that the instruments' position is to rely on the 'concrete' measure first and *only* if this is not possible can the 'abstract' approach be taken.[358] What loss does the buyer suffer and how should this loss be measured? The answer depends on the purpose for which the buyer has bought the goods. If the buyer bought the goods for resale, then under the 'concrete' approach it is the profit margin (or a part thereof) that the buyer planned to receive on a sub-sale that the buyer might claim as damages. The delay in delivery may either prevent the sub-sale (because sub-buyers reject the late delivery) or force the buyer to sell the goods at a reduced price. It may, however, not be possible to establish loss of an *actual* profit margin because the buyer has not yet concluded a sub-sale contract or because it is impossible to link contract goods with any particular sub-sale contract since the buyer is a large trader involved in a regular sale of the goods. In such cases, the 'abstract' measure may be appropriate[359] and the relevant formula is the difference between the

[354] There may be little difference between the two as 'concrete' cost of cure measures can only be awarded if the costs incurred were reasonable.

[355] See chs 2 and 3.

[356] It is also important to note the other suggested case where, as chs 2 and 3 have argued, damage to the performance interest can in principle be recoverable: namely, where an innocent party's contractual right is a valuable asset or a breach results in a loss of or damage to a valuable asset. The suggested examples within this category include those where there is a breach of the contractual 'non-compete' and 'confidentiality' clauses (see chs 2 and 3)). It is suggested that in addition to the methods of calculation discussed in the main text, the performance interest damages can be calculated with reference to the amount which the innocent party or a reasonable party in its position would have hypothetically negotiated and agreed to accept for releasing the other party from its obligations (known as 'negotiating damages' in English law (see *Morris-Garner v One Step (Support) Ltd* [2018] UKSC 20)).

[357] Suppose the buyer still persuades its sub-buyers to buy the goods at the same price at which they would have bought the goods had the goods been delivered on time. Under the 'concrete' approach to calculation, the buyer has suffered no loss (assuming no additional expenses were incurred in reselling the goods at a later date than planned). On a falling market, however, the 'abstract' approach may allow damages for the difference between the value of the goods at the due date and their value at the actual date of delivery (for a good illustration, see *Sally Wertheim v Chicoutimi Pulp Company* [1911] AC 301).

[358] It is submitted that the mitigation rule should still set the ceiling for recovery.

[359] This approach is analogous to the instruments' position where the contract is avoided (see above). For potential complexities in determining the market price, see, in English law,

value of the goods at the due date and that at the actual delivery date. The value at both dates is usually determined with reference to the market price.[360] This formula does not compensate the buyer for lost profit and awards damages for the difference in value of the goods resulting from the breach.

If the buyer bought the goods to use them in its manufacturing business, a delay may cause the manufacture to remain idle resulting in loss of profits which would otherwise have been earned. Alternatively, it may force the buyer to hire a substitute piece of equipment for the period of delay and thereby incur additional costs. The buyer may attempt to mitigate its loss by using its current stock to fulfil its business plans.[361] However, it may be the case that although loss of profit may thus be avoided, the buyer will suffer additional losses such as costs incurred in purchasing additional goods to restore the balance in its stock or even lost profits or lost opportunity to profit suffered due to the inability to fulfil other (potential or actual) orders which it would have satisfied had there been no delay. The buyer may also have to pay its workforce while the production remains idle or its materials may get damaged during the period of delay.

It is evident that different losses may flow from a delay in delivery and the calculation of damages depends on what losses are claimed. An 'abstract' formula, discussed above,[362] is generally irrelevant in such cases since '[t]he complaint of the buyer is not that he acquired an asset whose realizable value was diminished through the delay – for he did not intend to realize it at the due delivery date – but that he has been deprived of the use of the asset for the period of the delay and has thereby suffered inconvenience and/or lost income or increased expenditure in procuring the temporary use of comparable goods'.[363] Finally, in cases of delay, the buyer may often make a cover purchase as a precautionary measure and the benefits received from the use of the goods bought as cover[364]

Galaxy Energy International Ltd v Murco Petroleum Ltd (MV 'Seacrown') [2013] EWHC 3720 (Comm), that concerned a delay in delivering fuel oil on FOB terms (ie, late shipment). Experts disagreed about how the market price was to be determined for the purpose of the comparison between value of the oil on the contractual shipment date and the actual shipment date: namely, whether, to determine the market price on a given day based on the Platt's quotation for that particular day, or some combination of prior and/or future quotations. The latter option was chosen because that was how trades in the market were priced and because, with Platt's itself not being a market but a 'market reference for contracting pricing' (at [32]), that option provided a more reliable, accurate and fairer approach (at [48]).

360 For the considerations relating to the definition of a market and relevant market prices, see above.

361 See ICC No 8740, October 1996 (n 164).

362 See the text accompanying nn 359 and 360.

363 McKendrick (n 117) [14.34].

364 If the buyer manages to find a replacement for the period of delay and earn profits therefrom, these profits will either reduce the amount of profits lost during the period of delay or may even nullify the claim for lost profit if the cover has been found for the *entire* period of delay and if at least the same amount of profits as that which would have been earned but for the breach has been generated.

or the resale of those goods[365] need to be taken into consideration in calculating damages.[366]

5. OTHER CASES: LOST PROFITS

It is important to highlight some other cases, not covered above, which mainly involve loss of profit. These cases include those where: the contract is avoided but where neither the 'concrete'[367] nor the 'abstract'[368] formulae provided for by the instruments can be used; *or* the instruments' 'concrete' formula cannot be applied but the injured party does not invoke the instruments' 'abstract' formula and instead relies on another 'concrete' method of calculation. The legal basis for this calculation should be the instruments' general provisions on damages.[369]

So far as the seller is concerned, it may be that neither of the instruments' two specific formulae can be used because supply exceeds demand for the goods (lost volume).[370] To determine the amount of lost profit ('net profit') where no production has yet taken place and no costs have yet been incurred, the manufacturing costs that would have been incurred to produce the goods (including the overheads which can be reasonably attributed to this contract) will have to be subtracted from the seller's sales price ('gross profit').[371] If the seller has, by the time of the breach, relied on the contract, its overall damages can be calculated by determining the amount of 'net profit', adding costs actually incurred in relying on the contract, all other losses suffered as a result of the breach[372] and subtracting the amount of benefits received as a result of the breach.[373]

[365] This will be the case where the buyer had made a profit from purchasing and subsequently reselling the goods bought as cover.

[366] See Schlechtriem (n 97).

[367] Articles 75 CISG, 7.4.5 UPICC, and 9:506 PECL.

[368] Articles 76 CISG, 7.4.6 UPICC, and 9:507 PECL.

[369] Articles 74 CISG, 7.4.2 UPICC, and 9:501 PECL.

[370] See, generally, ch 3.

[371] See CIETAC 26 October 1993 (Frozen beef), available at cisgw3.law.pace.edu/cases/931026c1.html (where the seller claimed the difference between the price and costs of manufacture but where this claim was rejected due to the lack of evidence; the tribunal simply awarded damages in the amount of 10% of the contract price). See also ICC No 9078, October 2001, available at www.unilex.info ('The damage to be compensated is calculated as the difference between the hypothetical financial situation of the damaged party as it would have been had the breach of contract not occurred, and the financial situation of the Claimant party as it actually resulted (Differenztheorie). In this calculation, which is necessarily of a hypothetical nature, the lost gross income must be determined, and from that gross income all the costs connected or necessary for generating such gross income must be deducted, irrespectively of the nature of such costs, whether direct costs (for merchandise and labour) or indirect costs (fixed costs, such as administration, direct depreciation or cost of use of machinery and equipment).'

[372] These may include costs incurred in attempting to mitigate losses or damages paid to a supplier of raw materials rejected after the buyer's breach.

[373] Such benefits may include the value of what the seller has on hand (eg, raw materials not used due to the stoppage of production and whatever the seller has produced) or money received by the seller where it sold what has been produced for scrap.

For example, suppose the contract price was £20,000 and the seller would have incurred £12,000 to produce the goods. At the time of the breach, the seller has spent only £9,000 (out of £12,000). Suppose further that after the breach the seller sold whatever had been produced as scrap for £3,000 at the same time having spent £1,000 to find a buyer. The seller's damages can be calculated as follows: £8,000 ('net profit': £20,000 – £12,000) + £9,000 (production costs incurred) – £3,000 (price received from the sale of scrap) + £1, 000 (cost of searching for a buyer) = £15,000.

If the seller acts as an intermediary who manages to persuade its supplier to keep the goods at no charge after the buyer's breach and incurs no additional costs, its damages, in a true lost volume situation, consist of the difference between the price in its contract with its supplier and the price in the contract with the buyer.[374] Where the seller acquires the goods from its supplier and then resells them to a customer who would have bought the goods even if no breach had occurred, the seller should be entitled to damages for the 'net' profit margin it would have received had the buyer performed the contract.[375] The mitigation rule may require a lost volume seller to take measures to reduce its loss by either selling the goods on hand as scrap or on some secondary market at a lower price. Where this is possible, benefits actually derived or which would have been received had the seller mitigated its loss from such a resale, ought to be taken into account. Specifically, damages need to be calculated by subtracting such benefits from the amount of net profit and adding any costs the seller has incurred (or would have incurred had it acted reasonably) to mitigate its loss.[376]

The two formulae provided for by the instruments may also be irrelevant to the injured buyer. In general, this is so where there is no reasonable possibility of finding a replacement and/or there exists no current price for the goods. This situation may arise where: demand for the goods exceeds supply (loss of volume); the goods are highly specialised or even unique;[377] or the buyer's sub-sale contract requires the delivery of self-same goods. Where the buyer-manufacturer finds itself in a lost volume situation, damages for lost profits are usually calculated as the difference between the costs of manufacturing the goods and related costs, on the one hand, and the price at which the finished

[374] This situation may have taken place in ICC No 10274, 1999 (n 52) ('The sole arbitrator noted that the claimant was able to reach an agreement with the producer K that K would keep the remaining 300 mt of feed product A at no cost for claimant. Claimant had claimed the lost profit under the contract, which amounted to the difference between the price at which it had purchased feed product A and its anticipated sales price to respondent and the sole arbitrator awarded this amount').

[375] 'Net' profit is to be determined by subtracting from the purchase price (gross profit) all costs the seller would have incurred to purchase the goods from its supplier and to deliver them to the buyer.

[376] For a more detailed example of calculating damages in case of a lost volume car dealer see, RJ Harris, 'A General Theory for Measuring Seller's Damages for Total Breach of Contract' (1961–1962) 60 *Michigan L Rev* 577, 602–5.

[377] As was the case in Case No A40-564/16-175-6Б Arbitration Court Moscow (Russia) 24 October 2016, available at ras.arbitr.ru (in Russian), where the goods were designed specifically for the buyer's needs and requirements.

product is sold, on the other. For example, in one CISG case in determining the amount of 'net' lost profits flowing from the loss of volume in sales of air conditioners, the court subtracted from the sales price costs necessary to earn that profit including manufacturing cost, average commission to be paid, commercial/financial costs and royalty payments which had to be made.[378]

Take now the cases where the goods are specialised, making it impossible both to make a cover transaction and find the current price for the goods, or where otherwise the buyer cannot be reasonably expected to enter into a replacement transaction[379] (and consequently the instruments' 'abstract' formula based on the current price is also arguably inapplicable).[380] In these cases, the calculation of the buyer's lost profits depends on whether the buyer intended to use them as a profit earning asset or to resell them. In the latter case, lost profits need to be determined based on the difference between the costs of acquisition and the (actual or estimated) resale price or based on the estimated profit margin.[381] The calculation in the former case can be more complex and require taking account of the following considerations: whether there was some other possibility for the buyer to mitigate its loss; number and content of actual and potential orders[382] for the products to be manufactured; the period for which lost profits are claimed;[383] costs that would have been incurred to manufacture the final product; losses, other than lost profits, suffered as a consequence of the breach;[384] and benefits received as a result of the breach. Where the buyer's sub-contract requires the delivery of the very same goods as those under the contract with the seller, the buyer is again deprived of a profit margin with no possibility of cover and lost profits are to be measured as the difference between the contract price and the price in the sub-sale contract.[385] Leaving aside the issue of why the buyer is not able to find a replacement, it is important to note that, in some cases, to calculate the difference between the contract price and the price in a sub-sale contract, it may be necessary to make adjustments to one of the prices to make the two comparable. In one CISG case,[386] to make the sub-sale

[378] *Delchi Carrier SpA v Rotorex Corp* (n 31) (fixed costs were incorrectly held to be irrecoverable (see also *Delchi Carrier SpA v Rotorex Corp* 71 F.3d 1024 [2nd Cir. 1995].

[379] See Arbitration Court Stavropol Region 16 November 2017 (n 55).

[380] See the main text accompanying n 289.

[381] See Arbitration Court Stavropol Region 16 November 2017 (n 55), where the court determined the buyer's profit margin to be 10% of the price of the contract goods on the basis that 10% was considered to be a usual profit margin in international trade.

[382] Proving prices in potential orders can be difficult and require relying on the predictions as to the future price movements for the product in question.

[383] In principle, it is possible to claim lost profits for the period of working life of an asset (see, eg, McKendrick (n 117) [14.24]).

[384] These losses may include liability to customers for non-delivery and/or costs incurred in attempting to mitigate losses.

[385] See CIETAC 17 October 1996 (n 79) (no reasonable opportunity to mitigate losses as the goods under the contract with the seller and the sub-sales contract were the same goods in terms of specifications and place of manufacture (Korea)).

[386] See CIETAC 14 March 1996 (Dried sweet potatoes), available at cisgw3.law.pace.edu/cases/960314c1.html.

CIF price comparable to the FOB contract price, the tribunal deducted costs of freight and insurance from the CIF price. In some CISG cases,[387] whilst recognising that the buyer failed to mitigate its loss by procuring a substitute tribunals nevertheless awarded what seemed to them a reasonable profit margin under a sub-sale. It is suggested that this approach can only be justifiable[388] if the loss of profit would still have occurred even if the buyer had reasonably concluded a replacement transaction.[389]

Finally, as shown, the instruments' 'concrete' formula expressly provides that the difference between the contract price and the price in the replacement transaction can be claimed *after* the contract is avoided. But the injured party can make a replacement transaction *before* avoiding the contract. Where so, the question is whether the injured party is precluded from claiming the difference between the contract price and the price in a substitute transaction. This claim cannot be based on the instruments' 'concrete' formula due to its express requirements. However, it is submitted that contrary to some CISG cases,[390] there is no reason why such a calculation cannot be based on the instruments' general provision on damages[391] and this is the position rightly taken in some other CISG cases.[392]

[387] See ICAC No 406/1998, 6 June 2000, available at cisgw3.law.pace.edu/cases/000606r1.html.

[388] The decision would have been less questionable if the tribunal had applied art 76 CISG and it is not clear why it had not done so.

[389] This may be because the delay, caused by the need to find and make a replacement transaction, (reasonably) led the buyer to reduce the price in its sub-sale contract.

[390] See *Frischaff Produktions GmbH v Guillem Export SL* Appellate Court Valencia (Spain) 31 March 2005, available at cisgw3.law.pace.edu/cases/050331s4.html.

[391] Articles 74 CISG, 7.4.2 UPICC and 9:501 PECL. For a similar view, see Schlechtriem (n 97).

[392] See ICC No 8574, September 1996 (Metal concentrate), available at cisgw3.law.pace.edu/cases/968574i1.html; CIETAC 8 April 1999 (New Zealand raw wool), available at cisgw3.law.pace.edu/cases/990408c1.html. This position is also taken by the CISG Advisory Council (CISG-AC) No. 6, 'Calculation of Damages under CISG Article 74', available at www.cisg.law.pace.edu/cisg/CISG-AC-op6.html (see Rule 8).

9

Calculation of Damages (Part II)

1. GENERAL

THE PREVIOUS CHAPTER examined the difference between the two approaches ('concrete' and 'abstract') to calculating damages and the methods of assessment of what might be regarded as 'typical' losses in international sales transactions. While continuing to address the issues of the calculation of damages, this chapter explores the challenges posed by some specific situations, such as those arising in the anticipatory breach cases and long-term contracts, and by certain types of loss (such as currency losses, loss of a chance and damage to business reputation/goodwill). The chapter will conclude by addressing the question of the currency in which damages are to be awarded.

2. ANTICIPATORY BREACH

2.1. General

Calculating damages where a party commits an anticipatory breach is usually perceived as a challenging area of the law of damages. One reason is that because an anticipatory breach occurs before the due date for performance, there is a wider range of dates with reference to which damages can be potentially calculated. Not only are the due date for performance and the date of the avoidance of the contract candidates for this role, but also the date when an anticipatory breach actually occurs (that is, the date when the innocent party becomes aware of the other party's inability or unwillingness to perform). The consequences of choosing one of these dates can be serious because the amount of damages can vary significantly depending on the chosen date. The instruments' 'concrete' and 'abstract' formulae refer to the time of the avoidance of the contract.[1] There is little doubt that these formulae are applicable to the anticipatory breach cases. As explained,[2] both formulae are in line, albeit to a different extent, with

[1] For the discussion of the relevance of the time of taking over in art 76(1) CISG to anticipatory breach cases, see note 5 below.

[2] See ch 8.

the 'duty' to mitigate which should equally apply to the anticipatory breach situations.[3] These formulae reflect (again, to a different extent) the conduct expected of the injured party, *regardless of* whether an anticipatory or an actual breach is committed.

2.2. Relevant Time for Calculating Damages and the Problem of Over-compensation

The instruments' formulae[4] generally calculate damages with reference to the time of avoidance[5] which, in the anticipatory breach context, often precedes the due date of performance and the amount of loss thus calculated can be higher than the loss calculated with reference to the due date for performance. For example, where on a falling market the buyer's damages are calculated either based on a replacement transaction concluded after avoiding the contract but before the due date or based on the current/market price at the time of avoidance, damages thus calculated will be higher than those calculated with reference to the later due date. This may be seen as unsatisfactory because, as a consequence of the anticipatory breach, the buyer is put in a better position than if the contract had been performed. For this reason, when it comes to the 'abstract' calculation, some legal systems generally prefer to calculate damages with reference to the due date of performance.[6]

In response, it can be argued that such a result is a price to be paid for the law's recognition of the anticipatory breach doctrine, which provides certainty and security to the innocent party who finds itself in an insecure position before the due date of performance. Bearing in mind that the law requires the party to mitigate its loss (which usually means making a replacement transaction before the due date for performance), it would be impossible to calculate damages with reference to both the date when the party ought to have mitigated and the due date for performance because these would normally be different dates. Put differently, since the law wants the innocent party *both* to be able to claim damages based on an anticipatory breach *and* to mitigate its loss, calculating

[3] For the explanation of why the mitigation rule is applicable in the anticipatory breach cases, see ch 6.

[4] See arts 75 and 76 CISG, 7.4.5 and 7.4.6 UPICC, 9:506 and 9:507 PECL.

[5] According to art 76(1) CISG, if the goods have been taken over, the current price is to be determined based on the date of such taking over. At first sight, this provision may appear to be relevant to the anticipatory breach cases. Potentially relevant situations are those involving instalment contracts where the receipt of non-conforming goods gives good grounds to conclude that a fundamental breach will occur with respect to the remaining instalments (see art 73(2) CISG). However, art 76(1) seems to imply that its 'abstract' formula applies precisely to those goods which were *actually taken over* and, in the case of instalment contracts, the goods in the remaining instalments have not yet been taken over and therefore the 'taking over' part of art 76(1) will not be relevant.

[6] See, eg, MG Bridge, *The Sale of Goods*, 4th edn (Oxford, OUP, 2019) [12.65]–[12.66].

damages with reference to the due date for performance is impossible. This becomes evident where, typically after avoidance, the party makes a replacement transaction in a reasonable manner and within a reasonable time (satisfying the mitigation rule) and invokes the instruments' 'concrete' formula; where so, the due date for performance is automatically excluded since it is the price in the replacement transaction that will be relied upon.[7] Thus, subject to the discussion below, it is almost inevitable that the concern for over-compensating the innocent party will be over-ridden by the mitigation rule.

The concern for over-compensation may nevertheless be partly alleviated by interpreting the instruments' 'concrete' and 'abstract' formulae in accordance with their underlying rationale. So far as the 'concrete' formula is concerned, a replacement transaction needs to be on similar terms to those in the original contract.[8] In the anticipatory breach cases, this means that the innocent party needs to make every reasonable attempt to find a replacement transaction for the delivery[9] at the date fixed in the original contract.[10] Similarly, the 'abstract' formula is based on the assumption that the party is in the position to make a hypothetical replacement transaction which should be based, if reasonably possible, on similar terms to those in the original contract. This should be interpreted to mean the price for delivering the goods at the date fixed by the original contract *current at the time of avoidance*.[11] Such prices can sometimes be determined at the relevant forward or futures markets. This approach derives, to a significant extent, from the view that the contract itself is a commercial asset[12] which, although to be performed in the future, has a present value. This point seems particularly relevant here since the view that the contract is a commercial asset with a present value can justify the anticipatory breach doctrine.[13] Thus, even though the price in a replacement transaction or the current price may often be determined on a date before the contractual date of performance, these prices, being for future delivery, are the market's best guess as to what the price for the goods will be at the contractual due date.[14] This, it is hoped, alleviates the concern that because the price at the due date is not relied upon, the party might be put in a better position than what it would have been had the contract been performed.[15]

[7] See arts 75 CISG, 7.4.5 UPICC, and 9:506 PECL.

[8] See ch 8.

[9] Seller's resale or buyer's re-purchase, as the case may be.

[10] See P Schlechtriem, 'Calculation of Damages in the Event of Anticipatory Breach under the CISG', available at www.cisg-online.ch/cisg/FS%20Hellner.pdf.

[11] See ibid.

[12] Ibid.

[13] See D Saidov, 'Anticipatory Non-Performance and Underlying Values of the UNIDROIT Principles' (2006) 11 *Uniform L Rev* 795, 798.

[14] It is widely recognised that a market price incorporates the available information about the future (see Bridge (n 6) ch 12 note 358; S Waddams, *The Law of Damages,* 4th edn (Toronto, Canada Law Book Inc, 2004) 70).

[15] But see further the main text accompanying nn 30 and 34.

2.3. The Application of the 'Concrete' and 'Abstract' Formulae

Calculating damages for an anticipatory breach should not then be much different from the case of an actual breach, except that, as argued earlier, in the anticipatory breach cases the right to damages should be pre-conditioned to the avoidance of the contract not least because avoidance crystallises the parties' legal positions.[16] So, if an innocent party has sufficient grounds to suspect that the other party will commit a fundamental breach,[17] it can avoid the contract make a replacement transaction and claim the difference between the contract price and the price in the replacement transaction (the instruments' 'concrete' formula).[18] The requirement that a replacement transaction be made within a reasonable time after avoidance is integrally linked to the mitigation rule. This means that a contract needs to be avoided[19] and a replacement transaction must be made at the point in time that would lead to the lowest amount of damages. The buyer needs to avoid and re-purchase when the price is at its lowest and the seller needs to avoid and resell when the price is at its highest. In every case, the mitigation rule requires the innocent party to address two questions: (1) Should it avoid the contract and make a replacement transaction within a reasonable time after it becomes aware of the anticipatory breach?; or (2) Should it wait and observe the price movements before avoiding the contract and making a replacement transaction? This is a difficult position for the innocent party to be in as it has to predict the future price movements and calculate costs resulting from two alternative courses of action.

It is sometimes argued that because of the uncertainty inherent in market price movements, it can never be unreasonable for the innocent party to fail to predict the market price[20] and because the market price already factors into itself all available information, there can be 'no room for inquiring whether, in market conditions, the buyer's repurchase is reasonable'.[21] Under this approach, if immediately after anticipatory breach the buyer avoids the contract and makes a replacement transaction while the market was falling, the buyer should nevertheless be awarded a higher price difference, resulting from this replacement, than the one that would have resulted had it made a replacement later. This result is justified on two grounds. First, it introduces symmetry, for if the market had risen the seller would have been spared the higher amount of damages.[22]

[16] Otherwise, there is still a possibility that the contract may be performed at the due date. For further reasons, see ch 2 and D Saidov, 'Arts 71–73' in S Kröll, L Mistelis and P Viscasillas (eds), *The United Nations Convention on Contracts for the International Sale of Goods*, 2nd edn (München, CH Beck and Oxford, Hart, 2018) 933.

[17] See arts 72 CISG, 7.3.3 UPICC and 9:304 PECL.

[18] See *Downs Investments Pty Ltd v Perwaja Steel SDN BHD* [2000] QSC 421; Case No 99 O 123/92 District Court Berlin (Germany) 30 September 1992 (Shoes), available at cisgw3.law.pace.edu/cases/920930g1.html; Case No 11 O 210/92 District Court Krefeld (Germany) 28 April 1993 (Shoes), available at cisgw3.law.pace.edu/cases/930428g1.html.

[19] See further Saidov (n 16) 933.

[20] Waddams (n 14).

[21] Bridge (n 6) ch 12 note 358.

[22] See ibid, [12.66].

Second, the higher cost of an early replacement can be treated as a cost resulting from mitigation.[23] These arguments are attractive but they leave open the question of what should happen to the mitigation rule. Some, for example, take a somewhat extreme view by preferring to calculate damages with reference to the 'due date of performance' at the expense of virtually ignoring the mitigation rule.[24]

Indeed, it is often unrealistic to expect the innocent party to predict the price movements either because the market is highly fluctuating or because the contractual delivery date is too far in the future. In such cases, avoiding the contract shortly after anticipatory breach and making a replacement transaction soon after should be a reasonable mitigation measure and damages can be calculated 'concretely' with reference to that transaction. But there may still be situations where a party is in a position to make reasonable predictions about the likely market movements. It may well be that an experienced and well-informed buyer is in the position to expect, with a high degree of likelihood, either a rise[25] or fall in the market price.[26] This buyer may also be in the position to estimate the costs (eg, storage costs) it will incur if it buys the goods long before the due date. If so, the mitigation rule should, in principle, require the buyer to wait in order to buy the goods when the price falls and to reduce further costs. Such cases will be rare and given the difficulty of predicting future price movements it is *usually* reasonable for the innocent party to find a replacement transaction shortly after anticipatory breach.[27] A difficulty, faced by a court/tribunal, of determining whether the innocent party was in the position to reasonably predict the market movement may be partly alleviated by the fact that it is usually the breaching party who bears the initial burden of proving the innocent party's failure to mitigate.[28] If the breaching party fails to meet its burden of proof, damages can be assessed on the basis that the innocent party has acted reasonably.

Similar considerations apply to the instruments' 'abstract' formula which refers to the current price at the time of the avoidance of the contract. As explained, this provision should, in the first instance, be interpreted as referring to the price for future delivery at the date/period fixed by the original contract,

[23] Ibid; Waddams (n 14).

[24] Waddams (n 14).

[25] For example, it may be clear to an experienced trader that, due to bad weather conditions in a number of main tomato-producing countries and the resulting shortage of supply, the market price of tomatoes will be rising.

[26] For a similar view, see Schlechtriem (n 10) ('where performance is due in the future, the uncertainty of price developments in cases of anticipatory breach must be considered: the more certain price increases are, with the consequence that cover transactions should be undertaken promptly, the sooner a buyer aggrieved by the seller's anticipatory breach will be expected to avoid and cover').

[27] '[A] cover transaction should be allowed right (i.e. within a "reasonable" period) after avoidance, even if it subsequently turns out that waiting would have paid. Of course, in wildly fluctuating markets, the aggrieved party should not cover in the spot market at peak prices – but this advice is only to be followed if there is some likelihood of prices going down again' (ibid).

[28] See ch 6.

but current at the time of avoidance.[29] However, if no such prices can be found (eg, because there are no relevant forward or futures markets),[30] there is no reason why the current price at the time of avoidance,[31] for immediate delivery or for the delivery at some other date before the contractual delivery date, cannot be relied upon. The terms of a hypothetical replacement transaction need not be identical in all respects to the original contract.[32] It has also been argued[33] that where prices at the delivery date, fixed in the original contract, are forecasted to be higher than current prices, it is justifiable in the light of the mitigation rule, say, for the innocent buyer to avoid the contract at once and rely on the current price for immediate delivery at the time of avoidance.[34]

Where there is no price, available at the time of avoidance, for future delivery at the contractual due date,[35] there may be a risk that the instruments' 'abstract' formula would over- or under-compensate the innocent party. The price current at the time of avoidance may turn out to be lower or higher than the price at the due date of delivery, with the result that the difference between the two will put the innocent buyer into, respectively, a better or worse financial position than that in which it would have been had the contract been performed.[36] But a conclusion as to whether the party has in fact been over- or under-compensated can only be reached if court/arbitral proceedings and the assessment of damages

[29] This seems to have been the case in CIETAC 29 March 1996 (Caffeine), available at cisgw3.law.pace.edu/cases/960329cl.html, where damages were calculated with reference to the price current at the time when the goods were to be delivered.

[30] Forward markets will be relevant if the buyer bought goods for use while futures markets may be appropriate if the buyer bought the goods for the purpose of speculation (Waddams (n 14) 72).

[31] 'This follows the text of Article 76 as well as the rationale that the market price need not reflect all the terms of the avoided contract' (CISG Advisory Council (CISG-AC) Opinion No. 8, 'Calculation of Damages under CISG Articles 75 and 76', available at www.cisgac.com/file/repository/CISG_AC_Opinion_8_English.pdf, Comment 4.4.3).

[32] See ch 8; Schlechtriem (n 10).

[33] See Schlechtriem (n 10).

[34] The possible link between the avoidance of the contract and the mitigation rule needs to be borne in mind. The mitigation rule (or in any case, the instruments' general principle of reasonableness) should arguably dictate when the contract ought to have been avoided for the purpose of damages. It appears that in one CISG case the date when the contract was actually avoided (January or July 1994) was not significant because 'the current price for tomato concentrate from southern France was continuously *FF* 6.10/tin higher than as stipulated with the seller up to and including July 1994'. Although the mitigation rule is not expressly addressed, this holding nevertheless seems to reflect the court's implicit recognition of the rule and its connection with the avoidance of the contract. Damages were awarded under art 76 CISG (Case No: 1 U 143/95 and 410 O 21/95 Appellate Court Hamburg (Germany) 4 July 1997 (Tomato concentrate), available at cisgw3.law.pace.edu/cases/970704g1.html).

[35] As noted, the reliance on this price, on the market's best guess as to the prices at the date fixed by the contract, approximates, as much as possible, a hypothetical replacement at the time of avoidance to a hypothetical transaction had the assessment actually been made at the due date under the original contract.

[36] It has been suggested that there is nothing wrong with the innocent party being under-compensated as this is the risk the party takes when it claims damages under the 'abstract' formula at the time of avoidance and that the problem to be dealt with is the risk of over-compensating the party (Schlechtriem (n 10)). This view is, of course, open to criticism that it is based on an 'asymmetrical' treatment of the innocent party's position.

take place at or after the due date of performance. If the proceedings and the assessment of damages take place *before* the due date, there is no other choice but to award damages with reference to the current price at the time of avoidance (for immediate delivery or delivery at some other time before the due date), subject arguably to the time of avoidance being in line with the mitigation rule (or, in any case, with the reasonableness criterion flowing from the instruments' general principle of reasonableness).[37]

The problem of over- or under- compensation is relevant only where the proceedings and the assessment of damages take place *after* the due date when the prices at the due date become known. Where so, should the innocent party be entitled to damages based on the current price at the time of avoidance, even if they result in over-compensation? 'Yes' is the suggested answer.[38] This position provides legal certainty by staying true to the instruments' 'abstract' formula based on the current price at the time of the avoidance of the contract. It also provides security to the innocent party who is safe in the knowledge that: if after learning about an anticipatory breach it avoids the contract in line with the reasonableness criterion,[39] it will be entitled to damages under the 'abstract' formula; and no subsequently acquired knowledge will interfere in the assessment of damages. This position is also in line with the mitigation rule in the sense that the reasonableness criterion is evaluated not with the benefit of hindsight but based on what was reasonable at the relevant time, namely, after the innocent party learnt about the anticipatory breach.

The international instruments should not be interpreted as requiring the innocent party to necessarily resort to the 'concrete' or 'abstract' formulae, *expressly* provided for in the instruments.[40] There is no reason why the innocent party cannot choose to rely on other methods of calculation. The instruments' formulae may also be inapplicable even where the contract is avoided, such as where a replacement transaction, actual and hypothetical, is not possible. In one CISG case where the buyer avoided the contract before the due date for delivery but after it had become clear that the seller would not be able to provide a timely delivery of seasonal goods, the buyer was awarded damages for the lost profit it would have received from selling the goods at its retail store. The tribunal specifically stated that a replacement transaction was not possible as the goods needed to be ordered at least three to four months in advance to meet delivery deadlines and 'since the seller's anticipatory breach was on 29 March and the buyer required delivery for 5–7 April to meet the peak sale time …, the buyer would not have sufficient time to purchase replacement goods'.[41]

[37] See n 34.

[38] A different position is taken in this edition of this book, compared to that in the first edition.

[39] Flowing, as suggested, from the mitigation rule or, in any case, the instruments' general principle of reasonableness.

[40] That is, arts 75 and 76 CISG, 7.4.5 and 7.4.6 UPICC, 9:506 and 9:507 PECL.

[41] ICC No 8786, January 1997, available at cisgw3.law.pace.edu/cases/978786i1.html. In another case (Case No HG 95 0347 Commercial Court Zurich (Switzerland) 5 February 1997 (Sunflower oil), available at cisgw3.law.pace.edu/cases/970205s1.html), similar damages were awarded without any

Another challenging area is where, before the due date for performance, it becomes clear to the seller, who has not completed the manufacture of the goods, that the buyer will not perform the contract. What is the seller to do and how should damages be assessed? Although, in contrast with some legal systems,[42] the instruments do not contain a specific provision to this effect, it is suggested that the calculation of damages should depend on the mitigation rule. It may or may not be reasonable to complete the manufacture and damages need to be quantified based on what is reasonable in the circumstances. Reasonableness is to be judged not with the benefit of hindsight but according to the circumstances in which the seller found itself at the time of the anticipatory breach.[43] While there can be no hard and fast solution to this problem, it may be helpful to give a simple illustration.

Suppose that at the time of an anticipatory breach, the seller has only spent £2,000 as it had just begun to manufacture a piece of machinery for which the buyer agreed to pay £50,000. The costs of manufacture are £40,000. Knowing that a resale of the machinery will bring not more than £35,000, the seller nevertheless completes the manufacture, resells for £33,000 and claims £17,000 in damages. The seller's conduct is arguably unreasonable because it knew that if it completed the manufacture its loss would be in the range of £15,000 (£50,000 – £35,000), which is a higher amount than the loss it would have suffered if it had discontinued the manufacture (£12,000 (£10,000 + £2,000)).[44] If, however, the seller knew, at the time of the anticipatory breach, that it would be able to sell this machinery for £45,000, it is reasonable to complete the manufacture as damages thus calculated (£7,000 (£50,000 – £45,000 + £2,000)) are lower than the losses that would have been suffered had it stopped the manufacture. It will be incumbent on the seller to exercise care in making predictions about the current and future market prices and this is why it has been recommended that 'the lawyer and client should preserve evidence which formed the basis for the decision and document by letter or contemporaneous memoranda when and why the decision to complete or not to complete was made'.[45] It also follows from these examples that the main criterion for determining the reasonableness

inquiry into whether the innocent buyer could have reasonably made a replacement contract and it is clear that, in the light of the mitigation rule, this is not the correct approach. The award of these damages would only have been justifiable if there had been no reasonable opportunity to mitigate.

[42] § 2-704(2) UCC: 'Where the goods are unfinished an aggrieved seller may in the exercise of reasonable commercial judgment for the purposes of avoiding loss and of effective realization either complete the manufacture and wholly identify the goods to the contract or cease manufacture and resell for scrap or salvage value or proceed in any other reasonable manner.'

[43] For the same view, see JJ White and RS Summers, *Uniform Commercial Code*, 5th edn (St Paul, Minn, West Publishing Co, 2000) 296.

[44] Of course, any benefits received as a result of the breach must be taken into account. These benefits can include money received from selling whatever the seller manufactured by the time of the anticipatory breach as scrap. The seller may also channel its resources, initially allocated to the contract, in some other direction and any benefits thus received will have to be taken into consideration so long as they would not have been received had the buyer performed the contract.

[45] White and Summers (n 43) 297.

of a decision is the comparison between the amount of losses to be suffered if the manufacture is completed and those that will arise if the manufacture is discontinued – if the latter is a higher amount, the seller should generally complete the manufacture.[46]

Making a decision as to what is a reasonable course of action may be complicated by other factors and in some cases a decision to complete the manufacture may be reasonable despite the higher amount of resulting losses. This may be the case where the seller cannot afford to discontinue the manufacture because it might lose many skilled employees and some of them might even find jobs with the seller's competitors.[47] The nature of the materials used to manufacture contract goods can also be a factor relevant to determining a reasonable course of action for the seller to take. One CISG case,[48] albeit not involving anticipatory breach, provides a relevant example. The seller, an exporter of plastic products, agreed to manufacture and supply the buyer with cushions. After the buyer had failed to pay at the due date,[49] the seller continued the production and the tribunal held that doing so was unreasonable on the ground that the materials used in the production of contract goods were not specialised[50] and could have been put to some other valuable use. The tribunal stated that the seller had increased its own loss, which could have been prevented if the seller had stopped the production and used the production materials for some other valuable purpose.

3. LONG-TERM CONTRACTS

3.1. General

If the basis for claiming damages is a breach of a long-term contract, the calculation of damages may be complicated by various factors stemming from the nature of such contracts.[51] Because the performance of these contracts takes place over a long period of time, some important terms, such as the price or quantity of the goods, are unlikely to be definitively fixed for the entire duration of the contract. Calculating damages may be further complicated by some other contingencies, such as a party's right to avoid the contract upon the occurrence

[46] See ibid.

[47] See ibid.

[48] CIETAC 29 September 2000 (Cushion), available at cisgw3.law.pace.edu/cases/000929c1.html.

[49] The case is relevant here as the seller could have found itself in the same position as the one that arose in this case had the buyer committed an anticipatory breach.

[50] 'The PVC materials are not specially manufactured for the [contract] goods, but are generally used for the same kind of products.'

[51] For a recent examination of long-term gas sales agreements, see M Hammerson and E Richardson, 'Long-Term Gas Sales Agreements' in D Saidov (ed), *Research Handbook on International and Comparative Law Sale of Goods Law* (Cheltenham, Edward Elgar, 2019).

of a particular event or certain conditions,[52] which may require making predictions as to the likelihood of the occurrence of such events or of the exercise of the contractual right to avoid. The question may also arise whether an actual occurrence of the event is relevant to quantifying damages if the contract is avoided before the event but legal proceedings take place thereafter. Another problem is where a party is given an option, say, to buy or sell a particular quantity at a fixed price and a breach of contract leads to the loss of that option. Yet another difficulty stems from the need to project losses into the future and determine their present value. These examples are by no means exhaustive and this section addresses only some problems arising from the uncertainty inherent in long-term contracts.

3.2. Uncertain Price

Contracts may contain a rather uncertain mechanism for determining the price and arbitrators have been prepared to predict what the contract price would have been had the contract been performed.[53] In doing so, they have drawn assumptions about the parties' future conduct and taken into account events occurring subsequent to the conclusion of the contract. In one CISG case, involving two long-term contracts for the supply of raw aluminium,[54] the tribunal had to determine the contract prices for the remaining eight-year period. The contract provided that the parties were to fix the price 'every three months' on the basis of 'the competitive world market price'. The buyer argued that because the seller had sold the goods at preferential price levels in the past, the price for the remaining contract period should be fixed on the same preferential basis. This argument was rejected on several grounds.

First, the contract expressly referred to 'competitive market prices'. Second, the ownership and directorate of the seller had changed shortly before the seller breached the contract and the tribunal stated that it could be 'safely assumed that the new owners and the new directorate … would have requested the seller's management (sooner rather than later) to raise their export prices to the agreed "competitive world market" level during the next or following price negotiation rounds'. Third, 'the seller was created to accumulate hard currency trading profit outside Russia [and] [if the] seller wanted to make such hard currency trading profit in the future, this inevitably would have eroded [the] buyer's "preferential pricing" margin'. Finally, the seller was to receive a commission which would, at least in part, have been charged to the buyer. For these reasons, the

[52] See, eg, *British Gas Trading Ltd v Amerada Hess Ltd* [2006] EWCA Civ 900 (a depletion contract gave the seller the right to terminate if it became 'uneconomic' to continue production).

[53] For the instruments' provisions on price determination, see arts 55 CISG, 5.1.7 UPICC, 6:104–6:107 PECL.

[54] *Soinco v NKAP* Zurich Arbitration (Switzerland) 31 May 1996, available at cisgw3.law.pace.edu/cases/960531s1.html.

price was fixed at 'world price' levels determined with reference to those listed at the London Metal Exchange and adjusted to the terms of the contract.[55]

3.3. Uncertain Quantity

Contracts often fix the maximum and/or minimum quantities that can be delivered at the seller's or buyer's option. Where it is not possible to determine whether and how this option would have been exercised, a presumption can be raised that the party would have exercised this option in the way least burdensome or most beneficial to it. For example, where the buyer has the option of selecting the quantity within the specified range, a court/tribunal may decide that on a rising market the buyer would have ordered the maximum quantity. But if the buyer suffers from financial difficulties and/or the market price has been falling, a court/tribunal may hold that the buyer would have bought the minimum quantity. It should then be up to the innocent party to bring evidence to the contrary to rebut the presumption.[56]

Where no maximum or minimum quantities are fixed and where the seller agrees to sell any quantity ordered by the buyer or the buyer agrees to buy any quantity delivered by the seller (output contract), the innocent parties take a risk that the instruments' 'abstract' and 'concrete' formulae might not be applicable.[57] Suppose that the contract made in May 2018 provides that the farmer will sell its entire harvest in May 2020 to the buyer. It may be impossible for this farmer to find a replacement contract because the amount of harvest in May 2020 will not be known at the time of avoidance (say, August 2018) or within a reasonable time thereafter. Therefore, the instruments' 'concrete' formula is unlikely to be applicable unless the farmer manages to procure a similar (forward) output contract. For the same reason, the instruments' 'abstract' formula may be inapplicable unless there exists a current price for output contracts on similar terms. Subject to the mitigation rule, the farmer may be able to calculate its loss with reference to a lost profit margin based, say, on its previous activities or, if lost profits are too speculative, for loss of a chance to profit.[58]

3.4. Contractual Rights and Options

Besides providing for an option to deliver or order a specified quantity of goods, contracts may also confer other rights or options. The question whether

[55] '[T]o reflect transportation and other costs free Hungarian border' (ibid).
[56] For a more detailed discussion, see ch 8.
[57] See Schlechtriem (n 10).
[58] Under the UPICC, there is a possibility of damages being awarded on the basis of judicial discretion (see art 7.4.3(3) UPICC and ch 7).

a particular right would have been exercised in a hypothetical past or future is important to assessing damages. Two specific situations are addressed in this section. The first situation is where the contract provides that upon the occurrence of a particular event, one or both parties have the right to avoid the contract. Suppose that a seven-year textile supply contract provides that if the seller's country adopts the legislation requiring domestic exporters to sell hard currency, obtained from export transactions, to the state in exchange for a (weak) domestic currency, the seller can avoid the contract. If the buyer breaches the contract one year after it was concluded with the proceedings taking place shortly thereafter, how should the seller's damages be assessed? Subject to the rules of foreseeability and mitigation, can the seller claim profits for the remaining six-year period assuming that no such legislation would be adopted?

One answer is to postpone the assessment of damages until a later date if the applicable procedural rules so permit.[59] But if so, the seller will have to wait six years before there is any certainty regarding the amount of damages to which it is entitled. Assuming this solution is inapplicable or undesirable, the purpose of putting the party in the position in which it would have been had the contract been performed requires the probability of the occurrence of the relevant events to be incorporated into the calculation of damages. This would require the determination of the degree of likelihood of such legislation being adopted, the point in time when such legislation might be adopted and the likelihood that the seller would have avoided the contract.

The situation is different where the assessment of damages takes place *after* the occurrence of the relevant event.[60] Suppose that, although the buyer breached the contract one year after it had been made, the proceedings and the assessment of damages take place three years after the conclusion of the contract, which was when the aforementioned legislation was introduced and entered into force. It is sometimes argued that in the interests of certainty, finality and consistency,[61] it is preferable to ignore the actual occurrence of such events. This position is also supported by the argument that if the subsequent events *are* taken into account, this would create an incentive for the breaching parties to delay a dispute resolution process[62] and discourage them from reaching a settlement[63] in the hope that subsequent events triggering the reduction of damages will occur.[64]

[59] For the discussion of this possibility in some legal systems, see, eg, Waddams (n 14); also Note, 'Damages for Loss of Prospective Crops' (1920–1921) 34 *Harv L Rev* 662, 664.

[60] For examples in English law, see *Bunge SA v Nidera BV* [2015] UKSC 43; *Golden Strait Corp v Nippon Yusen Kubishika Kaisha* [2007] 2 WLR 691.

[61] '[C]ertainty ("generally important in commercial affairs"), finality ("the alternative being a running assessment of the state of play so far as the likelihood of some interruption to the contract concerned"), … consistency ("the idea that a party's accrued rights can be changed by subsequent events is objectionable in principle") …)' (Lord Bingham of Cornhill in ibid, 703).

[62] Ibid.

[63] See, eg, E Peel, *Treitel on The Law of* Contract, 15th edn (London, Thomson–Sweet & Maxwell, 2020) 1167, footnote 517.

[64] For a critical discussion of *Golden Strait Corp v Nippon Yusen Kubishika Kaisha* (n 60), see, eg, GH Treitel, 'Assessment of Damages for Wrongful Repudiation' (2007) 123 *LQR* 9.

While these arguments have some force, it is submitted that the subsequently acquired knowledge of the actual events must be taken into account to implement the compensatory purpose of damages and place the party in the position in which it would have been had the contract been performed.[65] If, in our example, it is established that the seller would have avoided the contract as soon as the legislation was introduced, damages for the six-year period would put the seller in a better position than that in which it would have been had there been no breach because after three years the contract would have ceased to exist.[66] Damages are to be awarded only up to the point when the seller would have terminated the contract.

The second situation is where the contract contains an option permitting (but not requiring) the seller to sell the goods ('put option') and the buyer to purchase the goods ('call option') at a price fixed in the contract.[67] Suppose that a long-term contract stipulates a procedure by fixing a 'quotation period' during which the buyer can exercise an option to buy aluminium at the price of $50 per ton.[68] If this contract requires the parties to agree on a price with reference to the 'competitive world prices'[69] which at a particular time fall below $50, the buyer has no incentive to invoke the option since the parties' agreement on the price is likely to be in the range below $50. Where 'world prices' are above $50 and the parties' agreement would have led to a price higher than $50, the buyer would benefit from this option. Calculating damages under such a contract would have to incorporate the possibility of the buyer's exercising that option. If the assessment of damages takes place after the period when the option could be exercised, the actual market movements during that time can be established and it can be ascertained whether damages are due for the loss of the buyer's right to exercise the option.

The assessment of damages is more difficult where the relevant period is in the future. One way to approach this situation is to argue that it is only if the price is predicted to rise that the buyer will suffer loss. If the court/tribunal takes the view that at the relevant time, the prices will remain at the level below $50, no damages for loss of an option would be due. This approach has been criticised on the basis that it ignores the nature of an option which, like an insurance policy, guards against uncertain future events. It has been suggested that by denying damages, even where it is predicted that future prices will be lower than the price underlying an option, courts disregard 'the fact that when a

[65] 'Certainty is a desideratum and a very important one, particularly in commercial contracts. But it is not a principle and must give way to principle ... The achievement of certainty in relation to commercial contracts depends ... on firm and settled principles of the law of contract rather than on the tailoring of principle in order to frustrate tactics of delay to which many litigants in many areas of litigation are wont to resort' (Lord Scott of Foscote in ibid, 709).

[66] In English law, see *Bunge SA v Nidera BV* (n 60).

[67] For a detailed discussion, see E Yang, 'Assessment of Damages for Breach of an Option' [2004] JBL 437.

[68] This seems to have been the case in Zurich Arbitration 31 May 1996 (n 54).

[69] See ibid.

party purchases an option, it is paying for the certainty that it will be protected from any market fluctuations, whether this could be predicted by the courts or not'.[70] This position is based on the view that an option has an *intrinsic* value and therefore, where the assessment takes place before the actual market price at the relevant date is known, damages need to be assessed on the basis that a party, by being deprived of its right to exercise an option, loses an asset.[71] From this perspective, damages need to be based on the replacement value of a similar asset, that is, of a similar option.

Recognising the possible difficulty of determining the value of a replacement option, the proponents of this view point to a formula for calculating that value which 'dispels the common misconception that the future value of an option can be accurately predicted using the present value as a benchmark' and tackles more accurately the problem of uncertainty of future price movement by taking account of 'the variance of the underlying asset's returns, the time remaining until the option's exercise and the option's exercise price'.[72] In comparison with the former approach, this approach provides greater security to the injured party and may be more in line with the function performed by an option in commercial contracts. For these reasons, this approach may provide a sound basis for rationalising the loss of an option. If the proposed mathematical formula[73] is able to provide an accurate assessment of an option's replacement value, it is arguable that it can be used under the international instruments.

3.5. Future Losses

In long-term contracts, damages will often be awarded for future losses the innocent party is predicted to suffer. In many cases, damages for loss of profits that would have been made in the hypothetical future will be claimed. When awarding damages for future losses, their value needs to be discounted to their present value.[74] Discounting requires the determination of the amount of compensable future losses which, in the case of lost profits, means that the amount of 'net' profits must be ascertained.[75] This amount then needs to be discounted to its present value by using an appropriate discount rate defined as the 'interest rate used to calculate future receipts or payments at their present value'.[76]

[70] Yang (n 67) 442–3.

[71] Ibid, 443–4.

[72] Yang (n 67) 444.

[73] For the proposed formula, see ibid, n 14.

[74] This has been done by some courts and tribunals applying the CISG (see *Mansonville Plastics (BC) Ltd v Kurtz GmbH* 2003 BCSC 1298; Zurich Arbitration 31 May 1996 (n 54)).

[75] The following formula is said to be commonly used to calculate the present value of future loss: $X/(1 + d)^n$ '[w]here X equals the amount of money to be discount, d is the discount rate and N equals the number of years' (White and Summers (n 43) 250).

[76] RL Dunn and EP Harry, 'Modeling and Discounting Future Damages' (2002) 193 *J Accountancy* 49, 50 ('For example, $1 put in the bank today at 5% interest will be worth $1.63 in 10 years. Therefore, the present value of $1.63 to be received in 10 years is $1 today at a 5% discount rate' (ibid)).

Although it is easy to formulate this principle, its implementation is far more difficult. The main reason stems from the difficulty of determining an appropriate discount rate as there is no agreement as to what its constituent elements should be. In general, a discount rate should take into account multiple factors, such as: the expected currency depreciation rate;[77] the risks associated with making profits by the business in question;[78] and the safe rate of return[79] the business is expected to make.[80] Determining a discount rate is a question of fact and it needs to be fixed in the light of all relevant circumstances.[81] In one CISG case,[82] a Canadian buyer contended that due to the delay in delivery it was unable to sell the product to a customer ('Korolite') in the United States and expand its market in that country. According to the decision:

> … the experts differed with respect to the appropriate discount rate. [The buyer's expert] chose a risk-free rate of 2.5% per annum, while [the seller's expert] chose a risk-based rate of 30%. [The latter] testified that a discount rate of 30% is basically a standard rate for startup businesses. In my opinion, an appropriate discount rate is between 20% and 25%. Although Korolite could be viewed as a startup company, its business is essentially an extension of [the buyer's] business and I believe that a discount rate of 30% is too high in the circumstances.

The next question is whether the amount of future loss needs to be discounted as of the date of judgment or the date of the breach. The question is important because the discount rate may be different on these two dates, especially if there is a substantial period of time between them. It is argued that the time of judgment is more appropriate since it is in line with the rationale underlying the need for discounting – that is, that the innocent party is able to invest the amount of a discounted award to receive, after the passage of time between judgment and the occurrence of future loss, the amount of future loss before discounting.

[77] 'The time value of money should also be taken into account in respect of future loss' *Mansonville Plastics (BC) Ltd v Kurtz GmbH* (n 74).

[78] See, eg, H Weisburg and C Ryan, 'Means to Be Made Whole: Damages in the Context of International Investment Arbitration' in Y Derains and RH Kreindler, *Evaluation of Damages in International Arbitration* (Dossiers of the ICC Institute of World Business Law, 2006) 165, 174; J Gotanda, 'Damages in Lieu of Performance Because of Breach of Contract' (Villanova University School of Law Working Paper No 2006-8, 2006) 73.

[79] See Dunn and Harry (n 76) 50.

[80] See further White and Summers (n 43) 251–53, who discuss the possibility of relying on several specific discount rates such as a 'risk-free' rate, lending rates based on the breaching party's credit rating and the injured party's rate of return. The commentators correctly reject a 'risk free' rate since earning profits is always accompanied by taking business risks and, for this reason, this rate is likely to over-compensate the injured party. The second rate is criticised because the present value of the injured party's losses is dependent on the credit rating of the breaching party and 'the legitimacy' of doing so is correctly doubted. The reliance on the latter rate is also put in doubt because it results in 'the lucky and efficient' being penalised since the more efficient the claimant, the higher is the discount rate.

[81] See RL Dunn, *Recovery of Damages for Lost Profits*, 6th edn (Alameda CA, Lawpress, 2006) 545.

[82] *Mansonville Plastics (BC) Ltd v Kurtz GmbH* (n 74).

Because the time of breach will always precede the time of judgment, the innocent party will not be able to go back in time to make an investment at the date of the breach.[83] Once a discount rate at the time of judgment is determined, it can be used to discount the amount of future losses, thereby fixing the final award of damages.

4. CURRENCY LOSSES[84]

4.1. Loss Flowing from the Change in the 'Internal Value' of Currency

A change in the 'internal' value or purchasing power of the currency can cause loss to the innocent party. Suppose the currency of payment is also the currency in which the aggrieved party operates. This is the case where, for example, a Finnish buyer delays payment to a German seller and the currency (euro) depreciates (ie, its purchasing power has decreased) during the period between when the payment was due and when it was actually made. In this case, the seller gets the amount which is nominally the same but the internal value or purchasing power of which is less than what it would have been on the due date. Provided that the requirements of limiting damages are met, the seller may be entitled to damages for this loss. However, an important question is whether the seller must show that it would have used the money for a purpose which was adversely affected by the late payment. For example, it can be argued that the seller does not suffer loss unless it shows that it would have purchased goods or services (or has in fact bought those goods or services) and would have paid (or has already paid) more than it would have if the payment had been timely. It may be that the seller's intention was to exchange the euros for Uzbek 'sums' and it may well be that the depreciation of the euro did not have an impact on the exchange rate between the euro and the 'sum'.[85]

Answering this question raises conflicting considerations. On the one hand, the logic underlying damage to the 'performance interest' may be interpreted as not requiring the seller to demonstrate that it would have used (or has used) the money for a particular purpose: it has received less than it was entitled to receive under the contract, and that is all that matters.[86] On the other hand, it can be argued that this approach over-compensates the seller. No problem arises if the

[83] For a similar view and more detailed discussion of this issue, see P Schulman, 'Economic Damages: Discounting Concepts and Alternatives' [1999] *Colorado Lawyer* 41, 44. See also KM Kolaski and M Kuga, 'Measuring Commercial Damages via Lost Profits or Loss of Business Value: Are these Measures Redundant or Distinguishable?' (1998–1999) 18 *J L Commerce* 1, 6–7.

[84] For the discussion of the recoverability of these losses, see ch 3.

[85] As discussed, there is no necessary connection between the internal and external values of a currency (see ch 3 with further references).

[86] For the discussion of the 'performance interest' loss, see chs 3, 8.

German seller can prove that it was going to use the euros to purchase goods or services. The depreciation of the euro is likely to affect its purchasing power and the seller is likely to need more euros to acquire identical goods or services than it would have needed on the due date or shortly thereafter.[87] The problem of over-compensation does arise, however, in the example above where it was seller's intention to exchange the euros for Uzbek 'sums' because the decline in the purchasing power of the euro did not affect its plans to purchase Uzbek 'sums'. It is argued that the innocent party's actual circumstances cannot be ignored and over-compensation should be avoided. In other words, the question whether damages for loss in the 'internal value' of the currency should be awarded must be resolved by having regard to the purpose for which the money was intended to be used.

4.1.1. Interest as a Tool for Compensating for Loss Flowing from a Change in the 'Internal' Value of Currency

It can be argued that when the aggrieved party suffers a currency depreciation loss as a result of delay in payment, the appropriate compensation should be made by awarding interest.[88] The instruments provide for the injured party's right to interest on the sum of money, the payment of which was delayed.[89] The interest rate takes account of the inflationary rate and the award of interest can function as a compensation for the currency depreciation loss.[90] It is submitted that interest and damages are not in opposition with each other[91] and what is crucial is that there must be no double recovery. In some cases, an award of interest may compensate for the inflationary loss, eliminating the need to award damages for this loss. An award of interest performs a number of functions,[92]

[87] Another factor that the seller may have to demonstrate is the date or period of time when it planned to use the money. Suppose the seller could not or would not have used the money earlier than the date when it received a late payment. In such a case, the seller cannot be considered to have suffered loss because had it been paid on time, it would not have used the money earlier than the date of actual payment, which is the date when the currency depreciated. Therefore, had the contract been performed the seller would have had to deal with the depreciated currency anyway.

[88] This was the position of a German court in a case governed by the ULIS. The court stated that 'a debtor in default must compensate for his delayed payment by paying interest, but not by balancing the currency devaluation' (Case No O 116/81 District Court Heidelberg (Germany) 27 January 1981, available at cisgw3.law.pace.edu/cases/810127g1.html).

[89] Article 78 CISG, art 7.4.9 UPICC, art 9:508 PECL.

[90] 'A higher interest rate is generally an expression of inflationary value of the money' (District Court Heidelberg 27 January 1981 (n 88)).

[91] Under the instruments, interest is distinct from damages. See, eg, B Nicholas, 'Art. 78 CISG' in CM Bianca and MJ Bonell (eds), *Commentary on the International Sales Law: The 1980 Vienna Sales Convention* (Milan, Giuffrè, 1987) 569; UPICC: 'the harm resulting from delay in payment of a sum of money is subject to a special regime' (Comment 1 on art 7.4.9 UPICC); PECL: 'Interest is not a species of ordinary damages. Therefore, the general rules on damages do not apply' (O Lando and H Beale (eds), *Principles of European Contract Law: Parts I and II* prepared by the Commission on European Contract Law (The Hague, Kluwer Law International, 2000) 450).

[92] An interest can: compensate for the loss of use of money (see AF Zoccolillo, Jr, 'Determination of the Interest Rate under the 1980 United Nations Convention on Contracts for the International

one of which is compensating for inflationary loss.[93] In particular, it has been pointed out that '[c]ommercial rates, such as the deposit rate ..., account for inflation by adjusting to economic conditions ... [T]he effects of inflation are already factored in the rate itself'.[94] Therefore, where the rate of interest reflects the inflationary rate, the award of interest fully compensates for the currency depreciation loss.[95] This may not always be the case. In some cases, the applicable interest rate may not fully reflect the rate of currency depreciation[96] and an award of interest does not then fully compensate the party for its loss. Where so, the party may claim damages for the part of the loss that was not compensated by interest. Full compensation is achieved partly by interest and partly by damages.[97] The injured party can always choose not to exercise its right to interest and resort exclusively to damages.[98] If so, damages must be calculated in a way that fully compensates for the currency depreciation loss.

4.2. Loss Flowing from a Change in the 'External' Value of Currency

The next type of loss to be considered is the loss caused by a change in the 'external' or international value of currency, that is, a change in the value of

Sale of Goods: General Principles vs. National Law' (1997) 1 *Vindobona J Int'l Commercial L Arbitration* 3, available at www.cisg.law.pace.edu/cisg/biblio/zoccolillo.html); be a preventive mechanism against undue enrichment of a debtor or against a debtor's use of money to which the creditor is entitled (see C Thiele, 'Interest on Damages and Rate of Interest under Article 78 of the United Nations Convention for the International Sale of Goods' (1998) 2 *Vindobona J Int'l Commercial L Arbitration* 3, available at www.cisg.law.pace.edu/cisg/biblio/thiele.html).

[93] '[I]nterest rates are in large part a function of anticipated inflation rates' (see K Rosenn, *Law and Inflation* (Philadelphia, University of Pennsylvania Press, 1982) 231); see also E Mackaay and C Fabien, 'Civil Law and the Fight Against Inflation – A Legal and Economic Analysis of the Quebec Case' (1983–1984) 44 *Louisiana L Rev* 723.

[94] JY Gotanda, 'Awarding Interest in International Arbitration' (1996) 90 *AJIL* 58.

[95] Interest rates can be even higher than the inflationary rates. See *Tessile 21 Srl v Ixela SA* District Court Pavia (Italy) 29 December 1999, available at www.cisg.law.pace.edu/cisg/wais/db/cases2/991229i3.html, where the court, applying the CISG, stated that '[n]othing [was] due by right of greater damages from monetary [depreciation] because ... the legal annual interest rates have always been greater than the rate of inflation'.

[96] See V Behr, 'The Sales Convention in Europe: From Problems in Drafting to Problems in Practice', available at www.cisg.law.pace.edu/cisg/biblio/behr.html; Lando and Beale (n 91) 450; J Dach, 'Conversion of Foreign Money: A Comparative Study of Changing Rules' (1954) 3 *AJCL* 170–1.

[97] Damages themselves may have to be calculated on the basis of the applicable interest rate. See Case No 12 U 39/00 25 Appellate Court Hamburg (Germany) 25 January 2008, available at cisgw3.law.pace.edu/cases/080125g1.html, where the buyer was awarded the sum, based on both arts 78 and 74 CISG, to compensate the buyer for the delay in the seller's payment of a contractual penalty ('Art. 78 and 74 CISG allow a creditor to claim interest which is higher than the statutory interest rate if he incurs corresponding expenses from lending. In the present case, [the Buyer's assignees] are entitled to claim an interest rate of 9% which they had to expend for a bank loan.').

[98] It can be argued that it is better for the injured party to claim interest when it amounts to or almost fully reflects the currency depreciation loss because, in contrast with damages, in a claim for interest neither the fact of loss must be proven nor any other requirement of limiting damages needs to be met.

one currency against another. This change may occur when one currency devalues[99] (ie, its value declines) or when one currency's value increases in relation to another currency.[100] Since international transactions often involve more than one currency, changes in the exchange rate can often result in a loss.[101] To identify cases where a change in the external value of the currency may so result, it needs to be borne in mind that currencies can be used in different capacities. The first capacity in which a currency can be used is that of being the currency of account or the currency of contract ('contract currency'). The contract currency is the currency in which an obligation is expressed and measured and it tells the debtor how much it has to pay.[102] A currency can also be used as a currency of payment, that is, the currency 'which must be used as a means of performing the obligation'.[103] The difference between the two is that the contract currency 'establishes the quantum of the obligation ("how much") while the [currency] of payment determines the mode of payment ("how", in what currency)'.[104] Only if the two are clearly differentiated is it possible to measure the value of the obligation, determine the proper means of its execution and accurately assess damages for its breach.[105]

One situation where exchange rate losses arise is where, between the payment due date and the actual date of payment, the contract currency has devalued against the payment currency or the latter has strengthened against the former resulting in the seller getting less in the currency of payment than what it would have received had the payment been made on time. Another situation is where the seller intends to exchange, or has in fact exchanged, the currency of payment

[99] It seems proper to use the term 'devaluation', rather than 'depreciation', in relation to decrease in a currency's value against another (see Mackaay and Fabien (n 93) 720 stating that '[t]he decline in the purchasing power of a currency is generally called depreciation. This term is not to be confused with devaluation, which is the decrease in the value of one currency in relation to another'; see also Rosenn (n 93) 3).

[100] 'Where a unit of account is devalued or depreciates, the rate of exchange is modified, but none of these other currencies can be said to be revalued or to appreciate. Conversely, where a unit of account is revalued or appreciates, in relation to other currencies, none of the latter is devalued or depreciates. Their value in terms of the particular unit of account affected by the change differs, but their value amongst themselves and their domestic values remain the same. In other words, the difference is relative, rather than absolute.' (C Proctor, *Mann on the Legal Aspect of Money,* 6th edn (Oxford, OUP, 2005) 75).

[101] See M Saldana, 'Cross Border Transactions', Practising Law Institute, Corporate Law and Practice Course Handbook Series (PLI Order N B0-003A, 1998) 369–70.

[102] See Proctor (n 100) 107, 109; J Dach, 'Money of Reference and Conversion of Money' (1956) 5 *AJCL* 517, *Procter & Gamble Co (The) v Svenska Cellulosa Aktiebolaget SCA* [2012] EWCA Civ 1413.

[103] Proctor (n 100) 190; Dach (n 102) 517; *Procter & Gamble Co (The) v Svenska Cellulosa Aktiebolaget SCA* (n 102).

[104] Dach (n 128) 517; see ICC No 7660, 23 August 1994 (Battery Machinery), where '[a]s a remedy against currency fluctuations, the contract price was valued in lira, but payment was due in DM', available at www.cisg.law.pace.edu/cisg/wais/db/cases2/947660i1.html.

[105] The distinction between the payment currency and the contract currency appears to have been important in *Celli SpA v Agrolang BV* Appellate Court Arnhem (Netherlands) 15 April 1997, available at www.cisg.law.pace.edu/cisg/wais/db/cases2/970415n1.html.

for another currency. The latter is often, but not always,[106] the seller's domestic currency. Thus, the seller may suffer loss where the value of its domestic currency changes in relation to the contract/payment currency (where these are the same currency) or against the payment currency (where the contract and payment currencies are different currencies), or even where the exchange rate has changed between the contract and payment currencies. If the buyer makes a late payment and the contract and payment currencies are the same currency,[107] the seller may suffer loss if the contract/payment currency has devalued against the seller's domestic currency, or if the latter has strengthened against the former between the time when the payment was due and when it was actually made.[108] The UPICC and PECL contain a specific mechanism outside the remedy of damages, which will, in many cases, compensate for this loss. The UPICC provide that where the contract and payment currency(ies) is/are different from the currency of the place of payment (often the creditor's domestic currency) and where it is impossible for the debtor to make a payment in the agreed currency, the creditor may require the debtor to pay in the currency of the place of payment.[109] If, then, the debtor does not pay on time, the creditor 'may require payment according to the applicable rate of exchange prevailing either when payment is due or at the time of actual payment'.[110] In a similar vein, the PECL provide that where the currency of payment is not specified and the contract currency is different from the currency of the place of payment, payment may be made in the currency of the place of payment.[111] If the debtor, in this case, does not pay on time 'the creditor may require payment in the currency of the place where payment is due according to the rate of exchange prevailing there either at the time when payment is due or at the time of actual payment'.[112] These provisions may serve the creditor well,[113] particularly if it intended to exchange the currency of payment into its domestic currency. In such cases, creditors may prefer to invoke these provisions rather than claim damages because by doing so no additional requirements, such as those to be met when claiming damages, are applicable.

[106] See, eg, *Société Française Bunge S.A. v Belcan N.V.* (*The 'Federal Huron'*) [1985] 3 All ER 378, where it was established that a French company, a trader of soya beans, conducted its financial affairs and operations in US dollars because soya beans were 'a dollar commodity'.

[107] Or if they are different currencies but there has been no change in the value of these currencies in relation to each other.

[108] 'S in London agrees to sell goods to B in Hamburg at a price of US$100,000 payable in London 28 days after shipment. The goods are duly shipped to B, who is three months late in paying the price. During this period the value of the US dollar in relation to the pound sterling (the currency in which S normally conducts his business) depreciates by 20 per cent. Assuming that these consequences of delay in payment could reasonably have been foreseen by B at the time of the contract, S is entitled to recover US$20,000 damages from B, in addition to interest, for the loss on exchange' (Lando and Beale (n 91) 451).

[109] See art 6.1.9(1), (2) UPICC and Comment thereon.

[110] Article 6.1.9(4) UPICC.

[111] Article 7:108(2) PECL.

[112] Article 7:108(3) PECL.

[113] See also Comment 1 on art 6.1.9 UPICC.

Since no similar provision is contained in the CISG, this loss can only be compensated by means of damages.[114] Unfortunately, in several cases, losses caused by a change in the external value of the creditor's domestic currency in relation to the contract/payment currency were held non-recoverable under the CISG. In one case,[115] the claimant claimed damages for the difference in the exchange rate caused by the government of its country substantially raising the rate of the national currency against the US dollar which was the contract currency. As a result, the return of an advance payment in US dollars by the respondent to the claimant caused the claimant loss in its domestic currency. The tribunal held that the change in the internal rate of the national currency against the US dollar was a creditor's 'domestic affair' and rejected the claim. In another case,[116] the tribunal rejected the claim for damages flowing from the change in the exchange rate between the Finnish mark (which appears to have been the creditor's currency) and the US dollar which was both the contract and payment currency.

It is argued that this approach, whereby such losses are treated as a creditor's 'domestic affair', should not be followed. The fact that the creditor's domestic currency (which is neither the currency of payment nor of contract) is involved, cannot preclude the exchange rate loss from being recoverable. As argued earlier,[117] this loss should be recoverable as a matter of law.[118] At the same time, the question whether the party has suffered loss should be decided having regard to the purpose for which the creditor's currency was intended to be used (or was used). As argued in relation to the inflationary losses, it is submitted that the purpose for which the currency was intended to be used should be ascertained to prevent over-compensation.[119] The creditor may have intended to exchange its domestic currency for a foreign currency. If the exchange rate between the

[114] The same point is made in CISG Advisory Council (CISG-AC) Opinion No. 6, 'Calculation of Damages under CISG Article 74', available at www.cisg.law.pace.edu/cisg/CISG-AC-op6.html.

[115] ICAC No 61/1993, 21 April 1994, available at cisgw3.law.pace.edu/cases/940421r1.html.

[116] ICAC No 442/1996, 26 February 1998.

[117] See ch 3.

[118] See Commercial Court Zürich (Switzerland) 5 February 1997 (n 41), where the court recognised that the German buyer who brought an action to recover the advance payment could in principle be compensated for losses suffered due to the change in the exchange rate between the US dollar (the currency of payment) and the DM, calculated as the difference between the exchange rate on the date of making an advance payment and the date on which it is returned, available at cisgw3.law.pace.edu/cases/970205s1.html; Case No C1 08 45 Higher Cantonal Court Valais (Switzerland) 28 January 2009, available at cisgw3.law.pace.edu/cases/090128s1.html, where the German seller recovered damages for the exchange rate loss, resulting from exchanging the Swiss buyer's late payment in Swiss francs into euros. The court, however, also held that the currency of payment ought to have been the euro (it is not clear whether the court also deemed the euro to have been the contract currency).

[119] See Case No 2 U 28/80 Appellate Court Hamm (Germany) 26 June 1980 (Shoes and bags), available at cisgw3.law.pace.edu/cases/800626g1.html, where the court stated that 'the loss can only be affirmed if it is certain that the creditor – had he received the open payment timely – would have used it in a particular way and that the unfavourable exchange rate there has a direct impact on him. This would be the case, i.e., if the creditor would have used the amount receivable in his own currency to repay his own debts in a different currency, which is now valued as a higher rate'.

creditor's currency and the foreign currency is such that the creditor has received a lower amount in the foreign currency than that it would have received had the payment been timely, it has suffered loss. If, however, between the due date and the actual date of payment, the exchange rate between the creditor's currency and the foreign currency has changed in a way causing the party to receive the same or even a greater amount in the foreign currency as/than it would have received had the payment been timely, there is no loss (eg, if the creditor's currency strengthened against the foreign currency). The foreseeability rule is of particular importance in this context and courts/tribunals need to ensure that the breaching party foresaw or was in the position to foresee that the injured party would exchange its domestic currency for a foreign currency and this may often not be the case.[120] In one CISG case, the court stated that '[u]sually, the creditor's currency [was] not converted into a different currency' and damages for this loss could be awarded 'if the creditor usually conduct[ed] his money transfers in a third currency and therefore always convert[ed] other currencies immediately after their receipt'.[121]

5. LOSS OF A CHANCE

Loss of a chance is recoverable under the UPICC[122] and this book has argued that the same should be the case for the CISG and PECL. It has been further suggested that for this loss to be recoverable, the chance must a 'real' or a 'substantial' one.[123] As explained, there are two categories of contract cases in which damages for loss of a chance can be claimed: (1) where a chance *itself* is the subject-matter of the contract;[124] and (2) where the subject-matter of the contract is not a chance but an ordinary sale of goods (but where the innocent party is unable to prove its lost profits flowing from the breach of contract). In this case, loss of a chance is a tool with which the law deals with the uncertainty

[120] But see *DT Ltd v B AG* Commercial Court St Gallen (Switzerland) 3 December 2002, available at cisgw3.law.pace.edu/cases/021203s1.html, where the court stated that '[w]ith regard to debtor's default, there is a valid factual assumption that the relevant creditor of a foreign debt might have immediately exchanged that amount into Swiss francs when it had received this payment at maturity'. See further C Proctor, 'Changes in Monetary Value and the Assessment of Damages' in D Saidov and R Cunnington (eds), *Contract Damages: Domestic and International Perspectives* (Oxford, Hart Publishing, 2008) 486–7, 495 for the discussion of the foreseeability test, in the context of English law, in cases where the creditor is obliged to surrender foreign currency receipts in exchange for its domestic currency.

[121] Case No 17 U 146/93 Appellate Court Düsseldorf (Germany) 14 January 1994 (Shoes), available at cisgw3.law.pace.edu/cases/940114g1.html. It seems that the court's statement was intended to go beyond the foreseeability rule and to address the issue of the recoverability of the loss flowing from the party's intention to convert its domestic currency into a foreign one. However, the court's arguments seem more relevant to foreseeability than to the recoverability of this loss as their relevance to the recoverability seems doubtful.

[122] See art 7.4.3(2).

[123] See ch 3.

[124] See *Chaplin v Hicks* [1911] 2 KB 786.

flowing from speculative losses and avoids an 'all-or-nothing' result in awarding damages. It is the second category of cases which is usually relevant in sale of goods cases and for this reason the calculation of damages for loss of a chance will be considered in the context of this type of case.

The quantification of loss of a chance is inevitably speculative and generally involves two stages: (1) the evaluation of the value of a possible benefit; and (2) the likelihood of obtaining it.[125] The greater the number of contingencies on which this likelihood depends, the lower the value of loss will be[126] and vice versa. Damages for this loss are to be calculated 'in proportion to the probability of its occurrence'.[127] Evaluating hypothetical actions of third parties, particularly where a number of contingencies are involved, can be difficult. Where several contingencies are involved, the relative weight of each contingency needs to be determined. It also needs to be ascertained whether contingencies are dependent on one another or are separate (independent).[128] In the former case, damages need to be assessed 'as a percentage of a percentage'.[129] Suppose the buyer asserts that due to the seller's breach, it has lost an opportunity of entering into a contract with a construction company which, in turn, intended to make a bid on the construction of a high-profile building.[130] Suppose also that the buyer claims damages for loss of a chance to earn profit for the entire expected period of constructing the building. The success of this claim is subject to a number of contingencies all of which are dependent on one another: a chance of making a contract with the construction company (in the first place), a chance of the company winning a bid, a chance of the buyer being retained as a supplier for the entire duration of the project. If a chance of earning the said profit is 'real or substantial', damages need to be calculated with reference to the percentages representing the likelihood of the occurrence of each of the contingencies. So, if the amount of profit is £10,000,000 and the chances of each of the events occurring are 50 per cent, 30 per cent, and 25 per cent, respectively, damages should amount to £375,000.[131]

The problems of valuing loss of a chance become more complicated where the innocent party claims that as a result of the breach, it has lost multiple chances, all of which are independent of one another and are mutually exclusive (alternative chances). Suppose that because of the seller's breach the buyer has lost a 30 per cent chance of winning a bid which would have led to the buyer concluding a contract with a resulting profit of £1,000,000. In the case of unsuccessful bidding, the buyer would have had a 50 per cent chance of securing a

[125] See Peel (n 63) 1153.
[126] See ibid.
[127] Article 7.4.3(2) UPICC.
[128] J Poole, 'Loss of Chance and the Evaluation of Hypotheticals in Contractual Claims' [2007] LMCLQ 63, 77.
[129] Ibid.
[130] See *Mansonville Plastics (BC) Ltd v Kurtz GmbH* (n 74).
[131] That is, 50% of 30% of 25%.

supply contract resulting in the profit margin of £500,000. Suppose also that the buyer would not have been in the position to perform both contracts and chances are mutually exclusive. It is suggested that damages need to be calculated on the basis that both *chances* were available to the injured party. In the given example, had there been no breach the buyer would have had *both* a 30 per cent chance of earning £1,000,000 (ie, £300,000) *and* a 70 per cent chance of having a 50 per cent chance of earning £500,000 (ie, £175,000). Therefore, the buyer needs to be awarded damages in the amount of £475,000.[132]

6. DAMAGE TO BUSINESS REPUTATION AND GOODWILL[133]

6.1. General

It is usually assumed that the most that can be done with respect to the assessment of damage to business reputation and goodwill is fixing a fair and reasonable sum.[134] It has also been suggested that great care needs to be exercised in awarding such damages and the sums awarded should be modest.[135] What is often stressed is that some degree of uniformity of awards be maintained as this is essential for preventing arbitrary awards, maintaining legal predictability and, more broadly, for a legal system to be credible and just.[136] With these concerns in mind, it has been suggested that setting a maximum amount of damages could be a way of introducing some order into the awards of damages for intangible losses.[137] How do these points fare in the context of the international instruments? It is certainly crucial for their long-term future that a uniform treatment of claims is maintained. At the same time, in the absence of some international institution responsible for monitoring their application, fixing the maximum amount is not a workable means of maintaining uniformity. Moreover, this solution is arbitrary and possibly unfair because in a particular case, it may be that the loss exceeds the fixed maximum amount.

[132] For an English case dealing with this situation, see *Inter-Leisure Ltd v Lamberts (a firm)* (1997) NPC 49.

[133] This section is a revised and partial version of D Saidov, 'Damage to Business Reputation and Goodwill under the Vienna Sales Convention' in Saidov and Cunnington (n 120).

[134] See, eg, A Burrows, *Remedies for Torts, Breach of Contract and Equitable Wrongs*, 4th edn (Oxford, OUP, 2019) 273.

[135] See McKendrick and Worthington, 'Damages for Non-Pecuniary Loss' in N Cohen and E McKendrick (eds), *Comparative Remedies for Breach of Contract* (Oxford, Hart Publishing, 2005) 321.

[136] '[J]ustice is not justice if it is arbitrary or whimsical, if that is awarded to one plaintiff for an injury bears no relation at all to what is awarded to another plaintiff for an injury of the same kind …' (*McCarey v Associated Newspapers Ltd and Others* (No 2) [1965] 2 QB 86, 108).

[137] See M Bridge, 'Contractual Damages for Intangible Loss: A Comprehensive Analysis' (1984) 62 *Can Bar Rev* 367.

So far as the argument in favour of fixing a fair and reasonable sum is concerned, it seems that this is precisely what courts and tribunals do where damages for this loss are awarded.[138] While maintaining a degree of uniformity of awards made on that basis may be possible in the context of a domestic legal system, it is much more difficult, if not impossible, to achieve even something remotely reminiscent of uniformity under the instruments, given the multiplicity of courts and tribunals applying them. The question arises therefore whether there are some other, more rational and reliable, means of quantification? If damage to reputation and goodwill is a 'true' loss, then in the light of developments in modern science and technology,[139] there must be some method of quantifying such damages with greater accuracy than fixing a reasonable sum. The discussion below will suggest some methods that can be used to quantify this loss.

6.2. General Measure

A general measure of damages is *the difference between the value of present and former reputations/goodwill*.[140] One difficulty relates to determining these two items of value. The precise moment at which the valuation takes place may also have an impact on the amount of the award. It may therefore be important to decide to which moments in time the words 'present and former' reputation/goodwill refer. One possibility is that they mean reputation/goodwill as they were *before* and *after* the breach. However, the reference to the time 'after the breach' may not always be appropriate since damage to reputation/goodwill can only occur when the relevant stakeholders become aware of the breach and its consequences and when that awareness negatively impacts on their perception of a company. The reference to reputation/goodwill after the breach may only be appropriate where the stakeholders' perceptions are being damaged as the breach occurs.[141] Conversely, in some other cases, there may be a substantial gap between the time of breach and the time when a negative impact on the

[138] See, eg, ICC No 3880, 27 September 1983 in S Jarvin and Y Derains, *Collection of ICC Arbitral Awards, 1974–1985: Recueil Des Sentences Arbitrales de la CCI* (The Hague, Kluwer Law International, 1990) 161.

[139] See *AM/PM Franchise Association v Atlantic Richfield Company* 526 Pa. 110, 128 (Pa., 1990) (where it was stated that those earlier decisions where recovery of goodwill had been disallowed were made at the time when 'market studies and economic forecasting were unexplored sciences' whereas '[w]e are now in an era in which computers, economic forecasting, sophisticated marketing studies and demographic studies are widely used and accepted').

[140] See Burrows (n 134) 273.

[141] This seems to have happened in an English case *Aerial Advertising Co v Batchelors Peas Ltd* [1938] 2 All ER 788, where the injured party hired the breaching party to advertise its goods by flying over various towns and trailing behind the aeroplane the words advertising the products. The latter, in breach of contract, flew over the crowded square during the Armistice service and the two minutes' silence, and it is likely that the damage to the innocent party's reputation largely occurred during that time.

stakeholders' perceptions occurs. For instance, a wholesaler may keep a large quantity of goods delivered by the breaching seller at its warehouse for several months before putting them on sale. In this case, damage to its reputation/goodwill will occur long after the breach when a certain number of customers become aware of the defects in the purchased products. In such a case, the reference to the time of breach is inappropriate and a later point in time at which injury to reputation/goodwill has occurred must be chosen. Thus, the general measure should be the difference between the value of reputation/goodwill *before and after the loss*.[142] However, it is not easy to determine a specific moment in time at which damage to reputation/ goodwill occurs and, ultimately, such a determination will depend on the particular circumstances. A workable solution needs to be based on the tangible manifestations of such a loss. Since in most cases customers will be regarded as the relevant stakeholders, the moment at or the period during which the injured party lost custom can perhaps provide a rough guideline.

6.3. 'Cost' Approach

One way to measure damage to reputation/goodwill is to estimate the costs incurred to repair the damaged reputation/goodwill. This measure was used in one CISG case where the buyer had taken measures and incurred expenses to regain its reputation as a supplier of canned food and to create 'new customer networks'.[143] In principle, this method can be used not only where an injured party has *actually* incurred costs to repair its reputation/goodwill but also where no such expenses have been made.[144] In both cases, the mitigation rule and/ or the instruments' general principle of reasonableness require a claimant to demonstrate that the costs of cure are reasonable[145] and the causation requirement may require that these costs be truly necessary for and directed at curing damage to reputation/goodwill.[146]

[142] In theory, 'before the loss' would probably mean the moment immediately preceding the loss and, if no reasonable estimation at that time is possible for practical reasons (due, eg, to the lack of information), the moment which is the closest in time to the loss and which affords a reasonable opportunity for the estimation can be taken as the basis for valuation. The words 'after the loss' should probably mean the time immediately after the loss and, in any event, not later than a reasonable time thereafter.

[143] Tampere Court of First Instance (Finland) 17 January 1997 (Canned food), available at cisgw3.law.pace.edu/cases/970117f5.html.

[144] See RF Reilly and RP Schweihs, *Valuing Intangible Assets* (New York, McGraw-Hill, 1999) 387.

[145] See the discussion on reasonableness of costs of cure and related issues in ch 8.

[146] It is not entirely clear whether such costs should be recovered as costs caused by the breach, in which case, the suggestion in the main text would be correct. However, it can also be argued that costs of curing damage to reputation/goodwill should not be recovered as costs caused by the breach but should be regarded as a method of calculating damage to reputation/goodwill and, in this case, the causal requirement does not apply to costs of cure but only requires that there be a causal connection between a breach and damage to reputation/goodwill (as opposed to a causal connection between a breach and costs of cure).

This method becomes more complicated if costs are understood as including 'opportunity costs',[147] that is, a lost opportunity to earn profit during the period of repairing reputation/goodwill. If so, and if a claimant also claims loss of profit, the duplication of recovery for lost profits must be prevented. Therefore, either 'costs' should not include lost opportunity to profit or the recovery of lost profit for the period of repairing the damaged reputation/goodwill should be denied.

6.4. 'Royalty'

Another method is to ask how much a third party would pay to lease a corporate name. Although this method is mostly used in the context of the valuation of brands, it has been suggested that it is possible to use this method to value reputation/goodwill.[148] If this is correct, the present value of all expected royalty payments under such licensing/leasing arrangements can be used to estimate a company's reputation.[149] This method would seem to dispense with the need to define reputation/goodwill as it refers to royalty rates insofar as the particular marketplace is concerned,[150] and market valuation has been said to correspond 'roughly to overall regard in which the company is held by its constituents'.[151] Quantifying damages would require the determination of the difference between the value of all royalty payments that would be payable *before* and *after* the loss. One potential difficulty relates to the availability of information regarding royalty rates. For example, because royalty data may be confined to a specific market or sector, it may not be easily extrapolated outside those boundaries.[152] What is the relationship between this valuation method and a claim for future lost profits? As noted, the royalty method aims to arrive at a value of reputation/goodwill in a particular market[153] and market value is generally viewed as reflecting a market's guess regarding the profits a company will make from a particular asset. Therefore, awarding damages for lost profits which can be attributed to reputation/goodwill along with damages calculated under the 'royalty' method can lead to an overlap. Specifically, because royalty rates are

[147] See Reilly and Schweihs (n 144).

[148] M Sussdorff, 'The Value to be Found in Corporate Reputation', available at intranet.csreurope.org/news/csr/one-entry?entry%5fid=114278.

[149] Ibid.

[150] See Reilly and Schweihs (n 144) 147, 152–53, 194 (treating the royalty relief method as a specific type of valuation based on the 'market approach' the purpose of which is to provide an estimate of a market value of an asset (see ibid, 147)).

[151] C Fombrun, *Reputation: Realizing Value from the Corporate Image* (Harvard Business School Press, Boston MA 1996) 91.

[152] R Shaw, 'Brand Valuation' (2004), available at www.mbpi.biz/Brand_Valuation.PDF (in the context of brand valuation).

[153] See, eg, Waddams (n 14) 82–83; *R.E.B. Inc v Ralston Purina Co.* 525 F.2d 749, 754–5 (C.A.Wyo. 1975); Dunn (n 81) 566.

often calculated as a percentage of *profits*, the amount arrived at by applying the royalty method would be precisely the amount which needs to be subtracted from the lost profit claim to avoid a double recovery.[154]

6.5. Market Value

Another well-known method of valuing business reputation/goodwill, based on market valuation, requires a calculation of the difference between the market value of a business[155] and the value of all its tangible and identifiable intangible assets. It has been suggested that the difference resulting from this calculation represents the value of business reputation/goodwill.[156] To calculate damages using this method, the value of reputation/goodwill has to be determined *before* and *after* the loss and then the value after the loss needs to be subtracted from the value before the loss. So far as the relationship of this calculation method with a lost profits claim is concerned, a possible overlap between them must be avoided. Damages to reputation/goodwill are calculated as a residual derived from market value and market value takes into consideration the market's expectation of profits a business will make.[157] Therefore, that part of future lost profits which can be attributed to reputation/goodwill cannot be awarded together with damages calculated under the 'market value' method.[158]

6.6. Income Approach

Yet another approach to valuing reputation/goodwill and damage thereto is based on the future profits a company would have been expected to earn *but for the breach*.[159] One specific method of calculating damages for lost reputation/

[154] See Reilly and Schweihs (n 144); Fombrun (n 151) 152–3, 194).

[155] Market value of a company can be determined either on the basis of an actual sale of business or of a constructed value (see Reilly and Schweihs (n 144) 387).

[156] See, eg, Reilly and Schweihs (n 144) 387. For further discussion and the proposal of a more complex formula, see R Bowd and L Bowd, 'Assessing a Financial Value for Corporate Entity's Reputation: A Proposed Formula', available at www.ribm.mmu.ac.uk/wps/papers/02-01.pdf.

[157] See, eg, Waddams (n 14) 82–83; *REB Inc v Ralston Purina Co* 525 F.2d 749 [10th Cir. 1975], 754–5 (C.A.Wyo. 1975); Dunn (n 81) 566; see also *Hydraform Products Corp v American and Aluminum Corp* 498 A.2d 339, 347 (N.H., 1985).

[158] It can be very difficult to determine the part of lost profits attributable to reputation/goodwill. Nevertheless, it seems that it can be determined in the following way. Under the 'market value' method, the value of reputation/goodwill is determined as a residual from market value. It seems possible therefore to determine the percentage of market value which can be attributed to the value of reputation/goodwill and then to discount the amount of future lost profits claimed by the same percentage. In other words, the amount of future profits is reduced in proportion to the percentage that the value of reputation/goodwill occupies within the overall market value of a business. It is the amount by which future lost profits are reduced which cannot be claimed together with damage to reputation/goodwill under the 'market value' method.

[159] See Reilly and Schweihs (n 144) 388; CISG-AC (n 114) para 7.4.

goodwill based on future lost profits has been used in some US cases[160] where it was suggested that in cases of non-conforming goods, damage to reputation/goodwill should be measured by future lost profits which the injured buyer would have made *not* from profits lost due to the sale of or a failed attempt to sell non-conforming goods, but due to the inability to provide *other* goods or services in the future. For example, if the buyer had purchased the goods to fulfil its sub-sale contract which were either rejected or bought at reduced prices, damages for lost profits caused by such rejection or resale at reduced price do not, under this approach, compensate for an injury to reputation/goodwill. Rather, it will be the profits the buyer was unable to make when it was in the position to provide conforming goods in *other future transactions unrelated to the initial sub-sale* that will be the basis for quantifying a damage to goodwill/reputation. The buyer will have to prove that had the seller performed the contract, the buyer would have made those *future* sales. This calculation method is based on the assumption that if the buyer's sales continue to decrease despite its ability to provide proper performance, this may be an indication of negative perceptions of its business held by existing and potential customers. Provided that a court/tribunal is satisfied that loss of future sales was caused by damage to reputation/goodwill, this method is sound and can be used to quantify this loss.

If a lost profit claim is brought together with a claim for lost reputation/goodwill calculated under this method, care is required to avoid double compensation. If a lost profit claim is for damage suffered directly as a result of the buyer's resale of or attempt to sell non-conforming goods, no overlap occurs between this claim and a claim calculated under the 'income approach' method. If, however, a claim for lost profit relates to future sales which the buyer could have made had the contract been performed, an overlap will occur.

7. CURRENCY OF DAMAGES

Given that an international sales transaction may involve several currencies, in which currency must an award of damages be? This question is also linked with that of the date with reference to which damages must be assessed. To understand the significance of these questions, the distinction between the internal and external values of currency needs to be recalled. The heart of the problem of the currency of damages lies in the fact that both internal and external values

[160] See *AM/PM Franchise Association v Atlantic Richfield Company* (n 139) ('goodwill damages refer to profits lost on future sales rather than on sales of the defective goods themselves'); *Sol-O-Lite Laminating Corp v Allen* 223 Or. 80, 353 P.2d 843, 849 (where goodwill was regarded as referring to 'the profits [the buyer] might have made on similar plastic he would have sold in the future or loss of profits on other items he would have sold had his customers not become disgusted with him').

of currency often change between the time when the loss was suffered and the date of judgment (award).[161]

Suppose the seller fails to deliver the goods and damages are measured 'abstractly' with reference to the market price.[162] As of the date of avoidance, the market price loss can be expressed either as 1,000 US dollars or as 65,000 Russian rubles (at the then existing exchange rate). By the time of judgment, however, the dollar has strengthened against the ruble and 1,000 dollars are now equivalent to 75,000 rubles. Should the buyer be awarded 1,000 dollars, 65,000 rubles, or 75,000 rubles? The first two sums represent the loss at an earlier date of avoidance and as between them the choice is merely between the two currencies. The third sum reflects not merely a choice in favour of a particular currency (ruble) but also a choice in favour of the date of assessment, that is, the date of judgment (award) as opposed to an earlier date of avoidance. It can be argued that if 75,000 rubles are awarded, the issue of currency of damages becomes much less important because the buyer receives the current equivalent of 1,000 dollars in rubles and, in this way, the award probably eliminates a potentially adverse change in the exchange rate.

The UPICC and PECL contain specific provisions regarding the currency in which to assess damages. The UPICC provide that 'damages are to be assessed either in the currency in which the monetary obligation was expressed or in the currency in which the harm was suffered, whichever is more appropriate'.[163] The PECL contain a similar, but not identical, provision to the effect that 'damages are to be measured by the currency which most appropriately reflects the aggrieved party's loss'.[164] The CISG, in contrast, does not expressly address this issue. The position in cases is far from uniform. One approach is to award damages in the currency in which loss was suffered.[165] According to another line of cases, damages ought to be awarded in the currency in which the contractual obligations were expressed[166] while in some other cases it was considered appropriate to award damages in the currency of payment.[167] Finally, on occasions, the currency of damages was treated as a matter of domestic law.[168]

[161] See, eg, Lando and Beale (n 91) 456 (viewing the issue of the currency of damages solely on the basis of the exchange rate fluctuations).

[162] See ch 8.

[163] Article 7.4.12.

[164] Article 9:510.

[165] See ICC No 9187, June 1999 (Coke), available at cisgw3.law.pace.edu/cases/999187i1.html.

[166] See *Downs Investments Pty Ltd v Perwaja Steel SDN BHD* (n 18); most probably, ICAC No 97/2004, 23 December 2004, available at cisgw3.law.pace.edu/cases/041223r1.html.

[167] District Court Berlin 30 September 1992 (n 18).

[168] *Delchi Carrier SpA v Rotorex Corp* 1994 WL 495787; also seemingly the position in Case No A56-108602/2017 Arbitration Court St Petersburg and Leningrad Region (Russia) 7 August 2018, available at ras.arbitr.ru (in Russian) ('It follows from the contract that the parties' monetary obligation was expressed in Euros. In these circumstances, an indication in a court decision of the amount of damages award in a foreign currency (Euro) does not contradict the legislation of the Russian Federation because the decision of the court … will be implemented in the currency of the Russian Federation – rubles.' (translated by the author)).

It is submitted that currency of damages is a matter governed by the CISG. Its provisions, as far as the exercise of the right to damages is concerned, should be regarded as exhaustive, precluding recourse to domestic law. Arguing otherwise would lead to an important aspect of the right to damages being left to the vagaries of domestic systems, undermining the Convention's requirement of uniformity in its application. Recognising this matter as being within the Convention's scope does not require embarking on a long journey in search of a relevant general principle.[169] General principles of full compensation and/or reasonableness can provide a basis for the position that damages are to be awarded in the currency which truly expresses and reflects the injured party's loss.[170] This approach, well known to many legal systems[171] and well established in international arbitration,[172] is no doubt fair and most appropriate in the light of the compensatory purpose of damages.[173] The UPICC can help by adding precision in formulating this principle under the CISG.

The real challenge lies not in justifying this principle but in applying it. One difficulty is that the principle contains only a general guideline which requires the balancing of various factors. How should the currency, in which the loss was suffered, be determined? The answer is relatively easy if the parties have expressed, explicitly or implicitly, their intention as regards the currency in which they wanted to settle their damages claims.[174] It must be stressed that while the contract currency may be a factor in establishing the parties' intention to settle their damages claims in that currency, there is no necessary connection between that currency and the one in which the loss was suffered.[175] Where no express or implied intention can be identified, the question of the currency in which that loss was suffered must be answered in the light of the particular circumstances.

[169] See art 7(2) CISG.

[170] See, similarly, M Djordjević, 'Arts 74–77' in S Kröll, L Mistelis and P Viscasillas (eds), *The United Nations Convention on Contracts for the International Sale of Goods*, 2nd edn (München, C.H. Beck and Oxford, Hart, 2018) 990.

[171] See Lando and Beale (n 91) 457.

[172] ICC No 6955, 1993 in JJ Arnaldez, Y Derains and D Hascher, *Collection of ICC Arbitral Awards, 1991–1995: Recueil des Sentences Arbitrales de la CCI* (The Hague, Kluwer Law International, 1997) 267, 295.

[173] See, similarly, I Schwenzer, 'Arts 74–77' in I Schwenzer (ed), *Schlechtriem and Schwenzer Commentary on the UN Convention on the International Sale of Goods (CISG)*, 4th edn (Oxford, OUP, 2016) 1084.

[174] For a similar view, see S Eiselen, 'Unresolved Damages Issues of the CISG: A Comparative Analysis' (2005) 38 Comparative Int'l L J Southern Africa 32, 41. See, in this regard, Case No 11 O 4261/94 District Court Kassel (Germany) 21 September 1995 (Wooden poles), available at cisgw3.law.pace.edu/cases/950921g1.html. In this case, a German buyer claimed damages for the loss of the profit margin on its sub-sale contract from a US seller. The court denied the buyer's request for damages in DM and awarded damages in US dollars on the ground that the contract currency in both the buyer's contract with the seller and its contract with its sub-buyer was the US dollar: 'Any profit or corresponding damage from non-performance could only accrue in [US dollars] in the first place. Giving further consideration to the principle of full compensation which applies under the CISG and the fact that [the Seller] has not objected to compensation in US dollars, the assumption is thus justified that the parties at least impliedly agreed on an execution of their relationship solely on the basis of that currency.'

[175] See Proctor (n 120).

One relevant factor is the currency in which the injured party usually operates or, in other words, the party's 'normal trading currency'.[176] Some English cases show that identifying this currency can be difficult, particularly where a multinational company is involved. Where so, it may be relevant to determine the currency in which the goods in question are traded. For example, in one case[177] a French trader of soya beans (amongst other commodities) was held to have suffered loss in US dollars, primarily because it treated soya beans 'as a dollar commodity'.[178] Where the party has actually incurred costs in a particular currency, that currency may often be decisive. In one CISG case,[179] where due to the delay in payment by the German buyer the French seller had to resort to credit, the court held that because the seller incurred costs in French francs, damages had to be awarded in that currency. For the same reason, in some other cases[180] where due to a non-conformity in the goods the buyer incurred additional costs arising from storage, inspection and liability to third parties in its domestic currency, damages were awarded in that currency. However, the currency in which the expenditure was incurred may not always be the currency in which loss was suffered if the injured party's normal business currency is different from that in which the loss was incurred. For instance, in one well-known English case,[181] although a French company incurred liability to third persons in Brazilian cruzeiros, French francs were the company's normal business currency and were used to purchase cruzeiros.[182]

As noted, the question whether the party is adequately compensated may depend on the date with reference to which a loss in that currency is to be assessed. Suppose that after the seller's breach a Russian buyer used 700,000 rubles to purchase 10,000 US dollars to pay damages to its customer. At the time of the legal proceedings, 750,000 rubles would be required to purchase 10,000 US dollars. If the ruble is held to be the currency in which the buyer suffered its loss because it is its normal trading currency, the question is whether to award the

[176] See ibid.

[177] *The Federal Huron* (n 106).

[178] '[T]he evidence is overwhelming that the cargo receivers treated soya beans as a dollar commodity. In purchases of raw beans the dollar was always the money of account ... [I]f the currency of any onward sale were not dollars, the proceeds of sale would be immediately converted into dollars and, if it were a forward sale, the cargo receivers would buy dollars forward as a hedge against depreciation of the foreign currency against the dollar' (ibid, 192).

[179] Case No 2 U 1230/91 Appellate Court Koblenz (Germany) 17 September 1993 (Computer Chip), available at cisgw3.law.pace.edu/cases/930917g1.html.

[180] See CIETAC 10 March 1995 (Polyethylene film), available at cisgw3. law.pace.edu/cases/950310c2.html; CIETAC (Copperized steel tubes) 5 July 1993, available at cisgw3.law.pace.edu/cases/930705c1.html.

[181] *Services Europe Atlantique Sud (Seas) v Stockholms Rederiaktiebolag Svea (The 'Folias')* [1979] AC 685.

[182] See also ICAC No 97/2004 (n 166) where the Russian buyer paid a penalty to its customers in rubles as a result of the seller's delay in delivery but damages were nevertheless awarded in US dollars because the dollar was the currency of the contract. It is, however, not entirely clear whether the tribunal viewed the contract currency as evidencing the parties' intention to settle damages claims in US dollars.

buyer 700,000 or 750,000 rubles. The question reflects the difficulty of making a choice between the time when the loss was suffered[183] and the date of judgment (or some other later date).[184] It is suggested that the date of judgment (award) is most appropriate under the international instruments.[185] This date is in line with the instruments' preference for the 'concrete' approach to calculating damages as it takes account of the developments which have taken place since the time of the breach and affected the injured party's *actual* position. This approach also ensures that the principle of full compensation is implemented most accurately.[186] The reliance on the date of judgment (award) may create an incentive for the injured party to cause delays to postpone the date of the judgment/award.[187] If, in our example, the Russian buyer correctly predicts that the value of the ruble will continue to fall against the dollar, it will benefit from damages at a later point in time. It is suggested, however, that the danger of speculation and delay can be countered by the mitigation rule which arguably requires the injured party to bring a claim in good time to avoid increasing its loss.

[183] In some cases, such as those involving the calculation of damages under the instruments' 'concrete' and 'abstract' formulae, the relevant date is that of the avoidance of the contract, or, under art 76 CISG where the goods were taken over, at the time of such taking over.

[184] An appropriate later date is the date when the payment of damages is actually made.

[185] The reason this date is preferred, as opposed to the date of payment of damages, is that it has shown to be a workable date in practice (see the statement by Lord Wilberforce in *Miliangos v George Frank (Textiles) Ltd* [1976] AC 443, 469) and seems more widely accepted than the date of payment.

[186] The date of judgment can, of course, lead to the innocent party getting less than what it would have received had damages been assessed based on the time of breach or shortly thereafter. Suppose that, in our example, the buyer paid 750,000 rubles to purchase 10,000 US dollars but at the time of judgment, due to the strengthening of the ruble against the dollar, it now has to spend 700,000 rubles to purchase the said amount in US dollars. It is suggested that the 'concrete' approach to calculating damages and the accompanying reliance on the date of judgment require that only 700,000 rubles be awarded as damages.

[187] For the discussion of incentives, see J Knott, 'A Quarter of a Century of Foreign Currency Judgments: The Wealth-Time Continuum in Perspective' [1994] LMCLQ 325, 344; R Bowles and C Whelan, 'Judgments in Foreign Currencies: Extension of the Miliangos Rule' (1979) 42 *MLR* 452, 455–8.

Bibliography

'Gap acts over Indian child labour', available at news.bbc.co.uk/2/hi/business/7098975.stm.

RR Anderson, 'Damages for Sellers under the Code's Profit Formula' (1986–1987) 40 *Southwestern L J* 1021.

——, 'Incidental and Consequential Damages' (1987) 7 *J L Commerce* 327.

PS Atiyah, *The Rise and Fall of Freedom of Contract* (Clarendon Press, Oxford, 1979).

RP Barbarowicz, 'Loss of Goodwill and Business Reputation' (1970–1971) 75 *Dickinson L Rev* 63.

DW Barnes, 'The Net Expectation Interest in Contractual Damages' (1999) 48 *Emory L J* 1143.

K Barnett, 'Gain-Based Damages' in R Halson and D Campbell (eds), *Research Handbook on Remedies in Private Law* (Cheltenham UK – Northampton, MA, USA, Edward Elgar, 2019).

G Baron, 'Do the UNIDROIT Principles of International Commercial Contracts form a New Lex Mercatoria?', available at www.cisg.law.pace.edu/cisg/biblio/baron.html.

J Basedow, 'Towards a Universal Doctrine of Breach of Contract: The Impact of the CISG' (2005) 25 *Int'l Rev L Economics* 487.

H Beale (ed), *Chitty on Contracts*, 33rd edn, vol 1 (London, Sweet & Maxwell, 2019).

HG Beale, *Remedies for Breach of Contract* (Sweet & Maxwell, London, 1980).

V Behr, 'The Sales Convention in Europe: From Problems in Drafting to Problems in Practice', available at www.cisg.law.pace.edu/cisg/biblio/behr.html.

P Benjamin, 'Penalties, Liquidated Damages and Penal Clauses in Commercial Contract: A Comparative Study of English and Continental Law' (1960) 9 *ICLQ* 600.

Benjamin's Sale of Goods (7th edn, Thomson–Sweet & Maxwell, London, 2006).

KP Berger, 'The Lex Mercatoria Doctrine and the UNIDROIT Principles of International Commercial Contracts' (1997) 28 *L and Policy Int'l Business* 943.

——, 'Transnational Commercial Law in the Age of Globalization', available at w3.uniroma1.it/idc/centro/publications/42berger.pdf.

L Bernstein, 'Opting out of the Legal System: Extralegal Contractual Relations in the Diamond Industry' (1992) 21 *JLS* 115.

——, 'Private Commercial Law in the Cotton Industry: Creating Cooperation through Rules, Norms, and Institutions' (2000–2001) 99 *Mich L Rev* 1724.

H Bernstein and J Lookofsky, *Understanding the CISG in Europe: a compact guide to the 1980 United Nations Convention on Contracts for the International Sale of Goods*, 2nd edn (Kluwer Law International, The Hague, 2003).

EL Black and TA Carnes, 'The Market Valuation of Corporate Reputation' (2000) 3 *Corporate Reputation Rev* 31.

MJ Bonell, *An International Restatement of Contract Law: The UNIDROIT Principles of International Commercial Contracts*, 3rd edn (Transnational Publishers Inc, Ardsley, NY, 2005).

——, 'Art. 7 CISG' in CM Bianca and MJ Bonell (eds), *Commentary on the International Sales Law: The 1980 Vienna Sales Convention* (Giuffrè, Milan, 1987).

——, 'UNIDROIT Principles 2004 – The New Edition of the Principles of International Commercial Contracts Adopted by the International Institute for the Unification of Private Law' (2004) 45 *Uniform L Rev* 5.

——, 'The UNIDROIT Principles of International Commercial Contracts and CISG – Alternatives or Complementary Instruments?', available at www.cisg.law.pace.edu/cisg/biblio/ulr96.html.

B Borisova, 'Commentary on the Manner in which the UNIDROIT Principles May Be Used to Interpret or Supplement Article 75 of the CISG', available at www.cisg.law.pace.edu/cisg/principles/uni75.html.

R Bowd and L Bowd, 'Assessing a Financial Value for Corporate Entity's Reputation: A Proposed Formula', available at www.ribm.mmu.ac.uk/wps/papers/02-01.pdf.
R Bowles and C Whelan, 'Judgments in Foreign Currencies: Extension of the Miliangos Rule' (1979) 42 *MLR* 452.
MI Braginskiy and VV Vitryanskiy, *Contract Law: General Provisions* (*Dogovornoye pravo: Obshiye polozheniya*) (Statut, Moscow 1998).
RA Brand, 'Exchange Loss Damages and the Uniform-Money Claims Act: The Emperor Hasn't All His Clothes' (1991/1992) 23 *L Policy Int'l Business* 1.
MG Bridge, 'Contractual Damages for Intangible Loss: A Comprehensive Analysis' (1984) 62 *Can Bar Rev* 323.
——, 'Mitigation of Damages in Contract and the Meaning of Avoidable Loss' (1989) 105 *LQR* 398.
——, 'The Evolution of Modern Sales Law' [1991] *LMCLQ* 52.
——, 'Expectation Damages and Uncertain Future' in J Beatson and D Friedmann (eds), *Good Faith and Fault in Contract Law* (OUP, Oxford, 1995).
——, 'Uniformity and Diversity in the Law of International Sale' (2003) 15 *Pace Int'l L Rev* 55.
——, 'Issues Arising under Articles 64, 72 and 73 of the United Nations Convention on Contracts for the International Sale of Goods' (2005–2006) 25 *J L Commerce* 405.
——, 'A Law for International Sales' (2007) 37 *Hong Kong L J* 17.
——, *The International Sale of Goods: Law and Practice*, 2nd edn (Oxford, OUP, 2007).
——, 'The Market Rule of Damages Assessment' in D Saidov and R Cunnington (eds), *Contract Damages: Domestic and International Perspectives* (Oxford, Hart Publishing, 2008).
——, (ed), *Benjamin's Sale of Goods*, 10th edn (London, Sweet & Maxwell – Thomson Reuters, 2019).
——, *The Sale of Goods*, 4th edn (Oxford, OUP, 2019).
LC Bulow, 'Consequential Damages and the Duty to Mitigate in New York Maritime Arbitrations' (1984) *LMCLQ* 625.
A Burrows, 'Contract, Tort and Restitution – A Satisfactory Division or Not?' (1983) 99 *LQR* 217.
A Burrows, *Remedies for Torts, Breach of Contract and Equitable Wrongs*, 4th edn (Oxford, OUP, 2019).
——, 'Are 'Damages on the *Wrotham Park* Basis' Compensatory, Restitutionary, or Neither?' in D Saidov and R Cunnington (eds), *Contract Damages: Domestic and International Perspectives* (Oxford, Hart Publishing, 2008).
——, 'Negotiating Damages' in C Mitchell and S Watterson, *The World of Maritime and Commercial Law: Essays in Honour of Francis Rose* (Oxford – New York, Hart, 2020).
J Cassels, *Remedies: The Law of Damages* (Toronto, Irwin Law, 2000).
M Chen-Wishart, *Contract Law*, 2nd edn (Oxford, OUP, 2008).
R Childress and R Burgess, 'Seller's Remedies: The Primacy of UCC 2-708(2)' (1973) 48 *New York University L Rev* 833.
Chitty on Contracts, 28th edn, Volume 1 (London, Sweet & Maxwell, 1999).
R Chun, 'Corporate Reputation: Meaning and Measurement' (2005) 7 *Int'l J Management Reviews* 91.
CISG Advisory Council (CISG-AC) Opinion No 5, 'The Buyer's Right to Avoid the Contract in Case of Non-Conforming Goods or Documents', available at www.cisg.law.pace.edu/cisg/CISG-AC-op5.html.
——, Opinion No 6, 'Calculation of Damages under CISG Article 74', available at www.cisg.law.pace.edu/cisg/CISG-AC-op6.html.
——, Opinion No. 8, 'Calculation of Damages under CISG Articles 75 and 76', available at www.cisgac.com/file/repository/CISG_AC_Opinion_8_English.pdf.
——, Opinion No 12, 'Liability of the Seller for Damages Arising out of Personal Injuries And Property Damage Caused by Goods and Services under the CISG', available at www.cisgac.com/cisgac-opinion-no12.
MR Cohen, 'The Basis of Contract' (1932–1933) 46 *Harvard L R* 553.

J Coleman, Book Review 'The Normative Basis of Economic Analysis: A Critical Review of Richard Posner's the Economics of Justice' (1981–1982) 34 *Stanford L Rev* 1105.

H Collins, *The Law of Contract*, 4th edn (London, Butterworths, 2003).

——, *Regulating Contracts* (Oxford, OUP, 1999).

Comment, 'Lost Profits as Contract Damages: Problems of Proof and Limitations on Recovery' (1955–1956) 65 *Yale L J* 992.

B Coote, 'Contractual Damages, *Ruxley*, and the Performance Interest' [1997] 56 *Cambridge LJ* 537.

RD Cooter, 'The Best Right Laws: Value Foundations of the Economic Analysis of Law' (1989) 64 *Notre Dame L Rev* 817.

AL Corbin, Corbin on Contracts: A Comprehensive Treatise on the Working Rules of Contract Law, Vol 5 (St Paul, Minn, West Publishing Co, 2002).

G Cuniberti, 'Is the CISG Benefiting Anybody? (Convention on Contract for International Sale of Goods' (2006) 39 *Vanderbilt J Transnational L* 1511.

R Cunnington, 'The Measure and Availability of Gain-Based Damages for Breach of Contract' in D Saidov and R Cunnington (eds), *Contract Damages: Domestic and International Perspectives* (Oxford, Hart Publishing, 2008).

J Dach, 'Conversion of Foreign Money: A Comparative Study of Changing Rules' (1954) 3 *AJCL* 155.

——, 'Money of Reference and Conversion of Money' (1956) 5 *AJCL* 512.

R Danzig, 'Hadley v. Baxendale: A Study in the Industrialization of the Law' (1975) 4 *JLS* 249.

C Debattista, Bill of Lading in Export Trade, 3rd edn (Haywards Heath, Tottel Publishing, 2009).

Deliberations at the 10th Plenary Meeting of the 1980 Vienna Diplomatic Conference, available at www.cisg.law.pace.edu/cisg/plenarycommittee/summary10.html.

R Demogue, 'Validity of the Theory of Compensatory Damages' (1917–1918) 27 *Yale L J* 585.

TA Diamond and H Foss, 'Consequential Damages for Commercial Loss: An Alternative to *Hadley v. Baxendale*' (1994–1995) 63 *Fordham L Rev* 665.

J Dietrich, 'Classifying Precontractual Liability: A Comparative Analysis' (2001) 21 *LS* 153.

M Djordjević, 'Arts 74–77' in S Kröll, L Mistelis and P Viscasillas (eds), *The United Nations Convention on Contracts for the International Sale of Goods*, 2nd edn (München, C.H. Beck and Oxford, Hart, 2018).

TA Downes, 'Nominalism, Indexation, Excuse and Revalorisation: A Comparative Survey' (1985) 101 *LQR* 98.

U Draetta, 'The Notion of Consequential Damages in the International Trade Practice: A Merger of Common Law and Civil Law Concepts' (1991) 4 *Int'l Business L J* 487.

RL Dunn, *Recovery of Damages for Lost Profits*, 6th edn (Alameda, CA, Lawpress, 2006).

RL Dunn and EP Harry, 'Modeling and Discounting Future Damages' (2002) 193 *J Accountancy* 49.

S Eiselen, 'Unresolved Damages Issues of the CISG: A Comparative Analysis' (2005) 38 *Comparative Int'l L J Southern Africa* 32.

——, 'Adopting the Vienna Sales Convention: Reflections Eight Years down the Line' (2007) 19 *SA Mercantile L J* 14.

——, 'Remarks on the Manner in which the UNIDROIT Principles of International Commercial Contracts May Be Used to Interpret or Supplement Article 74 of the CISG', available at www.cisg.law.pace.edu/cisg/principles/uni74.html.

MA Eisenberg, 'Probability and Chance in Contract Law' (1998) 45 *U California L Rev* 1005.

——, 'Symposium: A Tribute to Professor Joseph M. Perillo: The Duty to Rescue in Contract Law' (2002–2003) 71 *Fordham L Rev* 647.

MP Ellinghaus and EW Wright, 'The Common Law of Contracts: Are Broad Principles Better than Detailed Rules? An Empirical Investigation' (2004–2005) 11 *Texas Wesleyan L Rev* 399.

F Enderlein and D Maskow, *International Sales Law: United Nations Convention on Contracts for the International Sale of Goods, Convention on the Limitation Period in the International Sale of Goods* (New York, Oceana, 1992).

N Enonchong, 'Contract Damages for Injury to Reputation' (1996) 59 *MLR* 592.

RA Epstein, 'Beyond Foreseeability: Consequential Damages in the Law of Contract' (1989) 18 *JLS* 105.

EA Farnsworth, 'Legal Remedies for Breach of Contract' (1970) 70 *Columbia L Rev* 1145.

——, 'Damages and Specific Relief' (1979) 27 *AJCL* 247.

——, 'Precontractual Liability and Preliminary Agreements: Fair Dealing and Failed Negotiations' (1987) 87 *Columbia L Rev* 217.

——, 'Duties of Good Faith and Fair Dealing under the UNIDROIT Principles, Relevant International Convention, and National Laws' (1995) 3 *Tulane J Intl and Comparative L* 47.

——, 'An International Restatement: the UNIDROIT Principles of International Commercial Contracts' (1996–1997) 26 *U Baltimore L Rev* 1.

——, *Contracts*, 4th edn (New York, Aspen Publishers, 2004).

J Felemegas, 'The award of counsel's fees under Article 74 CISG, in *Zapata Hermanos Sucesores v. Hearthside Baking Co.* (2001)' (2002) 6 *Vindobona J Int'l Commercial L Arbitration* 30.

——, 'An Interpretation of Article 74 CISG by the U.S. Circuit Court of Appeals' (2003) 15 *Pace Int'l L Rev* 91.

F Ferrari, 'Comparative Ruminations on the Foreseeability of Damages in Contract Law' (1992–1993) 53 *Louisiana L Rev* 1257.

——, 'General Principles and International Uniform Commercial Law Conventions: A Study of the 1980 Vienna Sales Convention and the 1988 UNIDROIT Conventions on International Factoring and Leasing' (1998/99) 1 *Euro J L Reform* 217.

S Fisher and M Hains, 'Futures Market Law and Practice and the Vienna Sales Convention' [1993] *LMCLQ* 531.

HM Flechtner, 'The Several Texts of the CISG in a Decentralized System: Observations on Translations, Reservations and Other Challenges to the Uniformity Principle in Article 7(1)' (1997–1998) 17 *J L Commerce* 187.

——, 'Recovering Attorneys' Fees as Damages under the U.N. Sales Convention: A Case Study on the New International Commercial Practice and the Role of Case Law in CISG Jurisprudence, with Comments on *Zapata Hermanos Sucesores, S.A. v. Hearthside Baking Co.*' (2002) 22 *Northwestern J Int'l L Business* 121.

H Flechtner and J Lookofsky, 'Viva Zapata! American Procedure and CISG Substance in a U.S. Circuit Court of Appeal' (2003) 7 *Vindobona J Int'l Commercial L Arbitration* 93.

C Fombrun, *Reputation: Realizing Value from the Corporate Image* (Boston, MA, Harvard Business School Press, 1996).

CJ Fombrun, NA Gardberg and JM Sever, 'The Reputation QuotientSM: A multi-Stakeholder Measure of Corporate Reputation' (2000) 7 J *Brand Management* 241.

M Fontaine, 'Content and Performance' (1992) 40 *AJCL* 645.

C Fried, *Contract as Promise: A Theory of Contractual Obligation* (Cambridge, Mass, Harvard University Press, 1981).

D Friedmann, 'The Performance Interest in Contract Damages' (1995) 111 *LQR* 628.

LL Fuller and WR Perdue, Jr, 'The Reliance Interest in Contract Damages: 1' (1936–1937) 46 *Yale L J* 52.

LL Fuller and MA Eisenberg, *Basic Contract Law* (St Paul, Minn, West Group Publishing Co, 1981).

NM Galston and H Smit (eds), *International Sales: The United Nations Convention on Contracts for the International Sale of Goods* (New York, Matthew Bender, 1984).

Z Gao, *International Petroleum Contracts: Current Trends and New Directions* (London, Graham & Trotman, 1994).

NA Gardberg, 'Reputatie, Reputation, Réputation, Reputazione, Ruf: A Cross-Cultural Qualitative Analysis of Construct and Instrument Equivalence' (2006) 9 *Corporate Reputation Rev* 39.

BA Garner (ed) *Black's Law Dictionary*, 7th edn (St Paul, Minn, West Publishing Co, 1999).

AM Garro, 'The Gap-Filling Role of the UNIDROIT Principles in International Sales Law: Some Comments on the Interplay between the Principles and the CISG' (1994–1995) 69 *Tulane L Rev* 1149.

——, 'The Contribution of the UNIDROIT Principles to the Advancement of International Commercial Arbitration' (1994) 3 *Tulane J Int'l Comparative L* 93.

M Gebauer, 'Uniform Law, General Principles and Autonomous Interpretation' (2000) 5 *Uniform L Rev* 683.

CP Gillette, 'Reputation and Intermediaries in Electronic Commerce' (2001–2002) 62 *La L Rev* 1165.

CP Gillette and RE Scott, 'The Political Economy of International Sales Law' (2005) 25 *Int'l Rev L Economics* 446.

DM Goderre, 'International Negotiations Gone Sour: Precontractual Liability under the United Nations Sales Convention' (1997) 66 *U Cincinnati L Rev* 257.

DL Goetz, KL Moore, DE Perry, DS Raab and JS Ross, 'Article Two Warranties in Commercial Transactions: An Update' (1987) 72 *Cornell L Rev* 1159.

R Goode, *Commercial Law in the Next Millennium* (London, Sweet & Maxwell, 1998).

——, 'International Restatements of Contract and English Contract Law' in EZ Lomnicka and CGJ Morse (eds), *Contemporary Issues in Commercial Law – Essays in Honour of Professor AG Guest* (London, Sweet & Maxwell, 1997).

R Goode, H Kronke and E McKendrick, *Transnational Commercial Law: Text, Cases, and Materials*, 2nd edn (Oxford, OUP, 2015).

JY Gotanda, 'Awarding Interest in International Arbitration' (1996) 90 *AJIL* 40.

——, 'Awarding Costs and Attorney's Fees in International Commercial Arbitrations' (1999) 21 *Mich J Int'l L* 1.

——, 'Recovering Lost Profits in International Disputes' (2004) 36 *Georgetown J Int'l L* 61.

——, 'Damages in Lieu of Performance Because of Breach of Contract' (Villanova University School of Law Working Paper No. 2006-8, 2006, Paper 53).

——, 'Using the UNIDROIT Principles to Fill Gaps in the CISG' in D Saidov and R Cunnington (eds), *Contract Damages: Domestic and International Perspectives* (Oxford, Hart Publishing, 2008).

JC Gulotta, Jr., 'Anticipatory Breach – A Comparative Analysis' (1976) 50 *Tulane L Rev* 927.

AF Halaby, 'No Summary Judgement for You! One State's (Unjustified) Treatment of Contract Claims for Lost Profits' [1998] *U Miami Business L Rev* 57.

D Hamer, '"Chance Would Be a Fine Thing": Proof of Causation and Quantum in an Unpredictable World' (1999) 23 *Melbourne ULR* 557.

M Hammerson and E Richardson, 'Long-Term Gas Sales Agreements' in D Saidov (ed), *Research Handbook on International and Comparative Law Sale of Goods Law* (Edward Elgar, Cheltenham, 2019).

RG Hammond, 'Compensation for the Lost Value of Money: A Canadian Proposal' (1983) 99 *LQR* 68.

S Han, 'Principles of Asian Contract Law: An Endeavor of Regional Harmonization of Contract Law in East Asia' (2013) 58 *Villanova L Rev* 589.

D Harris, 'Incentives to Perform, or Break Contracts' (1992) 45 *Current Legal Problems* 29.

——, A Ogus, and J Phillips, 'Contract Remedies and the Consumer Surplus' (1979) 95 *LQR* 581.

D Harris, D Campbell and R Halson, *Remedies in Contract and Tort*, 2nd edn (Cambridge, CUP, 2002).

RJ Harris, 'A General Theory for Measuring Seller's Damages for Total Breach of Contract' (1961–1962) 60 *Michigan L Rev* 577.

——, 'A Radical Restatement of the Law of Seller's Damages: Sales Act and Commercial Code Results Compared' (1965–1966) 18 *Stanford L Rev* 66.

C Hawes, 'Damages for Defective Goods' (2005) 121 *LQR* 389.

HLA Hart and T Honore, *Causation in the Law*, 2nd edn (Oxford, Clarendon Press, 1985).

J Hellner, 'The Limits of Contractual Damages in the Scandinavian Law of Sales' (1966) 10 *Scandinavian L S* 37.

R Herber, 'Preamble and Arts. 1–7 CISG' in P Schlechtriem (ed), *Commentary on the UN Convention on the International Sale of Goods (CISG)*, 2nd edn (in translation) (Oxford, Clarendon Press, 1998).

JR Hicks, 'The Foundations of Welfare Economics (1939) 49 *Economic J* 696.

JS Hobhouse, 'International Conventions and Commercial Law: The Pursuit of Uniformity' (1990) 106 *LQR* 530.

M Hogg, 'Lost Chances in Contract and Delict – Golden Opportunities for Litigation' [1997] *SLT* 71.

JB Holisky, 'Finding the "Lost Volume Seller": Two Independent Sales Deserve Two Profits under Illinois Law' (1988) 22 *John Marshall L Rev* 363.

JO Honnold, *Uniform Law for International Sales under the 1980 United Nations Convention*, 3rd edn (Deventer, Kluwer Law International, 1999).

AM Honore, 'Causation and Remoteness of Damage' in K Zweigert and K Drobnig (eds), *International Encyclopedia of Comparative Law*, Vol 11 (The Hague, Martinus Nijhoff Publishers, 1971) ch 7.

T Honore, 'Causation in the Law', available at plato.stanford.edu/entries/causation-law.

P Huber, 'CISG – The Structure of Remedies' (2007) 71 *Rabels Zeitschrift für ausländisches und internationales Privatrecht* 13.

RE Hudec, 'Restating the "Reliance Interest"' (1981–1982) 67 *Cornell L Rev* 704.

A Hudson, 'Money as Property in Financial Transactions' (1999) 14 J *Int'l Banking L* 170.

R Hyland, 'On Setting Forth the Law of Contract: A Foreword' (1992) 40 *AJCL* 541.

Introduction to the 1994 edition in *UNIDROIT Principles of International Commercial Contracts 2004* (UNIDROIT, Rome 2004).

OS Ioffe, *Otvetstvennost' po Sovetskomu Grazhdanskomu Pravu* (Leningrad, LGU, 1955).

OS Ioffe, *Law of Obligations (Obyazatelstvennoye pravo)* (Moscow, Juridical Literature, 1975).

J Jackson, 'Global Economics and International Economic Law' (1998) 1 *JIEL* 1.

JH Jackson, WJ Davey and AO Sykes, Jr., *Legal Problems of International Economic Relations: Cases, Materials and International Regulation of Transnational Economic Relations*, 3rd edn (St Paul, Minn, West Publishing Co, 1995).

N Kaldor, 'Welfare Propositions of Economics and Inter-Personal Comparisons of Utility' (1939) 49 *Economic J* 549.

AW Katz, 'Remedies for Breach of Contract under the CISG' (2006) 25 *Int'l Rev L Economics* 378.

MB Kelly, 'Living without the Avoidable Consequences Doctrine in Contract Remedies' (1996) 33 *San Diego L Rev* 175.

T Kelly, 'How Does the Cookie Crumble? Legal Costs under a Uniform Interpretation of the United Nations Convention on Contracts for the International Sale of Goods' (2003) 1 *Nordic J Commercial L*, available at www.njcl.fi/1_2003/commentary2.pdf.

F Kessler and E Fine, 'Culpa in Contrahendo, Bargaining in Good Faith, and Freedom of Contract: A Comparative Study' (1963–1964) 77 *Harvard L Rev* 401.

J Klein, 'Good Faith in International Transactions' (1993) 15 *Liverpool L Rev* 115.

J Klein and C Bachechi, 'Precontractual Liability and the Duty of Good Faith Negotiation in International Transactions' (1994–1995) 17 *Houston J Int'l L* 1.

V Knapp, 'Arts. 74–77 CISG' in CM Bianca and MJ Bonell (eds), *Commentary on the International Sales Law: The 1980 Vienna Sales Convention* (Milan, Giuffrè, 1987).

J Knott, 'A Quarter of a Century of Foreign Currency Judgments: The Wealth-Time Continuum in Perspective' [1994] *LMCLQ* 325.

R Koch, 'Commentary on Whether the UNIDROIT Principles of International Commercial Contracts May Be Used to Interpret or Supplement Article 25 CISG', available at www.cisg.law.pace.edu/cisg/biblio/koch1.html#rki.

KM Kolaski and M Kuga, 'Measuring Commercial Damages via Lost Profits or Loss of Business Value: Are these Measures Redundant or Distinguishable?' (1998–1999) 18 *J L Commerce* 1.

AS Komarov, *Otvetstvennost' v kommercheskom oborote* (Moscow, Juridical Literature, 1991).

——, 'The Limitation of Contract Damages in Domestic Legal Systems and International Instruments' in D Saidov and R Cunnington (eds), *Contract Damages: Domestic and International Perspectives* (Oxford, Hart Publishing, 2008).

P Koneru, 'The International Interpretation of the UN Convention on Contracts for the International Sale of Goods: An Approach Based on General Principles' (1997) 6 *Minnesota J Global Trade* 105.

H Kötz, 'Civil Justice Systems in Europe and the United States' (2003) 13 *Duke J Comparative Int'l L* 61.

A Kramer, 'An Agreement-Centred Approach to Remoteness and Contract Damages' in N Cohen and E McKendrick (eds), *Comparative Remedies for Breach of Contract* (Oxford, Hart Publishing, 2005).

——, 'Remoteness: New Problems with the Old Test' in D Saidov and R Cunnington (eds), *Contract Damages: Domestic and International Perspectives* (Oxford, Hart Publishing, 2008).

AH Kritzer, 'Observations on the Use of the Principles of European Contract Law as an Aid to CISG Research', available at cisgw3.law.pace.edu/cisg/text/peclcomp.html.

——, 'Reasonableness', available at www.cisg.law.pace.edu/cisg/text/reason.html#schl.

H Kronke, 'The UN Sales Convention, The UNIDROIT Contract Principles and the Way Beyond' (2005–2006) 25 *J L Commerce* 451.

JT Landa, 'Hadley v. Baxendale and the Expansion of the Middleman Economy' (1987) 16 *JLS* 455.

O Lando, 'European Contract Law' (1983) 31 *AJCL* 653.

——, 'Assessing the Role of the UNIDROIT Principles in the Harmonization of Arbitration Law' (1994) 3 *Tulane J Int'l Comparative L* 129.

——, 'Comparative Law and Lawmaking' (2000–2001) 75 *Tulane L Rev* 1015.

——, 'Salient Features of the Principles of European Contract Law: A Comparison with the UCC' (2001) 13 *Pace Int'l L Rev* 339.

——, 'CISG and Its Followers: A Proposal to Adopt Some International Principles of Contract Law' (2005) 53 *AJCL* 379.

O Lando and H Beale (eds), *Principles of European Contract Law: Parts I and II* (prepared by the Commission on European Contract Law; The Hague, Kluwer Law International, 2000).

FH Lawson, *Remedies of English Law*, 2nd edn (London, Butterworths, 1980).

S Le Pautremat, 'Mitigation of Damage: A French Perspective' (2006) 55 *ICLQ* 205.

P Linzer, 'On the Amorality of Contract Remedies – Efficiency, Equity, and the Second Restatement' (1981) 81 *Columbia L Rev* 111.

P Lipton, 'Causation Outside the Law' in H Gross and R Harrison (eds), *Jurisprudence: Cambridge Essays* (Oxford, OUP, 1992).

Q Liu, 'Claiming Damages upon an Anticipatory Breach: Why Should an Acceptance Be Necessary?' (2005) 25 *LS* 559.

GG Letterman, *UNIDROIT's Rules in Practice: Standard International Contracts and Applicable Rules* (The Hague, Kluwer Law International, 2001).

PG Lewellyn, 'Corporate Reputation: Focusing on Zeitgeist' (2002) 41 *Business & Society* 415.

J Lookofsky, *Consequential Damages in Comparative Context: From Breach of Promise to Monetary Remedy in the American, Scandinavian and International Law of Contracts and Sales* (Copenhagen, Danmarks Jurist, 1989).

D Maskow, 'Article 58' in CM Bianca and MJ Bonell (eds), *Commentary on the International Sales Law: The 1980 Vienna Sales Convention* (Milan, Giuffrè, 1987).

CT McCormick, *Handbook on the Law of Damages* (St Paul, Minn, West Publishing Co, 1935).

H McGregor, *McGregor on Damages*, 20th edn (London, Sweet & Maxwell, 2019).

——, 'The Role of Mitigation in the Assessment of Damages' in D Saidov and R Cunnington (eds), *Contract Damages: Domestic and International Perspectives* (Oxford, Hart Publishing, 2008).

E McKendrick, *Goode on Commercial Law*, 5th edn (London, Penguin, 2016).

McKendrick and Worthington, 'Damages for Non-Pecuniary Loss' in N Cohen and E McKendrick (eds), *Comparative Remedies for Breach of Contract* (Oxford, Hart Publishing, 2005).

D McLauchlan, 'Expectation Damages: Avoided Loss, Offsetting Gains and Subsequent Events' Instruments' in D Saidov and R Cunnington (eds), *Contract Damages: Domestic and International Perspectives* (Oxford, Hart Publishing, 2008).

JG MacIntosh and DC Frydenlund, 'An Investment Approach to a Theory of Contract Mitigation' (1987) 37 *University Toronto L J* 113.

E Mackaay and C Fabien, 'Civil Law and the Fight Against Inflation–A Legal and Economic Analysis of the Quebec Case' (1983–1984) 44 *Louisiana L Rev* 719.

PJ McConnaughay, 'Rethinking the Role of Law and Contracts in East–West Commercial Relationships' (2001) 41 *Virginia J Intl L* 470.

U Magnus, 'General Principles of UN-Sales Law', available at www.cisg.law.pace.edu/cisg/text/magnus.html.

——, 'Remarks on good faith', available at www.cisg.law.pace.edu/cisg/principles/uni7.html.

The Rt Hon Lord Mance, *The Common Law and Europe: Differences of Style or Substance and Do They Matter?* Holdsworth Club Presidential Address delivered in Birmingham Law School on 24 November 2006, published by Holdsworth Club of the University of Birmingham, 2007.

A Michaud, 'Mitigation of Damage in the Context of Remedies for Breach of Contract' (1984) 15 *Revue Générale de Droit* 293.

JS Mill, 'Sedgwick's Discourse' in JM Robson (ed) *The Collected Works of John Stuart Mill, Volume X, Essays on Ethics, Religion and Society* (London, University of Toronto Press, Routledge and Kegan Paul Ltd, 1969).

L Mistelis, 'Is Harmonisation a Necessary Evil? The Future of Harmonisation and New Sources of International Trade Law' in I Fletcher, L Mistelis and M Cremona (eds), *Foundations and Perspectives of International Trade Law* (London, Sweet & Maxwell, 2001).

R Momberg and S Vogenauer (eds), *The Principles of Latin American Contract Law* (Oxford, Hart, 2017).

C Morris, 'On the Teaching of Legal Cause' (1939) 39 *Columbia L Rev* 1087.

A Mullis, 'Avoidance for Breach under the Vienna Convention; A Critical Analysis of Some of the Early Cases' in M Andenas and N Jareborg (eds), *Anglo-Swedish Studies in Law* (Uppsala, Iustus Förlag, 1999).

——, 'Recoverability of Lost Resale Profit and Compensation Paid to a Sub-Buyer under the Vienna Convention' at the Conference on 'Contract Damages: Domestic and International Perspectives' held in Birmingham, UK, June 2007.

——, 'Twenty-Five Years On – The United Kingdom, Damages and the Vienna Sales Convention' (2007) 71 *Rabels Zeitschrift für ausländisches und internationales Privatrecht* 35.

E Muñoz and DO Ament-Guemez, 'Calculation of Damages on the Basis of the Breaching Party's Profits under The CISG' (2017) 8 *George Mason J Int'l Commercial L* 201.

AG Murphey, Jr., 'Consequential Damages in Contracts for the International Sale of Goods and the Legacy of *Hadley*' (1989) 23 *Geo Wash J Int'l L and Econ* 415.

NE Nedzel, 'A Comparative Study of Good Faith, Fair Dealing, and Precontractual Liability' (1997) 12 *Tulane European Civil L Forum* 97.

B Nicholas, 'Rules and Terms – Civil and Common Law' (1973–1974) 48 *Tulane L R* 946.

——, 'Art. 78 CISG' in CM Bianca and MJ Bonell (eds), *Commentary on the International Sales Law: The 1980 Vienna Sales Convention* (Milan, Giuffrè, 1987).

——, 'Vienna Convention on International Sales Law' (1989) 105 *LQR* 201.

——, *The French Law of Contract*, 2nd edn (Oxford, Clarendon Press, 1992).

——, 'Fault and Breach of Contract' in J Beatson and D Friedmann (eds), *Good Faith and Fault in Contract Law* (Oxford, Clarendon Press, 1995).

Note, 'Damages for Loss of Prospective Crops' (1920–1921) 34 *Harv L Rev* 662.

Note, 'Damages – Loss of Profits Caused by Breach of Contract – Proof of Certainty' (1932–1933) 17 *Minnesota L Rev* 194.

——, 'The Requirement of Certainty in the Proof of Lost Profits' (1950) 64 *Harv L Rev* 317.

AI Ogus, *The Law of Damages* (London, Butterworths, 1973).

——, 'The Economic Basis of Damages for Breach of Contract: Inducement and Expectation' in D Saidov and R Cunnington (eds), *Contract Damages: Domestic and International Perspectives* (Oxford, Hart Publishing, 2008).

CG Orlandi, 'Procedural Law Issues and Law Conventions' (2000) 5 *Uniform L Rev* 23.

EW Patterson, 'The Apportionment of Business Risks through Legal Devices' (1924) 24 *Columbia L Rev* 335.

E Peel, *Treitel on the Law of Contract*, 15th edn (London, Thomson–Sweet & Maxwell, 2020).
IS Peretyorskiy and IB Novitskiy, *Roman Private Law (Rimskoye Chastnoye Pravo)* (Moscow, Yurist, 1999).
JM Perillo, 'UNIDROIT Principles of International Commercial Contracts: The Black Letter Text and a Review' (1994–1995) 63 *Fordham L Rev* 281.
EA Peters, 'Remedies for Breach of Contract Relating to the Sale of Goods Under the Uniform Commercial Code: A Roadmap for Article Two' (1963–1964) 73 *Yale L J* 199.
J Poole, 'Loss of Chance and the Evaluation of Hypotheticals in Contractual Claims' [2007] *LMCLQ* 63.
RA Posner, *Economic Analysis of Law*, 6th edn (New York, Aspen Publishers, 2003).
RJ Pothier, *A Treatise on Obligations, Considered in a Moral and Legal View* (Clark NJ, The Lawbook Exchange, Ltd, 1999).
R Powell, 'Good Faith in Contracts' (1956) 9 *Current Legal Problems* 16.
C Proctor, *Mann on the Legal Aspect of Money*, 6th edn (Oxford, OUP, 2005).
——, 'Changes in Monetary Value and the Assessment of Damages' in D Saidov and R Cunnington (eds), *Contract Damages: Domestic and International Perspectives* (Oxford, Hart Publishing, 2008).
J Ramberg, *ICC Guide to Incoterms 2000: Understanding and Practical Use* (Paris, ICC Publishing SA, 1999).
——, *International Commercial Transactions* (ICC Publication 624, 2nd edn (The Netherlands, Kluwer Law International, 2000).
——, *International Commercial Transactions*, 3rd edn (Stockholm, ICC – Norstedts Juridik, 2004).
RF Reilly and RP Schweihs, *Valuing Intangible Assets* (New York, McGraw-Hill, 1999).
K Rosenn, *Law and Inflation* (Philadelphia, University of Pennsylvania Press, 1982).
A Rosett, 'The UNIDROIT Principles of International Commercial Contracts: A New Approach to International Commercial Contracts, Part I' (1998) 46 (Supp.) *AJCL* 347.
——, 'Unification, Harmonization, Restatement, Codification, and Reform in International Commercial Law' (1992) 40 *AJCL* 683.
D Saidov, 'Methods of Limiting Damages under the UN Convention on Contracts for the International Sale of Goods' (2002) 14 *Pace Intl L Rev* 307.
——, 'Cases on the Sales Convention and the UNIDROIT Principles Decided in the Russian Federation: An Update' (2005) 9 *Vindobona J Int'l Commercial L Arbitration* 1.
——, 'Damages: The Need for Uniformity' (2005–2006) 25 *J L Commerce* 393.
——, 'Anticipatory Non-Performance and Underlying Values of the UNIDROIT Principles' (2006) 11 *Uniform L Rev* 795.
——, 'Standards of Proving Loss and Determining the Amount of Damages' (2006) 22 *J Contract L* 1.
——, 'Causation in Damages: The Convention on Contracts for the International Sale of Goods, the UNIDROIT Principles of International Commercial Contracts, the Principles of European Contract Law' in *Review of the Convention on Contracts for the International Sale of Goods (CISG) 2004–2005* (München, Sellier European Law Publishers, 2006).
——, 'Damage to Business Reputation and Goodwill under the Vienna Sales Convention' in D Saidov and R Cunnington (eds), *Contract Damages: Domestic and International Perspectives* (Oxford, Hart Publishing, 2008).
——, 'Remedies for a Documentary Breach: English Law and the CISG' in K Rowley, L DiMatteo, S Saintier and Q Zhou (eds), *Current Issues in Commercial Contracts: Transatlantic Perspectives* (New York, CUP, 2013).
——, Conformity of Goods and Documents – The Vienna Sales Convention (Oxford, Hart Publishing, 2015).
——, 'Arts 71–73' in S Kröll, L Mistelis and P Viscasillas (eds), The United Nations Convention on Contracts for the International Sale of Goods, 2nd edn (München, C.H. Beck and Oxford, Hart, 2018).
——, (ed), *Research Handbook on International and Comparative Law Sale of Goods Law* (Cheltenham, Edward Elgar, 2019).

——, 'Trade Usages in International Sales Law' in D Saidov (ed), *Research Handbook on International and Comparative Law Sale of Goods Law* (Cheltenham, Edward Elgar, 2019).

D Saidov and R Cunnington, 'Current Themes in the Law of Contract Damages: Introductory Remarks' in D Saidov and R Cunnington (eds), *Contract Damages: Domestic and International Perspectives* (Hart Publishing, Oxford, 2008).

M Saldana, 'Cross Border Transactions', Practising Law Institute, Corporate Law and Practice Course Handbook Series (PLI Order N B0-003A, 1998).

R Samek, 'Relevant Time of Foreseeability of Damages' (1964) 38 *Australian L J* 125.

PD Savkin (ed), *Praktika MKAS pri TPP RF: 2004–2016 – K 85-letiyu MKAS* (Moskva, Nauka Prava – Elektronnaya biblioteka, 2017).

P Schlechtriem, 'Calculation of Damages in the Event of Anticipatory Brach under the CISG', available at www.cisg-online.ch/cisg/FS%20Hellner.pdf.

——, 'Subsequent Performance and Delivery Deadlines – Avoidance of CISG Sales Contracts Due to Non-conformity of the Goods' (2006) *Pace Int'l L Rev* 83.

——, 'Damages, Avoidance of the Contract and Performance Interest under the CISG', available at www.cisg-online.ch/cisg/Schlechtriem_Damages_Avoidance.pdf.

——, 'Interpretation, Gap-Filling and Further Development of the UN Sales Convention', available at cisgw3.law.pace.edu/cisg/biblio/schlechtriem6.html.

——, *Uniform Sales Law: The UN-Convention on Contracts for the International Sale of Goods* (Vienna, Manz Verlag, 1986).

——, 'Effectiveness and Binding Nature of Declarations (Notices, Requests or Other Communications) under Part II and Part III of the CISG' (1995) *Cornell Review of the Convention on Contracts for the International Sale of Goods* 95.

C Schmitthoff, 'The Duty to Mitigate' [1961] *JBL* 361.

EC Schneider, 'Measuring Damages under the CISG', available at www.cisg.law.pace.edu/cisg/text/cross/cross-74.html.

——, 'Consequential Damages in the International Sale of Goods: Analysis of Two Decisions', available at www.cisg.law.pace.edu/cisg/wais/db/articles/schnedr2.html.

UG Schroeter, 'Has the UN Sales Convention Achieved its Key Purpose(s)?' in D Saidov (ed), *Research Handbook on International and Comparative Law Sale of Goods Law* (Cheltenham, Edward Elgar, 2019).

P Schulman, 'Economic Damages: Discounting Concepts and Alternatives' [1999] *Colorado Lawyer* 41.

I Schwenzer, 'Avoidance of the Contract in Case of Non-Conforming Goods (Article 49(1)(a) CISG)' (2005–2006) 25 *J L Commerce* 437.

——, 'Arts 74–77', in I Schwenzer (ed), *Schlechtriem and Schwenzer Commentary on the UN Convention on the International Sale of Goods (CISG)*, 4th edn (Oxford, OUP, 2016).

I Schwenzer and P Hachem, 'The Scope of the CISG Provisions on Damages' in D Saidov and R Cunnington (eds), *Contract Damages: Domestic and International Perspectives* (Oxford, Hart Publishing, 2008).

——, 'Arts 1–6 CISG' in I Schwenzer (ed), *Schlechtriem and Schwenzer Commentary on the UN Convention on the International Sale of Goods (CISG)*, 4th edn (Oxford, OUP, 2016).

RE Scott, 'The Case for Market Damages: Revisiting the Lost Profits Puzzle' (1990) 57 *The University Chicago L Rev* 1155.

JA Sebert, Jr., 'Remedies under Article Two of the Uniform Commercial Code: An Agenda for Review' (1981–1982) 130 *U Pennsylvania L Rev* 360.

Secretariat Commentary of the 1978 Draft Convention.

AP Sergeyev and YK Tolstoy, *Civil Law (Grazhdanskoye pravo)* (Prospect Publishing House, Moscow 1998) Part 1.

MG Shanker, 'The Case for a Literal Reading of UCC Section 2-708(2) (One Profit for the Reseller)' (1973) 24 *Case Western Reserve L Rev* 697.

R Shaw, 'Brand Valuation' (2004), available at www.mbpi.biz/Brand_Valuation.PDF.

D Sim, 'The Scope and Application of Good Faith in the Vienna Convention on Contracts for the International Sale of Goods', available at www.cisg.law.pace.edu/cisg/biblio/sim1.html#iiib.

D Simon and GA Novack, 'Limiting the Buyer's Market Damages to Lost Profits: A Challenge to the Enforceability of Market Contracts' (1978–1979) 92 *Harv L Rev* 1395.

EE Smith, JS Dzienkowski, JS Lowe, OL Anderson and GB Conine, *International Petroleum Transactions*, 2nd edn (Denver, Rocky Mountain Mineral Law Foundation, 2000).

J Smith, *The Law of Contract*, 4th edn (London, Sweet & Maxwell, 2002).

SA Smith, *Contract Theory* (Oxford, OUP, 2004).

R Speidel and K Clay, 'Seller's Recovery of Overhead Under UCC Section 2-708 (2): Economic Cost Theory and Contract Remedial Policy' (1972) 57 *Cornell L Rev* 681.

Status 1980 United Nations Convention on Contracts for the International Sale of Goods, available at www.uncitral.org/uncitral/en/uncitral_texts/sale_goods/1980CISG_status.html.

H Stoll, 'Damages: Article 74' in P Schlechtriem (ed), *Commentary on the UN Convention on the International Sale of Goods (CISG)*, 2nd edn (Oxford, OUP, 1998).

H Stoll and G Gruber, 'Arts. 74–77 CISG' in P Schlechtriem and I Schwenzer (eds), *Commentary on the UN Convention on the International Sale of Goods*, 2nd (English) edn (Oxford, OUP, 2005).

MG Strub, 'The Convention on the International Sale of Goods: Anticipatory Repudiation Provisions and Developing Countries' (1989) 38 *ICLQ* 475.

M Sussdorff, 'The Value to be Found in Corporate Reputation', available at csreurope.org/news/csr/one-entry?entry%5fid=114278.

JS Sutton, 'Measuring Damages under the United Nations Convention on the International Sale of Goods' (1989) 50 *Ohio State L J* 737.

K Takahashi, 'Right to Terminate (Avoid) International Sales of Commodities' [2003] *JBL* 102.

D Tallon, 'Arts. 79–84 CISG' in CM Bianca and MJ Bonell (eds), *Commentary on the International Sales Law: The 1980 Vienna Sales Convention* (Milan, Giuffrè, 1987).

——, 'French Report' in D Harris and D Tallon (eds), *Contract Law Today: Anglo-French Comparisons* (Clarendon Press, Oxford 1991).

C Thiele, 'Interest on Damages and Rate of Interest under Article 78 of the United Nations Convention for the International Sale of Goods' (1998) 2 *Vindobona J Int'l Commercial L Arbitration* 3.

P Todd, *International Trade Law* (London, Thomson–Sweet & Maxwell, 2003).

GH Treitel, *Remedies for Breach of Contract: A Comparative Account* (Oxford, Clarendon Press, 1988).

——, 'Assessment of Damages for Wrongful Repudiation' (2007) 123 *LQR* 9.

A Tunc, *Commentary on the Hague Conventions of the 1st of July 1964 on International Sale of Goods and the Formation of the Contract of Sale*, available at www.cisg.law.pace.edu/cisg/biblio/tunc.html.

UNCITRAL Digest of Case Law on the United Nations Convention on the International Sale of Goods (2004), available at www.uncitral.org/uncitral/en/case_law/digests/cisg.html.

United Nations Compensation Commission, Panel of the Commissioners, Panel F1, Recommendation S/AC.26, 23 September 1997, available at www.unilex.info/dynasite.cfm?dssid=2377&dsmid=13621&x=1.

H van Houtte, 'The UNIDROIT Principles of International Commercial Contracts' (1995) 11 *Arbitration Int'l* 373.

J Vanto, 'Attorney's Fees as Damages in International Commercial Litigation' (2003) 15 *Pace Int'l L Rev* 203.

H Veytia, 'The Requirement of Justice and Equity in Contracts' (1994–1995) 69 *Tulane L Rev* 1191.

MPP Viscasillas, 'UNIDROIT Principles of International Commercial Contracts: Sphere of Application and General Provisions' (1996) 13 *Arizona J Int'l and Comparative L* 380.

E Visser, 'Gaps in the CISG: In General and with Specific Emphasis on the Interpretation of the Remedial Provisions of the Convention in the Light of the General Principles of the CISG', available at www.cisg.law.pace.edu/cisg/biblio/visser.html.

A Von Mehren, 'General View of Contract' in *International Encyclopedia of Comparative Law*, Vol VII (Tübingen, Mohr; Alphen a/d Rijn, Sijthoff & Nordhoff, 1981).

AT Von Mehren and JR Gordley, *The Civil Law System: An Introduction to the Comparative Study of Law*, 2nd edn (Boston, Little, Brown & Co, 1977).

S Waddams, 'The Date for the Assessment of Damages' (1981) 97 *LQR* 445.

——, 'Damages: Assessment of Uncertainties' (1998) 13 *J Contract Law* 55.

——, *The Law of Damages*, 4th edn (Toronto, Canada Law Book Inc, 2004).

——, 'The Modern History of Remedies for Breach of Contract' in R Halson and D Campbell (eds), *Research Handbook on Remedies in Private Law* (Edward Elgar, Cheltenham UK – Northampton, MA, USA, 2019).

TW Waelde, 'Contract and Enforceability in International Business: What Works?', available at www.dundee.ac.uk/cepmlp/journal/html/vol5/vol5-8.html.

SL Wartick, 'Measuring Corporate Reputation: Definition and Data' (2002) 41 *Business & Society* 371.

DWM Waters, 'The Concept of Market in the Sale of Goods' (1958) 36 *The Canadian Bar Rev* 360.

EJ Weinrib, 'A Step Forward in Factual Causation' (1975) 38 *MLR* 518.

H Weisburg and C Ryan, 'Means to Be Made Whole: Damages in the Context of International Investment Arbitration' in Y Derains and RH Kreindler, *Evaluation of Damages in International Arbitration* (Dossiers of the ICC Institute of World Business Law, 2006).

MD Weisman and Clements, 'Protecting Reasonable Expectations: Proof of Lost Profits for New Business' (1991) 76 *Massachusetts L Rev* 186.

F Werro and EM Belser, 'Switzerland' in MJ Bonell (ed), *A New Approach to International Commercial Contracts: The UNIDROIT Principles of International Commercial Contract* (The Netherlands, Kluwer Law International, 1999).

JJ White and RS Summers, *Uniform Commercial Code*, 5th edn (St Paul, Minn, West Publishing Co, 2000).

T Wilhelmsson, 'Good Faith and the Duty of Disclosure in Commercial Contracting – The Nordic Experience' in R Brownsword, NJ Hird and G Howells (eds), *Good Faith in Contract: Concept and Context* (Aldershot, Ashgate, 1999).

M Will, 'Arts. 45–52 CISG' in CM Bianca and MJ Bonell, *Commentary on the International Sales Law: The 1980 Vienna Sales Convention* (Milan, Giuffrè, 1987).

G Williams 'Causation in the Law' [1961] *Cambridge L J* 62.

D Winterton, 'Two Conceptions of the 'Performance Interest' in Contract Damages' in R Halson and D Campbell (eds), *Research Handbook on Remedies in Private Law* (Cheltenham UK – Northampton, MA, Edward Elgar, 2019).

CT Wonnell, 'Efficiency and Conservatism' (2001) 80 *Nebraska L Rev* 643.

Lord Wright, 'Notes on Causation and Responsibility in English Law' [1955] *Cambridge L J* 163.

E Yang, 'Assessment of Damages for Breach of an Option' [2004] *JBL* 437.

J Yovel, 'Comparison between Provisions of the CISG (Measurement of Damages when Contract Avoided: Article 76) and the Counterpart Provisions of the PECL (Article 9:507)', available at www.cisg.law.pace.edu/cisg/text/peclcomp76.html.

——, 'Buyer's Right to Avoid the Contract: Comparison between Provisions of the CISG (Article 49) and the Counterpart Provisions of the PECL (Articles 9:301, 9:303 and 8:106)', available at www.cisg.law.pace.edu/cisg/text/peclcomp49.html#jyvii.

B Zeller, 'Interpretation of Article 74 – Zapata Hermanos Sucesores v Hearthside Baking – Where Next?' (2004) 1 *Nordic J Commercial L*, available at www.njcl.fi/1_2004/commentary1.pdf.

——, *Damages under the Convention on Contracts for the International Sale of Goods* (New York, Oceana, 2005).

JS Ziegel, 'The Remedial Provisions in the Vienna Sales Convention: Some Common Law Perspectives' in NM Galston and H Smit (eds), *International Sales: The United Nations Convention on Contracts for the International Sale of Goods* (New York, Matthew Bender, 1984).

——, Report to the Uniform Law Conference of Canada on Convention on Contracts for the International Sale of Goods, available at www.cisg.law.pace.edu/cisg/text/ziegel80.html.

AF Zoccolillo, Jr., 'Determination of the Interest Rate under the 1980 United Nations Convention on Contracts for the International Sale of Goods: General Principles vs. National Law' (1997) 1 *Vindobona J Int'l Commercial L Arbitration* 3.

Index

www.ingramcontent.com/pod-product-compliance
Lightning Source LLC
LaVergne TN
LVHW020057220926
848484LV00002BB/607
9781509922741